# Global Imbalances and the Evolving World Economy

# Global Imbalances and the Evolving World Economy

edited by

Jane Sneddon Little

Federal Reserve Bank of Boston
Boston, Massachusetts

This edited volume is based on a conference held in June 2006 by the Federal Reserve Bank of Boston.

Conference Series No. 51

This book was set in Sabon by Sztrecska Publishing and was printed and bound in the United States of America.

# Contents

# Acknowledgments

The Research Department of the Federal Reserve Bank of Boston and the editor thank all of the many people who contributed to the conference and to this book. To single out a few, we thank Patricia Geagan for superb management of the conference arrangements; she was ably assisted by Selva Baziki, Tom DeCoff, Donna Dulski, Nancy Gillespie, Ralph Ragsdale, and Teresa Foy Romano. As managing editor, Elizabeth Murry worked creatively with the authors to shape the preliminary conference presentations into final copy; her contributions were key. Suzanne Lorant and Tyler Williams put together the illustrations in the volume while Selva Baziki, Sheila Bodell, Heidi Furse, Adrienne Hathaway, Krista Magnuson, Teresa Foy Romano, Puja Singhal, Sally and Steve Sztrecska, and Julie Weinstein also made valuable contributions to the preparation of this book.

# 1

# Introduction

# Rebalancing Act: Global Imbalances in a Changing World

Jane Sneddon Little

In June 2006 when the Federal Reserve Bank of Boston conference on global imbalances took place, the world had been confronting unusually large current account imbalances for so long that international policymakers had almost stopped warning that these misalignments represented a major risk to the world economic outlook. Almost—but not completely. To avoid accusations of crying wolf, many analysts were continuing to include disruptive-adjustment scenarios involving sharp dollar depreciation, financial market crises, and global slowdowns in their published forecasts. But they had begun placing these warnings in boxes, outside the main text, where the reader could easily ignore these alternative scenarios. Today, while somewhat reduced and overshadowed by the (not unrelated) U.S. house price correction and its repercussions, these imbalances are still with us.[1]

How big a threat do these imbalances actually represent to the global economy? And how did these imbalances develop—with the United States, on one side, accounting for the bulk of the global deficit and a more variable group—currently China, Japan, Germany, and a collection of oil-exporting nations—accounting for the bulk of the global surplus, as shown in Figure 1.1? This state of affairs means that the United States has consumed more than it has produced and invested more than it has saved since 1991—a situation that has lasted well over 15 years. Equivalently, our trading partners, some of whom are very poor on a per capita basis, have willingly lent us, a wealthy country, the funds needed to import the resources to fill the gap—now equal to about 5 percent of our GDP, as illustrated in Figure 1.2. If the United

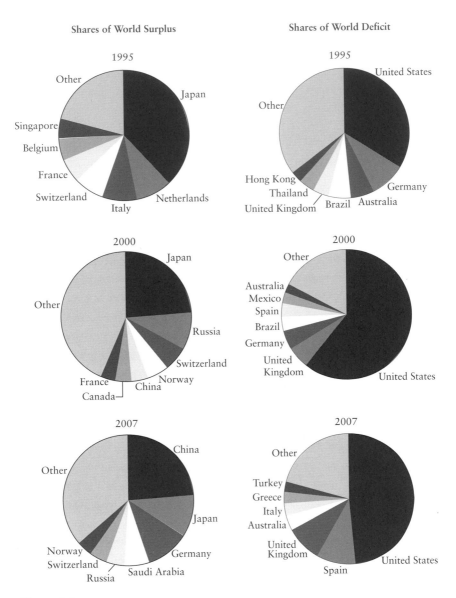

**Figure 1.1**
Global Current Account Imbalances, 1995, 2000, and 2007
*Source:* IMF *World Economic Outlook Database,* April 2008.
*Note:* Some 2007 data are IMF estimates.

States were a developing country, such behavior would have triggered a crisis long ago. But, of course, the United States is not a developing country.

In assigning blame, foreign policymakers tend to highlight American policy "mistakes" as having led to a decline in public and household saving rates in this country, while U.S. policymakers tend to point to Asian countries' "ill-advised" decision to manage their currencies in terms of the dollar. Such a dollar peg has led, they claim, to too much production with too little domestic consumption—a global savings glut, in other words, although some observers interpret this imbalance as a surplus-country investment dearth instead.

But cyclical imbalances are generally short-lived, and policy mistakes are usually quickly punished. By contrast, persistent imbalances may reflect something more fundamental than short-run policy errors. Indeed, such enduring imbalances may more likely reflect a major structural shift in the distribution of the world's resources associated with the arrival

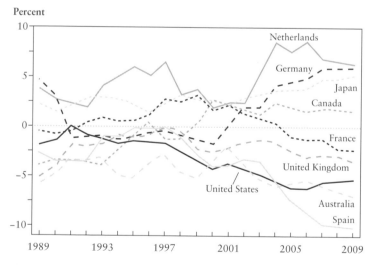

**Figure 1.2**
Current Account Balances as a Percent of GDP, Selected OECD Countries, 1989–2009
*Source:* OECD *Economic Outlook 82 Database.*
*Note:* 2008 and 2009 data are OECD projections.

of the new giants—China, of course, but also India and the ex-Soviet bloc countries—as key players in the global economy. In particular, the recent addition of hundreds of millions of Chinese and Indian workers to the globally active labor force represents a significant re-weighting of world labor markets. In addition, now Japan and Germany (and in a few decades, China) are stepping into an unprecedented demographic future of secular population decline. In scope and significance, these global resource shifts are not unlike the flows of capital and labor that accompanied the European migrations to the New World and the colonization of India and other regions in earlier periods. (See the following brief essay in this section for a discussion of the economic importance of the emerging giants.)

But in contrast with these previous episodes, this time around the capital flows are heading the "wrong way"—from fast-growing developing countries, where returns on investment would presumably be high, to mature wealthy countries. Is this situation sustainable? Simply stabilizing the U.S. current account deficit at its present level relative to GDP would require foreign investors to add U.S. assets worth about 5 percent of U.S. GDP to their portfolios year after year—an uncertain proposition.[2] But if these imbalances do turn out to be sustainable, is that outcome desirable? If not, will adjustment occur smoothly or in response to a crisis? How concerned should policymakers be? Opinions run the gamut from Apocalypse Now to Panglossian equanimity. What are the potential policy implications of these various scenarios?

In response to these puzzles and concerns, the Federal Reserve Bank of Boston organized a conference titled "Global Imbalances—as Giants Evolve," held in June 2006. Our hope in gathering academics, financial market participants, and policymakers from around the globe was to gain a better understanding of the fundamentals explaining these imbalances and to identify policy responses that might help ease the way to a smooth adjustment. This essay summarizes the conference presentations and discussions, some of which have been updated to take into account the potentially epochal events that have occurred since the conference was held two years ago.

## Déjà Vu?

Does history hold any lessons for the contemporary world economy? A wave of international activity between 1870 and 1913, often characterized as the "First Globalization," represents an earlier time when technological, economic, and political developments suddenly provided improved global access to previously untapped resources and the incentive to take advantage of them. The resulting flows of capital and people led to very persistent current account imbalances lasting through much of the period, a condition which offers some possible parallels to today's situation.

Beginning in the nineteenth century, improvements in shipping and communications technology and widespread adoption of the gold standard led to a surge in international migration, trade, and investment through the world's first truly global markets.[3] Steam replaced sail, the telegraph arrived in the 1830s, the first transoceanic cable was laid in 1866, and the Suez Canal opened in 1869. Driven by poverty, famine, religious persecution, and failed revolutions, the stream of people from the European core to sparsely populated British offshoots in North America, Australia, and New Zealand became a flood as 55 million people, one-quarter of the European population in 1850, emigrated between 1815 and 1924;[4] 60 percent of the migrants landed in the United States. Capital followed them to the New World, while investment in densely populated Asia accelerated as well. Throughout this period, Britain, the banker—and venture capitalist—to the world, ran a current account surplus that peaked at 9 percent of GDP. Britain was able to run this current account surplus despite a persistent trade deficit because it enjoyed significant income from massive foreign assets distributed throughout the empire. By contrast, the offshoot countries, settled largely by European immigrants and their offspring, ran persistent current account deficits. The United States recorded a current account deficit for most years between 1850 and 1890 as interest payments on its foreign debt more than offset a small trade surplus based on its shipping services. In other words, net flows of investment income played a key role in sustaining these long-term imbalances.

In Britain's case, its net investment earnings reflected both its large net asset position[5] and the gap between the interest it earned on those

## THE ECONOMIC IMPORTANCE OF THE EMERGING GIANTS

*by Selva Bahar Baziki*

By what criteria does one measure an emerging giant? Or determine which countries deserve that title? Everyone agrees that, by almost any measure, mainland China tops the list. But at the Boston Fed conference, Shankar Acharya and Richard Cooper argued that India should not be clubbed with China as a giant because India is less globally engaged and contributes little to current payments imbalances. In contrast, Surjit Bhalla sees India as "China with a 5- to 10-year lag." Other candidate giants—Brazil, Russia, and the entire regions encompassed by Africa and Eastern Europe—drew only occasional mention. Clearly, the economic concept of what constitutes an "emerging giant" has many dimensions, a few of which are discussed below and illustrated in the accompanying tables.

China and India are, respectively, the world's first- and second-largest countries by population size, second- and seventh-largest by land area, and third- and eleventh-largest by economic size measured at market exchange rates. In terms of purchasing power parity (PPP) exchange rates, which equalize the price of a common basket of goods across countries and put more weight on the portion of the basket that is not traded internationally, in 2005 China's economy ranked second in the world, and India ranked fourth. Together,

both countries account for more than 7 percent of the world's GDP. Each country, but China more than India, is a driver of the global economy: over the course of roughly 10 years since 1995, China's annual real GDP growth averaged 9.1 percent, contributing 12.8 percent to world output growth over that time span. India's average for the same period was 6.1 percent, and its contribution was a relatively modest 3.2 percent. In 2005 alone, Chinese GDP grew by 10 percent, and India's by 9 percent. Such rates are comparable to those of postwar Japan in the 1960s and South Korea in the 1980s. Although the growth rates in China and India are projected to decelerate, as both become increasingly prominent global players, their contribution to world output growth is forecasted to expand over the next 15 years.

Despite their already impressive economic size, China and India still fall well below the world average in terms of GDP per capita. In 2006, China's per capita GDP was $1,598, while India's was $634—roughly 25 percent and 10 percent, respectively, of the world average of $5,792 at market exchange rates. Using PPP exchange rates, which on the whole provide a better gauge of relative living standards than do the market-exchange-rate numbers, China's 2006 per capita income measures $4,500—almost 50 percent of the world average; at $2,393, India's was just over 25 percent.

To a degree, these low per capita incomes reflect these countries' histories of rapid

### Table 1 – GDP in Six Selected Countries[1]
### 2004

| Percent | Share of World GDP* | | Average Annual Real Growth Rate | | Average Contribution to World Growth | |
|---|---|---|---|---|---|---|
| | 2004 | 2020 | 1995–2004 | 2005–20 | 1995–2004 | 2005–20 |
| China | 4.7 | 7.9 | 9.1 | 6.6 | 12.8 | 15.8 |
| India | 1.7 | 2.4 | 6.1 | 5.5 | 3.2 | 4.1 |
| United States | 28.4 | 28.5 | 3.3 | 3.2 | 33.1 | 28.6 |
| Japan | 11.2 | 8.8 | 1.2 | 1.6 | 5.3 | 4.6 |
| Germany | 6.6 | 5.4 | 1.5 | 1.9 | 3.0 | 3.3 |
| Brazil | 1.5 | 1.5 | 2.4 | 3.6 | 1.5 | 1.7 |
| World | 100.0 | 100.0 | 3.0 | 3.2 | 100.0 | 100.0 |

[1]Table data comes from the World Bank *World Development Indicators*.

population growth. But fertility rates have come down in both countries, with the Chinese rate now below 2 births per woman, compared to the 3.6 average for the 1960–2005 period; India's rate is now 2.5 births per woman, compared to the 4.4 average for the 1960–2005 period. Population growth in both countries is currently stable at 0.6 percent a year in China, and 1.4 percent a year in India. The World Bank estimates that China's population will peak in 2032 at 1.5 billion people. Owing to its higher fertility rate, India will surpass China as the most populous country before 2032 and will reach 1.8 billion people by 2050.

With their populations stabilizing, rapid economic growth and capital deepening have allowed China's and India's still-low per capital incomes to rise rapidly in recent years. With per capita incomes up 58 percent in China and 30 percent in India between 1990 and 2000, these countries have become magnets for foreign direct investment intended to serve their growing middle classes as well as to expand their thriving export base. In 2006, China plus Hong Kong attracted 9 percent of direct investment flows—ranking a close third after the United States (13 percent) and the United Kingdom (10 percent). Considering developing countries alone, Russia, Brazil and India ranked second, sixth, and seventh, respectively.

Other important indicators of emerging giant status would have to include the supply of skilled and unskilled workers; the size of the domestic financial markets; the share of world trade, world payments imbalances, and official foreign exchange reserves; and demand for natural resources, like oil and coal, and the resulting contribution to carbon emissions and global warming. Obviously the list goes on and on, and many of these additional considerations were discussed during the conference.

Finally, as Stephen Bosworth notes, it may be good to consider how growing economic integration within East Asia or all of Asia—or among China, India, and Russia—is likely to have a multiplicative effect. Ideally, such integration will be politically stabilizing, but it will also clearly magnify the growing economic impact of these emerging giants.

### Table 2 – Main Indicators[2]
### 2006

| 2000 USD, unless stated otherwise | United States | EMU | Japan | China | India | World |
|---|---|---|---|---|---|---|
| Real GDP – trillions | 11.3 | 6.9 | 5.1 | 2.1 | 0.7 | 37.9 |
| Real GDP – rank | 1 | | 3 | 3 | 11 | — |
| Real GDP – share of world | 29.9% | 18.2% | 13.4% | 5.5% | 1.9% | — |
| Real GDP Growth YoY | 2.9% | 2.7% | 2.2% | 10.7% | 9.2% | 3.8% |
| GDP PPP[3] – trillions | 12.8 | 9.6 | 4.0 | 5.9 | 2.6 | 58.6 |
| GDP PPP – rank | 1 | | 3 | 2 | 4 | — |
| GDP per capita | 37,791 | 21,746 | 39,824 | 1,598 | 634 | 5,792 |
| GDP per capita – rank | 4 | | 3 | 102 | 131 | |
| GDP per capita PPP | 42,610 | 30,216 | 30,961 | 4,500 | 2,393 | 8,969 |
| GDP per capita PPP – rank | 5 | | 22 | 101 | 123 | |
| Population – millions | 299 | 317 | 128 | 1,312 | 1,110 | 6,538 |
| Population – rank | 3 | | 10 | 1 | 2 | — |
| Population growth rate | 1.0% | 0.5% | 0.0% | 0.6% | 1.4% | 1.2% |
| Fertility Rate[4] | 2.1 | 1.5 | 1.3 | 1.8 | 2.5 | 2.5 |
| Land Area – rank | 3 | | 61 | 2 | 7 | — |

[2]Data sources are the World Bank *World Development Indicators*, Organisation for Economic Co-Operation and Development, International Monetary Fund *International Financial Statistics*.
[3]All PPP figures are 2000 International Dollars.
[4]Fertility rate data is for 2004.
Rank excludes all Euro Area countries' individual ranks.

foreign assets and the interest it paid on its foreign liabilities. According to economic historians Christopher Meissner and Alan Taylor, this gap represented Britain's reward for risk-taking and its talent for financial innovation, as well as its reputation as a safe investment haven with secure property rights, economic stability, and deep, liquid financial markets. That the sun never set on the British Empire must have helped. But over time Britain's privilege as a financial pioneer dwindled as investors in other countries gradually adopted more sophisticated financial instruments and the emerging markets of the day grew less risky.

A century later, the United States is now the world's hegemon, a status—still largely intact despite the subprime mortgage-induced credit crisis—that again reflects a talent and taste for financial innovation and risk-taking as well as its economic strength and its financial and political stability. As a result, like nineteenth-century Britain, the United States has been earning more on its foreign assets than it pays on its foreign liabilities—by an amount that averaged 0.5 percent of GDP from 1981 to 2003, as estimated by Meissner and Taylor. Along with increased leverage, this privilege has allowed the United States to earn positive investment income on an annual basis through 2007 even as it recorded a growing net debt position for over 20 years, as shown in Figure 1.3. In other words, this country's net investment earnings have helped slow the growth in the U.S. current account deficit and contributed to its recent reversal.

But as happened in pre-World War I Britain, over time the U.S. privilege has declined, from 3 percent in the 1960s to 1 percent in recent years, according to Meissner and Taylor, as other countries have adopted U.S. financial practices. Combined with the growing U.S. net liability position, this loss of privilege could result in annual investment income turning negative and adding to the U.S. current account deficit. Thanks to the magic of compound interest, this small change, if continued, could significantly aggravate the stability issue, making the difference between a manageable payments deficit and an imbalance requiring a more painful adjustment.[6]

In this regard, however, the lessons from the First Globalization appear remarkably optimistic since, during that period, payments adjustment was surprisingly smooth. Indeed, Meissner and Taylor find that adjustment generally occurred without the severe GDP slowdowns typical of many post-World War II corrections. For the offshoot countries and other

U.S. Net Investment Income, 1976–2007

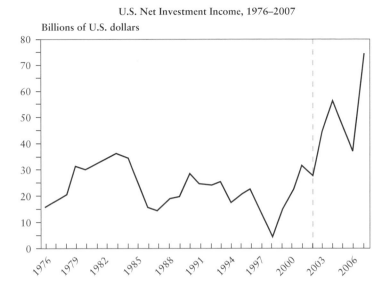

Net U.S. International Investment Position as a Share of GDP and as a Share of Domestic Financial Wealth, 1976–2006

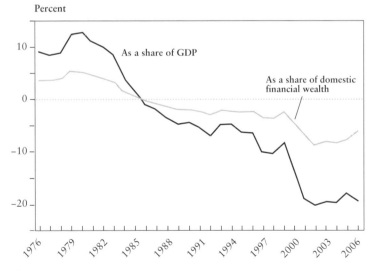

**Figure 1.3**
U.S. Net International Investment Position
*Source:* U.S. Bureau of Economic Analysis.
*Note:* Data from 2002 onward for U.S. net investment income are on a different conceptual basis than those prior to that time. Source data are not available to make similar adjustments to earlier years. Net U.S. international direct investment position is calculated at current cost.

borrowers that could credibly adhere to the gold standard, the reversal of payments imbalances did not generally involve a banking or currency crisis. Further, the nations that adopted the unforgiving gold standard as proof of good behavior did not suffer greater output losses during an adjustment than did the countries with flexible exchange rates, possibly because labor markets were also more flexible (and wages free to fall) in the early twentieth century. Overall, Meissner and Taylor argue that during the First Globalization, the capital-poor countries were able to run sustained deficits with smooth reversals as long as they invested the borrowed capital in productive ways that facilitated export growth and debt repayment. Today, Meissner and Taylor suggest, the United States' ability to avoid the hard landing and large dollar depreciation predicted by many analysts depends on our ability to maintain market confidence in this country's economic fundamentals.

Others are less agnostic on this point. Suzanne Berger questions whether foreign capital has in fact been used to build productive capacity in the United States, while John Helliwell warns that, in an era of multiple financial centers, the only way the United States can remain a magnet for foreign capital is to continue producing a steady stream of financial and other innovations and unusually high returns. If and when the luster disappears, disappointed investors are likely to flee—as happened in Asia in 1997–1998. And indeed, as the financial market distress triggered by the U.S. subprime credit crisis intensified in the third quarter of 2007 and the first quarter of 2008, U.S. net private portfolio flows turned notably negative.

## Labor Market Imbalances

As in the First Globalization, today's stubborn imbalances appear to be rooted (at least in part) in massive shifts in the size and location of the globally accessible labor supply. Indeed, the recent doubling of the globally active labor force may be one of the defining developments of our era. As Richard Freeman points out, until the end of the Cold War, China, India, and the ex-Soviet bloc countries were cut off from the world by trade barriers, capital controls, and restrictions on emigration. But with the collapse of the Soviet Union, China's turn toward market economics, and India's shift away from autarky, the supply of labor available to global producers roughly doubled from 1.5 billion to 3 billion people—though of this new supply of workers, a sizeable part remains in unproductive jobs located in rural areas and in state-owned enterprises, as suggested by Figure 1.4. While some argue that China is hardly a new player in the world economy, the country was largely closed to foreign investment from 1949 to the late 1980s. While postwar China first welcomed foreign investors in 1982, the 1989 Tiananmen tragedy scared them off. Almost a decade later, Y2K investments greatly improved Asia's global communications links, and China finally joined the World Trade Organization, earning its ultimate seal of approval, in 2001.

But the arrival of this additional labor supply did not increase the world's capital stock proportionately. Indeed, Freeman calculates that with the doubling of the global labor force, the capital-labor ratio fell to 61 percent of what it would have been had China, India, and the ex-Soviet bloc remained isolated. Naturally, newly arrived workers have benefited from the opportunity to work with capital and technology from the advanced countries. But comparably skilled workers in advanced countries find themselves in a weakened bargaining position vis-à-vis owners of capital everywhere and could face capital shallowing as well.

From the perspective of the American worker, China's daunting competitive threat reflects its remarkably low wages. According to the Bureau of Labor Statistics, average hourly compensation in China's manufacturing sector was just 67 cents in 2004, although anecdotal evidence suggests that Chinese wages have risen quite rapidly since then. But what producers really care about is relative labor costs adjusted for differences in productivity. And the gap between American and Asian labor costs per unit of output is much smaller than the gap between American and Asian wages. After adjusting for productivity differences, China is probably no more competitive overall than are high-income Hong Kong or Singapore—although the more productive foreign-affliated ventures in China's coastal provinces may have a significant competitive advantage. Still, history suggests that this gap between domestic and foreign unit labor costs tends to narrow over time as foreign productivity rises faster than productivity in the United States, but foreign wages rise even faster.

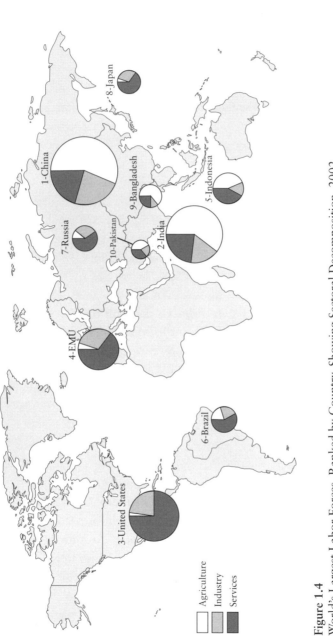

**Figure 1.4**
World's Largest Labor Forces, Ranked by Country, Showing Sectoral Decomposition, 2002
*Source:* International Labour Organization cited by the World Bank *World Development Indicators*; U.S. Department of State, *Key Labor Indicators*.
*Note:* The area of each pie is proportional to the size of the labor force of the selected region/country. Bangladesh's sectoral distribution data are for 2000; India's are for 2005.

While economists used to argue that American workers would always do well if only they invested in human capital and moved up the technology ladder to "better" jobs ahead of the foreign competition, China and India have not been following the economists' script. Rather these countries, particularly China, have been investing a surprising amount in education plus research and development (R&D) in order to "leapfrog" (to use Freeman's phrase) to higher levels of human capital and technical sophistication well ahead of schedule. As a result, Dani Rodrik finds that China's export bundle is far more sophisticated than one would expect given its low per capita income.[7] He attributes this success to China's industrial policy and its emphasis on technology transfer.

These Asian investments in human capital have produced some sobering statistics. While the United States accounted for 30 percent of world enrollment in higher education in the 1970s, as Freeman points out, this share had fallen to 14 percent by 2000. Similarly, in the 1970s, the United States produced 50 percent of the world's Ph.D.s, but it is expected to grant just 15 percent of the world's doctorates in 2010, when China alone will grant more Ph.D.s in science and engineering than the United States.[8] These developments are a matter of concern primarily because maintaining a leading role in high-tech sectors appears to require having a comparative advantage in scientists and engineers as well. Further, Freeman notes, innovation seems to depend on scale—on having a critical mass of researchers—rather than on achieving a given proportion of researchers in the workforce. While the United States is most unlikely to lose its critical mass or comparative advantage in high-tech industries any time soon, it could face growing challenges to its leadership role, at least in some sectors.

But beyond this competitive issue, as Freeman and Bhalla point out, we should rejoice that by bringing modern technology to all, globalization offers the prospect of "making poverty history." According to Judith Banister,[9] the real wages of urban manufacturing workers in China more than doubled between 1990 and 2002, while in India[10] real wages rose at a robust 4 percent a year in the second half of the 1990s.[11] As a result, rapid development has already lifted at least 450 million people out of $1-per-day poverty in China and India in the past 25 years.[12] But these declines in global income inequality have accompanied a highly visible increase in income inequality within China; these growing gaps are fueling social tensions, particularly in impoverished rural regions, as the Chinese government is acutely aware.

In the end, China and India will likely follow the path of developing countries before them. Wages and incomes will rise to rough parity with world levels. But the transition will take time. In South Korea, it lasted about 50 years, but the enormous scale of China's adjustment is even more daunting. Almost 200 million underemployed Chinese workers with huge incentives to move to better paid jobs in coastal urban areas remain in the countryside. Some 150 million have already moved, and more are following at the rate of more than 5 million a year by OECD estimates.[13] But because the Chinese government is concerned about urban overcrowding and unrest, it is using a variety of schemes like the Hukou system[14] to manage a migration that dwarfs the great European population movements of the nineteenth century. Still, if China's urban manufacturing wages continue to double every decade, Chinese wages will approach advanced country levels in about 30 years, according to Freeman's calculations. He estimates that it may take India 40 to 50 years to reach the same level. Other observers, including Alan Deardorff and Lawrence Lau, suggest that convergence may take even longer, given the remarkable degree of home bias in consumption and the size of China's labor surplus.[15]

Of course, if Chinese wages are likely to rise somewhat slowly, renminbi (RMB) appreciation offers an alternative way to narrow the gap between American or European and Chinese labor costs. But the Chinese government remains very cautious about allowing that process to occur. As this essay was being written in mid-2008, the dollar has fallen about 16 percent against the RMB since China ended its dollar peg in July 2005. This gradual decline reflects Chinese concern that rapid RMB appreciation might harm China's uncompetitive agricultural sector and stir political unrest in the countryside. It might also undermine the inefficient state-owned enterprises and the major banks whose assets are heavily weighted with loans to that sector of the economy. However, possibly because incomplete sterilization of Chinese foreign exchange market intervention has contributed to a disturbing increase in inflation, the

Chinese authorities have allowed the RMB to appreciate at a somewhat faster pace over the past year.

## The Essential Complements to Capital

The global distribution of labor and energy resources helps to explain the prevailing pattern of current account deficits and surpluses. But what explains the current pattern of capital flows? In particular, why are poor surplus countries willing to invest so much of their savings in the United States, a mature, wealthy country? Many analysts have found these wrong way flows to be a particular cause for concern.

Capital, a requirement for growth, embodies technology. But to make effective use of capital-cum-technology, as Brad DeLong reminds us, countries also need institutions like property rights, the rule of law, good management, good governance, and social and political security. Unfortunately, these complements to capital tend to be in relatively short supply in many developing countries.[16] So while economic theory suggests that capital ought to flow toward capital-poor countries, where the returns to investment should be high, in reality most developing countries are forced to raise most of their investment capital domestically. Making the task of raising capital intensities based on domestic savings alone all the more heroic, as DeLong points out, are the facts that in most developing countries population growth remains rapid and the real cost of capital remains high. Thus capital, or the lack thereof, represents a binding constraint on growth in many places.

During the First Globalization, to be sure, capital did flow from Britain to the offshoot countries and to the periphery as well, but, for the most part, these areas were under British rule. Indeed, the British East India Company literally governed India from the mid-1700s to the mid-1800s. And the offshoot countries were led by people who had brought British and other European institutions with them. Even so, in the nineteenth century the U.S. current account deficit generally amounted to about 0.5 to 1.0 percent of U.S. GDP, while investment spending equaled 20 percent of GDP. For the most part, in other words, foreign capital covered only a small portion of the required investment funds.

Today, by contrast, some analysts see net capital flows from China to the United States as a sign of a puzzling savings glut. But China's situation is not unique. Japan has run surpluses for years, with savings outstripping investment even in much of the 1950s. And since 1960 Malaysia and Indonesia have followed the Japanese path much of the time; see Figure 1.5. Perhaps world capital markets are just a lot less integrated than economists like to think. Indeed, while the financial market liberalization of the past two decades has led to large increases in gross capital flows to and from the developing nations, data on *net* capital flows suggest that global capital markets may be less integrated now than they were in the years before World War I—perhaps not in scale, but certainly in scope. Today, much capital flows among the rich nations, for diversification purposes, rather than from rich to poor regions as was the norm in the nineteenth century. Further, as DeLong points out, while the North American Free Trade Agreement encouraged a surge in U.S. direct investment in Mexico, rich Mexicans' concerns about monetary and political instability in their homeland produced even larger investment flows from Mexico to the United States. Similarly, DeLong notes, the Chinese government is purchasing insurance against social and political risk when it manages its exchange rate to ensure that exports grow fast enough to ensure absorption of the surplus labor flowing from the interior to the coasts.

But maybe these macroeconomic outcomes should only be expected. After all, according to Abhijit Banerjee and Colin Xu, in countries like China and India, even internal capital movements are highly constrained. In this regard, they cite the high cost of monitoring assets and collecting payments from small borrowers and the role of various institutions like the Hukou system and regional protectionism.[17] As a result of these impediments, interest rate spreads between deposit and loan rates or between loans to different borrowers can be enormous, even within a small geographic area,[18] and the marginal product of capital differs widely across regions and within narrow industries in both countries.

Yet, despite these many obstacles, and unlike portfolio capital, foreign direct investment (FDI) does flow to the developing countries on a net basis, as shown in Figure 1.6. And FDI carries technology, managerial skills, and growth-promoting institutions with it. In addition to serving

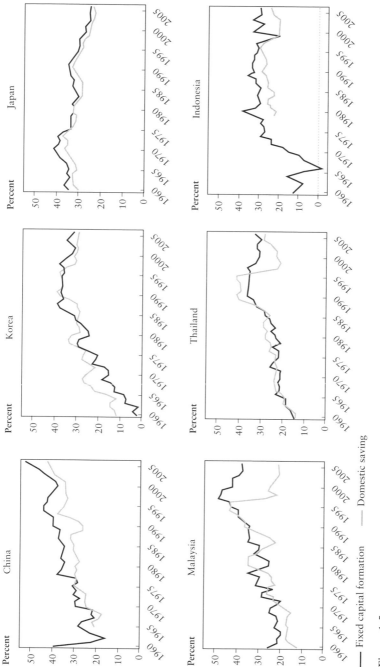

**Figure 1.5**
Fixed Capital Formation and Saving as a Percent of GDP in Selected Asian Economies, 1960–2006
*Source:* World Bank, *World Development Indicators.*

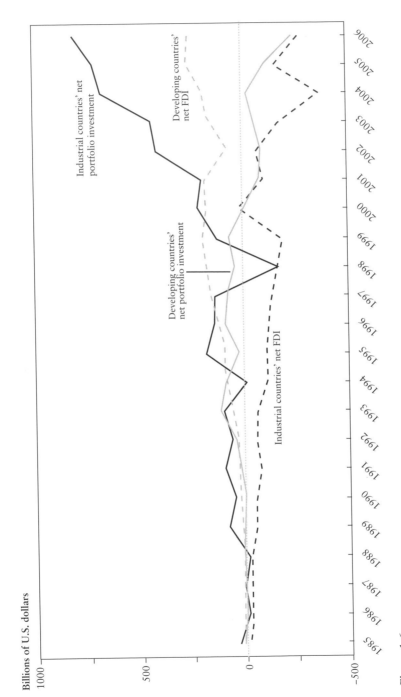

**Figure 1.6**
Industrial and Developing Countries' Net Portfolio and Net Foreign Direct Investment, 1985–2006
*Source:* International Monetary Fund, *Balance of Payments Statistics Yearbook*, Parts 2&3, 1992–2007.

as a conduit for the complements to capital, FDI is also more stable than portfolio flows, which are subject to sudden stops and reversals. Thus, as DeLong emphasizes, we should fervently hope—and governments should work to ensure—that gross and net FDI flows to the developing countries prove adequate to the task of providing these crucially important externalities.

### Explaining the Imbalance in Global Savings

The United States is clearly well endowed with the complements to capital. Why then does the United States, the "world's consumer of last resort," save so little? And why do the major surplus countries—currently China, Japan, Germany, and some of the oil-exporting nations—save so much? In 2006, U.S. gross national saving amounted to just 14 percent of GDP, one of the lowest ratios in the OECD, while Japan was saving almost twice and South Korea almost three times as much. In the context of the global imbalances, however, what really counts is the match or gap between domestic saving and domestic investment.

According to the U.S. national income accounts, between 1995 and 2007 the U.S. current account has deteriorated by about 4 percentage points of GDP. For the period as a whole, this development matched an increase in the gap between gross investment and private saving amounting to almost 4 percent of GDP, plus a small decline in government dissaving. But these numbers mask big swings in the government fiscal balance, which improved markedly in the late 1990s and then fell by almost 5 percent of GDP from 2000 to 2005. Within the private sector, net corporate saving is little changed, while personal saving has fallen near zero. Figure 1.7 shows the U.S. net savings rate between 1995 and 2006.

Yet Richard Cooper argues that when properly measured, U.S. households actually save a lot. Because "saving" is defined as consumption deferred today to raise consumption tomorrow, he believes that in the U.S. national income and product accounts, "saving" should actually include investment in education and durable goods as well as capital gains on wealth (which, thanks to ongoing financial innovations like mortgage equity withdrawals, have become ever more liquid). Adding in public and private pension claims,[19] American households have a good

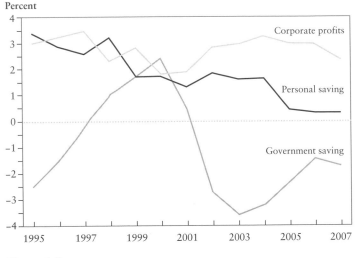

Percent

**Figure 1.7**
Net Saving by U.S. Public and Private Sectors as a Percent of GDP,
1982–2007
*Source:* U.S. Bureau of Economic Analysis
*Note:* Corporate profits includes inventory valuation and capital consumption
adjustments.

many sources of future income, he suggests—although, admittedly, the
uneven distribution of these resources may be cause for concern. But
overall, Cooper contends, it is not clear that the average U.S. household
needs to save more—or that it is likely to do so.

Similarly, corporate and government saving/investment are also poorly
measured by current national income accounting standards. Corporate
research and development (R&D), training, and branding are recorded
as intermediate business expenses, while government spending on R&D
and education are included in consumption, not investment. If U.S. spending on durable goods, education, and R&D were considered saving, then
U.S. "saving" would equal over 33 percent of GDP—hardly a sign that
the United States is shortchanging the future, in Cooper's view. Making
a similar measurement adjustment for other countries boosts their saving
rates as well, but generally by less than for the United States.[20] Still, while
it is useful to recognize that part of today's "consumption" spending is
actually "investment," it is spending nonetheless. Extra saving matched

by extra investment does nothing to improve the imbalance between saving and investment reflected in today's current account deficit.

Turning to why the major surplus countries save so much (relative to domestic investment) and invest a great deal in the United States, Cooper, DeLong, and others[21] point out that U.S. assets are attractive because over the long run the American economy remains robust and innovative and because U.S. financial markets offer liquidity, security, and stability—although the subprime mortgage crisis and related financial market distress may have raised questions about that reputation in recent months. In the major surplus countries, by contrast, investment opportunities are limited relative to the available savings—primarily because of demographic trends. Indeed, Cooper argues, the demographic differences among the world's nations are key considerations. Low population growth countries with declining numbers of young adults, like Japan and Germany, have limited need for investment in housing, education, and capital equipment, as the population pyramids in Figure 1.8 suggest. Moreover, as a result of its one-child policy, China will soon be a low population growth country as well, even though as a developing country it also faces huge housing and infrastructure needs. In China, therefore, investment is extraordinarily high—near 40 percent of GDP—but its savings rate is even higher because of China's inadequate social safety net and underdeveloped capital markets. Among the advanced economies, the United States is the demographic exception to the rule, as its fertility rate has remained relatively high, thanks to ongoing immigration on a significant scale.

Why are Japan and Germany not investing their surplus savings in the capital-poor developing countries, as economic theory suggests they should? Stated thus, the theory is just too simple, Cooper replies, because risk-averse investors seek a host of legal, political, and financial institutions, like the rule of law and secure property rights. Most low- and many middle-income countries do not offer these conditions, as discussed in the previous section, and as the recent rise of "resource nationalism" in many of the oil-exporting nations confirms.[22] By contrast, the United States does offer the required institutions—plus a higher return on investment than most other rich countries, at least as a general rule.

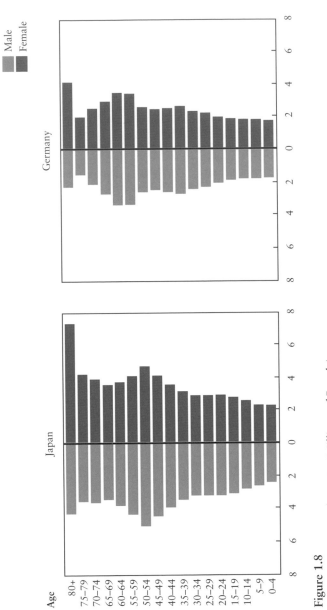

**Figure 1.8**
Population Pyramids, 2025 (Millions of People)
*Source:* U.S. Census Bureau.

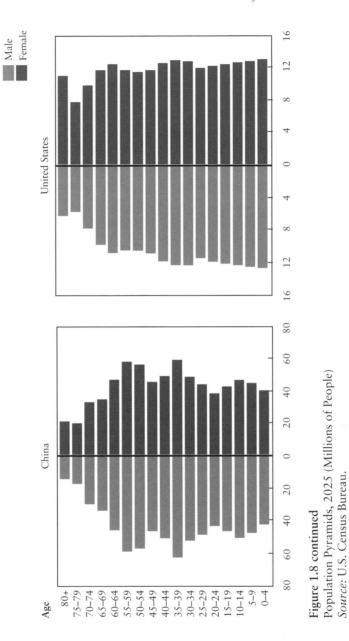

**Figure 1.8 continued**
Population Pyramids, 2025 (Millions of People)
*Source:* U.S. Census Bureau.

The demand for U.S. financial assets also reflects the fact that many, perhaps even most, countries are not comfortable with freely floating exchange rates, as Cooper, Peter Garber,[23] and Lawrence Summers all concur; thus, many governments choose to accumulate foreign exchange reserves and invest these in U.S. Treasury securities earning a modest return. In Cooper's view, these central banks are acting as financial intermediaries investing abroad on behalf of very conservative private savers (in Japan via the postal savings system) or on behalf of savers still facing capital controls (as in China). And even for developing China, the yield on U.S. government securities may not look so unattractive, given the country's current limited capacity to absorb capital. As symptoms of these limits, Larry Lau notes that the Chinese banking system continues to steer funds to unproductive projects, while the government keeps struggling to cool overheated investment spending.

Overall, in Cooper's judgment, a sizeable U.S. current account deficit is sustainable; indeed it may even be desirable. While the U.S. current account deficit clearly cannot continue to rise relative to GDP, it could certainly remain at a relatively high ratio to GDP for some years to come. Demographic trends in Europe, Japan, and parts of developing Asia will encourage those regions to accumulate external assets to draw down as the population ages. In contrast, the United States has notably different demographics. Although rich and politically mature, in a sense it remains a young and still developing country. The United States is also particularly good at inventing ways to exchange low-risk claims for high-risk assets. To be sure, some of these innovative assets can turn out to be unsound, as the subprime mortgage crisis has revealed. But even so, to date, surprisingly few U.S. financial institutions have had much trouble raising new capital from foreign investors, including sovereign wealth funds.[24] Seemingly, then, the world's savers still want to invest a significant portion of their savings in the United States, Cooper concludes.

But not everyone agrees with this assessment. Foremost among those with a less sanguine interpretation of recent trends in the U.S. saving-investment imbalance is Larry Kotlikoff. Admitting to little concern about the U.S. current account deficit[25] per se, he focuses instead on the disturbing decline in U.S. net investment and even faster decline in U.S. net saving relative to GDP.[26] Noting that government consumption has not been unusually high in recent years, Kotlikoff blames the fall in U.S. savings on increased private consumption, which now accounts for over 70 percent of GDP, its highest share since World War II. In particular, he points to an increase in consumption by the elderly, which he attributes to a fiscal policy that for decades has been transferring money from the young to the old via Social Security, Medicare, and Medicaid benefits. Citing Smetters and Gokhale, Kotlikoff emphasizes that with the aging of the baby boom generation, the present value of the fiscal gap—projected government receipts minus projected government expenditures—amounts to $63 trillion.[27] At some point, Kotlikoff warns, the U.S. government's looming fiscal gap will spook the financial markets; investors will unload U.S. government securities and dollars, U.S. interest rates and inflation will rise, and a disorderly correction will be under way.

But as several conference participants observed, most other advanced countries face equally difficult fiscal futures, for which—small comfort—they are no better prepared than is the United States. In addition, some attendees suggested that investors already assume that the U.S. government will find ways to modify—or renege on—its commitments to the elderly. More basically, as Guy Debelle reminded the group, current account deficits and fiscal deficits are distant cousins, not twins. Curing a fiscal deficit need not cure a current account deficit, or vice versa. In this regard, Cooper emphasized that while he is not worried about today's U.S. current account deficit, he strongly agrees with Kotlikoff that this country has a very serious fiscal problem related to Medicare—now that Americans have decided that death is increasingly "becoming an option."

## When Will Adjustment Occur, and How Might This Happen?
## A Continuum of Views

In mid-2006, at the time of the conference, the U.S. current account deficit equaled 6.1 percent of GDP; now in mid-2008 it is "only" 5 percent—still plenty large enough to trigger previous episodes of sudden stops and disorderly correction in other countries. Thus, it remains relevant to ask whether further adjustment of the current global imbalances will occur soon and abruptly or take place gradually over a more extended period.

Will the costs of this reversal be modest and concentrated in the United States, or will the adjustment result in a global slowdown? Indeed, the latter is a key concern as the world navigates the financial and real economic spillovers from the U.S. subprime mortgage crisis. Opinions at the conference, and even now, range along a continuum extending from Cooper's confident optimism to Kotlikoff's heightened anxiety.

Per force, adjustment—whenever it occurs—will require that U.S. output grow faster than U.S. demand. There is no other way that these imbalances can be reduced. Narrowing the current gap between U.S. gross domestic demand and output can occur only through some combination of slower U.S. demand growth, faster foreign demand growth, and dollar depreciation to encourage U.S. production and foreign consumption. In the face of further adjustment, foreign officials may stop suggesting that more U.S. saving, particularly by the government, is all that is needed to redress these imbalances. As Larry Summers noted, more U.S. saving without offsetting foreign stimulus would likely result in an unpalatable slowdown in world growth—as, mid-2008, we may be poised to find out.

Indeed, as signaled by the persistence of these ongoing global imbalances, most players appear to be reasonably satisfied with the current situation—at least for now. In addition to Cooper and Debelle, Dooley, Folkerts-Landau, and Garber (DFG) are prominent among the analysts arguing this more sanguine case. In the DFG view, developing countries seek to borrow capital, particularly FDI capital, at least on a gross basis. But to attract gross inflows in this postcolonial era, emerging countries have needed to accumulate net dollar collateral, which they have posted in the form of foreign exchange reserves. More importantly, China and much of Asia are convinced that they need export-led growth to absorb their supplies of underemployed labor. Indeed, China and many other Asian countries' vast underemployment and savings are the central driving forces in the Bretton Woods II system[28]—as signaled by world interest rates that have been unusually low, not high. U.S. savings may have fallen, in other words, but the increased supply of foreign savings has been the dominant development driving these sustained global imbalances. In the advanced countries, moreover, almost everyone has been pleased to enjoy real long-term interest rates and core inflation rates that have been somewhat lower—and equity and housing wealth that have been somewhat higher—than would otherwise have prevailed in the absence of such imbalances. In addition, producers who can access Asia's low-cost labor supply have been co-opted. They no longer clamor for protection and have largely abandoned labor to fight globalization on its own. For political and economic reasons, thus, the Bretton Woods II arrangement has already proved itself to be remarkably stable.

In the DFG view, eventual adjustment, when it comes, is likely to involve a slow rise in real interest rates as China becomes more fully integrated into world capital markets. They foresee that most of the adjustment in the U.S. trade account will occur as U.S. demand responds to these higher real interest rates. The dollar will depreciate against the RMB, but only gradually and moderately.[29] Reserve diversification by foreign officials would have little or no lasting effect on dollar-euro exchange rates because dollar-euro assets are close substitutes in the view of most private investors, DFG suggest.

While Cathy Mann tends to agree with DFG regarding the likely stability of the current imbalances, absent a "proper jolt," she questions the desirability of that outcome.[30] She builds her analysis around four Cs: consumption, codependency, complacency, and, possibly, crisis. Since the mid-1990s U.S. consumption has increased a good deal as a share of GDP, reinforcing the codependent relationship between the United States and its creditors. This codependency is based on unhealthy habits—an overemphasis on consumption in the United States and on production in China and Asia—that could last a long time. In China, these habits stunt financial market development and lead to a misallocation of still-scarce resources; in the United States, these habits create a dangerous buildup of foreign-owned debt and a risky reliance on a narrowing set of foreign official investors who could tire of accumulating dollar assets at any time. Mann warns against complacency—on the part of the private investors and policymakers as well.

In Mann's opinion, adjustment requires slower U.S. growth (not brought about by the integration of Asia into world capital markets but, as Mann proposed, by tighter monetary policy or, as has actually occurred, by increased risk aversion provoked by the subprime crisis) plus significant dollar depreciation. Indeed, airing a related and prescient scenario, William Dudley[31] suggested that U.S. household equity and real estate wealth were unlikely to continue growing at the unusually rapid rate of recent years. Thus, the American household saving rate would rise, and U.S. demand growth would weaken. As a result, U.S. interest rates would fall, triggering a depreciation of the dollar and, thus, a decline in the U.S. standard of living.[32] Hardly a disaster scenario, Dudley noted in mid-2006, but a plausible unwinding of the current imbalances.

In the end, Mann, joined by Larry Summers, Brad DeLong, and a growing minority as the conference progressed, was less certain than DFG and Richard Cooper that adjustment will occur without a crisis—especially since private investors exhibit occasional signs of waking from their complacency. But "crisis" is defined in the mind of the beholder, Mann suggests. How benign were the sharp (roughly 30 percent[33]) dollar depreciation of 1985–1987 and the ensuing balance of payments adjustment shown in Figure 1.9? Did these adjustments constitute a crisis? For the United States, clearly not. From Japan's perspective, however, the answer might be yes, since Japan's effort to curb yen appreciation at that time clearly laid the basis for its bubble economy in the late 1980s and the dismal period that followed. While Eswar Prasad was less ready than Mann and Kotlikoff to forecast a crisis, as a preventative measure, he urged policymakers to focus on what countries need most for their own internal balance. China, for instance, needs exchange rate flexibility to develop its domestic financial markets and use its capital more effectively, he suggests.

## What Is to Be Done in Uncertain Times?

What are the policy implications of today's still-large global payments imbalances? And how pressing is this question, now that the U.S. current account appears to be stabilizing? The improvement reflects the recent slowdown in U.S. relative to foreign growth and a 25-percent decline in the real broad trade-weighted dollar from its early 2002 peak to levels near its previous lows of 1978 and 1995. Looking ahead, forecasts for the U.S. current account over the next two years are mixed; most expect ongoing improvement, while others see stability or a return to somewhat larger deficits relative to GDP.

Index, March 1973 = 100

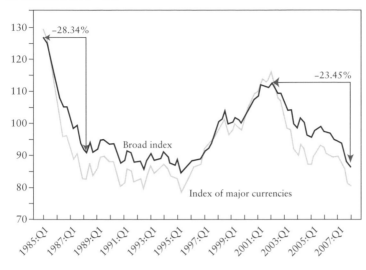

**Figure 1.9**
Real Trade-Weighted Exchange Value of the U.S. Dollar, 1985:Q1–2008:Q1
*Source:* Federal Reserve Board.
*Note:* Countries whose currencies are included in the Index for Major Currencies
are Euro Area, Japan, United Kingdom, Switzerland, Australia, and Sweden.
Broad Index has 19 additional currencies.

But whatever the immediate outlook, the current highly uneven distribution of world resources strongly suggests that today's payments imbalances could prove to be recurring and remarkably persistent. It will likely
take at least three decades for Chinese wages to reach world levels—somewhat less for Eastern Europe, somewhat more for India. Demographic
trends are unlikely to reverse, even with plausible changes in immigration
policies. And it seems improbable that the emerging giants will offer all
of the institutional features of mature financial centers any time soon. In
the meantime, a U.S. payments gap shrinking to 5 or even 4 percent of
GDP remains a substantial deficit, and would leave the world vulnerable
to a sudden bout of disorderly dollar depreciation.

What then should policymakers do to facilitate smooth—if gradual—
adjustment? Particularly if this rebalancing act is likely to be stretched
out, a primary concern for all must be maintaining the credibility of the
monetary, fiscal, and, more recently, supervisory authorities on both sides

of the surplus/deficit divide. For the developing countries, in particular, the main message is loud and clear: the importance of developing the good legal, political, and social institutions that comprise the essential complements to capital found in the world's financial centers. This theme, repeated throughout the conference, was echoed at the end by Larry Summers, who insisted that it is profoundly important that we find ways to get capital to flow in the "right" direction. Embracing FDI, which serves as a conduit for the complements to capital, was one specific policy prescription. Increased investment in human capital—health and education, especially in rural areas—was another.

Further, although a fixed exchange rate may well hinder the healthy evolution of a domestic money market in developing countries and clearly interferes with the conduct of an independent monetary policy, many of today's emerging giants continue to embrace this exchange rate regime for reasons ranging from a dependence on export-led employment growth to fears about reversible capital flows. Thus, as Summers put it, the "least expensive lunch" for these central banks may be figuring out how to invest their foreign exchange reserves more profitably.[34] In this context, new initiatives from China, the oil exporters, and some other emerging markets regarding reserve management via their sovereign wealth funds are an interesting and potentially promising development.

As for the United States, because monetary policy is a blunt instrument, most conference participants agreed that it would be nonsense for the Federal Reserve to engineer an outright recession to achieve, at most, a modest decrease in the U.S. current account deficit. Rather, as Governor Donald Kohn emphasized, the Fed makes its key contribution to orderly adjustment by maintaining investor confidence in its ability to deliver low, stable inflation. However, a few participants did note that an extended period of low U.S. interest rates undoubtedly contributed to the rise in equity and residential real estate prices in recent years and, thus, through the wealth effect, to strong(er) consumption and investment. Accordingly, Summers suggested that monetary policymakers should be catholic in choosing the set of variables they weigh in setting policy, including asset prices and exchange rates in particular.[35] For this reason, he argued, the current period is no time for the Fed to don a straitjacket by adopting an explicit inflation target.

Unlike monetary policy, fiscal policy is actually well suited to affecting saving behavior—public saving, obviously, but private saving as well. For instance, once the current house price correction is behind us, policymakers might want to rethink the extent to which we subsidize housing investment in this country. Maybe subsidizing one dwelling per household would be enough? After all, to facilitate repayment of this country's growing foreign debt, Congress might want to favor productive investment—in science education, say—rather than less productive investment in housing. Even more compelling is the need to deal with the very large fiscal deficits scheduled to arrive over the next 25 to 30 years with the aging and retirement of the baby boom generation, absent strong and prompt Congressional action.[36] Today, foreign investors are largely ignoring this country's irresponsible fiscal stance. Tomorrow, they just might take notice.

How workers in advanced countries fare will depend on the balance between the declines in real prices and in real compensation associated with the emergence of the new giants. Ideally, the global spread of innovative effort and new technologies will increase productivity, lower costs, and raise living standards everywhere. Thus, policymakers should aim to keep rising protectionism at bay by favoring labor over capital (which will be able to fend for itself). Examples of such policies include decoupling health insurance coverage from employment in the United States and encouraging improved labor standards in the developing countries.[37] Further, maintaining our competitiveness in coming decades will require the United States to invest more in education—in particular, in an education that gets students hooked on science and provides a less U.S.-centric view of the world. In addition, Ambassador Stephen Bosworth and Larry Summers both stressed the need for American students to gain a better understanding of Asian developments and perspectives.

In the end, U.S. policymakers must focus on what they can control, fixing what they can, accepting what they can't, and having the wisdom to know the difference.[38] China—practical and cautious—faces huge domestic challenges and is not likely to be much moved or hurried by U.S. Congressional or Administration pressures. India's challenges are equally daunting. In addressing what they can, U.S. policymakers might well start with what needs to be done for the domestic economy,

Millions of employees                    Thousands of U.S. dollars

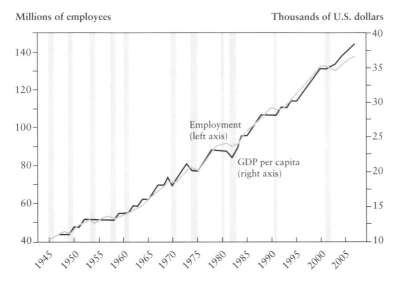

**Figure 1.10**
U.S. Total Nonfarm Employment and Real GDP per Capita, 1945–2007
*Source:* U.S. Bureau of Economic Analysis, U.S. Bureau of Labor Statistics,
U.S. Census Bureau.
*Note:* Gray bars indicate recession shading.

balancing the needs of current and future generations. As for what they
cannot control, U.S. policymakers may want to recall that despite—or was
it, in part, because of?—the re-emergence of postwar Europe and the arrival
of Japan and South Korea as major economies thereafter, U.S. employment
and living standards have continued to rise, albeit it with brief pauses,
relentlessly higher, as depicted in Figure 1.10. Thus, it seems safe to expect
that, despite the transitional challenges, as Chinese and Indian incomes
converge with world levels over the next 50 years, the impact on global
living standards will, on balance, be enormously positive.

## Notes

1. As discussed more fully later, the global labor supply conditions that contributed to the U.S. current account deficit and matching financial inflows helped
keep U.S. inflation and interest rates lower than otherwise would have been the
case, thus fanning the U.S. house price boom that began in the late 1990s.

2. As foreigners' U.S. assets rise, so too do U.S. interest payments on those assets; thus, stabilizing the current account—which includes interest payments—relative to output requires that the current account deficit grow no faster than nominal GDP. In these days of relatively low inflation, achieving nominal U.S. GDP growth of over 5 or 6 percent is no longer a sure bet.

3. Maurice Obstfeld and Alan M. Taylor, "Globalization and Capital Markets," in *Globalization in Historical Perspective*, ed. Michael D. Bordo, Alan M. Taylor, and Jeffrey G. Williamson (Chicago: University of Chicago Press, 2003), 121–183.

4. Robert Barde, Susan B. Carter, and Richard Sutch, "International Migration," in *Historical Statistics of the United States*, vol. 1, Population (New York: Cambridge University Press, 2006), 523–540.

5. British net foreign assets reached 200 percent of U.K. GDP in 1913.

6. Total return on U.S. foreign assets includes capital gains, which have been trending up by Meissner and Taylor's estimates. But since the source of these gains is not well understood, Meissner and Taylor warn against counting on continued increases.

7. Dani Rodrik, "What's So Special about China's Exports?" *China & World Economy* 14(5) (2006): 1–19.

8. Of course, many of the newly-minted Ph.D.s from U.S. universities will be granted to foreign students who may—or increasingly may not—decide to stay in this country.

9. Banister, Judith, "Manufacturing Earnings and Compensation in China," *Monthly Labor Review* 128 (2005): 22–40.

10. Glinskaya, Elena and Michael Lokshin, "Wage Differentials Between the Public and Private Sector in India" (Policy Research Paper 3574, World Bank, Washington, DC, 2005). Cited by Freeman.

11. By contrast, in the United States, real wages for nonfarm production workers rose by about 10 percent in total between 1990 and 2008.

12. Shaohua Chen and Martin Revallion, "How Have the World's Poorest Fared since the Early 1980s?" *The World Bank Research Observer* 19(2) (2004): 141–169. Bhalla estimates a much higher number in Surjit S. Bhalla, *Imagine There's No Country: Poverty, Inequality, and Growth in the Era of Globalization* (Washington, D.C. Institute for International Economics, 2002).

13. Anders Reutersward, "Labour Protection in China" (Social, Employment and Migration Working Papers No. 30, Organisation for Economic Co-operation and Development, Paris, 2005).

14. Hukou refers to China's household registration system, which operates to control access to public benefits like education, healthcare, and pension rights. Because the system generally limits such access to an individual's birth place, the government has used Hukou to guide labor mobility across China.

15. Shankar Acharya pointed out that only a small fraction of India's labor force is currently employed in the organized —as distinct from the informal—manufacturing sector. He blames a long history of dysfunctional labor laws.

16. In this connection, the recent passage of Communist China's new law strengthening property rights (first acknowledged in the Chinese constitution in 2004) is an intriguing development.

17. Other barriers might include India's caste system and the use of multiple spoken languages—15 in India and at least eight in China—which tend to foster the separate communities or trust networks that are the focus of Helliwell's recent work. See also Arvinder Singh, "Labour Mobility in China and India: The Role of Hukou, Caste, and Community" in *China and India: Learning from Each Other*, eds. Jahangir Aziz, Steven Dunaway, and Eswar Prasad (Washington, DC, International Monetary Fund, 2006), 241–261.

18. Banerjee mentions a basic deposit rate of 10 percent coexisting with a loan rate of 78.5 percent, and local loan rates varying between 48 percent a year and 5 percent a day (16,000 percent a year).

19. Cooper notes that the liabilities for private pensions have been an important spur to corporate saving in recent years.

20. Raising another measurement issue, Debelle noted that capital gains, which are more important for U.S. than for foreign investors, are not included in the current account but do show up in balance sheet measures like wealth. It is more appropriate, he argues, and much more reassuring, to measure U.S. net liabilities to foreigners against U.S. wealth rather than against U.S. GDP (see Figure 1.3).

21. See, for instance, Ricardo J. Caballero, Emmanuel Farhi and Pierre-Olivier Gourinchas, "An Equilibrium Model of 'Global Imbalances' and Low Interest Rates" (Working Paper 11996, National Bureau of Economic Research, Cambridge, MA, 2006).

22. Increased resource nationalism has led host countries, including Bolivia, Iran, Russia, and Venezuela to renegotiate access and revenue terms. Russia, for instance, has threatened to revoke oil and gas drilling licenses in Siberia and Sakhalin Island on the basis of "safety violations" and "environmental concerns." Investors also worry that Russia may be intent on renationalizing its energy sector.

23. As Peter Garber sees it, some bloc of countries of varying membership has always needed or wanted the stability of a fixed exchange rate; he expects they will continue to do so "for the foreseeable future." But once their domestic financial markets are more fully developed, and they are able to make a credible commitment to keeping inflation low and stable, some of these countries may find it easier to shift to a more flexible exchange rate regime.

24. Sovereign wealth funds are the professionally managed state-owned investment vehicles funded by foreign exchange assets and commodity export receipts that tend to invest in riskier assets than central banks have traditionally chosen for their foreign exchange reserves.

25. Or capital account surplus, as Kotlikoff prefers to call it, given his focus on saving and investment behavior.

26. By contrast, in this context, Cooper prefers gross to net measures of saving and investment, in part because it is gross investment that brings new technology.

27. This estimate uses rather conservative assumptions regarding health care costs and assumes that future generations face the same net tax rates as today's. See Jagadeesh Gokhale and Kent Smetters, "Fiscal and Generational Imbalances: An Update" in *Tax Policy and the Economy,* vol. 20, (Cambridge, MA: The MIT Press, 2006), 193–223.

28. The term "Bretton Woods II," coined by DFG, refers to the dollar exchange standard adopted at Bretton Woods, New Hampshire, in 1944 and in effect until the United States cut the dollar's ties to gold in 1971. In the original Bretton Woods arrangement, the United States maintained the dollar's value in terms of gold, and other countries pegged to the dollar. Under Bretton Woods II, a group of countries is choosing voluntarily to fix or closely tie their currencies to the U.S. dollar.

29. Supporting this point, Larry Lau argued that once capital controls are removed, private Chinese demand for U.S. dollar assets is likely to prove substantial. He also noted that, given the small share of domestic content in Chinese exports, it would take a large RMB appreciation to reduce Chinese exports notably.

30. Does the recent house price correction, begun in the United States but spreading beyond to some other advanced economies, represent a "proper jolt"? Mann concludes that determining the strength of the links between the subprime-led crisis in the United States and global external imbalances will require future research.

31. Executive Vice President, Markets Group, Federal Reserve Bank of New York.

32. Larry Summers describes a similar scenario with spillovers to global growth in a March 26, 2007, comment in the *Financial Times* (Lawrence Summers, "As America Falters, Policymakers Must Look Ahead," *Financial Times*, March 26, 2007) as well as in his essay in this volume.

33. From a peak in early 1985 to late 1987, the trade-weighted dollar fell almost 40 percent in real terms against other major currencies.

34. More recently, the Asian Development Bank has also urged central banks to invest their reserves in infrastructure, human capital, or financial assets earning more than U.S. Treasury securities. It points out that earning an additional 500 basis points on half of the region's reserves would yield a dividend equal to 0.8 percent of Asian GDP. Michiyo Nakamato, "Asia States Warned on Danger of Reserves: ADB Advises Investment Plans to Avoid Asset Bubbles," *Financial Times*, March 28, 2007, page 1. See also ADB, *Asian Development Outlook 2007*, March 2007.

35. By contrast, Shankar Acharya suggested prudential measures to address asset price concerns.

36. According to the U.S. Comptroller General's January 2007 testimony to the U.S. Senate Budget Committee, under conservative "intermediate" assumptions, expenditures for Social Security, Medicare, and Medicaid are projected to rise from 9 percent of GDP today to 15.5 percent in 2030. As a result, the fiscal deficit will likely deteriorate from near balance in 2001 to minus 20 percent of GDP ("out of control," as the Comptroller General sees it) by 2040. In early 2008 the "daunting" prognosis was essentially the same.

37. Suzanne Berger also proposed strengthening U.S. wage insurance programs to help counter the growing popularity of protectionist "remedies."

38. With apologies to Reinhold Niehbuhr as well as to Eswar Prasad, who advocated first setting one's own house in order—not only to reap the immediate internal benefits but also to strengthen the economy against future external shocks.

# 2

## Dancing with Giants: The Geopolitics of East Asia in the Twenty-First Century

# Dancing with Giants: The Geopolitics of East Asia in the Twenty-First Century

Stephen W. Bosworth

I am going to talk about what is happening in East Asia, the possible implications of these events, and how U.S. policy toward the region might be shaped. As a former U.S. diplomat, I spent much of my professional career in East Asia at a time when we had a very powerful and effective lodestar for American policy. We wanted to prevent the region's domination by any single power or combination of powers that could be hostile to the United States. This policy arose during the Cold War, and it was very similar to the approach that we took with regard to Western Europe. From a strategic point of view, these were judged to be the two regions which were most vital to the welfare and security of the United States.

In East Asia, this policy worked pretty well for a long time. While it was somewhat costly and somewhat expensive, it was nonetheless quite effective. But over the last couple of decades, U.S. policy toward East Asia has shifted rather dramatically, which I will summarize. In the interests of full disclosure, much of my discussion is drawn from a book, *Chasing the Sun: Rethinking East Asian Policy* (2006), which I co-authored with Morton Abramowitz.

First, over the last generation or so, East Asia has become a major economic power, and is still rising. East Asia now accounts for 25 percent or more of global exports, almost 25 percent of global imports, and 21 percent of foreign direct investment in the world. Perhaps the most gripping figure of all is that 63 percent of international reserves are held by the countries of East Asia.

Fifteen years ago, I never would have predicted the massive shift in global reserves from elsewhere in the world to East Asia. Over the last

25 years, this growth process has been occurring in tandem with China's marvelous rise. It has posted 25 years of double-digit growth that has lifted 200 to 300 million people out of abject poverty and into an urban-based and consumer-oriented middle class. Of course, simple arithmetic tells you that 600 to 800 million Chinese still live pretty much the way they did 25 years ago, which must be factored into any consideration of China's future prospects.

In the United States, there is presently a great debate over what China's fantastic rise poses for our nation's economy and security. There is disagreement over what China's goals might be and what it seeks to accomplish as its economic power grows. Clearly, as one looks at China, the future is not guaranteed; my co-author and I do not believe that one should blithely assume a linear progression over the next 25 years based on what has happened in China during the last 25 years. With that caveat, I think that China has acquired enormous momentum, both economically and socially. I certainly would not want to bet against China continuing this very rapid process of growth over another generation, but I think this will be harder to accomplish than the gains it has made over the last two decades.

China's growth has in turn fueled the growth of East Asia, and begun the dramatic process of knitting the East Asian economies together. When we started traveling in the region a couple of years ago, talking to people and doing interviews about what we might write about in this book, this was the most striking thing that we found. Asians, particularly in the aftermath of the 1997–1998 Asian financial crisis, began in very real ways to think about their economies as inextricably linked together. From an economic point of view, there is a remarkable degree of integration within East Asia. This has been a market-driven phenomenon sparked almost entirely by the private sector. This development stands, in some contrast, to what happened when Western European governments set a series of political goals concerning economic integration, and then the market and the private sector tried to act within that framework. In East Asia, governments have been entirely outflanked by what has been happening in the private sector. I think one of the reasons for this economic integration has been the manner in which China, starting in 1979, chose to modernize its economy. The very fateful decision by Deng Xiaoping was to open China to foreign direct investment gradually at first, and then speed it up. As foreign direct investment began to come into China, we started to see, particularly in the last decade, the establishment of production networks that now characterize much of the trade within East Asia. This is particularly true for the portion of trade accounted for by multinational corporations, both East Asian-based multinationals, and American- and other western-based multinationals.

East Asia's pace of integration has been quite remarkable. In 1981, 33 percent of East Asia's international trade occurred within the region. By 2005, that number increased to more than 50 percent. I would submit that is pretty dramatic and rapid progress, and showcases in many ways the power of the free market in East Asia, because for the most part, governments did not try to prevent this from happening. (On occasion, Taiwan tried to prevent it happening within inland China, but this is the exception to the rule.) But neither did governments explicitly do much to try to encourage it. This regional economic integration was a private sector, market-driven phenomenon. As this has developed, particularly within the last decade or so, we have begun to see the emergence of what I would describe as an East Asian regional identity. People who still think of themselves as Japanese, Korean, Singaporean, or Taiwanese now have also begun to think of themselves as East Asian. The people in these countries are growing more accustomed to moving back and forth in terms of employment from one East Asian economy to another. East Asian tourism is booming. Now you find the Chinese traveling all around the world, but particularly in East Asia, where the Chinese are as ubiquitous as the Japanese were a generation ago. South Korean property developers are building golf courses and resorts all along the coast looking to serve a market from China that is materializing quickly. There is a kind of consensus about what it means to be Asian. In some ways, the same thing happened in the early 1990s with the then-emerging debate over what constituted "Asian values." This coming together was rather harshly interrupted in the late 1990s by the Asian financial crisis. Now this broader regional identification is being revived, and I think is occurring in a way that is probably healthier and more sustainable over the long term.

This process of economic integration continues apace, but in part because of the experience of the Asian financial crisis, which they consider an unfortunate result of western-dominated international financial institutions. Particularly since 1998, at the governmental level the East Asians have been moving full speed ahead to try to put together new regionally based institutions, which they argue are necessary because they learned from the 1997–1998 debacle that they cannot count on outside forces to come and help them.

I say this without a issuing a value judgment as to whether they are right or wrong in making this assessment. One can argue about the general East Asian sentiment that international financial institutions did not do what should have been done. But they believe that this was the case, and the resulting response has been the very rapid growth of new East Asian institutions.

The Association of South East Asian Nations (ASEAN), which has been around since shortly before the end of the Vietnam War, has been the cornerstone in all of this. A new organization called ASEAN Plus Three has been put together with China, Japan, and South Korea. It has annual summit meetings, and ministerial meetings take place year-round. In late 2005, the first East Asian Summit was held. Now, for Americans, the strange thing about that summit meeting was that apparently our invitation got lost in the mail, because we were not included. Some of you may recall that back in the late 1980s and early 1990s, Malaysia's then-prime minister Mohamad Mahathir had a similar idea. He thought it would be nifty if the East Asians could get together without the U.S. elephant being in the room. Jim Baker, our Secretary of State at the time, thought that was about the worst idea he had ever heard, and engaged in a display of lightning and thunder to ensure that it didn't come off. Japan and South Korea, who at the time were the two biggest players on the East Asian stage, were persuaded that they should not support it, and so it never came to pass.

We interviewed Mahathir Mohamad in preparation for our book, and to say that this is a man who has seen vindication is an understatement. He is very pleased to see that an East Asian summit has been held without the participation of the United States. There is even considerable talk in the region about something called an East Asian community. Now, what that might mean remains very much to be defined. But, I think there is a growing feeling within the region that part of East Asia's destiny may well lie in a gradual but increasingly active series of commitments leading to something which could be called an East Asian community. There are substantial barriers and obstacles to that goal, as there were in the case of Europe. Perhaps in the case of East Asia the main one is the fact that China and Japan, the region's two largest powers, at the moment act as though they really cannot stand one another. Both countries have had very little success in reigning in their tendencies toward nationalism.

Nonetheless, even China and Japan talk to outsiders and to each other about the need for greater regional cooperation. It is not hard to figure out why they do this. For China, I think an open commitment to a more multilateral approach to the region, rather than picking off each country in the region one by one, is very much in keeping with their desire to reassure the rest of East Asia that it has nothing to fear from China's rise. In the case of Japan, as when the Lilliputians tried to deal with Gulliver, I think that many Japanese have concluded that it is good to tie China into a web of multilateral commitments and benefits in the hope that this will serve to restrain China's actions. It is also in some measure a way of institutionalizing Japan's current leadership position in the region.

We make no prediction about where this movement towards an East Asian community is likely to go. We do find that it is a very real phenomenon and not just a bunch of diplomatic palaver. They really mean this. There are people in all the capital cities of East Asia who are committed to continuing the process of building multilateral regional institutions.

Another significant change in the context in which East Asia now operates is that the attitude of the United States toward the region has changed dramatically. In great measure this change was precipitated by September 11 and by our excessive preoccupation, when viewed through East Asian eyes, with what we call the global war on terror. This focus, in the minds of many of East Asia, has caused the United States' attention to wander in terms of the key elements that really matter to the East Asians and, they would argue, should matter to us. The global war on terror of course has been greatly complicated by the Iraq War, which has been a further distraction.

There is a feeling in East Asia that the United States is not really paying much attention to them. This viewpoint is particularly prevalent in Southeast Asia, where countries like Indonesia, Singapore, Thailand, and Vietnam believe that we have really neglected them for most of this decade, except for occasional episodic fits of attention such as after the December 2004 tsunami. Throughout the region, there is a sense that we do not care about East Asia quite as much as we used to, particularly not as much as we did during the Cold War, but not even as much as we used to before the global war on terror became such a preoccupation for the United States.

In terms of American foreign policy, some things have not changed in East Asia, including the two most important items. One is the continuing problem of Taiwan, the Taiwan Straits, and the future of China's relationship with that wandering province. The second is the problem of North Korea, where we have had what in effect is our third nuclear crisis in the last decade and a half.

Those are two problems that almost everyone in East Asia agrees will continue to attract U.S. attention. There is a general feeling in East Asia that neither of those two problems can be effectively managed without the concerted attention and engagement of the United States.

I think that most Americans would agree with that assessment, although our attention does seem, to me at least, to have wandered substantially over the last few years with regard to North Korea, though not so much with regard to Taiwan. With Taiwan, of course, the problem is that for the last couple of decades we have always hoped and assumed that this problem would cure itself, largely through economic integration. The thinking held that as Taiwan's economy became more and more tied into mainland China, the prospect of conflict over the future of Taiwan would diminish. In some measure, I am still confident that is the case. But there is no question that the emergence of democracy in Taiwan has significantly complicated this issue. Not surprisingly, Taiwan believes that it should have the same chance to pursue its destiny that other countries have had. Certainly the current leadership in Taiwan—and I suspect the same will be true of the next generation of leaders—is increasingly convinced that time is not on Taiwan's side. The more time that goes by, the more unlikely it is that Taiwan would ever be able to have more autonomy than it has now; in fact its autonomy may well diminish over time as China's power grows, as the two economies become increasingly interdependent, and as the rest of the world comes to accept the reality that Taiwan is a province of China.

North Korea is a tougher problem because we have not paid it the sort of attention we should have. For years, the United States really has not had a consistent policy toward North Korea, and the Bush administration in particular has been caught up in an internal debate over how to handle the North Korean nuclear issue. One side advocates some form of negotiation, such as bilateral talks or through the so-called six party process, while the other side believes that no lasting solution to the problem of North Korea will come about without a change in the nature of the regime in North Korea, so their attention is focused on regime change.

There are some things I believe it is important that the United States do to take account of these changes in East Asia in order to manage our interests in the region during the next couple of decades. First of all, the United States should not resist the emergence of regionalism in East Asia. To the extent that regional institutions and the increasing integration of the regional economy ensure East Asia's economic progress continues and that no conflict emerges within East Asia, we should welcome these developments, which are in our self-interest. However, that is not to say that we should not insist that integration in East Asia has to occur with respect to the same kind of fundamental principles of the international system that, with varying degrees of success, we have insisted on receiving from the Europeans.

Obviously from our point of view, China is the key issue. Unless the United States can get its approach to China right, nothing else is going to matter all that much in East Asia. This is an enormously complicated proposition for the United States because of the ramified nature of our relationship with China. Dealing with the former Soviet Union was easy—we really did not have a relationship with the Soviet Union other than through a policy of mutually assured destruction. In the case of China, our economic interests are so ramified and so varied, and involve so many constituencies within the U.S. political process that managing the demands and preferences of all of those interests is a very, very demanding job. It is particularly demanding for the congressional branch of the U.S. government, which has consistently shown an inability to pursue an approach of coherence and consistency towards China.

Actually, I think that over the years, the U.S. executive branch has done far better than Congress in trying to follow a coherent path. With regard to China, we need coherence, we need consistency, and we need the right language. Too much of what we say to ourselves about China is designed to bring comfort to one or the other of our internal constituencies. This is not to say we should say only nice things about China, but we should be sure that what we say about China actually has some basis in reality and some basis in fact. I will not get into the question of our economic relationship with China, given that this topic has been discussed elsewhere at this conference. But a corollary to China's economic rise is what might be its military rise. Here I will state that I find it singularly unhelpful for the United States to be as concerned about the military rise of China as we seem to be.

If you look at U.S. military technology or military institutions, I argue that it will take 25 to 35 years before China, even if it decided to go all out, could possibly match what we can mount in terms of military technology. The United States is reaping the benefits of investments that we made during the height of the Cold War that are still continuing to pay off. We also have what seems to me to be a remarkable political ability to sustain very high levels of defense spending. China is increasing its defense spending, as might be expected given its economic performance, and it is true they are not nearly as transparent as we would like them to be about what they are spending it on. But I see no evidence that on the military side China is in any way trying to match the United States globally or even regionally. In fact, I think their defense spending is largely aimed at one thing, raising the ante for the United States in the event of conflict in the Taiwan Straits. They may have already come close to achieving that objective.

Japan is another issue that we must try to deal with. For many years Japan has been the United States' strategic ally in East Asia. I think Japan will continue to be the strategic U.S. ally in East Asia, both for better and for worse. We are not in total agreement with Japan on all questions, but we share a set of values and convictions more broadly with Japan than with almost any other country in the region. The major problem that I see with regard to Japan is that its relationships with the rest of East Asia are so bad that this adversely affects the U.S. interest in the region. This is not to say that the rest of East Asia is blameless with regard to their relationships with Japan, and I think that certainly China deserves severe criticism for its easy reliance on nationalistic rhetoric whenever it feels pressured on any issue. Japan is China's favorite whipping boy. By and large, it is still the case that the rest of Asia does not perceive that Japan has come to terms with the legacy of its behavior in the 1930s and during World War II. Fair or not, that assessment is the reality. As a result, while Japan is a powerful economy, while it has provided billions and billions in foreign assistance and trade to the rest of Asia, it receives remarkably little credit for this. Its political influence within the region is far, far less than one would expect, given its economic strength.

In our book, we advocate that the United States should quietly but deliberately take a less hands-off approach with regards to how Japan deals with and treats the rest of East Asia. The insistence of Koizumi, Japan's former prime minister, on visiting the Yasukuni Shrine, which honors some convicted Japanese war criminals, is but one example of the Japanese ability, due to internal politics, to raise the ire of its Asian neighbors in a way that is very much against Japan's enlightened self-interest.

On the question of what the United States should be doing with regards to North Korea, I think any policy would be better than no policy, which basically is what we have right now. I think that the key guide to what our policy should be to first consider whether it is something that South Korea and China would be able to support. I find it impossible to believe that the United States could pursue a successful policy toward North Korea that was opposed by the South Koreans. In truth, that is pretty much where we have been for the last four years, with predictable results. North Korea continues to run free in its production of fissile material, and presumably in its production of thermonuclear devices.

We should pay attention to the big countries in Southeast Asia, particularly Indonesia, which besides being a country of some 200 million people is also the world's largest Muslim country. I think that we have important stakes there, both politically and economically.

On the question of Taiwan, I think that if we could bring about some de-escalation of China's buildup of military hardware, that would be a remarkably important contribution. I must say, given the pressures on our current administration from our defense industry, and our subsequent pressures on the Taiwanese to purchase equipment that they don't always want to buy or believe that they need, I do not have much hope that we are going to be able to turn this around until after the 2008 election.

The promotion of democracy has become a central pillar of U.S. foreign policy around the world. In the case of East Asia, it is clearly an important consideration. Over the last fifty years or so, we have actually enjoyed a fair measure of success in the region. Japan was not a democracy in 1945, but now it is. South Korea is perhaps an even more dramatic case. Taiwan is democratic. Indonesia has made remarkable progress given where it was at the beginning of this decade. The Philippines has managed to have regular elections. It might fall a little short in terms of governance, but its election process works. In sum, democracy is advancing throughout the region. But I think our policy requires two adjustments. First of all, we should put more emphasis on governance in our conversations with the Asians, and not just focus on the framework of democracy, but on what a democratic government actually does. How does a democratically elected government validate its position with its own citizens? Second, I think we have to be realistic and bear in mind that while promoting democracy is a very important goal, it is not our only agenda in the region. We will forever have to measure that particular policy against what we are also trying to accomplish in other areas of our relationships. I think this type of policy trade-off is globally applicable, not just regionally applicable. While Americans feel very good about pursuing democracies in other countries, this poses a couple dangers. One is that we fall into a trap of self-righteousness and self-interest. The other is that sometimes we tend to pursue those interests without giving adequate attention to other interests that we may have.

Finally, how does East Asia see us? I think it is clear to all of us that East Asia does not see us nearly as positively as it did a decade ago, or even seven years ago before September 11. This change of sentiment, however, is not exclusive to East Asia, but is pretty much true of the entire world. In the case of East Asia, I think that goodwill—if it can be described as such—toward the United States can be regained. While it is probably going to take some time, it can be regained because, in many ways, what we have to offer East Asia is something that they very much want and appreciate. We just have to offer it in ways that are somewhat less self-centered and self-righteous, and somewhat more sensitive to their own views of the world and what they think they might need.

# 3
## Lessons from History

# Losing Our Marbles in the New Century? The Great Rebalancing in Historical Perspective

Christopher M. Meissner and Alan M. Taylor

The unending feedback of the dollars and pounds received by the European countries to the overseas countries from which they had come reduced the international monetary system to a mere child's game in which one party had agreed to return the loser's stake after each game of marbles.
—Jacques Rueff, 1961[1]

A remarkable amount of attention is now being paid to global imbalances, especially the growing U.S. current account deficit financed by increasing surpluses in the rest of the world, most notably in the Asian "dollar bloc" countries and among the oil exporting nations. The talk is no longer confined to obscure academic and policy debates. With insufficient space in his weekly columns to devote to the issue, in early February 2006 the *Financial Times*' Martin Wolf launched the "Economists' Forum" web site, stating that "the quantity of analysis devoted to the so-called 'global imbalances' is extraordinary. As is usual with economists, we have reached no conclusion. Yet what is happening is extraordinary enough to merit an attempt at least to clarify the basis of the disagreements." David Warsh considers the almost obsessive focus on the issue justified, since global imbalances constitute "the most exciting economic story of our times."[2]

Exciting and extraordinary it may be, but a relentless focus on trends from the recent past, on the current announcements of each quarter's balance of payments data, or on naïve extrapolations into the future has left one important perspective rather neglected: how can a more historically based long-term perspective inform our understanding of the contemporary issue of global imbalances at the start of the twenty-first century?

To address this question, we seek a meaningful comparison between past and present experience by focusing on the two modern eras of globalization: "then" being the period dating from 1870 to 1913, and "now" being the period since the early 1970s up to the present. We look at the special global macroeconomic position of each era's hegemons: Britain then, and the United States now. In adducing historical data to match what we know from the contemporary record, we proceed in the tradition of new comparative economic history to see what lessons the past might have for the present.

Although such an exercise in quantitative economic history could range far and wide, in this essay space limitations permit us only to look at what we consider two of the most controversial and pressing questions in the current debate.

First, are the current imbalances being sustained, at least in part, by return differentials? And if so, is this situation reassuring? If the United States can always earn some kind of privilege of this sort, then the degree of required adjustment will be reduced. Put another way, for any given trajectory of trade imbalances, we know that the current account and debt implications will look much more favorable or sustainable if such privileges persist. If not, any resulting adjustment difficulties will be that much more pronounced.

Second, how will any necessary adjustment take place? Will it be a hard or a soft landing? It is possible, again, that adjustments will happen smoothly. Depending on the extent to which expenditure shifts rather than switches, countries might avoid dramatic real exchange rate movements. If up and down shifts are coordinated across countries, or if switching is unhindered by trade policies or other frictions, then global demand might hold up, and a serious global recession might be averted. The fear is that adjustments might be much more abrupt, demanding large changes in real exchange rates. This situation could lead to politically awkward realignments of trade, and cause recession for one or more players in the game. If such a hard landing is likely, then policymakers face the challenge of devising suitable countermeasures to mitigate its effects.

Confronting these two questions, what insights can we take from the past?

To summarize our findings, on the persistence of privilege we find:

• Among G7 countries today, the United States is not unique in being able to enjoy a privilege in the form of higher yields earned on external assets relative to yields paid on external liabilities. This has been worth about 0.5 percent of GDP to the United States in the years 1981 to 2003. Similar privileges are detectable for Japan and the United Kingdom. France and Germany appear to have no privilege. Canada and Italy have negative privilege, or penalty.

• In the years 1870–1913, the previous financial hegemon, Britain, enjoyed a similar yield privilege, also amounting to about 0.5 percent of GDP.

• Measured as a differential in rates of yield, the U.S. privilege has been steadily declining since the 1960s, when it stood at around 3 percent per annum on all capital. It is now close to 1 percent per annum. Indirect measures may differ, and even the direct measures are subject to error. But if this trend continues, the United States will lose its privilege.

• Direct and indirect evidence on rates of yield for Britain in the past also suggests small and declining rates of yield privilege from the 1870s to 1910s, a similar pattern.

• For both the United States now and Britain then, declining rate of yield privilege meant that for a given leverage and a given composition of assets and liabilities, the income due to privilege (as a fraction of GDP) would have to shrink. In part this was offset either by expanding leverage (in the U.S. case today) or by shifting composition to riskier assets with higher returns (in both cases). These shifts may not be able to proceed without limit.

• It is often suggested that the United States might lose privilege if the net debt position grows too large. We find that rate of yield privilege has been correlated with the deterioration of the net external asset position in the postwar era.

• In the historical British case, leverage and indebtedness were not an issue. British net external assets roughly equaled gross external assets, and Britain became a very large net creditor. But a net credit position did not preclude a loss of privilege, suggesting that even if the United States could reverse its net debt position, this would not protect its privilege automatically.

• Rather, British experience suggests that over time, financial hegemons operating in a globalizing world face other pressures that squeeze privilege. Emerging markets mature and offer less outlandish risk-reward combinations, so the benefit of being a "loan shark" diminishes; the world becomes less risky as a whole; at the same time other rival financial centers emerge that can compete for lucrative business with the financial pioneer.

• Most of these perspectives bode ill for the persistence of privilege. But if we add capital gains to yields we can estimate a total return privilege for the United States. According to indirect estimates, total return privilege has risen since the 1960s. It also appears to have been steady in the 1980s and 1990s. Growing valuation effects have offset falling yield differentials, keeping up a total return privilege. It is unclear what mechanisms are driving these opposing trends.

• Looking at indirect evidence on total returns on the U.K. domestic and foreign portfolio 1870–1913, we also find a total return differential, but one that is very volatile over successive decades, and with very little systematic privilege overall.

• The large capital gains earned by the United States in the last 10 to 15 years are due to neither sustained price effects nor sustained exchange rate effects, both of which are close to zero on average; the effect is largely due to "other" capital gains. These remain a mystery, and until we understand them better, simple extrapolation of these trends may be ill advised.

On adjustment we examine the behavior of current accounts and the processes associated with current account reversals for a broad sample of countries between 1880 and 1913.

We attempt to verify whether there are any differences between the capital exporters like Britain, France, Germany, and the Netherlands, other core countries that import capital, areas that had recently been settled, also known as British offshoots (i.e., Australia, Canada, New Zealand, and the United States), and less-developed peripheral nations. Throughout we compare our findings to those from Edwards (2004) from the thirty years between 1970 and 2001.

In particular we look at summary statistics regarding the size of current accounts and incidence of reversals; the ability to sustain current account deficits or surpluses; connections between current account reversals, exchange rate movements, and financial crises; and patterns of movement of macroeconomic aggregates in the wake of large current account reversals, including the growth effects of reversals.

• We find that more-developed countries and the offshoots were able to run higher current account deficits more persistently, and that these countries had very different patterns of adjustment.

• In particular their current account reversals were generally associated with smaller real exchange rate fluctuations and less adjustment in the government surplus.

• Overall, we do not find overwhelming evidence that current account reversals had negative consequences for the aggregate growth of income per capita in the core or periphery. (Although many reversals involved serious crises that surely did have major distributional impacts.)

• Moreover, we are able to test some modern hypotheses with the historical data in ways that have not previously been done. We assess whether openness to international trade, financial and institutional development, and currency mismatches played a role in adjustment.

• We find little evidence that currency mismatches, openness to international trade, or the level of institutional and financial sophistication (proxied very roughly by higher income per capita) altered the severity of output losses associated with reversals in the nineteenth century.

• Nevertheless we do find some evidence that core Western European countries and the offshoots had lower growth losses in the adjustment process. Some countries even managed to see income rising in the face of reversals because previous investment was so productive. This offsets the negative growth experiences of other countries in the periphery leading to the finding that current account reversals were not systematically associated with output losses in this period.

## Minimizing Adjustment: Are We Losing Our Marbles?

As has been noted frequently in current and past debates about global imbalances, some countries may enjoy a special privilege—an excess return on assets relative to liabilities—allowing them to sustain larger trade deficits in equilibrium. For example, if all borrowing occurs at a constant world interest rate, then, absent default or other forms of capital gains, a nation's long-run budget constraint would require a net debtor like the United States to run future surpluses to extinguish the debt, requiring a large trade balance improvement. But if investment income surpluses can be earned even as a net debtor, as has been the case for the United States in recent decades, then the required degree of trade balance adjustment is mitigated.

Of course, this kind of scenario can cause umbrage among the creditors: those nations in the rest of the world who run persistent net trade surpluses are "winners" in a mercantilist sense, but gain nothing from this situation as they give back, in the form of net investment income flows, their "marbles" to the "loser," to use Jacques Rueff's memorable terminology. Rueff and his colleagues were bothered by the United States' ability to use this strategy during the heyday of the Bretton Woods era (Despres, Kindleberger, and Salant 1966). This French irritation was expressed in Valery Giscard d'Estaing's reference to "exorbitant privilege," a phrase frequently misattributed to de Gaulle (Gourinchas and Rey 2007, 12).

Why do these seemingly esoteric debates over return differentials matter so much? The differentials may seem small at first, and their contribution to overall capital and trade flows rather minimal, but it turns out that even small changes in the assumptions about the future path of these differentials can be the difference between seemingly manageable and seemingly disastrous paths of future national indebtedness. Or, put another way, these return differentials can be the deciding factor between a scenario in which drastic exchange rate adjustment is needed, and one where only a minor correction is required. How can small differentials make such a big difference? The reason is simple—compounding small differences for a long time can make a huge difference to outcomes further down the road.

In pioneering contributions, Lane and Milesi-Ferretti (2003, 2004, 2005a, 2005b), confronted the important question as to how a nation's external wealth evolves and how adjustment takes place. Their data, from the 1970s onward, provides important evidence on this subject. An even longer-run perspective on the postwar U.S. experience will be afforded by the soon-to-be released data of Gourinchas and Rey (2007). More recently, as global imbalances have grown over the last 10–15 years, a wave of policy analysis has followed these leads and has focused on the trends evident in the U.S. balance of payments. For example, in a comparative study of several models that project future imbalances and U.S. external wealth, we find the following predictions (see Kitchen 2006, Table 1, based on Roubini and Setser 2004; Higgins, Klitgaard, and Tille 2005; Cline 2005):

• In "optimistic" scenarios where the United States continues to enjoy differentials in its favor of 500 basis points on income yields on foreign direct investment, and of 200 basis points on capital gains on all forms of external wealth, then by 2016 the U.S. net international investment position is likely to have a net debt in the range of –40 percent to –60 percent of GDP, with an income balance between –1.5 percent and +0.2 percent of GDP. The U.S. current account deficit might then be about –4 percent to –5 percent of GDP.

• In "pessimistic" scenarios, all else equal, where its privilege disappears and these differentials vanish, the United States may end up with an external debt position in excess of –100 percent of GDP, and an income balance between –3 percent and –7.2 percent of GDP. The current account might then be about –10 percent to –15 percent of GDP.

The range of these estimates depends on various other assumptions in the models studied, such as the speed at which the U.S. trade balance improves, and these estimates assume that all imbalances are accommodated by financing from the rest of the world. Still, the numbers are illustrative only, and the point is this: whether the United States' current privileges persist or not will make a big difference to future outcomes. An adverse outcome has the potential to double or triple our net debt position and our income payments to the rest of the world in ten years' time.

So a country's privileges are worth worrying about, and the realization that these favorable circumstances may prove ephemeral in the long run is increasingly a cause for concern. Despite past trends, Geithner (2006) warns that "nevertheless, going forward, the scope for positive net factor payments from abroad and sizeable valuation effects is limited." Should we worry? Or, to reframe the question as Rueff might have said: will the United States lose its marbles, sooner or later? For suggestive evidence, we compare past and present experience.

*Measuring Privilege*

We examine four ways of thinking about privilege. Suppose that at the end of the previous year, a country has external assets $A$, external liabilities $L$, and a net foreign asset position, $NFA = A - L$. In the current year, the country can earn an investment income flow that exceeds what would be predicted based on the world average rate of yield $r$ if its rate of yield on assets is higher $(r_A > r)$, or its rate of yield on liabilities lower $(r_L < r)$ than the world average. This implies that net property income from abroad ($NPIA$) is

$$NPIA = r_A A - r_L L = [\ \underbrace{(r_A - r)}_{\substack{\text{rate of yield} \\ \text{privilege on assets} \\ \text{if } > 0}}\ A + \underbrace{(r - r_L)}_{\substack{\text{rate of yield} \\ \text{privilege on liabilites} \\ \text{if } > 0}}\ L] + r(A - L)$$

$$> r(A - L) = \underbrace{rNFA}_{\substack{\text{NPIA in the case} \\ \text{of zero privilege}}}$$

Scaling by $GDP$ we may write

$$(1)\quad \frac{NPIA}{GDP} = r\left[\frac{NFA}{GDP}\right] + \underbrace{\left[(r_A - r)\frac{A}{GDP} - (r_L - r)\frac{L}{GDP}\right]}_{\substack{\text{yield privilege} \\ \text{as \% of GDP}}}.$$

The term in brackets represents the yield privilege, measured as a fraction of GDP (say, in terms of percent). This privilege arises whenever there is an advantage accruing to the country in the form of favorable yields; that is, whenever $r_A > r$ or $r_L < r$.

These yield privileges matter because they affect a country's wealth in the long run, and hence the adjustments necessary to satisfy the nation's long-run budget constraint. They show up in the current account (CA) since these yields are part of $NPIA$, which is one component of $NFIA$, or net factor income from abroad (the so-called income account).[3]

As an accounting identity, the change in external wealth $W$ can be disaggregated into earnings on the trade balance $TB$, plus net unilateral transfers $NUT$, plus net labor income from abroad $NLIA$, plus net property income from abroad $NPIA$, plus capital gains $KG$. The last two items can then be thought of as the total returns on external wealth, as follows:

$$(2) \quad \Delta W = \underbrace{-FA}_{\substack{\text{net import of assets} \\ \text{(-financial account)}}} + \underbrace{KG}_{\substack{\text{capital gains on} \\ \text{external assets and liabilities}}} = \underbrace{CA + KA}_{\substack{-FA \\ \text{(BOP identity)}}} + KG$$

$$= \underbrace{TB + (NLIA + NPIA) + NUT + KA}_{\text{CA definition}} + KG$$

$$= TB + \underbrace{NUT + KA}_{\text{transfers}} + \underbrace{NLIA}_{\text{net labor income}} + \underbrace{(r_A A - r_L L)}_{\text{net property income}} + \underbrace{(\gamma_A A - \gamma_L L)}_{\text{capital gains}}$$

$$= TB + NUT + NLIA + KA + (\rho_A A - \rho_L L)$$

where $r$ denotes yields, $\gamma$ denotes capital gains, and $\rho$ denotes total returns (whether for assets or liabilities, as indicated by subscripts).

Thus, setting aside transfers and labor income ($NUT+NLIA+KA$) in the last equation (or treating them as exogenous), the evolution of external wealth is critically affected by the total rates of return (rates of yield plus rates of capital gains) on assets and liabilities. The higher are the privileges (in yields or capital gains), the larger is the deficit that can be run on the trade balance in the long run, all else equal—and, hence, the smaller is the adjustment needed for a country that is temporarily running a trade deficit at a larger nonsustainable level.

We can use many approaches to explore these effects. Several methods have been proposed in the extant literature. All of these approaches are closely related to one another, so we need to pause and take stock of these possible options.

1. *Perform a naïve comparison of income flow and asset position.* This is a simple way to illustrate privilege. Following equation (1) we can do a simple bivariate regression of $y=NPIA/GDP$ on $x=NFA/GDP$. The slope is an estimate of $r$ and the intercept an estimate of the yield privilege term in brackets. The relationship can also be seen using an $x$-$y$ scatterplot. Creditors with interest receipts sit in the positive quadrant, debtors with payments in the negative quadrant. In the other quadrants we find the paradoxical cases of debtors with receipts and creditors making payments. If an observation sits well above (or below) the diagonal with slope $r$ through the origin, then we can say the country has a privilege (or penalty). We use this method as a simple descriptive tool in this paper, since the relevant data are widely available for past and present periods.[4] This method makes certain assumptions that may not always hold: the intercept need not be constant, and changes over time might be detect-

able either due to changes in the balance sheet ($A$ and $L$) or in the yield differentials. A fixed intercept only measures the average privilege. The slope may also change, for example, if there are changes in inflation, since the slope is a nominal not a real yield.

2. *Perform a direct calculation of privilege.* A direct computation of rates of yield on assets is found by taking investment income credits from balance of payments data, divided by total assets obtained from net international investment position (NIIP) data. The rate of yield on liabilities equals investment income debits, taken from balance of payments data, divided by total liabilities obtained from NIIP data.[5] This method can be applied to disaggregated asset classes when disaggregated data on income flows and positions are available. For example, disaggregation shows that the current U.S. yield privilege is driven by foreign direct investment yield differentials (see Higgins, Klitgaard, amd Tille 2005). This method can also be extended  to include capital gains when capital gains data are available. A leading example of this approach using current U.S. data is Kitchen (2006). He finds a large total return privilege in recent years, partly due to yields and partly due to capital gains of unidentifiable origin. The method cannot be applied historically in the aggregate because gross position data are not available for the past; however, microeconomic data do permit some comparisons.

3. *Perform an indirect calculation of privilege.* This could be done by ignoring reported income flow data and instead using market data to compute returns for synthetic portfolios. These should match actual portfolios as closely as possible, for instance by using portfolio-weighted stock market data. This method does not suffer, then, from errors in investment flow data (as in the accrual basis used for computing interest flows; see Buiter 2006). It should also avoid problems resulting from underreporting of investment income (the likely major source of the global current account deficit). However, this approach also relies on assumptions that the weights are correct and that returns and valuation changes derived from stock and bond indexes track those of the actual portfolio. The most fragile calculations are the imputations of returns to foreign direct investment, especially for privately held companies. Subject to these caveats, and after a lot of work, imputed yields and imputed capital gains on synthetic asset and liability positions can be estimated. A leading example is Gourinchas and Rey (2007), who find that the United States has enjoyed a large and growing privilege in total returns since the

1950s. Some of this increase is due to a growing return differential in all asset classes, and some is due to a composition shift toward higher yielding but riskier assets.

4. *Compute a privilege-adjusted net foreign asset position.* This approach is not a new concept, but just a reworking of the second method discussed. Instead of focusing on the return differentials, this method replaces the official (market value) measures of assets $A$ and liabilities $L$, with adjusted measures $A^*$ and $L^*$ so that under a uniform world rate of yield $r$, the modified positions yield the actual income flows seen, that is, $r_A A = rA^*$ and $r_L L = rL^*$. Hence, in cases of privilege, where $r_A > r$ or $r_L > r$, external assets increase and liabilities shrink, $A^* = r_A A/r > A$ and $L^* = r_L L/r < L$. This method can also be applied to disaggregated asset classes. While this approach does not consider capital gains (meaning total returns), in principle it could be extended in that way. This method was proposed by Hausmann and Sturzenegger (2006), who arbitrarily set $r$ equal to 5 percent. They find that whereas the conventional NFA position of the United States has deteriorated, its adjusted NFA position, NFA* = A* − L*, reveals virtually no change since the 1970s. Given that the foreign direct investment component contains all of the yield differential, inevitably it is in this component that almost all of the adjustments occur en route to A* and L*.

While none of these methods proves ideal in practice, due to a combination of theoretical and empirical concerns, taken together these approaches offer corroborating evidence when the underlying data are fragmentary, so we shall not rely on any single approach in the analysis that follows, as we try to identify U.K. and U.S. privilege then and now.[6]

### Some Simple Estimates of Privilege

Following method 1, we begin with the simplest of comparative exercises. Looking across time and space, we see whether countries are able to earn more on the investment income account than would be predicted under an assumption of a uniform world real interest rate. To do this we run a regression

$$(3) \quad \frac{NPIA}{GDP} = \beta \left[ \frac{NFA}{GDP} \right] + \alpha_i + u_{it} \, ,$$

which is the econometric analog of equation (1).

For the time being we assume that the slope is constant across any sample (we allow this to vary later). We also assume that the intercept is constant over time, but we allow it to vary across countries. The slope is an estimate of the world average rate of yield $r$ in equation (1), and the intercepts are estimates of a country's average yield privilege as a fraction of its GDP.

Figure 3.1 shows a simple example of this naïve method calculated for the United States using data for the 1981–2003 period. The slope is 2.3 percent, a measure of the world average rate of yield. The intercept is 0.5 percent of GDP, a sign that the United States enjoyed an average level of privilege equal to about 0.5 percent of GDP over two decades. The details of the corresponding regression (3) appear in Table 3.1, panel (a), column 1. The result is not surprising: since the mid-1980s the United States has been a net debtor, but for more than two decades it has main-

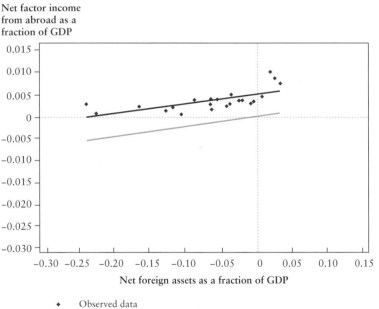

**Figure 3.1**
U.S. Privilege Relative to GDP, 1982–2003
*Source:* Authors' calculations based on various sources (see the section on Data Methodology, this chapter).

tained a positive, albeit declining, investment income balance: in Figure 3.1 the U.S. data points for this period sit in the paradoxical zone in the upper-left quadrant of the scatterplot. The points line up along the line of best fit. One way to see the extent of U.S. privilege is to plot the line of best fit and a parallel line through the origin. The vertical distance between the two equals the privilege or intercept, which is worth on average 0.5 percent of GDP.

Having noted the existence and extent of U.S. privilege, we focus on two comparative questions: is this privilege unique by contemporary global standards? And is it unique by historical standards? Some answers are shown in the remainder of Table 3.1 and later in Figures 3.2 and 3.3.

Most conjectures about the source of a country's privilege tend to focus on certain characteristics of the privileged nation. Hegemonic explanations tend to stress economic or military strength. Institutional "safe haven" explanations stress a country's record of property rights (security from expropriation risk) and economic stability (security from inflation or other risks). Purely economic explanations would stress the special abilities of a country's financial or investment sector to provide know-how, or other intangible but economically valuable services. A country's position as a financial center could also be important in cases where concentration and size matter, for example, in the provision of market depth and liquidity. Reserve currency status also might matter. Where else but the United States might such privileges be found in the contemporary world economy?

As a first step, we think it natural to look at a group of other large, advanced countries: the G7. Table 3.1, column 3 reports regression (3) for the G7, including the United States. Unreported results for the G7 excluding the United States, and for each remaining G7 country individually, yield qualitatively similar findings. Compared to column 1, the slope reveals a world rate of yield of 2.5 percent. But the intercepts are revealing. The United States again has a privilege that is still 0.5 percent of its GDP. Yet so too do Japan and the United Kingdom.[7] France and Germany have intercepts of 0.2 percent of GDP, which are slightly positive but not statistically significant. Canada and Italy have negative intercepts, a sign that these nations are incurring penalties that are statistically significant, respectively, –2.5 percent and –0.8 percent of GDP.

**Table 3.1**
Privilege: Relative to GDP

(a)  Estimates

Dependent Variable is NFIA/GDP

| | United States 1981–2003 | | G7 1981–2003 | | United Kingdom 1870–1913 | |
|---|---|---|---|---|---|---|
| | (1) | (2) | (3) | (4) | (5) | (6) |
| NFA/GDP | 0.023 (4.16)** | 0.001 (0.08) | 0.025 (4.39)** | 0.015 (1.98)* | 0.040 (16.51)** | 0.039 (16.16)** |
| INFL*NFA/ GDP | | 0.915 (1.76) | | 0.332 (2.12)* | | 0.019 (0.90) |
| U.S. | 0.005 (9.95)** | 0.005 (10.46)** | 0.005 (4.96)** | 0.005 (4.87)** | | |
| U.K. | | | 0.006 (5.38)** | 0.005 (5.22)** | 0.006 (1.89) | 0.007 (1.99) |
| CAN | | | −0.026 (11.78)** | −0.025 (11.53)** | | |
| FRA | | | 0.002 (1.49) | 0.002 (1.56) | | |
| DEU | | | 0.002 (1.82) | 0.002 (1.77) | | |
| ITA | | | −0.008 (7.09)** | −0.008 (7.04)** | | |
| JPN | | | 0.006 (5.32)** | 0.006 (5.50)** | | |
| Observations | 23 | 23 | 161 | 161 | 44 | 44 |
| R-squared | 0.45 | 0.52 | 0.89 | 0.90 | 0.87 | 0.87 |

(b)  Frequency of Privilege/Penalty†

| | | | | | | |
|---|---|---|---|---|---|---|
| U.S. | 100% / 0% | 100% / 0% | 100% / 0% | 100% / 0% | | |
| U.K. | | | 76% / 9% | 71% / 9% | 80% / 0% | 85% / 0% |
| CAN | | | 32% / 68% | 32% / 68% | | |
| FRA | | | 56% / 24% | 56% / 18% | | |
| DEU | | | 66% / 16% | 66% / 16% | | |
| ITA | | | 32% / 68% | 32% / 65% | | |
| JPN | | | 94% / 0% | 94% / 0% | | |

Absolute value of t statistics in parentheses
* Significant at 5 percent
** Significant at 1 percent
† Observations more than 2 s.d. above/below r NFA/GDP, where r is the slope estimate.

To illustrate these patterns, Figure 3.2 shows a scatterplot diagram using the same axes as Figure 3.1. A diagonal line through the origin is plotted with a slope equal to the estimated common value of *r*. For countries with a zero intercept, all points should sit on this line, which we might call the "neutral line" where neither penalty nor privilege is present. Points above this line correspond to privilege, those below to penalty, using our terminology. To permit comparison with Figure 3.1, the U.S. points in Figure 3.2 are depicted with an "x" symbol. All of the U.S. points sit in a zone well above the neutral line. Only a fraction of the non-U.S. points sit in this neutral zone, and many are close to or below the diagonal line.

To add a little more detail to this description, panel (b) of Table 3.1 computes an indicator variable based on the regressions in panel (a). We compare the distance between each point and the neutral line, and com-

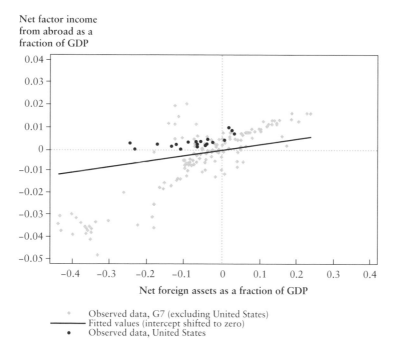

**Figure 3.2**
Privilege of G7 Countries Relative to GDP, 1981–2003
*Source:* Authors' calculations based on various sources (see the section on Data and Methodology, this chapter).

pare it to the standard deviation of the fitted value. If the point is 2 standard deviations or more above the neutral line, we label this country-year observation as being in the privilege zone; if it is 2 standard deviations below we label it as in the penalty zone.[8]

Columns 1 and 3 confirm that the United States has been in the privilege zone 100 percent of the time during the 1981–2003 period. The rest of the G7 countries have spent more time either in the neutral or in the penalty zone. Japan has spent 94 percent of this time period in the privilege zone, and the United Kingdom 76 percent. During this period, France and Germany are in the privilege zone 56 percent and 66 percent of the time, respectively, but also clocked a nontrivial amount of time in the penalty zone. Canada and Italy spend two-thirds of this time period in the penalty zone.

To sum up, among the G7 countries, privilege can be often be found outside the United States, particularly in the cases of Japan and the United Kingdom. Although not hegemonic military powers like the United States, these two countries are both global financial centers and issue important global currencies.

What about historical precedents? Several conjectures in the current debate surrounding contemporary global imbalances lead us to focus on the experience of Britain in the 1870–1913 period as a case study of privilege in the past. In this era, Britain was the undisputed hegemonic political and military power of its time, held a global empire, and despite the economic rise of the United States and other competitors, was still a leading industrial power. It was also, famously, a "banker to the world" before that term was gradually applied more to the United States in the years after 1914. The British pound sterling was the most important key currency of the period preceding World War I. How relevant is comparing the United Kingdom then and the United States now for this paper? Many commentators have speculated on the similarities between the financial privilege that Britain enjoyed in the late nineteenth century and that enjoyed by the United States in the period following World War II, noting the ways in which this privilege relaxed Britain's long-run budget constraint and eased adjustment. For example, James Foreman-Peck writes that:

The international use of sterling raised British and world incomes by foreigners effectively giving Britain interest-free loans by holding sterling, and by sterling's enhancement of world liquidity. . . . By analogy with the role of the U.S. dollar after 1945, the key currency system contained the seeds of its own destruction. . . . British industry had to export less in order to buy a given quantity of imports than if sterling had not been a reserve currency. The adjustments of prices in the British economy and of the industrial structure, necessary to maintain a balance of payments equilibrium, were reduced. If Britain had been forced to adjust faster the structure of her industry, not only would the eventual adjustment have been less wrenching, but the rate of industrial growth in the late nineteenth century may have been higher (Foreman-Peck 1983, 169–170).

So let us examine the empirical evidence for British privilege in the four decades before World War I. Table 3.1, column 5 repeats our regression analysis for the United Kingdom in the years 1870 to 1913, the so-called age of high imperialism when Britain rose to preeminence as the world center of global finance. The results are quite similar to those seen for the contemporary United States in column 1. A slope of 4 percent represents the estimated rate of yield. An intercept of 0.6 percent of GDP suggests that the United Kingdom did enjoy some privilege during this period. Panel (b) indicates that during this time, the United Kingdom was in the privilege zone 80 percent of the time, and otherwise in the neutral zone. The corresponding scatter diagram appears in Figure 3.3.

However, two key differences, and one similarity, stand out when comparing Britain then and the United States now.

First, as a fraction of GDP, between 1870 and 1913, Britain's yield privilege was only marginally statistically significant, and this at the 10 percent confidence level, not the 5 percent level.

Second, as is apparent from a brief review of Figure 3.1 and an examination of Figure 3.3, Britain was in a very different position to the United States today. During the 1870–1913 period, Britain was a large net creditor: its NFA was positive, constantly increasing, and approached 200 percent of GDP by the period's end. But today the United States is a large net debtor, with its NFA falling below zero in the early 1980s and nearing –30 percent of GDP as of 2003. The United Kingdom in this earlier period inhabited the normal upper-right quadrant in Figure 3.3, but the United States inhabits the paradoxical upper-left quadrant shown in Figure 3.1.

Net factor income
from abroad as a
fraction of GDP

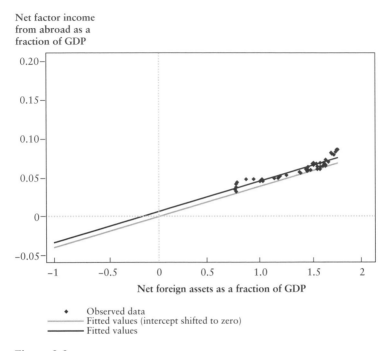

Net foreign assets as a fraction of GDP

◆      Observed data
─────── Fitted values (intercept shifted to zero)
─────── Fitted values

**Figure 3.3**
U.K. Privilege Relative to GDP, 1870–1913
*Source:* Authors' calculations based on various sources (see the section on Data
and Methodology, this chapter).

Third, we note that the extent of the privilege enjoyed by the United
Kingdom then and the United States now was quite volatile, measured as
a fraction of GDP. Treating the privilege as the gap between the actual
observed NFIA/GDP and that predicted by the fitted line constrained to
pass through the origin, the implied measures of privilege are shown in
Figure 3.4. Both figures show a distinct W shape.

To use the terminology of Higgins, Klitgaard, and Tille (2005), both of
these countries have at times enjoyed a "series of fortunate events" taking their investment income balance far above trend in certain periods. In
the early 1870s, U.K. returns were high after a loan boom, before a wave
of crises and defaults hit emerging markets, and investment returns fell.
The same pattern was witnessed in the 1890s, before and after the Baring
crash. This volatile pattern highlights the possibility of recurring "peso
problems" (see Buiter 2006) even for a country with privilege: risky

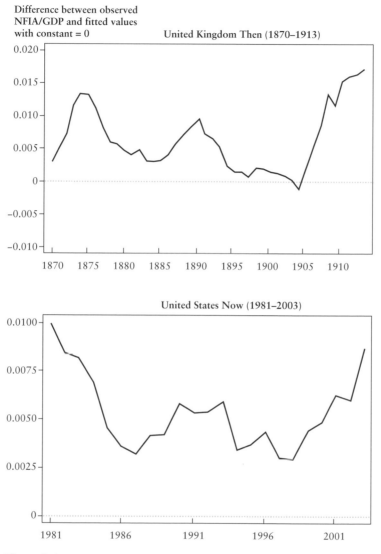

Figure 3.4

Privilege Relative to GDP, United Kingdom Then and United States Now
*Source:* Authors' calculations based on various sources (see the section on Data and Methodology, this chapter).

foreign assets may generate supranormal returns for a time, but these trends may not be sustainable.

In the current case of the United States, some of the same factors are possibly at work, along with exchange rate effects. Net income yields were low during the strong dollar periods of the mid-1980s and the late 1990s, and these were also times of default for many emerging market bonds. The recent uptick in privilege for the United States in 2000–2003 echoes that experienced by the United Kingdom in 1905–1913. But if the clock had been stopped earlier in each case—in 1905 for United Kingdom, and 2000 for the United States—then an unmistakable downward trend in privilege would be evident.

Before proceeding it should be noted that in the regressions reported so far, we have been analyzing a nominal yield $r$ based on the slope estimates in regression (3). Should such nominal yields be stable? This is, for example, the implicit assumption made by Hausmann and Sturzenegger (2006), who use a constant arbitrary 5 percent discount rate; that is, a "price-earnings" ratio of 20 for all assets. An alternative approach would recognize that $r$ is a rate of nominal yield, and that it might fluctuate systematically with the rate of inflation $\pi$. In this case we might be better off estimating a variant of equation (3):

$$(4) \quad \frac{NPIA}{GDP} = \beta \left[ \frac{NFA}{GDP} \right] + \theta \left[ \pi \frac{NFA}{GDP} \right] + \alpha_i + u_{it} \, .$$

If the Fisher effect holds for all assets and their yields, then in equation 4 the coefficient $\theta$ should equal unity. But this may not be the case in practice. If loans payments are tied to a floating rate of interest, the pass-through of inflation to yields will depend on the speed of market adjustment and the accuracy of expectations. If fixed income yields are tied to a fixed interest rate, no change in yields will occur. In principle, this situation ought to be resolved by changes in the market value of the underlying debt, but from an empirical standpoint it is doubtful that all such loans and debts are properly revalued in the data. Thus, we do not impose a unity restriction on $\theta$ (for if we did, it would be rejected) when we estimate (4) in columns 2, 4, and 6 of Table 3.1, panel (a). The bottom line is unchanged, however. The measures of privilege by country are only slightly affected when this simple inflation adjustment is carried out, as all the findings based on columns 1, 3, and 5 are valid.

The lesson from these simple calculations is that the privilege the United States enjoys today is not unprecedented by contemporary standards. We even find evidence of a historical precedent in the case of Britain between 1870 and 1913, during the first age of globalization. In the following sections we look at some of the details that lie behind these simple comparisons, trying to understand what was going on in the past for the British case, and what is taking place in the present for the U.S. case, though still using the G7 as background to this analysis of the United States.

### Disappearing Privilege Then and Now?

We first turn to the trend in privilege over time. The privilege term in (1) need not be constant, of course. Two factors operate to affect the size of this term. First, consider the differential between rates of yield on assets and liabilities: the bigger the rate of yield differential, the bigger the privilege term. Second, consider leverage: if there are yield differentials, these can be exploited by enlarging the size of the nation's balance sheet, increasing $A$ and/or $L$.

The implication of both these considerations is that if a country faces declining yield differentials on its portfolio, then to preserve its privilege one of two things must happen.

First, there might be a reweighting of the country's asset and liability portfolios that raises aggregate differentials via composition effects. For example, if debt and fixed income assets yield less than equity or foreign direct investment, a country will earn more if it sells foreigners less high-yield home equity and more low-yield home debt. A country also earns more if it purchases more high-yield foreign equity and less low-yield debt. It has been suggested, for example, that recent political maneuvers to block foreign takeovers in a number of countries could reflect, in part, this sort of concern.

Second, an increase in leverage may occur, which helps offset a fall in differentials. For example, if the yield differentials are cut in half, then the same amount of investment income can be attained by doubling the size of the national balance sheet; that is, by doubling $A$ and $L$.

While these two kinds of responses would show up in macroeconomic aggregates, these would represent a manifestation of microeconomic decisions by investors. Either way, each individual investor, and in aggregate the privileged country, takes on more risk, either by engaging in a quest for yield or by ramping up leverage.

The interplay between these two forces could be of importance both in the past and the present. For example, we will show that rate of yield differentials appear to have shrunk progressively for the two hegemons in the periods we study: Britain during the 1870–1913 period and the United States in the postwar period. This development appears to have been true in the aggregate portfolios, even allowing for the fact that in the search for yield, both countries are thought to have reweighted their portfolios toward riskier and higher yielding equity assets over time.

In Table 3.2 we repeat the analysis of Table 3.1 for the United States now and the United Kingdom then, but include an "early" indicator to

**Table 3.2**
Privilege: Relative to GDP, Early Versus Late

| Dependent Variable is NFIA/GDP | United States 1981–2003 | United Kingdom 1870–1913 |
|---|---|---|
| | (1) | (2) |
| NFA/GDP | 0.013 (1.75) | 0.051 (11.41)** |
| EARLY | 0.002 (1.69) | 0.009 (2.93)** |
| United States | 0.004 (3.45)** | |
| United Kingdom | | –0.011 (1.69) |
| Observations | 23 | 44 |
| R-squared | 0.86 | 0.99 |

Absolute value of t statistics in parentheses
* Significant at 5 percent
** Significant at 1 percent
EARLY = 1 when year is less than or equal to 1880 (United Kingdom) or 1992 (United States).

test for an early period of "high privilege" in the sample; pre-1880 for the United Kingdom and pre-1992 for the United States. We find evidence that U.K. and U.S. privilege, as a fraction of GDP, was much higher in the early years compared to the late years. For the United Kingdom, privilege was 0.9 percent of GDP higher before 1890, a difference significant at the 1-percent level. For the United States, privilege was 0.2 percent higher before 1992, but the difference is of borderline significance using a 10-percent (two-tailed) test. These results offer the first suggestion that yield privilege can be difficult to sustain. What message lies behind these results?

We begin with the historical example of Britain. An important fact to remember is that we do not possess gross asset and liability positions for this period, so direct calculation of the privilege term in (1) and its components is not feasible, ruling out method 2. Instead we can turn to methods 3 and 4: look at market yield data on portfolio assets, or perform an adjusted NFA calculation.

We begin with the simpler adjusted NFA approach. We employ an arbitrary 4 percent discount rate and infer the British-adjusted NFA position. To perform this calculation, we take the net investment income each year from 1870 to 1913, multiply by 25, and call this NFA*. We can compare this with NFA, the conventional measure of the net position derived by economic historians by accumulating the current account and adding it to some known absolute position data for a given benchmark year.

The result of this comparison is shown in Figure 3.5. We recall that Hausmann and Sturzenegger's NFA* is not a new concept—it is just another way of expressing yield differentials and the privilege associated with them. By implication, if these privileges are big, then NFA* should deviate very significantly from NFA—in a positive direction for a privileged country, and in a negative direction for a penalized country.[9]

In contrast to recent U.S. experience, for the earlier British case Figure 3.5 shows no evidence of any substantial deviations from 1870 to 1913. The two measures NFA* and NFA track each other very closely. Given the isomorphism between yield differentials and the size of the NFA adjustment, this finding gives an indirect test of the presence of yield differentials in the British case. Minimal or nonexistent differences between NFA and NFA* imply minimal or nonexistent British yield privilege.

Net Foreign assets as a percent of GDP

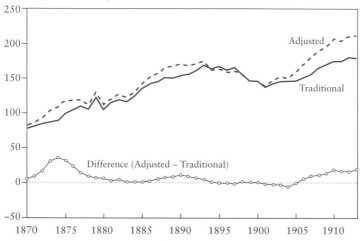

**Figure 3.5**
The United Kingdom's Minimal Privilege, 1870–1913
*Source:* Authors' calculations based on various sources (see the section on
Data and Methodology, this chapter).
*Note:* This figure uses a 4 percent discount rate (or a Hausmann-Sturzenegger
PE ratio of 25) based on the estimated yield in Table 3.1.

Should we believe an indirect test? One reason for doubt is that the
source data for the British investment income data series is rather conjec-
tural. Imlah (1958, 59–64) had no records on actual investment income
flows and instead imputed annual U.K. NFIA based on estimates—some
might say educated guesses—about the rate of return on the British overseas portfolio. The rate was then applied to an estimate of the British
NFA position, which was equally fragile, not least because it depended
in part on cumulated NFIA as an element in cumulated CA (Imlah 1958,
64–81). In other words, in the above calculations, all the indirect method
does is reveal what Imlah thought the British rate of return on external
assets was doing from year to year.

To probe further, we might like to get additional and more precise
direct or indirect evidence on yields. Unfortunately, the direct method is
impossible in the aggregate data, as noted, so the best hope right now is
the indirect method 3. However, data limitations mean we cannot repli-
cate Gourinchas and Rey (2007) until we have yield and position data for

the British portfolios, or at least a large share of these. But fortunately we do have some more recent yield measures that ought to be more accurate than Imlah's conjectured yields from fifty years ago.

For a sample of British companies at home and abroad, realized rates of profit were computed by Davis and Huttenback (1986). Their important findings for the 1870 to 1913 period are summarized in Figure 3.6. In the early years of this period, Britain enjoyed very high returns on its overseas investments, notably its investments in its empire, something the authors attribute to Britain's role as a pioneer in the business of foreign investment in the 1870s and 1880s. However, these high returns soon evaporated. By 1900 and later, foreign nonempire investment, empire investments, and domestic investments were all showing similar rates of yield.[10]

Concerning government debt obligations, we know that ex ante yields experienced dramatic convergence from 1870 to 1913, as shown in Figure 3.7. We recall again the peso problem; ex post yields were surely

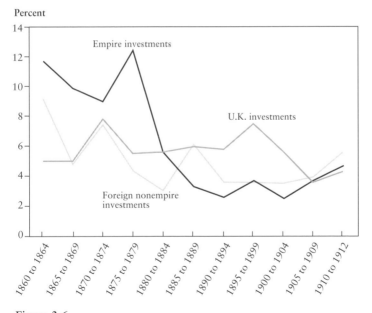

**Figure 3.6**
Rate of Yield on Selected U.K. Investments in Home and Overseas Firms, 1870–1913
*Source:* Davis and Huttenback (1986).

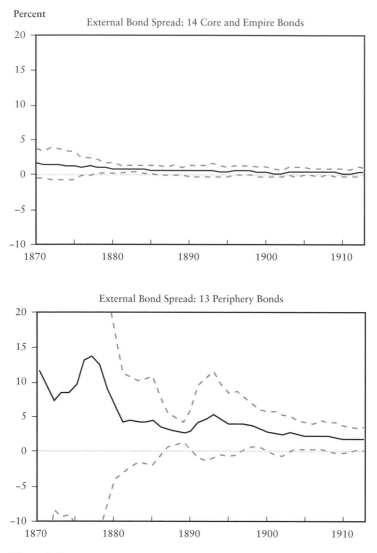

**Figure 3.7**
Yield to Maturity on Sovereign Bonds, 1870–1913
*Source:* Obstfeld and Taylor (2004).

never so high and some of this convergence was probably due to the diminution of risk premia. We might expect ex post returns to have converged rather less.

From this fragmentary evidence—the lack of privilege suggested by the adjusted NFA calculation and the suggestive evidence on yield differentials—we might conclude that the British faced declining yield differentials even when at the apex of their economic and military power, and even when London stood as the world's undisputed financial center, a locus of investment know-how, and an unimpeachable safe haven. True, the British did expand their balance sheet dramatically (as we saw in Figure 3.3), and they did shift to more risky assets in the private sector and in nonempire emerging markets as time went by. But apparently these maneuvers were not enough to deliver a strong and persistent measure of privilege relative to GDP: as we saw in Table 3.1, the British intercept was positive but had only weak statistical significance.

One theme that must be emphasized and reiterated throughout this paper is that when trying to predict the future, naïve extrapolation from the past is ill advised, whether the past constitutes the last 20 years or the 1870–1913 period. Still, the British experience in the late nineteenth century cautions against ever assuming that privilege is automatically perpetuated. Perhaps the British did have some initial advantages in the 1870s and 1880s that delivered privilege. But these circumstances did not last. Other countries like France, Germany, and later the United States entered the fray to compete with Britain in overseas investment, and the British share of world overseas assets shrank from 78 percent in 1855 to 50 percent in 1914 (Obstfeld and Taylor 2004). As an explanation for this decline, Britain may have lost its pioneer advantages in some markets, and in other countries risk premia may have fallen as the institutional environment improved.

Bearing these cautionary words in mind, we turn to the experience of the United States since the 1960s. Now, the direct method 2 is feasible to use, and we need not beat about the bush with indirect evidence. Figure 3.8 illustrates the bottom line regarding rates of yield using U.S. Bureau of Economic Analysis (BEA) data. Rates of yield on assets and liabilities (in nominal dollar terms) obviously peaked in the late 1970s and early 1980s as U.S. inflation reached its postwar peak. But the important issue for us is not the level of these rates of yield, but the differential—which, fortunately, is naturally purged of any effects of inflation.

The yield differential appears at the bottom of Figure 3.8. Its trend is unmistakably downward. We can also see that U.S. yield differentials tend to rise and fall in line with the strength of the dollar: the dollar value of yields on overseas assets tends to be low (relative to the yield paid on liabilities) when the dollar is strong. In the mid-1980s and again in the mid-1990s, the U.S. yield differential is low. This is not surprising when there are deviations from purchasing power parity in the short run. A good deal of foreign investment income is denominated in local currency, and its dollar value will be depressed when the dollar is strong.

Figure 3.8 helps us understand the indignant stance of the French in the early 1960s: at that time the U.S. yield differential was a whopping 3 percent or 300 basis points (bps). Since 1975 it has barely risen above 2 percent. Since 1995, it has averaged about 1.5 percent, reaching a low of under 1 percent or 100 bps in 1999. Over this period the rate of yield privilege has fallen by about 200 bps. Many fewer marbles are being returned these days, compared to how the game was played during the Bretton Woods era.[11]

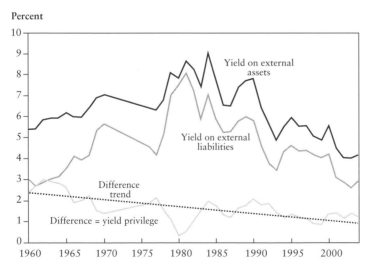

**Figure 3.8**
U.S. Rates of Yield and Differentials, 1960–2003
*Source:* U.S. Bureau of Economic Analysis.

Table 3.3 and Figure 3.9 show how the United States stacks up against the rest of the G7 where the yield differential is computed from 1981 onward using a dataset that is comparable across countries.[12] Table 3.3 shows that among the G7 countries, the United States has enjoyed a large and statistically significant rate of yield differential of about 167 bps on average. But since 1981 two other countries have enjoyed positive and significant yield differentials: Japan (112 bps) and, ironically, France (80 bps). Italy (–52 bps) and Canada (–139 bps) have had adverse rate of yield differentials.[13]

Figure 3.9 exposes the volatility of this differential over time and also reveals a declining trend: the United States began with quite high levels of privilege relative to the rest of the G7 (where on average, differentials have been about zero), but the trend over time has been an inexorable convergence of the U.S. yield differential toward zero. Regression analysis confirms that the U.S. yield differential has a negative and statistically significant time trend (in the G7, only the United Kingdom has enjoyed a positive and statistically significant time trend in this yield differential). Again, as in Figure 3.8, we see that the U.S. yield differential has been declining, with this trend only abating in periods when the dollar is weak.

Only time will tell what the long-term outcome will be, but the recent uptick in the differential in 2000–2003 is the source of much controversy.

**Table 3.3**
G7 Rate of Yield Differentials (Assets versus Liabilities), 1981–2003

|        | Obs. | Mean     | Std.Error | [95-percent confidence interval] | |
|--------|------|----------|-----------|----------------------------------|---------|
| U.S.   | 23   | 0.0167*  | 0.0018    | 0.0130                           | 0.0204  |
| U.K.   | 23   | 0.0009   | 0.0010    | –0.0011                          | 0.0030  |
| CAN    | 23   | –0.0139* | 0.0021    | –0.0182                          | –0.0096 |
| FRA    | 23   | 0.0080*  | 0.0015    | 0.0049                           | 0.0111  |
| DEU    | 23   | 0.0032   | 0.0016    | –0.0002                          | 0.0066  |
| ITA    | 23   | –0.0052* | 0.0015    | –0.0083                          | –0.0021 |
| JPN    | 23   | 0.0112*  | 0.0013    | 0.0084                           | 0.0140  |

* significant at the 5-percent level

Percent

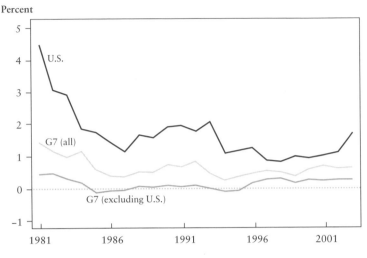

**Figure 3.9**
U.S. versus G7 Rate of Yield Differentials, 1981–2003
*Source:* Lane and Milesi-Ferretti (2004).
*Note:* G7 (excluding the United States) and G7 (all) are averages weighted
by positions; that is, total income divided by total position for all 6 or 7
countries, expressed in U.S. dollars.

A longer run perspective seems to indicate that although that uptick is
there, the longer run trend for the United States is likely one of vanishing
yield differentials or disappearing privilege, just as in the British case a
century before.

### *Maintaining Privilege via Leverage?*

At the start of this section we showed that the United States has managed
to maintain a nontrivial privilege that has averaged about 0.5 percent
of GDP over the last two decades. Close scrutiny of Figure 3.1 suggests
that, relative to the fitted values, privilege relative to GDP has been fairly
stable over the years, with a slight upward blip evident in the years after
2001 (the points farthest to the left on the scatterplot). This blip is largely
driven by the aforementioned uptick in yield differentials observed in
2000–2003.

Yet, notwithstanding a couple of such blips, we have also seen that
over time U.S. yield differentials followed a downward trend since
1981. So, looking at equation (1), we reach the immediate conclusion

that the United States has only been able to maintain its privilege as a fraction of GDP by raising its leverage to offset the diminution in yield differentials.

Figure 3.10 explores this mechanism further. Using BEA and U.S. historical statistics data going back to the 1960s, we examine the actual path of the yield privilege as a fraction of GDP, and its counterfactual path under the assumption that rate of yield differentials had been *constant* at their average 1960s values throughout the period (about 300 bps). In the counterfactual example, yield differentials would thus be much higher in later years than was actually seen.[14]

Figure 3.10 shows what we would expect. We know that the United States has been increasing its leverage dramatically since the 1960s. If the U.S. balance sheets had expanded thus with constant 1960s average yield differentials over the *entire* period, then in 2003 the privilege, rather than being about 1 percent of GDP, would have been about 2 percent. Put another way, if leverage massively increases over several decades, then

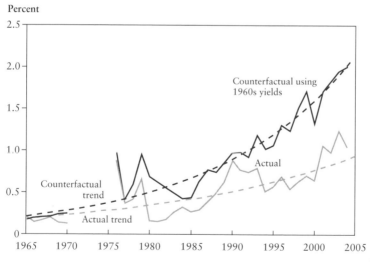

**Figure 3.10**
Actual versus Counterfactual U.S. Investment Income as a Percent of GDP, 1965–2004
*Source:* Authors' calculations based on various sources (see the section on Data and Methodology, this chapter).
*Note:* "Actual" shows declining yield differentials; "Counterfactual" shows constant yield differentials at 1960s levels.

it is not that reassuring when we find privilege merely holding steady as a fraction of GDP (Hausmann and Sturzenegger 2006). If U.S. yield differentials—the ultimate basis of the privilege—were stable, then privilege ought to have exploded relative to GDP, counterfactually, as in Figure 3.10. The reason these did not increase is that the yield differentials are narrowing. From this perspective, U.S. privilege is disappearing.

When we focus on this trend, subject to the caveat about naïve extrapolation, there are two reasons why the future outlook for the United States is surely less rosy. First, if the yield differential keeps shrinking, then astronomic and implausible explosions in leverage would be needed to maintain U.S. privilege at its current level as a fraction of GDP; if the differential reaches zero, privilege will vanish. Second, the 2000–2003 blip may or may not be sustainable, and some or all of it is due to transitory effects—overseas earnings are boosted by a weakening dollar, there has been a tax amnesty, there have been low interest rates on debt liabilities, and so on (see Higgins, Klitgaard, and Tille 2005).

One might add a third observation. Correlation does not imply causation, but this shrinkage in the yield differential obviously does coincide with the United States sliding from a net creditor position to a net debtor position, as shown in Figure 3.11. If there is a causal link here, and differentials shrink as net debt increases, then a Laffer curve type of argument tells us that at some point the United States will reach (or may already have reached) a point of maximum privilege relative to GDP.

### Capital Gains

So far, the paper's main focus has been on the yield differentials that underpin privilege in equation (1). However, the evolution of wealth is also affected by capital gains, as seen in equation (2). So even if a country suffers a decline in yield differentials, it might be of no consequence for the long-run budget constraint if this decline is offset by an increase in the capital gain differential; thus adjustment may be avoided if capital gains offset any change in yields.

The evidence on capital gains is even more fragile and fragmentary than for investment income yields, but we will make a few observations. Using indirect measures of total returns, Gourinchas and Rey (2007) find evidence that U.S. total return differentials (for assets minus liabilities)

Percent

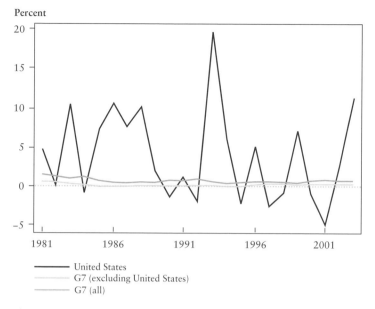

**Figure 3.11**
Total Rate of Return Differentials: United States Versus G7
*Source:* Lane and Milesi-Ferretti (2004).
*Note:* G7 (excluding the United States) and G7 (all) are averages weighted
by positions; that is, total income and capital gain divided by total position,
for all 6 or 7 countries, expressed in U.S. dollars.

may have grown in the post-Bretton Woods period as compared to the
Bretton Woods period. Given that the total return differential equals the
yield differential plus the capital gain differential, this says that the capital gain differentials must have grown enormously, since we know from
the above that yield differentials have shrunk. If anything, in the Bretton
Woods era the United States incurred a penalty on the capital gains differential, averaging about –2 percent of GDP. Then, once the floating
rate period began, the United States enjoyed positive valuation effects.
It is tempting to infer that it was the breakdown of the gold-backed
dollar standard—and the ability of the United States to reap exchange-
rate-driven capital gains—that caused this shift. But as we shall see in a
moment, as an explanatory mechanism, the exchange rate channel seems
weak. The data show that capital gains on external wealth moved in
favor of the United States in every year until the turn of the millennium,

when the U.S. stock market approached a peak. Capital gains were then zero or negative for several quarters.

Another perspective is presented by Kitchen (2006). He examined trends only since 1989 using direct BEA measures, and in that shorter window no firm time trends emerge, leading him to conclude that a positive 2 percent rate of capital gain differential in favor of the United States is the norm in recent years.

We raise two questions here. First, if this capital gain differential is flat, will it offset a declining yield differential trend, should that trend continue? Obviously the answer is no, even if such a constant differential can be assumed to continue. Second, where are these capital gains coming from? This turns out to be a dark secret. Kitchen (2006) relates how the BEA classifies valuation effects as arising from three factors: first, "prices" (meaning changes in prices of assets in the currency of denomination); second, "exchange rates" (this barely affects liabilities, but reflects changes in the dollar values of nondollar assets due to changes in currency values); finally, "other" is the remaining category.

It turns out that since 1989 the price component of capital gains has delivered a rate of return of about 1.5 percent on both external assets and liabilities: no differential there. On average, annual exchange rate changes have been zero (but large in some years). The positive differential in the rate of capital gains on assets versus liabilities has, on average, been entirely due to the final mysterious "other" category: about 100 bps on assets and 100 bps on liabilities (with both in favor of the United States for a total differential of 200 bps). What comprises this "other"? Apparently "discussions with BEA staff indicate that the source of much of this 'other' valuation change is simply unidentified" (Kitchen 2006, 16), a claim which prompts Cline (2005) to call these gains "statistical 'manna from heaven.'" The inability to account for this unidentified source of the capital gains is quite worrying. We ought to feel slightly uneasy if we cannot really understand these gains, and we should feel very uneasy about the idea of extrapolating from something we cannot understand.[15]

Notwithstanding the mystery surrounding the source of these capital gains, have these been enough to offset the declining U.S. yield differential? Table 3.4 and Figure 3.11 show that they have. These figures repeat

Table 3.4
G7 Total Rate of Return Differentials (Assets versus Liabilities), 1981–2003

|        | Obs. | Mean    | Std.Error | [95-percent confidence interval] | |
|--------|------|---------|-----------|---------|---------|
| U.S.   | 23   | 0.0369* | 0.0117    | 0.0127  | 0.0612  |
| U.K.   | 23   | 0.0025  | 0.0060    | –0.0099 | 0.0149  |
| CAN    | 23   | –0.0006 | 0.0151    | –0.0319 | 0.0307  |
| FRA    | 23   | 0.0019  | 0.0091    | –0.0170 | 0.0207  |
| DEU    | 23   | –0.0062 | 0.0058    | –0.0183 | 0.0059  |
| ITA    | 23   | –0.0034 | 0.0087    | –0.0215 | 0.0147  |
| JPN    | 17   | 0.0009  | 0.0186    | –0.0385 | 0.0403  |

* significant at the 5-percent level

the format of Table 3.3 and Figure 3.8, but show the total rate of return differentials for the G7, not just the rate of yield differentials. The difference is just capital gains, and since the capital gains are a volatile measure (partly accounted for by nature, partly due to measurement error) these data have much higher variance. The bottom line is that switching to total rates of return places the United States in a unique position as the only privileged country among the G7.

Table 3.4 shows that among the G7 countries, the United States has enjoyed a large and statistically significant rate of total return differential of about 370 basis points on average.[16] Of the U.S. total return differential, we have already seen that about 167 bps was due to yields, so the remaining 203 bps is due to capital gains.[17] On average these two parts of the differential have played an almost equal role. But the trends of the two components are obviously different. The trend in the total return differential is flat (which is confirmed by regression analysis). But because Figure 3.8 showed that the rate of yield differential was closing, the result here implies that the differential in the rate of capital gains must be widening.

It would be interesting to see how trends in capital gains (or total returns) evolved in the past for the case of Britain from 1870 and 1913. Unfortunately, the limitations of the current historical macroeconomic data preclude any calculation of gross valuation effects, even with the limited degree of precision we accept today. Imlah (1958, 59–81) ignored capital gains entirely, and assumed that gains and losses roughly cancelled out. However, as with our earlier discussion of yields, we can make use of some more recent data based on samples of traded securities.

Edelstein (1982) has computed total returns for home and foreign portfolios of equity and debenture assets in the U.K. portfolio in the late nineteenth century. The summary data in Figure 3.12 suggest no discernible trend movement in the yield differential between home and foreign assets. Indeed, a noticeable differential is apparent only for debentures (including both government and private bonds and debt), suggesting that even as ex ante differentials converged, ex post differentials were rather steady.

There is suggestive evidence here that Britain then, like the United States now, made a transition from "banker" to "venture capitalist" mode, whereby returns to investors increasingly took the form of capital gains rather than yield differentials. So the good news from the past for the U.S. position today is that such a relatively painless transition is possible, although it is worrisome that the U.S. data provide us with no comprehension of where these gains originate. The bad news is that U.K. return differentials were quite volatile in the long run—a decade or so of large positive differentials can be followed by another decade with a large negative differential. To repeat, naïve trend extrapolation is unwise.

### Summary: Privilege has its Memberships

Over the last half-century, the United States has gradually become the world's largest debtor and the world's largest creditor nation. Over that same period, official data show that the United States has earned higher yields (and higher total returns) on its external assets than the rest of the world has earned on U.S. external liabilities. Yet the rate of the yield differential has fallen, from 300 bps in the early 1960s to maybe 150 bps today. And if some of this remaining 150 bps is due to understated income payments to foreigners, the gap today could in reality be nearing zero (see Gros 2006).

Percent

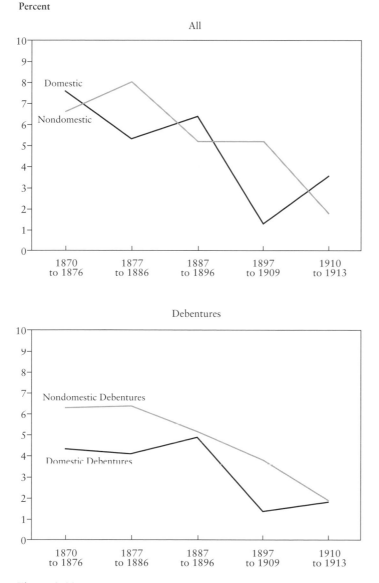

Figure 3.12
U.K. Total Rates of Return for Samples of Securities, 1870–1913
*Source:* Edelstein (1982).

It appears that by expanding its leverage, the United States has offset diminishing yield differentials to prop up its privilege as a fraction of GDP. Yet the future extrapolation of this trend is doubtful: the net external position cannot trend up forever, and if the yield differential continues to trend down, no amount of leverage will help. At the present time a significant contribution from ill-defined capital gains is propping up the U.S. measures of privilege, and more research will be required to verify and identify these mysterious additions to U.S. external wealth.

Compared to the United States today, a century ago Britain enjoyed a similar hegemonic position—economically as well as geopolitically. Britain also appeared to enjoy some modest privilege at times between 1870 and 1913. But this privilege could not be sustained, even from a massive net credit position. International financial competition, the global quest for superior yields, and the maturing of emerging markets all put a squeeze on British privilege. Similar forces are at work today that are affecting the United States. In both eras the hegemons possibly gained privilege during the "pioneer" phase of globalization, but for the British at least, holding on to its privilege proved elusive in the long run.

As privilege shrinks from, say, 2 percent of GDP to 1 percent or to zero, this enlarges yet further the eventual adjustment needed to bring a high trade deficit to a sustainable long-run level. With the trade deficit around 6 percent of GDP, the adjustment grows from 4 percent to 5 percent to 6 percent, given near balance on the income account.

### Scenarios for the Inevitable Adjustment: The Good, the Bad, and the Ugly

The second part of this paper examines the implications of how large adjustments to the current external balances may play out, again with an eye to history.

#### Data and Methodology

We use a panel data set for over 20 countries between the years 1880 and 1913 to address the questions posed above. Our data come from various sources, including those used in recent work on crises by Bordo, Eichengreen, Klingebiel, and Martínez-Peria (2001) and subsequently updated by Bordo and Meissner (2007). We also make use of the extensive data generated by Obstfeld and Taylor (2003). Our data for current accounts comes from Jones and Obstfeld (2001). Data for the Netherlands come from Smits, Horlings, and van Zanden (2000) and for Chile from Braun et al. (2000). In the places where the Jones and Obstfeld data set did not have information available, we used the trade balance (exports minus imports), following the practice in previous studies such as Adalet and Eichengreen (2007) and Catão and Solomou (2005).

We define the core countries to include Belgium, Denmark, Norway, Sweden, and Switzerland. During this period, these were high-income countries with robust institutional features, but which also imported a fair amount of capital. France, Germany, Great Britain, and the Netherlands, also in the core, are classified as a group of capital exporters and/or financial centers. Since surplus countries often had different experiences in adjustment, we leave these countries out of the core group when we analyze the adjustment process in detail. Furthermore we place Australia, Canada, New Zealand, and the United States into an "offshoots" category. These regions were extensive capital importers, were settled by immigrants of European origins, and also had a special institutional heritage, being members (or once having been members) of the British Empire. The periphery is defined to include Argentina, Austria-Hungary, Brazil, Chile, Egypt, Finland, Greece, India, Italy, Japan, Mexico, Portugal, Russia, Spain, Turkey, and Uruguay. We divide the remainder of the world in this manner because the periphery was, on average, poorer, less financially developed, had institutions that were less conducive to economic growth, and relied extensively on external financing due to its low per capita incomes and deficient pools of domestic savings. At the same time, most of the nations in the periphery had floating exchange rate regimes for significant portions of the period and only a few spells being on a gold standard. At times we separate countries simply into the rich and poor. We define the rich countries to be those with an income per capita in 1913 higher than $2,892, which was the median level of per capita income in 1913.

### Current Account Evolution over Time

In Figures 3.13 and 3.14 we illustrate the distribution of current account surpluses using box and whisker plots. These show the median, the 25th and 75th percentile, and the key outliers at either end of the distribution. These plots also exhibit the adjacent values for each category of country.[18]

Figure 3.13 shows that the core countries had persistently higher surpluses than the other nations, although there are quite a few more outliers at each end of the distribution in the core. The offshoots have a skewed distribution. There are many more country years of deficit than of surplus in the offshoot nations. There are also fewer outliers than in the other two categories. The periphery countries seem to be much more bunched toward the middle as the outside values on the bottom end are far fewer in number. Figure 3.14, which separates countries by whether they are rich, an offshoot, or poor, shows a similar picture. Rich countries again have a much more varied experience than either of the two other categories.

Figures 3.15 through 3.17 represent the time series properties of current accounts in each group of countries for the 1880–1913 period. Figure 3.15 shows the unweighted average current account surplus in the core, offshoots, and the periphery. Figure 3.16 divides the countries of the world into the categories of rich, offshoots, and poor. It is clear that there

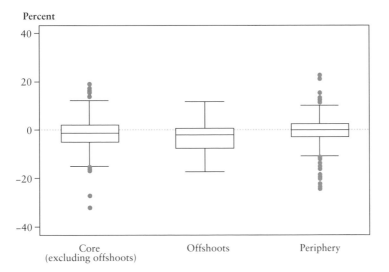

**Figure 3.13**
Current Account Surplus for All Countries as a Percent of GDP, 1880–1913
*Source:* Authors' calculations based on various sources (see the section on Data and Methodology, this chapter).

Percent

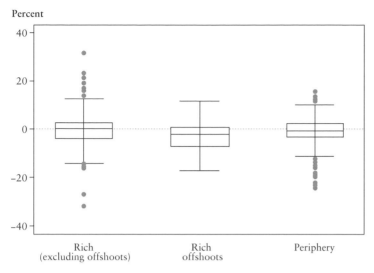

**Figure 3.14**
Current Account Surplus for Rich versus Poor Countries as a Percent of GDP,
1880–1913
*Source:* Authors' calculations based on various sources (see the section on Data
and Methodology, this chapter).

Percent

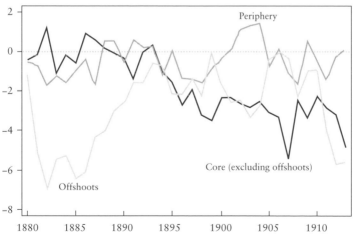

**Figure 3.15**
Current Account Surplus as a Percent of GDP in Periphery, Offshoots, and
Core, 1880–1913 (Unweighted Averages)
*Source:* Authors' calculations based on various sources (see the section on
Data and Methodology, this chapter).

Percent

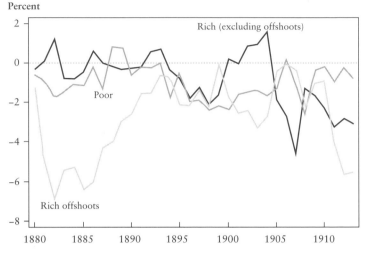

**Figure 3.16**
Current Account Surplus as a Percent of GDP in Rich and Poor Countries,
1880–1913 (Unweighted Averages)
*Source:* Authors' calculations based on various sources (see the section on
Data and Methodology, this chapter).

Percent

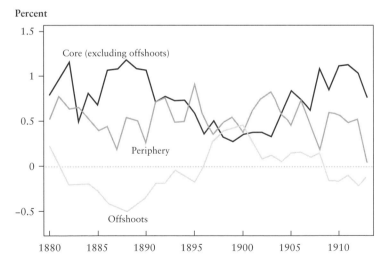

**Figure 3.17**
Current Account Surplus as a Percent of GDP, Core, and Periphery,
1880–1913 (GDP-Weighted Averages)
*Source:* Authors' calculations based on various sources (see the section on
Data and Methodology, this chapter).

is a strong inverse correlation between current account movements in the periphery nations and in the core. When surpluses in the core countries are high, the periphery tends to move into deficit. These cycles are well known in the historical literature and coincide with movements in the global, and especially the British, business cycle (see Fishlow 1986). In particular, when British investment (usually in residential housing) was high, British capital stayed home and the trade balance in the periphery turned positive. As investment cooled in Britain, capital ventured abroad and allowed for significant increases in the current account deficits of the peripheral nations.

Downturns in the global economy (meaning in Great Britain and in the Western European core, which together made up the principal export markets for the periphery) coincide with increased current account deficits in the periphery as export markets fizzled.[19] Reversals from deficits to surpluses in the periphery are often associated with economic recovery in the core countries, as capital flows emanating from the core dried up during cyclical downturns in the core regions. But such reversals in this period tended to be largely healthy in the sense that these were the natural conclusion of a cycle whereby capital flowed into the less-developed regions to fund infrastructure and other productive investment. When export markets ripened in the core, exports from the peripheral nations increased, helping to repay obligations previously incurred and smooth the adjustment process.

Figure 3.17, showing the *weighted* averages of current account deficits, illustrates these co-movements even more clearly. Although weighting in this way should balance out deficits and surpluses, this is not the case depicted here. For most years a downward shift equivalent to 0.5 percent of GDP would make it so that there was global balance. The reason this does not happen in the sample period of 1880 to 1913 could be because of missing current account information for a small portion of the world's total output. Nevertheless, this figure shows that the total surplus of the core or the total deficit of the periphery was not usually higher than 1 percent of GDP. However, this figure does obscure the large and persistent surpluses previously discussed in the case of Britain.

*Current Account Persistence*
Early work by Bordo, Eichengreen, and Kim (1998) used AR (1) regressions of the current account to compare persistence of the current account

in the past and present. They found that current account imbalances were significantly more persistent in the past than these have been recently. Taylor (2002) ran separate regressions for 15 countries allowing for dynamic error correction. We generalize these regressions by pooling the data and implementing the following type of vector error correction model

$$\Delta \frac{CA_{it}}{GDP_{it}} = \beta_i \frac{CA_{it-1}}{GDP_{it-1}} + \gamma_i \Delta \frac{CA_{it-1}}{GDP_{it-1}} CA_{it-1} + \mu_i + \delta_t + \varepsilon_{it} .$$

Our sample is slightly larger than that in Taylor (2002). Here, the country-specific $\beta_i$s represent the adjustment coefficients for each country in the sample. A small adjustment coefficient (in absolute value) implies that current accounts persist at levels far from their long-run values longer than for countries with larger absolute values. Figure 3.18 plots these coefficients and reveals a ranking compatible with previous qualitative assessments. The first batch of countries (from right to left) include the financial centers like Britain, France, and Holland. In the next group of countries, we find the extensive capital importers that ran persistent deficits such as Australia, Canada, and the United States. The implied half-life for current account deficits is roughly three years. Countries further out on the periphery that tended to indulge in revenue financing using the international capital markets, or which were smaller and more susceptible to changes in the moods of the capital markets, such as Chile, Finland, Japan, and Uruguay, witnessed significantly faster adjustment. Their average coefficient of roughly –0.6 implies a half-life of roughly nine months, or three-fourths of a year. The bottom line is that during the 1880–1913 period, many important capital importers were in fact able to run highly persistent deficits, and that surplus countries persistently ran current account surpluses.

We also tested whether several country attributes might be associated with the observed persistence of current account deficits. Specifically, we allowed the adjustment parameter to vary with the level of exports relative to output, the lagged level of output per capita, and the level of the government's currency mismatch. Countries with higher levels of exports for a given level of output (used as a proxy for the level of total trade to GDP) could be expected to have an easier time adjusting in the future, and hence capital markets might be expected to keep the money

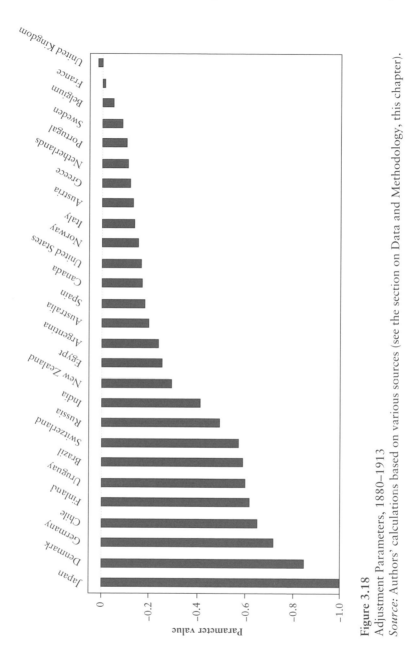

**Figure 3.18**
Adjustment Parameters, 1880–1913
*Source:* Authors' calculations based on various sources (see the section on Data and Methodology, this chapter).

flowing in the face of global shocks. On average, such countries would be expected to run more persistent imbalances.

A similar logic might be applied to countries with higher per capita income. At the same time, a higher share of British surplus capital was attracted to higher income per capita countries because investment opportunities were better in these wealthier countries. This division, along expected investment returns, then attempts to control somewhat for differences between imbalances derived from development finance and those associated with stop-gap external funding of frivolous government budget deficits. Fishlow (1986) made such a distinction and argued that the latter type of funding could quickly turn around as markets realized borrowing costs were growing more rapidly than revenue streams or the real economy. Fishlow also argued that countries using foreign capital for development finance could bide their time in the face of slowing export demand by borrowing even more from the international capital markets as these countries' financial sustainability was not necessarily in doubt. Markets could be expected to fulfill this role in the short term, as revenue and profits would be expected to be higher in the medium term. Similarly, if expectations of faster growth relative to world averages were strongest in the wealthy offshoot countries, their current account imbalances could be well justified.

We also checked whether countries with a fixed exchange rate or currency mismatch problems on the aggregate balance sheet had any observable differences in persistence. The logic of including a control for whether the country had a gold standard or not is that flexible exchange rates are typically argued to provide shock absorbers and thus equilibrate more quickly any potential imbalances through much faster changes in the real exchange rate. We define the economy's currency mismatch to be the level of outstanding debt payable in foreign currency or in a fixed amount of gold specie, minus the total reserves in the country normalized by the level of exports (cf. Bordo and Meissner 2007). Countries with larger mismatches could also face confidence problems if, in the event of a current account reversal, the real exchange rate depreciated and made the real burden of repayment more difficult and hence repayment more risky.

To control for all of these risk factors, we ran a regression similar to that above but included interaction terms between the lagged level of the current account and the lagged value of these various controls. If the interaction is found to be positive, it would suggest that the adjustment parameter would move toward zero, and hence that such a variable made it easier to sustain current account imbalances. Table 3.5 shows that countries that have higher per capita output have more persistent current account imbalances. This is further evidence that the capital exporters and the rich offshoots ran more persistent imbalances. Results regarding the exchange rate regime seem inconclusive. The interaction effect is not highly statistically significant nor is the coefficient on the interaction term very large. This is also the case for the terms including an interaction with openness to exports or the currency mismatch variable. Table 3.6 shows the years of high current account deficits and surpluses for various countries between 1880 and 1913.

### Current Account Reversals

We now turn to an analysis of the impact of current account reversals on short-run economic growth. Our preferred measure of a reversal is similar to that used in Edwards (2004). We define a reversal as occurring if, in a given year, the current account relative to GDP increases by more than 4 percentage points, and in the previous year the country was in deficit.

Table 3.7 shows the incidence of these "4-percent reversals." Financial centers have *no* reversals in the period between 1880 and 1913. Tabulations show that the core countries, excluding the financial centers, had twelve reversals accounting for 3.92 percent of the country-year observations for this group. The periphery nations had 21 reversals, or 3.86 percent of the country-year observations within this group. So it would appear that outside of the financial centers such as Britain, France, Germany, and the Netherlands, there is little difference between the raw frequency of reversals in the core or periphery nations. In rich countries, excluding the financial centers, the frequency of reversals is double that which take place in the poor countries. In 5.6 percent of the country-years, there is a reversal in the rich countries, while the number is 2.3 percent in poor countries. Together with the previous findings, this result suggests that the distribution of reversals in rich countries might have been highly uneven.

Table 3.8 shows the average levels of the current account balance relative to GDP in each of the three years before a reversal, the year of the

**Table 3.5**
Current Account Adjustment and its Determinants

| Regressors | (1) |
| --- | --- |
| Current Account $t - 1$ | −2.26 [0.72]** |
| Change in the Current Account $t - 1$ | −0.12 [0.09] |
| Current Account × Gold Standard $t - 1$ | −0.20 [0.10] |
| Current Account × ln(Real GDP per capita) $t - 1$ | 0.27 [0.09]** |
| Current Account × Exports/GDP $t - 1$ | 0.00 [0.00] |
| Current Account × Currency Mismatch $t - 1$ | 0.04 [0.04] |
| Gold Standard | −1.23 [1.89] |
| ln (Real GDP per capita) | −0.91 [0.41]* |
| Exports/GDP | −0.12 [0.03]** |
| Currency Mismatch | 0.19 [0.08]* |
| Change in log of the real exchange rate | −3.67 [2.73] |
| Constant | 11.75 [14.90] |
| Number of observations | 516 |
| R-squared | 0.24 |

Notes: Dependent variable is change in the ratio of the current account to GDP. The regression includes country fixed effects and year dummies. Robust clustered standard errors are in parentheses. See the text for precise definitions of variables.
* p-value < 0.1; ** p-value < 0.05; *** p-value < 0.01

**Table 3.6**
Years of "High" Deficit and "High" Surplus

| Country | High Deficit Years |
|---|---|
| (a) Years of "High" Deficit | |
| Australia | 1881–1892 |
| Belgium | 1904–1913 |
| Chile | 1884–1890 and 1909–1913 |
| Finland | 1895–1900 |
| Greece | 1880–1889 and 1891–1906 |
| Switzerland | 1886–1911 |

| Country | High Surplus Years |
|---|---|
| (b) Years of "High" Surplus | |
| Brazil | 1900–1911 |
| Egypt | 1886–1897 |
| Netherlands | 1884–1895 |
| New Zealand | 1893–1903 |
| United Kingdom | 1905–1913 |
| Uruguay | 1900–1904 |

reversal, and the three following years. We obtain these coefficients from a regression of the ratio of the current account to GDP on three leads of the reversal indicator, the contemporaneous reversal indicator, and three lags. Figure 3.19 shows how the average values of four different groups evolved over the cycle of reversal and recovery. The behavior of core and offshoot countries seems different than the periphery nations' experience. The core countries run higher deficits than other types of countries. Absent this, there seems to be little significant difference between the various types of breakdowns we use.

We also checked more carefully whether if once a reversal had occurred, it was sustained. The answer is yes, for the most part. We say a reversal is sustained if three or five years after the reversal occurred, the current account surplus is still higher than the year immediately before the reversal. Out of 31 reversals, 27 exhibited a sustained turnaround in this

**Table 3.7**
Countries and Years of Current Account Reversals

| Country | Years of 4-Percent Reversals |
| --- | --- |
| Argentina | 1885, 1891, 1912 |
| Australia | 1887, 1891, 1893, 1899, 1904, 1905 |
| Belgium | 1881, 1889, 1908 |
| Brazil | 1886 |
| Chile | 1888, 1898 |
| Denmark | 1886 |
| Egypt | 1909 |
| Finland | 1893, 1901 |
| Greece | 1883, 1885, 1893, 1897, 1904, 1906, |
| Japan | 1891, 1895, 1906 |
| New Zealand | 1883, 1909 |
| Spain | 1905 |
| Uruguay | 1908, 1913 |

Notes: See the text for the definition of a 4-percent reversal.

manner three years after the event. After five years, four of the 29 country-year observations had witnessed a relapse. These statistics reveal that current account reversals were, if anything, more likely to be sustained in the past than in the last 30 years. Edwards (2004) found that between 68 and 83 percent of reversal episodes were sustained, which is slightly lower than our findings.

Another interesting question concerns the relationship between financial crises and current account reversals. Edwards (2004) found that countries experiencing a current account reversal had a significantly greater probability of suffering a large change in the exchange rate (meaning a currency crisis) than countries that did not have a reversal. The idea that currency crises or sharp changes in the exchange rate could be associated with current account reversals is intuitive. In a reversal, all else remaining the same, the price at which domestic goods are exchanged for foreign goods typically must fall with the associated expenditure switching and reduction. If a reversal is associated with a sudden stop of capital inflows

Table 3.8
Average Current Account Levels Before and After a Reversal

| Regressors | Pooled (1) | Core Excluding Fin. Ctrs. and Offshoots (2) | Offshoots (3) | Periphery (4) | Gold Std. Ctry.-Years (5) | Non-Gold Ctry.-Years (6) |
|---|---|---|---|---|---|---|
| Current Account Reversal $t + 3$ | -4.79 [1.33]** | -8.10 [3.45]* | -6.27 [2.57]* | -4.24 [1.75]* | -4.27 [1.32]** | -5.83 [2.85]* |
| Current Account Reversal $t + 2$ | -5.75 [1.34]** | -7.48 [2.65J]** | -6.91 [2.46]** | -5.21 [1.82]** | -5.38 [1.28]** | -6.30 [2.85]* |
| Current Account Reversal $t + 1$ | -7.88 [1.19]** | -12.77 [6.11]* | -7.58 [1.84]** | -7.19 [1.28]** | -8.17 [1.46]** | -7.21 [1.93]** |
| Current Account Reversal | -1.39 [1.05] | -3.24 [2.57] | -1.28 [1.81] | -1.31 [1.44] | -1.13 [0.96] | -1.83 [2.38] |
| Current Account Reversal $t - 1$ | -2.55 [1.33] | -7.52 [4.02] | -1.33 [2.12] | -2.50 [1.73] | -1.45 [1.65] | -3.81 [2.15] |
| Current Account Reversal $t - 2$ | -3.72 [1.08]** | -7.52 [2.16]** | -1.80 [1.57] | -3.80 [1.41]** | -3.65 [1.07]** | -4.00 [2.08] |
| Current Account Reversal $t - 3$ | -2.40 [1.14]* | -3.43 [0.24]** | 0.45 [1.49] | -3.38 [1.63]* | -1.56 [0.83] | -3.34 [2.13] |
| Number of observations | 728 | 138 | 112 | 366 | 521 | 207 |
| R-squared | 0.17 | 0.17 | 0.30 | 0.20 | 0.13 | 0.32 |

Notes: Dependent variable is the level of the current account. All regressions include country fixed effects. Robust clustered standard errors are in parentheses. See the text for precise definitions of variables.
* p-value < 0.1; ** p-value < 0.05; *** p-value < 0.01

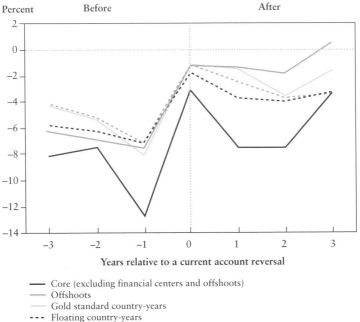

Percent    Before    After

Years relative to a current account reversal

— Core (excluding financial centers and offshoots)
— Offshoots
— Gold standard country-years
- - - Floating country-years
- - - Periphery

**Figure 3.19**
Current Account Balances as a Percent of GDP Before and After a Reversal
(Averages for Various Groups)
*Source:* Authors' calculations based on various sources (see the section on
Data and Methodology, this chapter).

and reserves are depleted, then the nominal exchange rate could also
fall for the reasons contemporary models of the exchange rate suggest.
On the other hand, real depreciation via deflation might be a possibility,
especially in the gold standard period when many countries had fixed
exchange rates under the gold standard. Bordo (2005) discusses how the
price-specie flow mechanism operated and suggests that adjustment was
often smooth in this period.

In the rosiest of adjustment scenarios, originally analyzed by Feis
(1930) and later Fishlow (1986), current account reversals are relatively
smooth. Early investments give rise to higher incomes, which allow for
increased savings. These adjustment periods are also times in which earlier investments made using imported capital begin to pay off. Dividends
reaped by the capital exporters from earlier investments are used to fund

purchases of goods and services from yesterday's capital importers. These proceeds are used to pay interest and principal on earlier debts incurred and the cycle repeats itself. The historical literature suggests that adjustment may have been more difficult in debtor countries that used external funding for "revenue" purposes than in regions that put funds toward further development of the economy and marketable exports.

In our data over the 1880 to 1913 period, the majority of current account reversals are *not* associated with currency crises and banking crises.[20] For the handful of debt crises in our period, there are few reversals surrounding such events. There are no debt crises concurrent with a reversal. Greece had a reversal in the year before its 1894 debt default. Tabulations show that only three of the 33 reversals in our data set are associated with currency crises in the same year. These three are Argentina in 1885, Chile in 1898, and Greece in 1885. The banking crises that have concurrent reversals are Australia in 1893, Chile in 1898, and Uruguay in 1913.

There is a possibility that this result is sensitive to the window of observation. So we created a five-year window for each type of crisis. This indicator equals one if there was a currency, banking, or debt crisis in the current year or within the previous two or next two years. Measured this way, seven out of the 33 reversals are associated with the five-year currency crisis window. Ten out of 33 reversals are associated with the five-year banking crisis window. As it happens, only two of the 33 reversals are associated with our five-year window for debt crises.

There does not seem to be overwhelming evidence of an association between currency crises and exchange rate reversals in this period. This is particularly so for the richer countries that adhered credibly to the gold standard. Reversals such as those which took place in Australia (1891), Belgium (1881), Denmark (1886), Finland (1893), and New Zealand (1893), to name a few, had no currency crisis associated with them. Most of these countries managed to hold on to their gold-based exchange rates despite suffering reversals and even banking crises. In this period, periphery countries that financed deficits with external borrowing and had mismanaged currencies seem more susceptible to being served up crises along with reversals. This begs the question of what the connection is between the real exchange rate and movements in the current account.

Obstfeld and Rogoff (2004) suggest that today a real effective depreciation of the U.S. dollar of over 30 percent would have to arise to allow for enough expenditure switching to rebalance recent U.S. trade deficits. Their model is an endowment economy and does not appear to allow for factors affecting economic growth. This conclusion would seem to bias the result in favor of large exchange rate swings.

The historical literature is not conclusive on the subject. New research by Catão and Solomou (2005) argues that the elasticity of the trade balance (defined as the difference of the log of exports and the log of imports) with respect to the real effective exchange rate was roughly 1. Their sample is for a group of 15 countries between 1870 and 1913. We examine this question slightly differently by presenting regressions of the change in the logarithm of the real exchange rate (where the nominal exchange rate is local currency units per pound sterling) on the contemporary reversal indicator, three lags of the reversal indicator, and country fixed effects. The regression equation takes the following form:

$$\Delta RER_{it} = \sum_{j=1}^{j=3} \gamma_k CA\_REV_{it+j} + \sum_{k=0}^{k=3} \gamma_k CA\_REV_{it-k} + \mu_i + \varepsilon_{it},$$

where $CA\_REV$ equals 1 when there is a current account reversal. Table 3.9 shows the short-run coefficients for six different specifications. Column 1 pools the data while columns 2, 3, and 4 split the sample by core excluding the financial centers, offshoots nations, and periphery countries. Columns 5 and 6 compare the experience of country-year observations for those nations on the gold standard and for those nations off the gold standard. Figure 3.20 plots these coefficients. Figure 3.21 plots the actual sample average and median change in the real exchange rate from three years before to three years after a current account reversal.

Overall there is some support consistent with the classical price-specie adjustment process. This is most easily seen in the plot of the median real exchange rates. Here we see mild appreciation in the run up to a reversal and mild depreciation after the reversal.

Table 3.9 and our plots reveal that countries see real appreciation in the years that precede a current account reversal. The cumulative sum of all post-reversal coefficients is usually positive, implying that *mild* depreciations on the order of 2 to 8 percent are associated with the years fol-

Table 3.9
Changes in Real Exchange Rates Before and After Current Account Reversals

| Regressors | Pooled (1) | Core Excluding Fin. Ctrs. and Offshoots (2) | Offshoots (3) | Periphery (4) | Gold Std. Ctry.-Years (5) | Non-Gold Ctry.-Years (6) |
|---|---|---|---|---|---|---|
| Current Account Reversal $t + 3$ | -0.01 [0.01] | 0.03 [0.02] | -0.01 [0.01] | -0.02 [0.02] | -0.02 [0.01] | 0.01 [0.02] |
| Current Account Reversal $t + 2$ | 0.01 [0.02] | -0.05 [0.01]** | -0.01 [0.01] | 0.03 [0.03] | -0.02 [0.02] | 0.08 [0.04] |
| Current Account Reversal $t + 1$ | -0.02 [0.01] | -0.01 [0.01] | 0.01 [0.02] | -0.04 [0.02]* | 0 [0.01] | -0.07 [0.04] |
| Current Account Reversal | -0.02 [0.01] | -0.01 [0.01] | 0 [0.01] | -0.04 [0.02] | 0.01 [0.01] | -0.09 [0.03]** |
| Current Account Reversal $t - 1$ | 0 [0.01] | -0.01 [0.02] | 0.02 [0.01]* | -0.01 [0.02] | 0.01 [0.01] | -0.01 [0.03] |
| Current Account Reversal $t - 2$ | 0 [0.02] | 0.01 [0.01] | -0.01 [0.02] | 0 [0.03] | 0 [0.01] | 0 [0.04] |
| Current Account Reversal $t - 3$ | 0.03 [0.01]* | 0.02 [0.02] | -0.01 [0.01] | 0.05 [0.02]* | 0 [0.01] | 0.07 [0.02]** |
| Number of observations | 689 | 140 | 112 | 353 | 495 | 194 |
| F-Statistic | 1.11 | 3.60*** | 1.77* | 1.77* | 0.83 | 3.03*** |
| R-squared | 0.02 | 0.09 | 0.06 | 0.04 | 0.01 | 0.11 |

Notes: Dependent variable is the change in the real exchange rate. Robust clustered standard errors are in parentheses. See the text for precise definitions of variables.
* $p$-value < 0.1; ** $p$-value < 0.05; *** $p$-value < 0.01

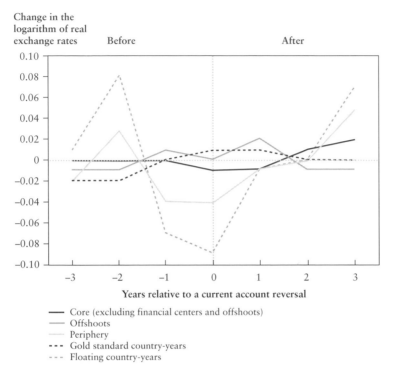

Change in the
logarithm of real
exchange rates        Before                                    After

**Figure 3.20**
Real Exchange Rates Before and After Current Account Reversals (Averages
for Various Groups)
*Source:* Authors' calculations based on various sources (see the section on
Data and Methodology, this chapter).

lowing reversals. There is an appreciable difference between countries on
the gold standard and countries that are not. Reversals in the non-gold
countries exhibit larger real depreciations after a few years. Deficits are
associated with large appreciations that continue into the year of reversal. In gold standard countries, the concomitant depreciation seems much
smoother and smaller over the years encompassing the reversal and following the reversal. This result contrasts with findings by Freund and
Warnock (2007), who looked at similar data between 1980 and 2003.
They argued that the movement of the real exchange rate did not depend
on whether the deficit was large or small. Our findings suggest that the
offshoot countries, which ran the most persistent and highest deficits on
average, had significantly smaller depreciations in the reversal period
than did the periphery and the floating countries.

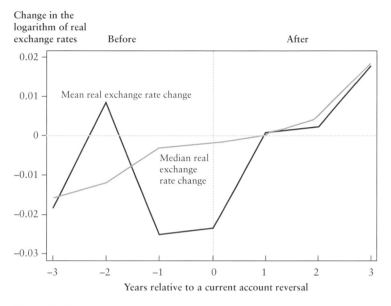

Change in the
logarithm of real
exchange rates

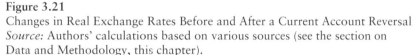

Years relative to a current account reversal

**Figure 3.21**
Changes in Real Exchange Rates Before and After a Current Account Reversal
*Source:* Authors' calculations based on various sources (see the section on
Data and Methodology, this chapter).

There are few coefficients on the reversal indicators that are individually statistically significant. However, tests of the hypothesis show that
the four coefficients are jointly significant and show that the current and
lagged values are together statistically significantly different from zero
in most specifications, except for the pooled sample and for the gold
standard country-years. Our conclusion is that the process of adjustment
associated with a reversal entailed a mild depreciation in both the core
and periphery countries, and in gold versus non-gold countries. Many
possible explanations for such a pattern exist that contrast with current
findings. Stabilizing capital flows, rather than destabilizing speculative
flows, and more extensive price flexibility may have allowed for smoother
adjustment and fewer panics, conditions that resemble the first generation variety of currency crises. Finally, rising incomes associated with
these large investment flows also seem to have helped ease the burden of
adjustment, so that aggregate demand changes were not associated with
large price swings. This explanation vindicates somewhat an Ohlinian
view of the conventional transfer problem.

*Patterns of Reversals*

In this section we analyze the adjustment process in detail. Mechanically, current account adjustments must be associated with a rise in national savings relative to total investment. The route by which countries get to adjustment, however, can vary quite significantly. Countries with fiscal deficits could be forced to eliminate such deficits in the face of capital flow reversals. This situation could lead to sharp falls in output as consumption and investment decline. But not all current account deficits emanate from government deficits and often these deficits reflect high investment in productive enterprises in excess of domestic savings. In such countries, a burst of exports based on earlier investments could facilitate exchange rate adjustment, sometimes even offsetting the required reduction in consumption for consumers and government alike. This can occur as incomes expand and finance the additional savings needed to improve the balance. Nevertheless, Edwards (2004), Adalet and Eichengreeen (2007), and Freund and Warnock (2007) suggest that reversals have been associated with growth slowdowns. These samples are either entirely from the post–1970 period or heavily weighted to describe events post–1913. Given what we have found and our reading of the historical literature, there is reason to believe that prior to 1913 the growth impact of reversals might not have been so pernicious.

In the discussion that follows, we attempt to see whether the various types of countries, which had very different reasons for their current account imbalances, had different adjustment paths. We have data for 15 countries on investment and savings, but the sample is larger when we look at the government surplus, and expands appreciably more when we analyze the growth impact of reversals.

Table 3.10 shows how changes in the ratio of private savings to GDP are associated with changes in the current account balance. We regress the savings ratios on the contemporaneous and lagged changes in the current account. We also include the lagged level of the dependent variable, the average growth rate of the world's economies, the lagged growth rate of per capita income, and country fixed effects.[21] For comparisons we include standardized beta coefficients for the contemporaneous changes in the current account. These coefficients are equal to the estimated coefficient multiplied by the ratio of the standard deviation of the change in

Table 3.10
Dynamics of the Ratio of Savings to GDP

| Regressors | Pooled (1) | Core Excluding Fin. Ctrs. and Offshoots (2) | Offshoots (3) | Periphery (4) |
|---|---|---|---|---|
| S/GDP $t-1$ | -0.23 [0.05]** | -0.02 [0.02] | -0.17 [0.06] | -0.21 [0.03]** |
| Change in Ratio of Current Account to GDP | 0.78/0.49 [0.09]** | 0.71/0.73 [0.01]** | 0.85/0.56 [0.17]* | 0.83/0.54 [0.22]* |
| Lagged Change in Ratio of Current Account to GDP | -0.13 [0.07] | 0.04 [0.06] | -0.15 [0.06] | -0.04 [0.09] |
| Average Growth Rate of GDP All Countries | -0.01 [0.09] | 0.09 [0.01]* | 0.07 [0.10] | -0.04 [0.11] |
| Lagged Growth in per capita GDP | -0.03 [0.04] | -0.03 [0.03] | -0.02 [0.10] | -0.06 [0.05] |
| Constant | 3.10 [0.78]** | 0.37 [0.26] | 2.06 [0.86] | 2.27 [0.24]** |
| Number of observations | 471 | 96 | 96 | 151 |
| R-squared | 0.41 | 0.55 | 0.44 | 0.45 |

Notes: Dependent variable is the change in the ratio of domestic savings to GDP. All regressions include country fixed effects. Robust clustered standard errors are in parentheses. See the text for precise definitions of variables. Absolute values of standardized beta coefficients are listed in row 2 after the estimated coefficients.
* p-value < 0.1; ** p-value < 0.05; *** p-value < 0.01

the current account in the sample to the standard deviation of the dependent variable.

Unsurprisingly there is a positive relationship between the savings ratio and current account reversals in all types of countries. However, there is also a difference between the core countries and the other groups. In the core nations, the savings ratio is more sensitive to changes in the current account measured by its beta coefficient than in the offshoots and the periphery. In the offshoot and periphery countries, there is no discernible difference between the impact of changes in the current account on the savings rate.

Table 3.11 shows the association of the investment to GDP ratio with the current account. The estimating equation follows a parallel specification for the savings equation. Investment declines as the current account strengthens, but there are very significant differences between our various groups of countries. In the core and the periphery, investment clearly falls and makes up in the adjustment process what the rise in savings did not. In the offshoot countries, the coefficient on contemporaneous investment is statistically indistinguishable from zero. Nevertheless the sensitivity of investment to changes in the current account in the following year is nearly the same as in the periphery in the contemporaneous year. While the lag structure is slightly different, the coarseness of the data should be taken into account, and it is likely that investment moved in a similar way both in the offshoots and the periphery. The conventional wisdom is that savings, possibly out of higher incomes, prevented adjustment from being too choppy in the burgeoning offshoots. The data back this up and suggest that the rise in savings makes up for the majority of the compression in the current account, with investment declines accounting for about half as much of the compression.

Changes in public savings make up for the rest of the adjustment, as Table 3.12 demonstrates. Here the dependent variable is the ratio of government surplus to GDP. The point estimates suggest significant differences between our three groups of countries. In the periphery, where borrowing was frequently undertaken to plug fiscal gaps during the 1880–1913 period, we see that reversals would tend to be associated with a rise in the government surplus. In the core, and in the offshoots, the point estimates on the contemporaneous current account terms are both negative and statistically indistinguishable from zero.

Table 3.11
Dynamics of the Ratio of Investment to GDP

| Regressors | Pooled (1) | Core Excluding Fin. Ctrs. and Offshoots (2) | Offshoots (3) | Periphery (4) |
|---|---|---|---|---|
| I/GDP $t-1$ | -0.23 [0.06]** | -0.10 [0.04] | -0.17 [0.11] | -0.30 [0.06]** |
| Change in Ratio of Current Account to GDP | -0.17/0.18 [0.06]* | -0.27/0.38 [0.00]** | -0.07/0.06 [0.17] | -0.24/0.26 [0.08]* |
| Lagged Change in Ratio of Current Account to GDP | -0.18 [0.04]** | 0.01 [0.06] | -0.25 [0.05]* | -0.19 [0.11] |
| Average Growth Rate of GDP All Countries | 0.08 [0.05] | 0.11 [0.01]** | 0.05 [0.14] | 0.10 [0.06] |
| Lagged Growth in per capita GDP | 0.01 [0.05] | -0.01 [0.03] | -0.03 [0.09] | 0.03 [0.09] |
| Constant | 3.25 [0.89]** | 1.43 [0.68] | 3.00 [2.30] | 3.65 [0.83]* |
| Number of observations | 471 | 96 | 96 | 151 |
| R-squared | 0.17 | 0.23 | 0.12 | 0.24 |

Notes: Dependent variable is the change in the ratio of investment to GDP. All regressions include country fixed effects. Robust clustered standard errors are in parentheses. See the text for precise definitions of variables.
Absolute values of standardized beta coefficients are listed in row 2 after the estimated coefficients.
* p-value < 0.1; ** p-value < 0.05; *** p-value < 0.01

Table 3.12
Dynamics of the Government Surplus Divided by GDP, 1880–1913

| Regressors | Pooled (1) | Core Excluding Fin. Ctrs. and Offshoots (2) | Offshoots (3) | Periphery (4) |
|---|---|---|---|---|
| Govt. Surplus/GDP $t-1$ | -0.77 [0.11]** | -0.71 [0.19]* | -0.31 [0.08]* | -0.83 [0.12]** |
| Change in Ratio of Current Account to GDP | 0.05/0.05 [0.03] | -0.02/0.04 [0.04] | -0.02/0.06 [0.03] | 0.10/0.08 [0.05]* |
| Lagged Change in Ratio of Current Account to GDP | -0.02 [0.07] | -0.08 [0.04] | 0.06 [0.03] | -0.04 [0.11] |
| Average Growth Rate of GDP All Countries | -0.06 [0.04] | -0.02 [0.01] | 0.06 [0.08] | -0.18 [0.09] |
| Lagged Growth in per capita GDP | 0.08 [0.02]** | 0.04 [0.01] | 0.02 [0.02] | 0.12 [0.03]** |
| Constant | -0.85 [0.12]** | -0.26 [0.06]* | -1.37 [0.45] | 0.07 [0.11] |
| Number of observations | 619 | 123 | 119 | 268 |
| R-squared | 0.41 | 0.36 | 0.23 | 0.46 |

Notes: Dependent variable is the change in the ratio of the government surplus to GDP. All regressions include country fixed effects. Robust clustered standard errors are in parentheses. See the text for precise definitions of variables. Absolute value of standardized beta coefficients are listed in row 2 after the estimated coefficients.
* p-value < 0.1; ** p-value < 0.05; *** p-value < 0.01

Together these tables point out that in the distant past century, the major part of the adjustment process came through increased savings. At this research stage we are unable to say whether these increases came out of higher incomes generated by previous investments in plant and infrastructure, or whether these savings are a result of a decline in aggregate demand. Based on the historical literature, we suspect that in the periphery countries it is more likely that we would see declines in aggregate output in the wake of current account reversals. This is because much of the borrowing was not spent on productive enterprises. Even when it was productive, it was invested in development of single commodity export industries that were vulnerable to large price shocks, like guano or coffee. The fact that government deficit financing played a larger role in the periphery countries would tend to damage output growth as well. First, because much of the government expenditure went to pay for current outlays rather than investments, and second, because this type of deficit borrowing is susceptible to crises of confidence, which precipitate relatively large exchange rate swings (as we have seen for the floating periphery in Figure 3.20). These conditions add up to balance sheet crises, as described in Bordo and Meissner (2007).

Tables 3.13 and 3.14 show the impact on per capita output growth of current account reversals. Adalet and Eichengreen (2007) argue that reversals have been associated with lower growth in per capita income and Edwards found a similar result for the post–1970 period. Comparing our results directly to Adalet and Eichengreen is difficult because they pool the data between 1880 and 1997. They do not report separate coefficients for each period and follow a slightly different specification by using the average value of growth in the three years after a reversal as the dependent variable.

In Table 3.13 we follow the specifications from Tables 3.10 through 3.12 and use the growth rate of income per capita as the dependent variable. We also include contemporaneous and lagged changes in the current account balance, the change in world GDP, lagged domestic growth, and country-level fixed effects. We find little evidence that changes in the current account are associated with changes in the conditional growth rates of per capita output. This is true for the pooled sample as it is in each of the subsamples. This result suggests that current account

**Table 3.13**
Growth Dynamics Versus the Current Account, 1880–1913

| Regressors | Pooled (1) | Core Excluding Fin. Ctrs. and Offshoots (2) | Offshoots (3) | Periphery (4) |
|---|---|---|---|---|
| Change in Ratio of Current Account to GDP | 0.09 [0.10] | 0.11 [0.07] | -0.03 [0.14] | 0.17 [0.13] |
| Lagged Change in Ratio of Current Account to GDP | -0.02 [0.06] | 0.06 [0.04] | 0.29 [0.31] | -0.07 [0.07] |
| Average Growth Rate of GDP All Countries | 0.40 [0.13]** | 0.11 [0.06] | 1.16 [0.48] | 0.17 [0.17] |
| Lagged Growth in per capita GDP | -0.24 [0.04]** | -0.07 [0.09] | -0.22 [0.09] | -0.25 [0.07]** |
| Constant | 1.13 [0.20]** | 1.44 [0.10]** | 0.14 [0.71] | 1.41 [0.28]** |
| Number of observations | 756 | 155 | 128 | 345 |
| R-squared | 0.09 | 0.04 | 0.21 | 0.10 |

Notes: Dependent variable is the growth rate of GDP per capita. All regressions include country fixed effects. Robust clustered standard errors are in parentheses. See the text for precise definitions of variables.
* p-value < 0.1; ** p-value < 0.05; *** p-value < 0.01

reversals were not, on average, costly in terms of lost output during the first era of globalization.

The virtuous cycle of investments, growing local capacity, and import absorption in the surplus countries seems to be a stylized fact backed up by a broad statistical analysis of all available data. Moreover, as we have seen, only about one-third of the current account reversals were associated with financial crises. As it happens, even these events do not seem to have been important enough in the overall sample to conclude that these reversals are associated with output losses.

In Table 3.14 we check the robustness of these results by using indicators for our 4-percent reversals rather than the changes in the current account as the key regressors. Here again we find no overwhelming evidence of slower growth during reversal episodes. In the pooled sample, none of the coefficients on reversals are individually statistically different from zero, and jointly they are also statistically insignificant.

Looking at the point estimates, we find the following results. In the core countries, growth is above average in the year of a current account reversal. In the offshoot countries, growth is lower by about 2 percentage points two years after a reversal, but there is no difference in growth rates in the year of and one year after a reversal. In the periphery, growth appears to be lower one year after a reversal. Again the coefficient is only statistically significant at a generous 90 percent level of confidence. The results here again contrast with those of Freund and Warnock (2007). In the last 30 years they found that larger exchange rate movements led to lower output losses. Since we know the core and the offshoot countries clung to the gold standard while the periphery typically floated, it appears that, if anything, on average the gold standard countries with rigid exchange rates had higher growth rates than the periphery countries.[22] Taking the cumulative sum of the point estimates suggests that the wealthier offshoot countries do have a larger dip in output in the wake of reversals than do the rest of the periphery countries. This result is almost surely driven by the severe economic crisis in Australia in the 1890s that was analyzed most recently in Adalet and Eichengreen (2007).

In columns 6 through 8 of Table 3.14, we test whether openness to trade, the level of GDP per capita, and currency mismatches affected output losses in the face of a current account reversal. We do so by sepa-

Table 3.14
Growth Dynamics and Current Account Reversals, 1880–1913

| Regressors | Pooled (1) | Core Excluding Fin. Ctrs. and Offshoots (2) | Offshoots (3) | Periphery (5) | Openness (6) | Wealth (7) | Mismatch (8) |
|---|---|---|---|---|---|---|---|
| Current Account Reversal $t$ | -0.52 [0.88] | 1.09 [0.21]** | -1.14 [2.82] | -0.67 [1.30] | -2.72 [2.82] | -3.49 [7.24] | -1.12 [1.14] |
| Current Account Reversal $t-1$ | -0.60 [0.99] | 0.27 [0.15] | 0.02 [4.04] | -0.95 [0.53]* | — | — | — |
| Current Account Reversal $t-2$ | -0.13 [0.84] | -0.75 [0.60] | -2.71 [0.90]* | 1.20 [0.91] | — | — | — |
| Current Account Reversal $t-3$ | 0.85 [1.14] | -0.30 [0.54] | -0.27 [2.55] | 2.34 [1.80] | — | — | — |
| Current Account Reversal $t$ × Exports/GDP | — | — | — | — | 0.08 [0.10] | — | — |
| Current Account Reversal $t$ × Lagged GDP per Capita | — | — | — | — | — | 0.38 [0.97] | — |
| Current Account Reversal $t$ × Currency Mismatch | — | — | — | — | — | — | 0.77 [1.03] |
| Exports/GDP | — | — | — | — | 0.01 [0.02] | — | — |
| Lagged GDP per Capita | — | — | — | — | — | -3.32 [0.97]** | — |

| | (1) | (2) | (3) | (4) | (5) | (6) | (7) |
|---|---|---|---|---|---|---|---|
| Mismatch | — | — | — | — | — | — | -0.15 [0.14] |
| Average Growth Rate of GDP per capita all countries | 0.44 [0.13]** | 0.10 [0.05] | 1.26 [0.51] | 0.25 [0.16] | 0.44 [0.13]** | 0.46 [0.13]** | 0.55 [0.16]** |
| Constant | 0.75 [0.20]** | 1.31 [0.09]** | 0.05 [0.68] | 0.84 [0.28]* | 0.57 [0.43] | 26.23 [7.44]** | 0.75 [0.23]** |
| Number of observations | 730 | 150 | 124 | 332 | 787 | 787 | 582 |
| R-squared | 0.03 | 0.02 | 0.18 | 0.02 | 0.03 | 0.04 | 0.06 |

Notes: Dependent variable is the growth rate of GDP per capita. All regressions include country fixed effects. Robust clustered standard errors are in parentheses. See the text for precise definitions of variables.
* p-value < 0.1; ** p-value < 0.05; *** p-value < 0.01

rately interacting each of these controls with the contemporaneous reversal indicator. Edwards (2004) argued that more open economies were less likely to suffer growth slowdowns after a reversal. In theory a larger currency mismatch could make it so that a larger primary surplus would be needed to maintain fiscal sustainability in the face of a currency depreciation. An interaction between per capita output and the reversal indicator is an ad hoc comparison, but asks the data whether stronger institutions and better financial development allowed for easier adjustment. In column 6 we find that the interaction term with export openness is positive, but the marginal effect of a reversal at any level of openness is not highly statistically significant. Columns 7 and 8 are equally inconclusive. The impact of reversals does not appear to depend on the level of real output per capita nor on the level of the currency mismatch.

Tables 3.13 and 3.14 suggest that in the first golden age of financial globalization, current account reversals were not unambiguously associated with growth disasters. On the whole, the weight of evidence is for a benign view of current account reversals. If savings were rising and moving more than investment fell during reversals, then this would suggest that a vast majority of reversals were accompanied by enough expenditure shifting (meaning increases in net exports) so as to allow for continued trend growth. This evidence therefore suggests that prior to 1913, current account reversals were just part of a series of mostly amicable games of marbles *à la* Rueff.

### Summary: Smooth or Choppy Adjustment?

Our overall assessment about current account reversals arises from a period that witnessed profound international integration in trade and capital markets. This global economic integration had the industrial powerhouse of Western Europe behind it, promoting capital imports in the periphery to further enhance domestic economic growth. The lending cycles often discussed in the literature are prevalent and emblematic of this largely symbiotic relationship. Current account reversals did occur and roughly one-third of these adjustments were accompanied by large swings in exchange rates in the years preceding or following these reversals. However, capital markets were much more stabilizing in the past. These financial markets reacted to local events rather than to global events, and hence crises were less contagious (cf. Mauro, Sussman, and Yafeh 2006). That being the case, current account imbalances persisted especially where markets had the confidence that due care was being taken to ensure that profitable investment returns would eventually result.

When reversals did come in this earlier period, these were mostly accompanied by mild exchange rate fluctuations on the order of 2 to 8 percent over the adjustment phase—nowhere near the 30 percent effective fluctuations that are envisaged by contemporary predictions of adjustment for the current U.S. imbalances. In this earlier era, growth in exports and higher productive capacity overcame the compression in government expenditure and investment that accompanied reversals and created reversal episodes that were not the growth mishaps that seem to be occurring more frequently these days. Why are the effects so different from era to era? Current account deficits and financial globalization in developing countries these days has often been associated with fiscal excess and misguided development attempts in places where supporting fundamentals such as human and social capital were weak and institutions were unpropitious. This description most resembles what happened in the nineteenth century in the peripheral regions. But recently greater contagion and capital market spillovers have also contributed to international capital markets that seize up and lose liquidity even for good risks. Because of the maturity mismatch problem that afflicts countries, many projects go underfunded during the downswing of the cycle. Looking forward after having looked backward, we believe the key determinant of whether current account reversals in the present day will be smooth or not will depend on continued confidence in the international capital markets, and continued efforts to improve future productive capacity in debtor nations. In this case, the eventual and inevitable reversal will more likely be smooth and gentle rather than abrupt and abrasive.

## Conclusions

In this paper we have used a comparative economic history approach to study two hotly debated aspects of the current global imbalances: privilege and adjustment.

We find that the special and privileged position of the United States in the global economy of the late twentieth century appears to be on the wane. We make comparisons with the last imperial and hegemonic power, Britain in the late nineteenth century, and find some parallels with the U.S. situation today. Although Britain was a net creditor, its ability to extract privilege appears to have been a phenomenon largely resulting from its status as a global financial pioneer in the 1860s and 1870s. After that period, yield differentials between home and foreign assets closed, and total returns differentials between home and foreign assets fluctuated above and below zero from decade to decade.

For the United States today, as compared to the 1960s, yield privilege appears to be draining away, falling from almost 3 percent to less than 1 percent, despite the rise of riskier foreign investment portfolios. The only reason that privilege has grown as a fraction of GDP is that the leverage has massively increased, with the United States, like many other countries, vastly expanding its external balance sheet through large gross flows since the 1980s. Naïve trend extrapolation is always unwise, but it is especially unwise for considering privilege as a fraction of GDP, because the underlying trends are countervailing, and cannot be expected to carry on forever in the same way. The only offsetting factor is that U.S. capital gains on external wealth appear to be very strong in recent years, but the origin of these is a mystery and their extrapolation even more subject to doubt. If privilege continues to disappear as it has in the past, then, all else equal, an even larger adjustment will be needed.

What can history teach us about adjustment of current account imbalances? We have examined the experience of a large sample of countries and compared their adjustment experiences with those from the recent past. There are striking differences between the results from the recent period and those from the past. Most notably current account deficits were often highly persistent while the adjustment process was not always as fraught with the economic distress economists typically predict today.

Part of this suggests that persistent current account deficits backed by sound investments will pay dividends, and expenditure switching and reduction will not have to be as abrupt as is commonly implied. The large and liquid capital market of London channeled local funds to emerging markets via fixed income investments, and it managed to discriminate between good and bad borrowers. This led to differences in the willingness with which future deficits could be funded. It followed that the deficits in the fast-growing but capital-poor countries were sustainable and these nations had rather smooth adjustments. This is to say that if history is any guide, the extent to which a hard landing will follow today's current imbalances could hinge importantly on the confidence of the capital markets, which is ultimately likely to be driven by the fundamentals.

■ *Meissner thanks the Bank of England staff for valuable conversations. Taylor thanks the John Simon Guggenheim Memorial Foundation for its support. The paper was prepared while Taylor was a visiting professor at London Business School, which he thanks for its support. We also thank Michael Bordo and Maurice Obstfeld for helpful discussions. Michael Edelstein, Philip Lane, Gian Maria Milesi-Ferreti, and Hélène Rey generously helped us with data. We have received helpful comments from Luis Catão, Michael Edelstein, Marcus Miller, Federico Sturzenegger, Gian Maria Milesi-Ferreti, seminar participants at the Bank of England, Birkbeck College, and many of the conference participants. In particular, we thank our discussants John Helliwell and Suzanne Berger for their thoughtful responses. The usual disclaimer applies.*

## Notes

1. See Jacques Rueff, "The Gold-Exchange Standard: A Danger to the West," *The Times* (London), June 27–29, 1961 (translated from the original article published in *Le Monde*, Paris, on the same dates).

2. For Warsh on Wolf, see http://www.economicprincipals.com/issues/05.04.10. html. For the Wolf forum, see www.ft.com/forumwolf. For up to the minute discussions, see http://www.rgemonitor.com/blog/setser/. For a recent overview, see Eichengreen (2006).

3. Due to data restrictions, as a first approximation we shall sometimes treat net labor income from abroad (NLIA) as zero, in which case net property income from abroad (NPIA) equals total net factor income from abroad (NFIA); this treatment is necessary when using contemporary IMF International Financial Statistics data (which do not present separate data on labor income remittances).

4. This method assumes the income balance data are reliable, although there are two concerns that for the United States these data may be biased by artificially high receipts (due to tax shifting to overseas affiliates) and artificially low payments (due to underreporting of income on foreign direct investment in

the United States). The first point need not be an issue for adjustment if this is achieved via transfer pricing, since there is then an offsetting item in the trade balance, as noted by Philip Lane and others; the second point may be an issue, since the U.S. income position is likely being misreported, as noted by Daniel Gros and others (see http://www.rgemonitor.com/blog/setser/). Admittedly there may be other biases in the income balance. Globally, IMF International Financial Statistics data for 2003 show the world has a deficit on trade of 1.6 percent of reported imports (if this is underreporting on the import side it is likely trade tax evasion), but the deficit on the income balance is 6.8 percent of reported credits, suggesting a bigger problem with underreported foreign income. If such a bias applied to the United States in 2004, it would add about $25 billion to U.S. NFIA, a rough doubling.

5. As with the previous method, this method assumes the income flow data are correct. But it also requires that the position data be correct, and here there is even greater controversy. Since NIIP data are usually built up from survey reports, the accuracy and consistency of the reporting is open to question. As we shall see later in this section, there are large changes in NIIP data from year to year that are simply not accounted for by financial flows, exchange rate changes, and price changes.

6. Of the four methods, method 4, recently proposed by Hausmann and Sturzenegger (2006), has probably attracted the most controversy. Opinions are divided on the so-called dark matter hypothesis. It is uncontroversial that the adjusted NFA positions are nothing more than a different way of looking at yield privilege (as the formulae show, there is a direct mapping from yield differentials and gross positions to NFA*). What is still disputed is whether these differentials are an expression of unmeasured exports such as liquidity services, insurance services, or know-how (see, e.g., Buiter 2006 or Brad Setser's blog). Hausmann and Sturzenegger (2006) do find a strong correlation between their dark matter measure (the gap between NFA* and NFA) and foreign direct investment, which is consistent with other research identifying foreign direct investment as the main source of yield differentials (Cline 2005; Higgins, Klitgaarde, and Tille 2005; Kitchen 2006). Disaggregation can illuminate the sources of differentials and how these change over time, but in this paper we look only at aggregate yield differentials and use the adjusted NFA positions solely for that purpose.

7. The existence of such a privilege for the United Kingdom was recently noted by Nickell (2006).

8. The missing category, within two standard deviations of the diagonal, is the neutral zone.

9. For example, when Hausmann and Sturzenegger (2006) find that the U.S. path for NFA* is level while the path for NFA plunges precipitously, they are merely restating in a different metric what Gourinchas and Rey (2007) called the "famous observation that the large increase in U.S. net liabilities to the rest of the

world has not been accompanied by a commensurate increase in net income payments;" that is to say, investment income balances have not lined up with the net asset position, so the privilege intercept is positive in (1), as in Figure 3.1.

10. As explained in Davis and Huttenback (1986, p. 84), these measures do not include capital gains, so in this context they are termed rates of yield, in contrast to rates of total return that include capital gains.

11. Another way of looking at this is to note that at the end of the period the nominal yield on assets was 4 percent, and that on liabilities 3 percent, which matches the ratio of 1.3 computed by Gourinchas and Rey (2007); but back in the 1960s, a time of comparable low inflation, the figures were about 3 percent and 6 percent, a ratio of 2.

12. We use the IMF IFS for investment income data proxied by NFIA, and Lane and Milesi-Ferretti (2004) for data on external positions.

13. There may be other countries outside the G7 that have enjoyed a yield privilege in recent times. For example, in an analysis of uncovered interest parity, Switzerland appears to have had a systematic negative risk premium with respect to OECD countries (Kugler and Weder 2005).

14. For the purposes of the counterfactual, we attribute 50 percent of the difference in the yield differential to the yield on assets, and 50 percent to the yield on liabilities.

15. One possible source of these mysterious gains is simply mismeasurement. For example, the statistical discrepancy in the balance of payments is often quite large. As an accounting principle, it appears routine to fold this discrepancy into financial accounts (see e.g. Lane and Milesi-Ferretti 2004, Nickell 2006). This accounting implicitly treats the current account side as the fully reliable measure. In practice, this distribution of the error is unlikely to be correct. Since valuation effects are simply the difference between reported external wealth changes and (minus) the financial account, falsely attributing a part of the statistical discrepancy to the financial account will bias the measure of capital gains.

16. For all other countries, zero is within the 95-percent confidence interval, and mean total return differential range between at most +25 bps (United Kingdom) and –62 bps (Germany).

17. This is presumably driven by those "other" capital gains identified by Kitchen (2006), who found a very similar 210 bps differential.

18. These are found by calculating the upper and lower quartiles. Call them p75 and p25. The interquartile range iqr is then p75 - p25. The adjacent values are the highest value not greater than p75 + 3/2 iqr and the lowest value not less than p25 - 3/2 iqr.

19. However, Britain had a persistent trade surplus with India.

20. We use crisis dates from Bordo, Eichengreen, Klingebiel, and Martínez Peria (2001) that were slightly updated in Bordo and Meissner (2007).

21. Since $T$ is large (34) for most countries in our panel, the Hurwicz-Nickell bias from including fixed effects and the lagged dependent variable is small, so we eschew generalized method of moments (GMM) and other esoteric methods.

22. This assertion holds up to more formal testing. When we interact the reversal indicator with the change in the real exchange rate, the marginal effect is not statistically different from zero.

## References

Adalet, Muge, and Barry Eichengreen. 2007. "Current Account Reversals: Always a Problem?" In *G7 Current Account Imbalances: Sustainability and Adjustment*, ed. Richard H. Clarida, 205–245. Chicago: University of Chicago Press.

Bordo, Michael D. 2005. "Historical Perspectives on Global Imbalances." Working Paper 11383. Cambridge, MA: National Bureau of Economic Research.

Bordo, Michael D., Barry Eichengreen, and Jong Woo Kim. 1998. "Was There Really an Earlier Period of International Financial Integration Compared to Today?" In *The Implications of Globalization of World Financial Markets*, ed. Bank of Korea. Seoul: Bank of Korea.

Bordo, Michael D., Barry Eichengreen, Daniela Klingebiel, and Maria Soledad Martínez-Peria. 2001. "Is the Crisis Problem Growing More Severe?" *Economic Policy* 16(32): 53–82.

Bordo, Michael D., and Christopher M. Meissner. 2007. "Financial Crises, 1880–1913: The Role of Foreign Currency Debt." In *The Decline of Latin American Economies, Growth, Institutions and Crises*, ed. Sebastian Edwards, 139–194. Chicago: University of Chicago Press.

Braun, Juan, Matías Braun, Ignacio Briones, José Díaz, Rolf Lüders, and Gert Wagner. 2000. *Economia Chilena 1810–1995: Estadisticas Historicas*. Santiago: Pontificia Universidad Catolica de Chile Instituto de Economia.

Buiter, Willem. 2006. "Dark Matter or Cold Fusion?" Global Economics Paper No. 136. London: Goldman Sachs.

Catão, Luis A.V., and Solomos N. Solomou. 2005. "Effective Exchange Rates and the Classical Gold Standard Adjustment." *American Economic Review* 95(4): 1259–1275.

Cline, William R. 2005. *The United States as a Debtor Nation*. Washington, DC: Institute for International Economics.

Davis, Lance E., and Robert A. Huttenback, with Susan Gray Davis. 1986. *Mammon and the Pursuit of Empire: The Political Economy of British Imperialism, 1860–1912*. Cambridge: Cambridge University Press.

Despres, Emile, Charles Kindleberger, and Walter Salant. 1966. "The Dollar and World Liquidity: A Minority View." *The Economist*, February 5, 526–529.

Edelstein, Michael. 1982. *Overseas Investment in the Age of High Imperialism.* New York: Columbia University Press.

Edwards, Sebastian. 2004. "Thirty Years of Current Account Imbalances, Current Account Reversals, and Sudden Stops." *IMF Staff Papers* 51 (Special Issue): 1–49.

Eichengreen, Barry. 2006. "Global Imbalances: The New Economy, the Dark Matter, the Savvy Investor, and the Standard Analysis." *Journal of Policy Making* 28(6): 645–652.

Feis, Herbert. 1930. *Europe: The World's Banker.* New Haven, CT: Yale University Press.

Fishlow, Albert. 1986. "Lessons from the Past, Capital Markets and International Lending in the 19th Century and the Interwar Years." In *The Politics of International Debt,* ed. Miles Kahler, 37–93. Ithaca, NY: Cornell University Press.

Foreman-Peck, James. 1983. *A History of the World Economy: International Economic Relations Since 1850.* New York: Harvester Wheatsheaf.

Freund, Caroline, and Frank Warnock. 2007. "Current Account Deficits in Industrial Countries: The Bigger They Are, The Harder They Fall?" In *G7 Current Account Imbalances: Sustainability and Adjustment,* ed. Richard Clarida, 133–162. Chicago: University of Chicago Press.

Geithner, Timothy F. 2006. "Policy Implications of Global Imbalances." Remarks at the Global Financial Imbalances Conference at Chatham House, London, January 23, 2006. Federal Reserve Bank of New York.

Gourinchas, Pierre-Olivier, and Hélène Rey. 2007. "From World Banker to World Venture Capitalist: U.S. External Adjustment and the Exorbitant Privilege." In *G7 Current Account Imbalances: Sustainability and Adjustment,* ed. Richard II. Clarida, 11–55. Chicago: University of Chicago Press.

Gros, Daniel. 2006. "Foreign Investment in the U.S. (II): Being Taken to the Cleaners?" Working Document No. 243. Brussels: Centre for European Policy Studies.

Hausmann, Ricardo, and Federico Sturzenegger. 2006. "Global Imbalances or Bad Accounting? The Missing Dark Matter in the Wealth of Nations." Working Paper. Cambridge, MA: Kennedy School of Government, Harvard University.

Higgins, Matthew, Thomas Klitgaard, and Cédric Tille. 2005. "The Income Implications of Rising U.S. International Liabilities." *Current Issues in Economics and Finance* 11(12).

Imlah, Albert H. 1958. *Economic Elements of the Pax Brittanica.* Cambridge, MA.: Harvard University Press.

Jones, Matthew T., and Maurice Obstfeld. 2001. "Saving, Investment, and Gold: A Reassessment of Historical Current Account Data." In *Money, Capital Mobility, and Trade: Essays in Honor of Robert Mundell,* ed. Guillermo A. Calvo, Rudi Dornbusch, and Maurice Obstfeld. Cambridge, MA: MIT Press. Data available at http://www.nber.org/databases/jones-obstfeld/.

Kitchen, John. 2006. "Sharecroppers or Shrewd Capitalists? Projections of the U.S. Current Account, International Income Flows, and Net International Debt." Unpublished manuscript, Office of Management and Budget.

Kugler, Peter, and Beatrice Weder. 2005. "Why Are Returns on Swiss Franc Assets So Low? Rare Events May Solve the Puzzle." Discussion Paper No. 5181. London: Centre for Economic Policy Research.

Lane, Philip R., and Gian Maria Milesi-Ferretti. 2003. International Financial Integration. *IMF Staff Papers* 50: 82–113.

Lane, Philip R., and Gian Maria Milesi-Ferretti. 2004. "The Transfer Problem Revisited: Net Foreign Assets and Real Exchange Rates." *Review of Economics and Statistics* 86(4): 841–857.

Lane, Philip R., and Gian Maria Milesi-Ferretti. 2005a. "Financial Globalization and Exchange Rates." IMF Working Papers 05/3. Washington, DC: International Monetary Fund.

Lane, Philip R., and Gian Maria Milesi-Ferretti. 2005b. "A Global Perspective on External Positions." IMF Working Papers 05/161. Washington, DC: International Monetary Fund.

Mauro, Paolo, Nathan Sussman, and Yishay Yafeh. 2006. *Emerging Markets and Financial Globalization: Sovereign Bond Spreads in 1870–1913 and Today.* Oxford: Oxford University Press.

Nickell, Stephen. 2006. "The U.K. Current Account Deficit and All That." Unpublished paper. London: Bank of England.

Obstfeld, Maurice, and Kenneth Rogoff. 2004. "The Unsustainable U.S. Current Account Position Revisited." Working Paper No. 10869. Cambridge, MA: National Bureau of Economic Research.

Obstfeld, Maurice, and Alan M. Taylor. 2003. "Sovereign Risk, Credibility and the Gold Standard, 1870–1913 versus 1925–1931." *Economic Journal* 113(487): 241–275.

Obstfeld, Maurice, and Alan M. Taylor. 2004. *Global Capital Markets: Integration, Crisis, and Growth.* Cambridge: Cambridge University Press.

Roubini, Nouriel, and Brad Setser. 2004. "The U.S. as a Net Debtor: The Sustainability of the U.S. External Imbalances." Unpublished manuscript. New York: Stern School of Business, New York University.

Smits, Jan-Pieter, Edwin Horlings, and Jan Luiten van Zanden. 2000. "Dutch GNP and its Components, 1800–1913." GGDC Research Memorandum No. 5. Groningen, Netherlands: Groningen Growth and Development Centre, University of Groningen.

Taylor, Alan M. 2002. "A Century of Current Account Dynamics." *Journal of International Money and Finance* 21(6): 725–748.

## Appendix: Data Sources and Notes for our Current Account Econometric Study

The sample of countries in our current account study are: Argentina (SI), Australia (SI), Austria-Hungary, Belgium, Brazil, Canada (SI), Denmark (SI), Egypt, Finland (SI), France (SI), Germany (SI), Greece, India, Italy (SI), Japan (SI), Netherlands (SI), New Zealand, Norway (SI), Portugal, Russia, Spain (SI), Sweden (SI), Switzerland, United Kingdom (SI), United States (SI), and Uruguay.

Not all countries appear in each of the 34 years which we analyze. (SI) indicates the subset of 15 countries that are included in the regressions with the savings and investment ratios.

**Current Accounts:** Current accounts for Australia, Canada, Denmark, Finland, France, Germany, Italy, Japan, Norway, Russia, Sweden, the United Kingdom, and the United States are taken from Jones and Obstfeld, *Saving, Investment, and Gold: A Reassessment of Historical Current Account Data*, available at http://www.nber.org/databases/jones-obstfeld/.

For the Netherlands, the source is Smits, Horlings, and van Zanden (2000) at http://nationalaccounts.niwi.knaw.nl/start.htm. The current account is calculated as GNP–GDP + Net exports of merchandise and services.

For Chile, the current account statistics come from Braun, Briones Díaz, Lüders, and Wagner (2000), while GDP statistics are obtained from Obstfeld and Taylor (2003).

For all other countries we used the trade balance as a proxy for the current account balance.

**GDP and GDP per capita**: Data underlying Obstfeld and Taylor (2003)

**Real Exchange Rates**: Data underlying Bordo et al. (2001).

**Savings and Investment Ratios**: Taylor (2003)

**Government Surplus**: Data underlying Bordo et al. (2001).

**Exports GDP**: Data underlying Obstfeld and Taylor (2003)

**Currency Mismatch**: Data underlying Bordo and Meissner (2007).

# Comments on "Losing Our Marbles in the New Century? The Great Rebalancing in Historical Perspective" by Christopher M. Meissner and Alan M. Taylor

Suzanne Berger

In August 1914 the first great wave of globalization crashed to an abrupt and totally unexpected end, as the outbreak of war suspended trading in all major markets. A financial journalist on the scene recalled a year later:

It came upon us like a thunderbolt from a clear sky. At the end of July, 1914, any citizen of London who was asked what a moratorium meant would probably have answered that there was not such a word. Possibly he might have said that it was a large extinct woolly beast with big tusks. If he was exceptionally well-informed in matters of finance he would have replied that it was some sort of device used in economically backward countries for blurring the distinction between *meum* and *tuum*. On the second of August we had a moratorium on bills of exchange. On the sixth of August we had a general moratorium....The machinery of credit broke down in both hemispheres, and London, as its centre, had to be given time to arrange matters under the new conditions. After all, you cannot have credit without civilization, and at the beginning of last August civilization went into the hands of a Receiver, the God of Battles, who will, in due course, bring forth his scheme of reconstruction. (Withers 1915, 1–3)

How the international economy's current account imbalances during the first globalization—with surpluses of nearly 9 percent of GDP in Britain, and very large ones as well in France, Germany, and Netherlands (Bordo 2005)—would have been resolved in the absence of World War I is a question that can never be answered definitively. Even once the God of Battles had settled scores, national barriers to the flow of capital, labor, goods, and services across borders did not come down for another 70 years. The general lesson of this tragedy is one that sheds doubt on any notion about the irreversibility of globalization or the triumph of economic interests over politics. But within the confines of the globalization story as it played out before the First World War, there are lessons to be learned from observing the processes of economic and political strain and adjustment. A return to the earlier period suggests, too, that today there are lessons to be learned from the debates among economists then and from considering, in retrospect, whether or not their contemporary analyses and quarrels ultimately identified the most important dangers to the openness and stability of the international economy.

Current debates over the international flows of capital, goods, and services center around the puzzle of privilege—the possibility for some countries to enjoy "an excess return on assets relative to liabilities allowing them to sustain larger trade deficits in equilibrium"—as Christopher Meissner and Alan Taylor define privilege in their contribution to this conference. Why do foreigners, at apparently such low rates of return, continue to invest so heavily in the United States? Why do American investments abroad apparently earn higher returns than investors from other nations derive operating in the same countries? How sustainable is a state of affairs in which the U.S. current account deficit in 2007 was 5.3 percent of GDP, resulting in a debt that over time will place a large share of the country's capital stock in foreign hands? Absent any agreement on the basic mechanisms and relationships underlying the present situation, and absent even any agreement on the existence or not of a serious problem for public policy, scenarios of readjustment in the early twenty-first century diverge widely.

During the first globalization that took place between 1870 and 1914, the mystery at the heart of economists' debates over capital flows was the reverse image of today's situation. A century ago the puzzle was why investors from advanced economies poured capital into peripheral and underdeveloped economies like Tsarist Russia, the Ottoman Empire, Argentina, and Paraguay, even when their savings might have earned about the same returns at home in less risky environments that were better insulated against dramatic reversals of fortune. Even though the British were far better positioned to do well overseas than were investors from other countries, at least in the prewar years after 1900, the British "savvy investor" abroad would not have done better than his more conservative compatriot who kept his money home (Eichengreen 2006). As Edelstein (1982) and Davis and Huttenback (1986) show, rates of return on British investments at home and abroad in the period 1870–1913 varied considerably over time and even from decade to decade; ultimately the rates of yield for investments made domestically, across the British Empire, and in other foreign locations converged.[1]

For France, which was second only to Britain in the magnitude of the capital it sent abroad during the first globalization, there is the same puzzle of why so much domestic savings was invested overseas; this question stirred up rancorous divisions among economists that spilled over into political debates about whether to institute capital controls (see Cameron 1961 and Berger 2003). For many liberal French economists at the time, there was no debatable issue at all: people invested abroad because the returns on foreign investments were higher than those earned on domestic issues (see Testis 1907, Théry 1908, Brion 1912). But even the mainstream economists of the day, who saw nothing more at work than the expected differences between investing in an old economy with a stagnant demography and investing in large emerging dynamic econo-mies like Russia, calculated that the differences between returns at home and abroad were small. In 1905 Paul Leroy-Beaulieu, a celebrity econo-mist of the era, made the case for buying foreign securities by reason-ing that it was just too risky for anyone but experts and the very rich to invest in domestic industries. As for portfolio investment, though the rate of return on foreign issues was only a half point higher than on domestic securities, "disdain for a half percent is turning your nose up at wealth" (Leroy-Beaulieu, 1905, 107–108). Returns varied widely by period. Calculations on the rates of return of French investment abroad show some of the same patterns as those for British foreign investment: those investors who seized overseas opportunities early often did a lot better than latecomers. But as the advice of Leroy-Beaulieu to the neo-phyte investor implied, over the four decades before the First World War, the gap between the rates of return over any number of years was not so great in either direction that individuals could readily figure out whether their best investments would be made at home or abroad. Indeed, by some estimates, the French would have done better investing in France. Harry Dexter White (1933) calculated 1899 yields on French foreign and domestic securities relative to the price of issue, and found that at 4.28 percent, the yield on domestic securities was higher than on foreign ones, which earned 3.85 percent. Similar conclusions for the period emerge in Lévy-Leboyer (1977) and Lévy-Leboyer and Bourguignon (1985).[2]

If massive French capital exports were not simply the response to clearly advantageous rates of return, what does explain this phenomenon? As the economists and politicians who challenged the liberal view saw it, the basic error of the liberal proponents was thinking of the world as one in which individuals choose from an array of rates of return. Eugene Letailleur, under the pseudonym Lysis, published a series of articles starting in 1906 that launched the great debate over the outflow of French capital.[3] He argued that it was the institutions of French capitalism that shaped the choices and responses of investors. Far from reflecting the absence of good investment opportunities in France, he contended that bank-led export of capital was one of the principal *causes* of France's slow growth and industrial stagnation. Commercial banks channeled individual savings into foreign investment (because, unlike German banks, French banks had only weakly developed links to domestic industry), earned large commissions from the sale of foreign securities, and manipulated the margins between the rates at which they negotiated foreign loans and the prices at which they sold them to customers. Between 1897 and 1903, for example, a third of Credit Lyonnais's profits came from the sale of Russian securities. From this institutional perspective, individual investors choose only among the investment options they find already in place. So the real reasons behind the massive capital flows from France were the structures of French capitalism and the institutions of French commercial banking.

In the debate over capital exports, another camp argued that money flowed out of France because the government used foreign investment as a lever to increase its power in international politics. As one economist, Maurice Brion, explained, capital exports were a kind of substitute for French weaknesses overall—for the country's sluggish economy and for its inadequate military capabilities. These exports of capital were "the latest form of French influence in the world" (Brion 1912). Take the case of Russia, which absorbed a quarter of all French overseas investment—after the 1870 Franco-Prussian war, French diplomacy was preoccupied with trying to build alliances that would break France's international isolation. French governments of every political stripe saw loans to Russia and foreign direct investment in that country as ways of advancing the cause of a Franco-Russian alliance (Kennan 1984). So French politicians and bureaucrats did whatever they could to promote these flows, and officials even collaborated with Tsarist agents in France to bribe financial journalists to write glowing accounts of the prospects of the Russian economy, even at such unpropitious moments as during the 1905 revolution (Raffalovitch 1931). As loan followed loan and French politicians and senior civil servants began to grasp the disastrous condition of Russian state finances, they also realized that French holdings of Russian assets had become so large that the ruin of the debtor would be a disaster for the creditor (see Girault 1973)—a dilemma still quite familiar to us today. Whatever the enthusiasm of the French state for foreign investments as an instrument of influence abroad, the role of government as a determinant of capital outflows seems a weak explanation because governments had extremely limited powers in this domain. The French government could veto the listing of foreign issues on the Paris exchange, but private investors found this obstacle easy enough to circumvent by going to the stock exchanges in Brussels or even Berlin. And as for positive inducements for investing at home or abroad, the French government basically had no levers at its command to influence such decisions.

Over the decade before the outbreak of war, as the French economists' debates over the determinants of capital outflows continued—were these due to market forces, institutions, or government policy?—these controversies fed into party politics and into a set of legislative proposals for capital controls. As nationalist passions heated up, it seemed that refusing to allow German securities to list on the Paris stock exchange was not enough; laws were introduced to require any foreign borrower of French funds to commit to buying goods from France (or to buy more goods or particular goods from France rather than from Germany—this latter proposal was provoked by Argentina's use of a French loan to buy armaments from Thyssen). Such protectionist legislative proposals were repeatedly defeated. Both with respect to the decisions of private investors and with respect to the use of French monetary reserves to support the gold standard, France before World War I kept its borders open to international trade.

Against a rising tide of nationalism, the political defense of French openness turned out to depend on two improbable allies: the economic liberals, for obvious reasons, and the French Socialist Left. The Left's commitment to free trade, to open borders for immigration, and to capital mobility is difficult to understand on any purely interest-based rationale. Unlike Britain, where food prices depended significantly on imports, French workers still ate French bread. French workers found themselves competing with immigrants for jobs in sectors like construction and mining. As the Left clearly understood, the heavy flow of capital abroad weakened job creation at home, and also created the prospect of new competitors in the future. Yet in the debates and parliamentary votes on openness, the Left rejected the implementation of market controls. Even when the Socialist leader Jean Jaurès opposed new loans to Russia in 1907, during a period of particularly harsh Tsarist repression, he insisted that Socialists had no principled objection to investing capital abroad: "It would be impossible, and not at all desirable, to forbid French capital to participate in this [cross-border] movement, at a time when the whole world is caught up in this process of economic growth and transformation."[4]

What sustained the Left's commitment to France's role as a provider of capital in the international economy was first, the belief that the gold standard and open borders were necessary foundations of a capitalist economic order. As Polanyi expressed it, "where Marx and Ricardo were at one, the nineteenth century knew not doubt" (Polanyi 1957, 25). Equally important, the Left's support for open frontiers for capital mobility derived from its internationalist ideology: the basic idea that nationalist autarchy was antithetical to a program of uniting workers across borders, and assuring a decent life for people around the world. These socialist convictions meant that the brotherhood of workers should be extended to include even Italian and Polish immigrants, whose presence in the French job market might drive down wages, and even to Russian workers, whose jobs in a French-owned factory in Russia replaced jobs that might have been created at home. In fact, the Socialist Left voted against increasing trade protection, against immigration restrictions, and against capital controls. These internationalist convictions were anchored by the alliances that the Socialists had made with Republicans and economic liberals in the violent French political battles at the turn of the century (the Church-State conflict, the Dreyfus Affair) against right-wing nationalists.

The Left's internationalism was one of the earliest and permanent casualties of World War I. By the end of the war in France, across the political spectrum, nationalism had conquered the field.[5] When issues involving the use of French reserves to support the gold standard, or capital mobility, or trade, or immigration returned to the political agenda in the 1920s, the political alliances that had sustained openness in the first era of globalization could not be recreated. In contrast to the prewar situation, when only 5 percent of France's overseas holdings were invested in French territories, after the war nationalist economic policies prompted a retreat of French foreign investment in order to take advantage of the protective economic barriers erected around French colonies. Coupled with a political backlash against foreign economic interests, these nationalist forces made the prewar economists' debates over capital accounts seem very distant and irrelevant. With the collapse of the political alliances that had once sustained open-market economic policies, in the interwar period the French were never again politically able to engineer the necessary domestic adjustments that would have allowed their reserves to be systematically mobilized to support a gold exchange standard (Bordo 2005).

In 1919 John Maynard Keynes described the illusions about the relationship between politics and economics that the experience of the war had demolished. Before the war, the British had regarded internationalization of their economy as:

normal, certain, and permanent, except in the direction of further improvement, and any deviation from it as aberrant, scandalous, and avoidable. The projects and politics of militarism and imperialism, of racial and cultural rivalries, of monopolies, restrictions, and exclusion, which were to play the serpent to this paradise, were little more than the amusements of [the Englishman's]daily newspaper, and appeared to exercise almost no influence at all on the ordinary course of social and economic life, the internationalisation of which was nearly complete in practice. (Keynes 1919, chapter 2)

But after the First World War an altogether different understanding of national borders emerged. Protectionism came to seem an essential component of national defense against Germany's economic resurgence. The notion that Britain would inevitably flourish in an international trade regime with free flows of capital, goods, and services seemed suddenly revealed as outdated and illusory wishful thinking.[6] Many of the French who had participated in the prewar debates and had advocated an unfettered regime of free capital flows also looked back on their earlier positions as naïve, and on the nationalists whom they had once held in contempt as having been, at the end of the day, the true realists.

Just as the political alliance between the economic liberals and the internationalists before the First World War had underpinned the French commitment to open borders for capital flows, in the United States today the political balances preserving economic openness depend on compromises among unlikely allies. But these alliances are fragile and under increasing strain. The reservations voiced by the Democratic candidates in the 2008 presidential primary campaigns about the Doha round negotiations and about the North and Central American Free Trade Agreements are responses to a rising tide of protectionist sentiment. The American public's concern and anger over outsourcing, offshoring, and possible foreign takeovers of U.S. assets (China National Offshore Oil Corporation, Dubai Ports World) have escalated dramatically. The entry of sovereign wealth funds into the capital of large banks and investment firms has fueled anxieties about the penetration of foreign state-controlled actors into positions of influence and control in the American economy. Foreign influence seems to threaten U.S. economic autonomy at the same time as a flood of poisoned toothpaste, pet food, heparin, and lead-painted toys harms American consumers. China is the focus of much of this political agitation, and Congressional leaders from both parties are threatening retaliatory measures against Chinese imports unless China revalues its currency. As Stephen S. Roach, Morgan Stanley Chief Economist, summed up the political atmosphere after testifying before Congressional committees in May 2007, "the protectionist train has left the station" (Roach 2007).

The realistic basis for much of this public anxiety may be thin. Why the agitation about the 1000 percent plus rise in imports of Chinese bras after the end of textile quotas, when bras are no longer manufactured in the United States? Why the political backlash over the offshoring of jobs when the Bureau of Labor Statistics finds very few U.S. jobs that have been terminated because of transfer overseas?[7] Or over the outsourcing of some research and development to China and India when, even setting aside the prominent cases of fraud and theft of intellectual property, reports from the field shows that the capabilities in these dynamic emerging economies for producing innovative research are still embry-onic (OECD 2007, Wilsdon and Keeley 2007)? But the fact is that in the United States public concerns about outsourcing and offshoring have now taken on a political life of their own, with little direct or immediate connection to the underlying economic realities. As Figure 3.22 shows, the rise and fall of media attention to the shifts of capital and employ-ment across borders now has little relation (at least in the short term) to the fall of domestic job creation or to the rise in layoffs. In a climate of economic recession and anxieties over employment, these sentiments are very likely to expand into greater pressure for protection.

If a great political backlash against globalization, with China as its focal point, is in the making in the United States, what if anything can be done about this situation? A return to the lessons of the first global-ization suggests two lines of reflection. First, one might wonder about the impact of real exchange rate readjustments and the value of the dol-lar (which in some of the scenarios envisaged in current debates about global imbalances are extreme) producing pressure for expansion of the U.S. tradeable goods and services industries. If, as Meissner and Taylor suggest, the smoothness of an eventual capital account reversal depends in large measure on building productive capacity in debtor countries, we need to examine the prospects for this taking place in the United States. Would creating more U.S. manufacturing jobs vent some of the protec-tionist steam that has built up along with the expansion of the balance of trade deficit? Will it actually be possible to restore manufacturing sector jobs that have been lost? Or have the industries that once provided such employment now become so uncompetitive or broken up by the fragmen-tation of production and the relocation of production around the world that these jobs cannot be recreated in the United States? If the expansion of the trade sector of the U.S. economy is not to take place in manufac-turing but in services, how much room is there for the type of growth that will substantially reduce the current account deficit? And which groups of workers in the American population are likely to be able to qualify for such services-sector jobs? The record of success for programs designed to retrain workers is so dismal that most of the new workers for any new jobs in tradeable services would almost surely be new entrants to the job market (coming out of somehow-improved U.S. secondary and tertiary educational institutions.) If the adjustment strategies to rebalance the

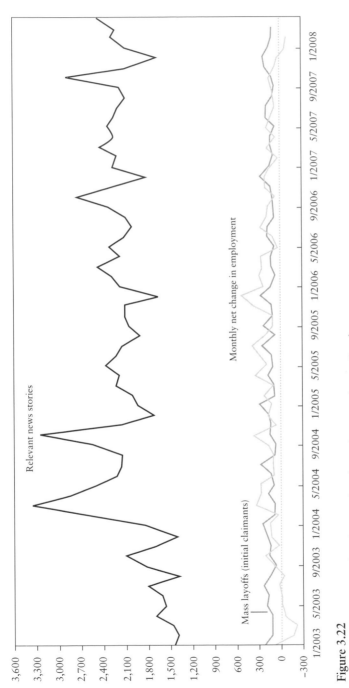

**Figure 3.22**
Media Attention to Shifts of Capital and Employment Across Borders

United States' current account deficits and trade deficits are supposed to generate more public support for the forces of globalization, there still remain quite a few problems to be addressed and solved.

Second, if the debates among today's economists over the sources of the current global imbalances and the scenarios and strategies of readjustment run the risk of focusing on the economic fundamentals and missing the political clamor rising outside in the streets—exactly what their predecessors did in the great debates over capital flows in the first globalization—what *should* economists now be focusing on to try and forestall the worse political outcomes? Here, my modest proposal would be to consider the public policies that might serve to bolster the U.S. economic system against surges of protectionist sentiment and come up with concrete strategies that would allow us to pay for these policies. Today in the United States anxieties about globalization are exacerbated by the fact that losing one's job usually means losing healthcare for one's family, often retirement benefits, and—over the past few years—the likelihood of having to settle for a new job that pays less than the old one. There are already a large number of proposals on the table, like wage insurance, for dealing with these issues. But implementation has been very weak. For example, the 2002 Alternative Trade Adjustment Assistance (ATAA) program that provides wage subsidies to workers over age 50 who lose jobs because of open trade policy, and are rehired at jobs paying lower wages, covered only 3,864 individuals during the period 2003–2005 (Rosen 2008, 3). What it would take to move ahead on these fronts undoubtedly belongs to a different subfield in the economics discipline than the one in which debates on global balances focus on whether Hausmann-Sturzenegger dark matter explains the apparent positive net income account in the U.S. balance of payments. But there are certainly few intellectual or political challenges as important as figuring out how to design and accommodate policies that could consolidate broad American public support for economic openness within a federal budget that needs to be brought out of deep deficit.

## Notes

1. Meissner and Taylor display the Davis and Huttenback calculations in Figure 3.6 in their paper, and the Edelstein calculations on slide 14.

2. For Germany, Richard Tilly (1991) calculated that over the period 1874–1914, the annual rate of return on Prussian government issues (consols) was 4.3 percent; on domestic industrial shares, 9.35 percent; and on foreign securities traded on the Berlin exchange, 6.7 percent. For Germany as for Britain and France, these averages reflect great fluctuations over different years during this 40-year period.

3. The articles were collected in Lysis (1912), *Contre l'Oligarchie Financière en France*.

4. Jean Jaurès, speech to the Chamber of Deputies, February 8, 1907, *Journal Officiel*, p. 338.

5. For the Communist Left, of course, internationalism became synonymous with the defense of the Soviet Union.

6. See also Frank Trentmann, *Free Trade Nation* (2008), chapter 6, on the massive disillusionment about free trade in Britain after the First World War.

7. Bureau of Labor Statistics, U.S. Department of Labor, "Extended Mass Layoffs Associated with Domestic and Overseas Relocations, First Quarter 2004," June 10, 2004, http://www.bls.gov/news.release/reloc.nr0.htm.

## References

Berger, Suzanne. 2003. *Notre Première Mondialisation: Lecons d'un échec oublié*. Paris: Seuil.

Berger, Suzanne. 2005. *How We Compete*. New York: Doubleday.

Bordo, Michael D. 2005. "Historical Perspective On Global Imbalances." Working Paper 11383. Cambridge, MA: National Bureau of Economic Research.

Brion, Maurice. 1912. *L'Exode des Capitaux Francais à l'Etranger*. Paris: Arthur Rousseau.

Cairncross, A.K. 1953. *Home and Foreign Investment, 1870-1913*. Cambridge: Cambridge University Press.

Cameron, Rondo. 1961. *France and the Economic Development of Europe, 1800-1914: Conquests of Peace and Seeds of War*. Princeton, NJ : Princeton University Press.

Davis, Lance E., and Robert A. Huttenback. 1986. *Mammon and the Pursuit of Empire. The Political Economy of British Imperialism, 1860-1912*. Cambridge: Cambridge University Press.

Edelstein, Michael. 1982. *Overseas Investment in the Age of High Imperialism, The United Kingdom 1850-1914*. New York: Columbia University Press.

Eichengreen, Barry. 2006. "Global Imbalances: The New Economy, the Dark Matter, the Savvy Investor, and the Standard Analysis." *Journal of Policy Modeling* 28(6): 645–652.

Girault, Rene. 1973. *Emprunts Russes et Investissements Français*. Paris: Armand Colin.

*Journal Officiel*. 1907. February 8.

Kennan, George. 1984. *The Fateful Alliance*. Manchester: Manchester University Press.

Keynes, John Maynard. 1919. *The Economic Consequences of the Peace*. New York: Harcourt Brace.

Leroy-Beaulieu, Paul. 1905. *L'Art de Placer et Gérer Sa Fortune*. Paris: Delagrave.

Lévy-Leboyer, Maurice. 1977. "La Balance des Paiements et l'Exportation des Capitaux Français." In *La Position Internationale de la France*, ed. M. Lévy-Leboyer, 75–142. Paris: Editions de l'Ecole des Hautes Etudes en Sciences Sociales.

Lévy-Leboyer, Maurice, and François Bourguignon. 1985. *L'Economie Française au XIXe Siècle*. Paris: Economica.

Lysis [pseudonym of Eugene Letailleur]. 1912. *Contre l'Oligarchie Financière en France*. Paris: Albin Michel.

Organisation for Economic Co-operation and Development. 2007. *OECD Review of Innovation Policy: China*. Paris: OECD.

Polanyi, Karl. 1957. *The Great Transformation*. Boston: Beacon Press.

Raffalovitch, Arthur. 1931. *"…L'Abominable Vénalité de la Presse…" D'Après les Documents des Archives Russes (1897–1917)*. Paris: Librairie du Travail.

Roach, Stephen. 2007. "Past the Point of No Return." May 11. Available at http://www.morganstanley.com/views/gef/archive/2007/20070511-Fri.html

Rosen, Howard. 2008. "Strengthening Trade Adjustment Assistance." Policy Brief PB08–2. Washington, DC: Peterson Institute for International Economics.

Testis [pseudonym of Raphael-Georges Lévy]. 1907. *Le Rôle des Etablissements de Crédit en France. La Vérité sur Les Propos de Lysis*. Paris: Revue Politique et Parlementaire.

Théry, Edmond. 1908. *Les Progrès Economiques de la France: Bilan du régime douanier de 1892*. Paris: L'Economiste Europeen.

Tilly, Richard. 1991. "International Aspects of the Development of German Banking." In *International Banking*, ed. R. Cameron and V. Bovykin, 90–112. Oxford: Oxford University Press.

White, Harry Dexter. 1933. *The French International Accounts, 1880–1913*. Cambridge, MA: Harvard University Press.

Wilsdon, James, and James Keeley. 2007. "China: The Next Science Superpower?" In *The Atlas of Ideas*, eds. Charles Leadbeater and James Wilsdon. London: Demos. Available at http://www.demos.co.uk/publications/atlaschina/.

Withers, Hartley. 1915. *War and Lombard Street*. London: Smith, Elder & Co.

# Comments on "Losing Our Marbles in the New Century? The Great Rebalancing in Historical Perspective" by Christopher M. Meissner and Alan M. Taylor

John F. Helliwell

For someone of a certain age, losing one's marbles is about things other than the gross domestic product (GDP) or the balance of payments, so when I first saw the title of the Meissner and Taylor paper I thought they were going to be impolite about the current state of debate and policy relating to the U.S. current account and the exchange rate for the dollar. I was quite mistaken. Instead, this urbane and creative paper adds greatly to the range and quality of comparative data and analysis of current account reversals over the past 120 years.

For decades the use of metaphors in international finance has been so rampant as to deserve inspection by *The New Yorker's* team of metaphor blockers. There was Machlup's wardrobe theory of the demand for foreign exchange reserves, and in the current literature so ably synthesized and extended by Meissner and Taylor, there is even an appeal to "dark matter," which turns out to refer to cosmology rather than witchcraft, although some commentators (for instance, Buiter 2006) on the dark matter approach would think the witchcraft interpretation to be more appropriate.

When Meissner and Taylor talk of having marbles, they are referring to the advantages of being a country with reserve-currency status. This marbles metaphor was inspired by 1961 article in *Le Monde* by the French economist Jacques Rueff, who was in the first instance worried about the long-term implications of balance of payments deficits by the issuers of reserve currencies—especially under the then-operating gold-exchange standard.[1] While Rueff concentrated most on what he saw as the inevitable collapse of such a system, he was also concerned about both the moral hazard and the excess returns to the core country in the effectively dollar-based Bretton Woods system. The moral hazard worry was that U.S. dollar reserves would be built up by European and other central banks (their winnings in a mercantilist game of marbles), after which the United States would eventually devalue their increasing dollar debts through the U.S. dollar inflation and/or dollar devaluations that would eventually be forced upon dollar-holding countries at the periphery of the Bretton Woods system. And as long as the system remained in place, the United States would benefit from the super-seigniorage accruing to the core country in a fixed exchange-rate system. Under the marbles metaphor, the pressure required to support the system was one part moral suasion on the part of the anchor country (for other central banks to insist on gold settlement would destroy the system), but a decade after Rueff's complaint came more heavy-handed measures. These included the so-called Nixon Shock of August 15, 1971, which imposed import surcharges that were to remain in place until exchange rates were realigned to U.S. preferences.[2]

Meissner and Taylor ask whether, in the forthcoming "great rebalancing," this time the United States will lose its marbles. Answering this question requires that the notion of the game being played be recast, including its rules and whatever new extralegal twists might be devised to get or keep marbles as the rebalancing progresses. This time, compared to the end of the Bretton Woods system in the early 1970s, there is little reference to the United States devaluing the foreign-held marbles.[3] Why the change in emphasis? First, because anyone who now holds U.S. dollar assets does so of their own free will, and not because the rules demand that they do so. Second, almost everyone now expects that the U.S. dollar will in fact fall further in the course of the great rebalancing, so there should be no surprises there. Third, and perhaps most important, there is still widespread belief (in contrast to the 1960s and 1970s) that the United States will do whatever is required to keep domestic inflation rates modest. Thus current holders of U.S. dollar assets think that they will avoid any serious erosion of their real claims on goods and services, at least on goods and services sold in the United States.

If the Bretton Woods-era metaphor does not apply to the current situation of imbalances, then what marbles are at stake, and how can these be retained or lost by the United States in the new century? In the current rebalancing game, I assume the potential U.S. marble losses will take one of two forms: either through losing the current capacity to generate much higher earnings on U.S. investments abroad than are paid on U.S. liabilities to foreigners, or through experiencing some sort of abrupt hard landing involving nasty macroeconomic consequences.

Meissner and Taylor's paper considers both of these possible forms of losses, and so shall I in these comments upon it. The first form is more in keeping with the zero-sum nature of a game of marbles. The second form, a sudden hard adjustment, may involve losses for all interested parties, a scenario reminiscent of any schoolyard game gone sour, with bad tempers and a possible punch-up. The two forms are linked, and if the proponents of dark matter are correct, then very large U.S. current account deficits are possibly sustainable for far longer than most analysts forecast. This outcome would lessen the likelihood of large and immediate changes in U.S. domestic demand and output, or in the external value of the dollar. Conversely, if the excess return privilege were to evaporate suddenly, then the required adjustment would be that much larger, and correspondingly harder to achieve in a smooth manner.

One of the chief innovations of Meissner and Taylor's paper is to consider both issues in historical context. Their primary reference for the excess rate of return (or "privilege") calculations is the United Kingdom in the late nineteenth and early twentieth centuries, but they also calculate contemporary privilege estimates for the other G8 countries. Based on their analysis of privilege, Meissner and Taylor find no grounds for thinking that today's levels of U.S. current account imbalances are sustainable in the long run. There are several key reasons for this opinion. First, they argue that the currently high rate-of-return differential favoring U.S. assets over U.S. liabilities is a blip in a generally downward trend. Second, a century ago U.K. net foreign income from investments was driven predominantly by positive current accounts and by large and growing net foreign asset positions (reaching 200 percent of GDP by 1913). By contrast, the comparably measured U.S. net foreign asset position is by now well into net liability territory. Third, as long as the U.S. current account remains in significant deficit, the rate of return differential favouring U.S. assets abroad has to be continually increasing, but the trend they find is in the other direction.

Meissner and Taylor agree with Gourchinas and Rey (2005) that some part of the recent increase in U.S. privilege is due to the country's increasingly leveraged position, which is effectively a change from banker to merchant banker, or a situation even further out on the high-risk end of the spectrum. Some analysts have noted that there is quite a lot of leverage inherent in much of U.S. direct investment abroad, with acquisitions and even greenfield projects being largely financed by local banks.

The possibility of generating good ideas for Americans to produce foreign profits while requiring little by way of net capital inflow from the United States lies behind the optimism of those like Hausmann and Sturzenegger (2006). Proponents of this view see this sort of leverage as underpinning the continuing U.S. net investment income from abroad. Like any leveraged position, the situation can turn vicious if and when the profits are not high enough to service the debt. It has long been thought that much of the measured privilege of the United States relative to Canada—Meissner and Taylor report (in their Table 3.1) that the United States has a yield differential (assets versus liabilities) of +1.7 percent, while Canada has one of -1.4 percent— is due to U.S. investments in Canadian branch plants, since Canada has long had the highest share of its business capital stock controlled from outside the country, with the United States as the predominant investor. This privilege of the core versus the periphery underlies much of the Canadian economic historian Harold Innis' staples-based core and periphery theories of North American economic development.[4]

Meissner and Taylor's historical analysis of the macroeconomic consequences of current account rebalancing uses a panel data set, including 33 current account reversals (exceeding 4 percent of GDP) from 13 countries over the period between 1890 and 1913. They find that the more-developed countries and their offshoots were able to run current account deficits more persistently, and had smaller real exchange rate fluctuations and growth reductions in the aftermath of current-account reversals. Meissner and Taylor find no evidence, looking across countries in their historical sample, that increased openness to trade altered the severity of output losses. This makes them more sanguine than are some students of recent data (for instance, see Freund and Warnock 2005) about the possibilities for achieving significant current account reversals without serious macroeconomic consequences.

Which of the earlier historic examples are most relevant today? It is important to distinguish, as do Meissner and Taylor, between the gold standard and the flexible exchange rate cases. Under the gold standard, fewer financial crises were associated with current account recoveries, and real exchange rates have smaller swings, in contrast to the cases taking place under flexible exchange rate regimes. The smaller real exchange rate movements under the gold standard are to be expected, since both then and now real exchange rate shifts are largely driven by changes in nominal exchange rates, which are more volatile than prices of goods and services. Today, flexible exchange rates are the norm, and more real exchange rate volatility is the order of the day, whether or not current account transitions are taking place.

In their interpretation of the historical experience, Meissner and Taylor emphasize that current account reversals occurred most smoothly in those cases where the original deficits were triggered by direct investment, often in natural resources in offshoot economies, and where the current account reversals were fueled by exports, usually resource-based, whose development had been financed by the original investment. When matching imports of goods and capital are part of a foreign direct investment boom, and the subsequent net exports are matched with capital service payments, there is little call for real exchange rate changes.

In these same resource-based offshoot economies, the situation is different in response to changes in the relative prices of the primary products. In such "Dutch disease" cases, terms of trade changes are inevitable, and force real adjustments. In 1950 there was good reason, when agricultural exports from Australia (primarily wool) comprised 90 percent of total exports and 25 percent of GDP, that the Australian dollar moved closely with the price of wool, a situation which foreshadowed the petro-currencies of today (see Helliwell 1984, 1991). I make the parallel between Australia in 1950 and the United States today because in both cases capital was flowing from rich countries to even richer countries. In 1861, real output per capita in Australia was 5 times as high as in Canada, 20 times as high as in Japan, and 40 percent higher than in Great Britain, from which migrants, goods, and capital were flowing in search of wool and gold (see Helliwell 1984, 1985).

Today there are large movements of migrants, goods, and capital to the United States from many other countries. What is the contemporary parallel with the long-ago lure of the Australian outback? And is this current situation sustainable? Here I combine the consideration of privilege with that of the adjustment process, since I agree with Meissner and Taylor that these two issues are inevitably linked. The primary reason for the linkage is not that any fixed rate of privilege could forever offset the requirements of servicing a growing net debt, because this is impossible. Rather, the link is because any long-run continuing sustainability would require an increasing appetite for investment in the United States. More importantly, because expectations about future international differences in real returns are, in a flexible exchange rate world, what drive the dynamics of the adjustment process, these expectations establish the probabilities of hard and soft landings.

Those analysts who think that the United States' current account deficits are sustainable will be heartened by the Meissner and Taylor finding that richer capital importers in the pre-1913 period had a better chance of sustaining current account deficits for longer periods of time, and of reversing these situations without crisis. What is the current lure of the United States as a global magnet for investment? A decade ago, the mid-1990s high-tech boom was thought to provide the underpinnings for larger net foreign investment in the United States. To some extent, this impetus probably remains the case, although productivity levels and rates of growth in these high-tech industries are notoriously hard to measure. However, the fact that U.S. investments abroad still earn materially more than foreign investments earn in the United States must mean that the hopes of foreign investors for supernormal returns from their U.S. investments are on average not being realized, or at least not yet.

Are there other relevant issues that might have deserved mention in the Meissner and Taylor paper? Given its length and high average value, a general answer must be "no," but it might be worth flagging some items for future consideration. First, one of the important components of the contemporary U.S. balance of payments account is migrants' remittances abroad. These payments have grown very rapidly, especially to Mexico, and are now about as large, as a share of GDP, as is net U.S. financial income from abroad. Hausmann and Sturzenegger (2006) use a 5 percent rate of return to capitalize a $30 billion net financial income into a net U.S. external financial capital (dark matter) of $600 billion, or 5 percent of GDP. The 2005 U.S. balance of payments account shows net private foreign remittances of $50 billion (see BEA 2008), most of which are workers' remittances (see Congressional Budget Office 2005). A similar calculation for human capital "grey matter," based on remittances, would yield a net foreign human capital debt as great as the net foreign financial asset position calculated by Hausmann and Sturzenegger. This human capital component is embodied mainly in recent migrants, so the net remittances to foreigners might be expected to stop growing as and when the share of foreign-born workers in the United States halts its recent growth. The larger the share of foreign citizens residing in the United States who effectively are guest workers, the larger will be the fraction of their income that is likely to be repatriated.

There is a related issue posed by the growing international trade in services, especially that recent development described as offshoring. In a narrow sense, services obtained offshore count directly as components of imports, and hence toward the current account deficit. In the larger picture, these services may be deemed to be part of an increase in international supply-chain slicing necessary to maintain the growth of average incomes in the world's richest country. As international convergence in per capita incomes becomes applicable to an increasing share of the world's population, terms of trade losses for the richest countries are an inevitable by-product of this process. This is because the countries converging from below inevitably face higher real values for their currencies as part of the adjustment process, although this process may be forestalled during a period (which may be lengthy in the cases of China and India) in which there are still large reserve armies of the unemployed. But throughout most of this adjustment process, factor costs remain higher in the richer nations, and there is continuing pressure to spin off parts of the production process to countries where these tasks can be done more cheaply. If India now represents a cost-effective back office, and by a sufficient margin, then offshoring will be a growing part of the unfolding adjustment process.

If the United States is to remain a magnet for foreign capital inflows, it must be for one of two reasons: either there are key franchise values that exist or can be more easily created there, or else there is no other credible place to store liquid assets. Both of these possibilities lie at the core of the debates about privilege so ably summarized by Meissner and Taylor. In the Bretton Woods era, the pivotal country had a special position, and this unique status provided some basis for continuing privilege. However, the Meissner and Taylor analysis of the pre-1913 returns for Great Britain, which was then at the center of the gold standard and world financial markets, showed modest and declining estimates of privilege. They thereby invite us to conclude that, in today's world of flexible exchange rates and multiple financial centers, the United States is likely to need some fresh sources of franchise value in financial intermediation, as well as in the production of goods and other services. Failing these innovations, then if increasing shares of world portfolios are to be invested in the United States, foreign investors are likely to require higher returns, either currently or in the future, if these present imbalances are to be sustained.

Meissner and Taylor are largely skeptical about there being enough new franchise values in the United States—the Boeings, Coca-Colas, and Microsofts of the twenty-first century—to rationalize continued global net acquisition of claims on the United States. To evaluate the future prospects of this prediction, it would be useful to further unpack recent historical returns, including the mysterious "other" components of the capital gains so critical to the calculation of dark matter. The parallel with Australia a century ago shows that prospects of gold, or other tremendous returns, are enough to get people and investments to flow, and the U.S. economy has had real productivity levels and growth rates to underpin parallel hopes. But the Australian gold boom ended, like all booms do, when there was enough, or more than enough, capital and labor to exploit any high-return investments. When the luster disappears, disappointed investors, especially those following the pack, may flee, just as they did from Asia in 1998.

Meissner and Taylor have done a splendid job of making the history of the last great globalization relevant to the current great rebalancing. In their admirably understated way, they have argued that there is no credible evidence supporting the status quo, and have shown that the savings and investment patterns that mark today's U.S. current account deficit pose more problems for adjustment than were confronted by Great Britain when the offshoot countries reversed their current account deficits so painlessly a century ago. I agree with Meissner and Taylor on both counts, and have learned much from their evidence and explanations.

In conclusion, is it possible to build on their broad sweep of evidence, and ask if there are systemic implications for the twenty-first century? Thirty-five years ago, Rueff considered fixed exchange rates based on the dollar to be inferior to gold, or some alternative fixed base. Robert Mundell (1973), in his review of Rueff's book, argued that the appropriate alternative was a global currency unit. But in the ensuing decades, the systemic competition has been won by a third option: flexible exchange rates among the major currencies, with peripheral countries choosing from a range of possibilities. Is this arrangement for the better? I think so, for several reasons. First, as I have already noted, the flexible exchange rate system reduces the need for foreign exchange reserves, removes the obligation to accumulate key currencies, and encourages a more symmetric global system. (But, I hear you asking, if this is true, why are so many public and private agents acting as though the Bretton Woods system were still in place? Why do they keep accumulating U.S. marbles? If I knew I'd tell you.)

Second, as global income convergence continues among countries (even if often not within them), substantial increases in the real exchange rates of developing countries are inevitable, and rising external values for flexible exchange currencies may be preferred to domestic inflation as a means of adjustment. Third, for similar reasons, flexible exchange rates may facilitate adjustment for countries subject to terms-of-trade shocks, especially those driven by cyclical movements of energy and other resource prices. Finally, and most relevant to the great rebalancing in prospect, there is more scope for gradual changes in portfolio mixes as different agents change their minds at different times. On this last point there is a reverse possibility, however, as was seen in 1998. If the degree of exposure exceeds the extent of informed opinion, then the possibility for herding behavior is real. On this score, we'll have to wait and see.[5] But in cases of great uncertainty about appropriate exchange rates, such as that in the early 1970s, there may not be any viable alternative to flexible exchange rates.

## Notes

1. "The unending feedback of the dollars and pounds received by the European countries to the overseas countries from which they had come reduced the international monetary system to a mere child's game in which one party had agreed to return the loser's stake after each game of marbles." (Rueff 1961, reprinted in Rueff 1972, 22)

2. Econometric analysis of these measures was the subject of my presentation to the September 1971 conference of the Federal Reserve Bank of Boston on financial relations between the United States and Canada, as described in Helliwell (2005).

3. In 2008, as the United States is trying to deal simultaneously with financial disarray, possible recession, and rising inflation, this possibility is looming larger in public discussions.

4. Innis apparently knew how to work to good effect from the periphery better than most, as he was elected president of the American Economic Association in 1952, the only president in the Association's history who was not a U.S. resident.

5. The rise and post-conference collapse of the U.S. subprime mortgage market can perhaps be added to the list of recent examples.

## References

Buiter, Willem. 2006. "Dark Matter or Cold Fusion?" Global Economics Paper No. 136. London: Goldman Sachs.

Bureau of Economic Analysis. 2008. "U.S. International Transactions: First Quarter of 2008." *Survey of Current Business* 88(7): 66–67.

Congressional Budget Office. 2005. "Remittances: International Payments by Migrants." Washington, DC: Congressional Budget Office.

Freund, Caroline, and Frank Warnock. 2005. "Current Account Deficits in Industrial Countries: The Bigger They Are the Harder They Fall?" Working Paper No. 11823. Cambridge, MA: National Bureau of Economic Research.

Gourinchas, Pierre-Olivier, and Hélène Rey. 2005. "From World Banker to World Venture Capitalist: U.S. External Adjustment and the Exorbitant Privilege." Working Paper No. 11563. Cambridge, MA: National Bureau of Economic Research.

Hausmann, Ricardo, and Federico Sturzenegger. 2006. "Global Imbalances or Bad Accounting? The Missing Dark Matter in the Wealth of Nations." CID Working Paper 124. Cambridge, MA: Harvard University Center for Economic Development.

Helliwell, John F. 1984. "Natural Resources and the Australian Economy." In *The Australian Economy: A View from the North*, ed. R.E. Caves and L.R. Krause, 81–126. Washington, DC: Brookings Institution.

Helliwell, John F. 2005. "From Flapper to Bluestocking: What Happened to the Young Woman of Wellington Street?" *Bank of Canada Review* Winter 2005–2006: 26–35.

Mundell, Robert A. 1973. "The Monetary Consequences of Jacques Rueff: Review Article." *Journal of Business* 46(3): 384–395.

Rueff, Jacques. 1961. "The Gold-Exchange Standard: A Danger to the West." *The Times* (London), June 27–29.

Rueff, Jacques. 1972. *The Monetary Sin of the West*. New York: Macmillan.

# 4

## Labor Market Imbalances

# Labor Market Imbalances: Shortages, Surpluses, or What?

Richard B. Freeman

There are two competing narratives about how the labor market in the United States will develop over the next decade or two. One view is that the country faces an impending labor shortage due to demographic forces reducing the growth of U.S. labor supply. The other holds that the country faces an impending surplus of labor due to globalization increasing the supply of competitors for U.S. workers.

The Impending Shortage narrative, which has attracted attention from business and policy groups, is that the retirement of the baby boomer generation will create a great labor shortage. Slower growth of new entrants from colleges and universities, an increased proportion of young workers from minority groups, and inadequate training in science and math will produce a shortage of the skills the United States needs to maintain itself as the world's leading economy. The message to policymakers is to forget about the sluggish real wage growth of the past three decades, the deterioration in pensions and employer-provided healthcare, and fears of job loss from offshoring or low-wage imports. Instead focus on helping business find workers given the impending shortage.

These shortage claims stress problems in attracting U.S. citizens into science and engineering. Many leaders of the scientific establishment and high-tech firms have complained that the United States faces a future shortfall of scientists and engineers and have asked for governmental policies to address this problem. The National Academy of Sciences (2006), the Association of American Universities (2006), and the Government-University-Industry Research Roundtable of the National Academy of Sciences (2003) have issued reports arguing for increasing the supply of scientific and engineering talent in the United States. The heads of Intel, Microsoft, and other high-tech firms have spoken out on this issue as well. Responding to the business community, in his 2006 State of the Union Address President Bush announced the American Competitiveness Initiative to stress the importance of investing in our science and engineering workforce.

But the claim of coming labor shortages goes beyond science and engineering. Demographic projections of the U.S. labor supply that show a sharp reduction in the growth of the workforce through 2050, as shown in Table 4.1, have aroused concern in the business and policy community. Reporting the consensus from the Aspen Institute's Domestic Strategy Group (2003), David Ellwood stated that "CEOs, labor leaders, community leaders, all came to the unanimous conclusion that we will have a worker gap that is a very serious one" (cited by Overholt 2004). A 2003 *Fortune* headline declared "Believe It or Not, a Labor Shortage Is Coming" for virtually all workers (Fisher 2003).

**Table 4.1**
U.S. Labor Supply, 1950–2000, and Projected Labor Supply, 2000–2050

|      | Labor Supply in millions | Change in millions |
| ---- | ------------------------ | ------------------ |
| 1950 | 62.2                     | —                  |
| 1960 | 69.6                     | 7.4                |
| 1970 | 82.8                     | 13.2               |
| 1980 | 106.9                    | 24.1               |
| 1990 | 125.8                    | 18.9               |
| 2000 | 140.9                    | 15.1               |
| 2010 | 157.7                    | 16.8               |
| 2020 | 164.7                    | 7.0                |
| 2030 | 170.1                    | 5.4                |
| 2040 | 180.5                    | 10.4               |
| 2050 | 191.8                    | 11.3               |

Source: 2000–2050, Toossi (2002); 1950–1990, United States Census, http://www.census.gov/statab/hist/02HS0029.xls.

Believers in the impending shortage story generally favor increased immigration, particularly of highly skilled workers through H1B and other visas; increased spending on education and technological innovation; and guest worker programs to keep a sizeable flow of less-skilled but legal immigrants coming to the country. Proponents of the shortage scenario regard many of these immigrants as complements rather than substitutes for U.S. workers. Greater education and training of U.S. citizens, particularly of disadvantaged minorities, is advocated as well.

The Globalization Surplus narrative, which has attracted attention as part of the discussion about how the current mode of globalization is playing out, takes the opposite tack. Unlike the shortage story, this tale holds that the spread of capitalism around the world, particularly to China and India, has generated a labor surplus that threatens wage rates in advanced and higher-wage developing countries. Trade, offshoring, global sourcing of jobs, and flows of capital to the low-wage giants combine to reduce the demand for workers in manufacturing and tradable services in advanced countries and in moderate-income developing countries.

At first, the advent of huge numbers of workers from China and India into the global capitalist system seemed to offer a boon to most workers in advanced countries. The labor force is less skilled in the emerging global giants than in the advanced economies. According to the Heckscher-Ohlin model, skilled workers in the advanced countries would benefit from the new trading opportunities, while only the relatively small number of unskilled workers in these economies would lose. If all workers in the North were sufficiently educated, they would avoid competing with low-paid foreign labor and would benefit from the low-priced products produced in the developing countries. Competition from low-wage workers in China and India might create problems for apparel workers in South Africa and Central and Latin America but not for machinists in the advanced North. The "North-South" trade model that analyzes how technology affects trade between advanced and developing countries implied that trade would benefit workers in the North, who had exclusive access to the most modern technology. More low-wage workers in the developing world would lead to greater production of the goods in which the South specialized, driving down their prices.

Tell it to Lou Dobbs! The offshoring of computer jobs, the United States' trade deficits even in high technology sectors, and the global sourcing strategies of major American firms have challenged this sanguine view. The economic entry of China, India, and the ex-Soviet Union shifted the global capital-labor ratio massively against workers. Expansion of higher education in developing countries has increased the world's supply of highly educated workers and allowed the emerging giants to compete with the advanced countries, even in the leading edge sectors that the North-South model assigned to the North as its birthright.

In this paper I assess these two competing visions, particularly the demographic and economic projections on which they are based. I reject the notion that the retirement of the baby boomers and slow growth of the U.S. workforce will create a future labor shortage. Instead, I favor the argument that the increased supplies of skilled labor in low-wage countries will squeeze highly skilled as well as less-skilled U.S. workers. I examine the problem of attracting homegrown American talent to science and engineering in the face of increasing supplies of highly qualified students and workers from lower-wage countries. Going beyond the United States, I argue that the expansion of global capitalism to China, India, and the former Soviet bloc has initiated a critical transition period for workers around the world. As the low-income countries catch up with the advanced countries, the pressure of low-wage competition from the new giants will battle with the growth of world productivity and the lower prices from goods produced in low-wage countries to determine the well-being of workers in higher income economies. While U.S. wages will not be set in Beijing, how workers fare in China, India, and other rapidly developing low-wage countries will become critical to the position of labor worldwide.

## A Great Labor Shortage: An Angler's Tale

The most alarmist claims that the U.S. labor market faces a great worker shortage in the foreseeable future begin with the notion that total gross domestic product (GDP) should increase in the future at a rate comparable to the growth rate witnessed in the recent past. From 1980 to 2005, U.S. real GDP grew by 3.1 percent annually, with 1.4 percent due to the growth of labor supply and 1.7 percent due to the growth of labor productivity. The growth of the labor force is projected to drop in half, to 0.7 percent per year, which makes the 3.1 percent growth of GDP unsustainable absent increases in labor productivity above historical levels. To maintain past levels of GDP growth with 1.7 percent growth of labor productivity between 2005 and 2030, the United States would need 30 million workers more than the Bureau of Labor Statistics (BLS) has projected for that year's labor supply. The cry of impending shortages is the result of this type of analysis.

Despite the attention given to calculations of this kind, these predictions make little sense in terms of social welfare. From the perspective of standard welfare analysis, making a given growth rate of GDP the touchstone of economic policy is a cart-before-the-horse approach. As a wealthy country, the United States can increase GDP whenever it wants by admitting more immigrants. A massively larger labor supply would increase GDP but would reduce GDP per capita and real wages. The standard metrics for assessing how well an economy performs, GDP per capita, or productivity per hour worked, are more appropriate indicators of economic success than the volume of GDP irrespective of the size of the nation's population or workforce.

Still, these alarmist analyses do direct attention toward two important demographic developments. The first is that, barring a huge change in immigration policy, the U.S. workforce will grow more slowly than it has in the past half century or so. The second is that the labor force growth will be concentrated in minority groups that have historically obtained less education and thus possess lower work skills than the majority population. As a result, shortage analysts fear that the growth of skilled labor will decline and produce bottlenecks in production that could reduce growth of GDP per capita. Many argue that the United States could avoid these problems by investing in education and training in high-technology areas such as science and engineering, particularly among the disadvantaged minority groups who may otherwise not gain sufficient skills to do well in the economy.

Table 4.1 shows the number of people in the U.S labor force from 1950 to 2000 and the projected size of the labor force from 2000 to 2050. From 1950 to 2000, the U.S. labor force grew by 78.7 million persons, or 127 percent. From 2000 to 2050, the projected growth of the labor force is 50.9 million persons, or 36 percent. This deceleration in the rate of growth is likely to be greatest from 2010 through 2030, when just 12.4 million additional persons are expected to join the U.S. labor force. The major reason for this reduced increase in the workforce is the ongoing retirement of the baby boomers, that cohort born between 1946 and 1964, taking place during these two decades. As the Chamber of Commerce's 2006 *State of American Business* report stated "We are staring right in the face of a severe worker shortage as 77 million baby boomers prepare to retire in the next few years— with a fewer number of younger workers available to replace them" (p. 13).

The rapid growth of the American workforce in the 1950s and 1960s came largely from increased numbers of woman workers. From 1970 through the 1990s, labor force growth came from immigration as well as from the continued influx of women into the workforce. In the 2000–2050 period, growth of the U.S. workforce is expected to come disproportionately from Hispanics and African Americans—groups with below-average education levels. The share of the U.S. population from disadvantaged minorities (African Americans, Hispanic, American Indians, Alaska Natives) is projected to rise from 25 percent in 2000 to 37 percent in 2050. Some analysts worry that as a result the U.S. workforce will become less skilled unless the country adopts new policies to help these groups improve their educational skills and attainment.

There are two problems with basing projections of future labor market imbalances on impending demographic developments. First, in the past, demographic changes have not been consistently associated with changes in labor market conditions, even for the young workers whose positions are most sensitive to changing market realities. As a case in point, labor supply grew slowly in Europe in the 1980s and the 1990s without creating a labor shortage or reducing high levels of youth unemployment. In the United States, young persons' wages fell relative to older workers when the baby boomers hit the job market in the 1970s (Freeman 1979, Welch 1979), but the wages of the young workers did not increase relative to older workers when smaller youth cohorts entered the market in the 1990s. The employment and earnings of young workers depends more on macroeconomic conditions, wage-setting institutions, and technological developments than on demography. Second, the United States is not a closed economy dependent only on domestic labor to produce goods and services. In the global economy, demographic and labor conditions in other countries affect the U.S. labor market. Globalization gives U.S. firms access to labor overseas through foreign direct investment, offshoring, or subcontracting, and access to foreign-born labor that immigrates to the United States. Hence, the claims of a coming labor shortage must be assessed in a global context.

As a first step toward doing this, I examined United Nations (UN) data on the actual and projected change in the population of a broad working age group of 15-59-year-olds (summarized in Table 4.2). Consistent with the BLS projections, the numbers in Table 4.2 show that the *increase* in the U.S. population among 15-59-year-olds drops from 44 million additional persons during 1975–2000 to 20 million during 2000–2025 and to 21 million from 2025 to 2050. But the projected declines in this age group are much greater in Western Europe and Japan. As a result, among these advanced countries the U.S. share of this working-age population rises from 50 percent to 62 percent. As for the two major highly populous developing countries, China's population aged 15-59 years is projected to rise through 2025 and then fall, as the single child policy affects the

**Table 4.2**
Trends in the Working Population Aged 15–59 Years

| Country/Region | 1975 | 2000 | 2025 | 2050 |
|---|---|---|---|---|
| United States | 132 | 176 | 196 | 217 |
| Western Europe | 99 | 113 | 100 | 86 |
| Japan | 71 | 79 | 65 | 49 |
| U.S. share of (%) | 44 | 48 | 54 | 62 |
| China | 497 | 829 | 913 | 787 |
| India | 335 | 594 | 869 | 939 |
| World | 2223 | 3636 | 4818 | 5404 |

Source: United Nations Population Division, DESA, *World Population Ageing 1950–2050*. http://www.un.org/esa/population/publications/worldageing 19502050./index.htm.

size of cohorts; India's population is expected to increase throughout the 2000–2050 period. The ratio of the Chinese population to the U.S. population will barely change from 2000 to 2050. For the world as whole, the UN projects that the number of persons aged 15–59 will increase massively, so that if enough of these persons gain appropriate labor skills, it would take a massive increase in demand for labor to generate labor shortages.

## Doubling the Global Workforce is Like Swallowing a Whale

Demographic trends aside, the global labor market changed greatly in the 1990s due to the addition of China, India, and the ex-Soviet bloc to the world economic system. During the Cold War era, these countries had trade barriers, self-contained capital markets, and little immigration to the advanced countries—all of which isolated their labor markets from those in the United States and the rest of the capitalist global world. The collapse of Soviet communism, China's decision to "marketize" its economy, and India's rejection of autarky greatly increased the supply of labor available to the global capitalist system. I estimate that if China, India, and the ex-Soviet bloc had remained outside of the global economy, there would have been about 1.46 billion workers in the global economy in 2000; see Figure 4.1. There were 2.93 billion workers in the global economy in 2000 because those countries joined the rest of the world; since 2.92 billion is twice 1.46 billion, I have called this transformation "The Great Doubling" (Freeman 2005b).

The effect of this huge increase in the world's workforce changed the balance between labor and capital in the global economy. Multinational firms could suddenly hire or subcontract work to low-wage workers in China, India, and the ex-Soviet bloc instead of hiring workers in the advanced countries or in other developing countries with higher wages. As result of the doubling of the global workforce, I estimate that in 2000 the ratio of capital to labor in the world economy fell to 61 percent of what it would have been in 2000 if China, India, and the ex-Soviet bloc had not joined the world economy. The reason the global capital-labor ratio fell was that China, India, and the ex-Soviet bloc did not bring much capital with them when they joined the global economy. India had

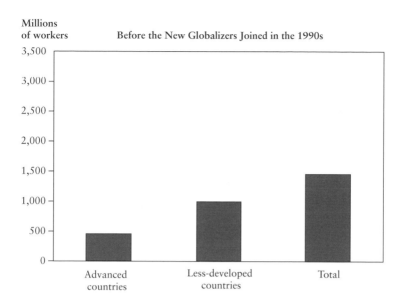

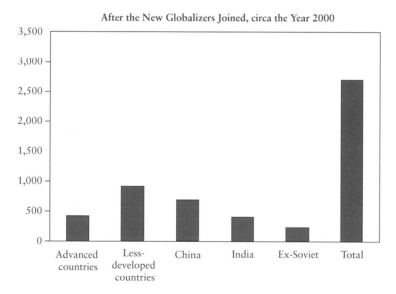

**Figure 4.1**
The Global Labor Supply Before and After the New Globalizers Joined
the World Economy
*Source:* Tabulated from International Labour Organization data, laborsta.ilo.org.

little capital because it was one of the lowest income countries in the world. China was also very poor and destroyed some of its capital stock during the Maoist period. The former Soviet empire had a high investment rate and was wealthier than China or India, but invested primarily in military goods and heavy industry instead of in computer-driven technologies or in the production and delivery of consumer products. One lesson from German reunification was that much of the civilian capital stock in the old Soviet bloc was either outmoded or so pollutant as to be basically worthless.

Gaining access to the capital stock and technology in the advanced countries has greatly benefited workers in China, India, and, to a lesser extent, in the ex-Soviet bloc. Firms in advanced countries offshore jobs to India, fund joint ventures in China, import manufactured goods from China, set up research facilities in India and China, and subcontract production to them and to other low-wage countries. In Europe, German manufacturers set up plants in Eastern Europe, where wages are far below those in Germany, and look longingly at Ukraine, where wages are even lower than in Eastern Europe. By giving firms a new supply of low-wage labor, the doubling of the global workforce has weakened the bargaining position of workers in the advanced countries and in many developing countries as well. Firms threaten to move facilities to lower-wage locations or to import products made by low-wage workers if their current work force does not accept lower wages or less favorable working conditions, demands to which there is no strong labor response. The result is a very different globalization than the International Monetary Fund, the World Bank, and other international trade and financial organizations envisaged two decades ago when they developed their policy recommendations for the integration of the world economy.

### What about Skills and Technology?

The difference between the skills of workers in the United States and those in low-wage countries was in the forefront of the debate over the impact of the North American Free Trade Agreement with Mexico on U.S. workers. Proponents of the treaty argued that the United States would gain high-skilled jobs from increased trade with Mexico, while at the same time it exported less-skilled low-wage jobs to Mexico. All U.S. workers had to do to benefit from globalization was to invest more in human capital. The proponents also promised that the ensuing boom in Mexico would reduce the flow of illegal immigrants to the United States, and thus lessen labor competition at the bottom of the U.S. job market. The argument that the United States and other advanced countries should gain skilled jobs while losing less-skilled jobs would seem to apply even more strongly to China and India than it did to Mexico. The average Chinese and Indian worker has lower skills than the average Mexican worker because so many of the former are peasants with limited education—relatively few have university training. Perhaps the right way to consider these workers are as *complements* rather than *substitutes* for American workers, foreign workers who will increase U.S. demand for educated labor relative to less-educated labor, and thus create a greater potential shortage of skills in the United States.

Yet the current global labor market has not developed according to this scenario, which relies on differences in human capital endowments and the presumed inability of low-wage countries to educate many persons to world standards. Instead, countries around the world, including the new giants, have invested heavily in higher education, so that the number of college and university students and graduates outside the United States has grown rapidly relative to the number in the United States. Table 4.3 shows that the U.S. share of enrollment in higher education declined

**Table 4.3**
U.S. Share of Highly Educated Workers, 1970–2000 and 2010

| U.S. Global Share of College Enrollments (%) | |
|---|---|
| 1970 | 30 |
| 2000 | 14 |

| U.S. Global Share of Science and Engineering Ph.D.s | |
|---|---|
| 1975 | 40 |
| 2010 | 15 |

Source: Freeman 2006a

dramatically from the 1970s through the 2000s. In 1970 approximately 30 percent of university enrollment worldwide was in the United States. In 2000, the U.S. proportion of university enrollment worldwide was 14 percent. Similarly, at the Ph.D. level, the U.S. share of doctorates produced globally has fallen from about 50 percent in the early 1970s to a projected level of 15 percent in 2010. Some of the growth of higher education overseas has been the result of European countries rebuilding their university systems following the destruction of World War II, and of Japan and South Korea investing in university education. By the mid-2000s, several European Union countries and South Korea were sending a larger proportion of their young citizens to university than was the United States (OECD 2005).

But highly populous low-wage countries have also invested heavily in higher education. Brazil, China, India, Indonesia—almost any country you can name—have more than doubled university student enrollments in the 1980s and 1990s (Freeman 2006b). China has made a particularly large investment in science and engineering, so that by 2010 it will graduate more Ph.D.s in science and engineering than the United States. While the quality of graduate training is higher in the United States than in China, it will surely improve in quality over time. India has produced many computer programmers and engineers.

To find out how well graduates in developing countries can compete with those from advanced countries in the global labor market, in 2005 the McKinsey Global Institute asked recruiters for multinational firms the proportion of graduates from developing and transition economies that they viewed as good job candidates. The recruiters came up with numbers ranging from 10 percent to 20 percent, depending on the occupation and country. Strong English language skills were a key factor in this assessment, so many of the workers that the multinationals did not feel met their requirements could undoubtedly do world-class work for firms in their own countries and languages. But even 10 to 20 percent of an increasing number of graduates from developing countries adds immensely to the supply pool from which multinationals fill vacancies.

In sum, the early 1990s notion that skilled workers in the United States need not worry about competition from equally skilled workers in low-income countries because developing countries have fewer graduates per capita does not fit with current reality. With an increased supply of highly educated persons from low-wage developing countries, multinational firms can offshore high-skilled work and hire graduates from universities worldwide. At the same time, large numbers of highly educated immigrants can come to the United States to work.

### Scientists and Engineers as a Special Case?

As noted, the scientific and technological establishment believes that the United States confronted a shortfall of science and engineering workers in the early to mid-2000s. But past experience with expected shortages of scientists and engineers suggests that we view such claims skeptically. The first time the United States worried about shortfalls in the science and engineering workforce was in the late 1950s and early 1960s, prompted by the Soviet Union's surprise launch of Sputnik in 1957. Congress responded by enacting the National Defense Education Act of 1958 and by increasing federally funded research and development, much of it focused on aeronautics and space. The immediate result of the increase in research and development was a rapid rise in the earnings of scientists and engineers, so the U.S. labor market confirmed the shortage claim. Given the time required for the new fellowships and higher wages to increase the supply of scientists and engineers, the supply/demand balance had indeed shifted in favor of workers.

The next two claims of shortages failed, however, to reflect reality. In the early 1980s, the National Science Foundation announced a shortage in scientists and engineers that turned out to be unjustified. The projected shortage was based on policymakers' erroneous use of data, which produced angry articles and editorials in *Science* and *Nature*, among other publications. As best one can tell, the claimed shortage came from a desire to reduce the cost of scientists and engineers to large firms (Weinstein n.d.). In the early 1990s, leaders of the scientific community again proclaimed an incipient shortage of scientists and engineers. Richard C. Atkinson, then president of the American Association for the Advancement of Science, predicted that by the year 2000, demand for scientists in the United States would outstrip supply by almost 400,000 persons (1990). But throughout the decade, indicators of the state of the labor market (salaries, unemployment rates, the number of graduates and postdocs relative to tenure track job in academic institutions, and so on) for scientists and engineers showed no evidence of a shortage. From 1990 to 2000, earnings rose more slowly in science and engineering than in law, medicine, and related professions. While the booming 1990s did produce a shortfall of computer programmers and related specialists, this shortage disappeared in ensuing years as firms offshored work to lower-wage countries, notably India. The BLS subsequently reduced its projected increases in employment for computer and mathematical scientists over the next decade by 500,000 workers (Freeman 2006b). From the perspective of young persons choosing a career, prospects in science and engineering seemed highly uncertain and less lucrative than prospects in business, finance, law, or medicine.

During the 1990s boom, the United States greatly increased the employment of scientists and engineers. It did so despite fairly constant numbers of graduates in science and engineering among U.S. citizens or permanent residents. Much of the increased science and engineering employment took the form of "importing" large numbers of foreign-born students and workers in these disciplines. Table 4.4 shows how the share of foreign-trained workers in the U.S. labor market for scientists and engineers grew in this decade. The most telling statistics are that by 2000, over half of postdoctoral workers and of Ph.D. scientists and engineers below the age of 45 years were foreign born. The large increase in the proportion of bachelor's degree scientists and engineers from overseas is

**Table 4.4**
Huge Supplies Outside U.S. Raise Foreign-born Shares of Scientists and Engineers

|              | 1990 (%) | 2000 (%) |
| ------------ | -------- | -------- |
| Bachelor's   | 11       | 17       |
| Master's     | 19       | 29       |
| Ph.D.        | 24       | 38       |
| Ph.D.s <45   | 27       | 52       |
| Postdocs     | 51       | 60       |

Source: Freeman 2005a

also striking, however, since there are many more workers in these fields with bachelor's degrees than with master's degrees or doctorates. Some of the foreign-born workers obtained their education in the United States and stayed here to work. But most of the scientists and engineers with bachelor's degrees employed in the United States—and roughly half of those with higher degrees—graduated overseas and came to fill jobs in this country.

The lesson from the 1990s regarding increased employment of science and engineering workers is clear: if the U.S. economy demands more highly skilled workers during the period of projected slow labor force growth, it can increase supplies by admitting more immigrants trained in fields with rising labor demand, as it did in the 1990s. The rising supply of highly educated persons overseas, many of whom major in science and engineering, suggests that as long as the United States is an attractive place to work and is open to immigration, it *cannot* experience a shortage in the science and engineering workforce.

This does not mean that the United States does not have a potential problem in the supply of its citizens going into science and engineering fields. It is possible that the country relies excessively on foreign-born talent in these areas. This dependence could risk a sudden decline in supply due to political problems, visa restrictions (as occurred for international graduate students post-9/11), or other factors outside the job market. Moreover, to the extent that native-born workers are more attuned to American economic and social realities, reduced numbers of scientists and engineers born in the United States could weaken the connection between science, engineering, and business that has made the United States a paragon of turning scientific knowledge into technological and business innovation. I would recast concern about shortages of science and engineering workers in the United States from supposed shortages of overall supply, an assertion which finds no support in labor market data, to concern about the balance between native- and foreign-born scientists and engineers in the workforce. If the problem is this balance, there are clear policies that could make science and engineering careers more lucrative and attractive to Americans. More spending on research and development would raise demand and wages relative to opportunities in other occupations. Provision of more and higher-valued scholarships and fellowships would increase the supply of American workers entering these fields (Freeman, Chiang, and Chang 2005). Allocation of a larger share of research grants to young researchers as opposed to senior researchers would make the fields more attractive to young Americans. But as in the 1950s, this would require actual government spending, not just moral suasion.

## The Challenge of Human Resource Leapfrogging

In the North-South model that trade economists use to analyze how technology affects trade between the advanced North and the developing South, the advanced countries monopolize cutting-edge innovative sectors while developing countries end up producing traditional products. The greater the rate of technological advance and the slower the spread of the newest technology to low-wage countries, the higher paid are workers in the North relative to workers in the South. The comparative advantage of advanced countries in high-technology sectors is rooted in those countries having more scientists, engineers, and other highly educated workers, relative to the overall workforce, than do developing countries.

In these sorts of analyses, the spread of higher education and modern technology to low-wage countries can reduce advanced countries' comparative advantage in high-tech sectors and adversely affect workers in the advanced countries as a result. Any country with a comparative advantage in a given sector can lose when another country can compete successfully in that sector. The increase in supply reduces the price of exports, with a potential loss of income for the original dominant exporter. If a foreign competitor gains comparative advantage in industries that have particularly desirable attributes—that employ large numbers of highly educated workers and offer great opportunities for rapid technological advancement—the country with the initial advantage has to shift resources to less desirable sectors: those with lower chances for productivity growth, with fewer good jobs, and so on.

The usual assumption regarding high-tech sectors is that only advanced countries have the educated workforce necessary for competing in these industries. In the 1980s, Americans got worked up when Japan seemed to be producing better high-tech products than the United States. In the 1990s, the United States worried about the competition between Airbus and Boeing in the manufacturing of aircraft. No one entertained the notion that China or India would become major players in high technology leading-edge industries. In *Global Trade and Conflicting National Interest* (2001), Gomory and Baumol argue that trade between low-wage and high-wage countries invariably benefited both groups, while one country's advance could harm another through trade between countries with similar levels of development.

Yet the advance of China and India into high-tech sectors has made these analyses obsolete. China has moved rapidly up the technological ladder and has greatly increased its high tech exports. Over 750 multinational firms have set up research and development facilities in China. And in what is purported to be the next big industrial technology, nanotechnology, China's share of scientific research papers has risen greatly, making it one of the major centers of research in this area. India has not invested as much in science and engineering as China, but it has achieved a strong international position in information technology, and has also attracted major research and development investments, particularly in Bangalore.

How can low-income countries with few scientists and engineers relative to their entire workforces compete in high-technology industries?

These countries have moved to the technological frontier because success in high-tech fields depends on the absolute number of scientists and engineers, rather than on the relative number of science and engineering workers that belong to the overall workforce. It is not how many engineers per person that produces a technological breakthrough as much as the total number of engineers working on the problem. Put differently, there is an economy of scale in research, development, and innovation that enables large populous countries to reach the scientific and technological frontier. China and India can have a large footprint in high tech because they will have many highly educated scientists and engineers, not because they approach the advanced countries in science and engineering workers per capita. I have called the process of moving up the technological ladder by educating large numbers "human resource leapfrogging" since it uses human capital resources to leapfrog comparative advantage from low-tech to high-tech sectors, contrary to the assumption of the North-South model. The low wages in these large populous countries, moreover, makes them formidable competitors for an advanced country because it gives them a potentially large cost advantage in attracting investment centered on research and development.

The bottom line is that the spread of modern technology and education to China and India will undo some of the advanced countries' monopoly in high-tech innovation and production. The North no longer has the lock on high tech that lies at the heart of the North-South model.

### The Transition to the New Global Labor Market

The triumph of global capitalism has brought or will bring modern technology and business practices to most of humanity. Barring disaster, the world is on a historic transition to a truly global economy and labor market that should produce rough income parity among nations and make poverty history. The way the transition proceeds will have immense consequences for workers throughout the world. Workers in the countries that are new entrants to the global economy should do better, since capital and modern technology will flow to these locations, raising wages and introducing modern sector employment. Developing nations where wages exceed those in China and India face a big problem, as these countries will have to find their place in the global economy without engaging in head-on competition with the giants in low-wage industries. Workers in the United States and other advanced countries will benefit from the low-priced goods from China and India, but will suffer from enhanced labor market competition.

Joining the global capitalist system has improved the economic position of workers in China and India. These two countries have been leaders in economic growth and in the reduction of poverty. In China, poverty has fallen sharply from the 1980s to the present, despite China having one of the largest rises of inequality in the history of the world; this result makes China arguably the best case for trickle-down economics in the world. The earnings of Chinese workers in the urban sector have increased greatly. Estimated rates of change in real earnings vary across surveys and groups, but invariably show increases in real wages for virtually all groups of workers. Using data from the Chinese Labor Statistical Yearbook, Bannister (2005) estimated that the real earnings of urban manufacturing staff and workers more than doubled between 1990 and 2002. The annual rate of increase of real earnings was 6.7 percent. Data on the structure of wages show that increases in wages have been greater for the more educated and skilled workers than for other Chinese workers.

But during the 1990s, growth in China did little to advance the economic position of peasants. The rising inequality and lack of political freedom and of legitimate channels of protest presents a challenge to China and to the global transition process. There is a danger that if or when the Chinese economy runs into economic problems, this will create social disorder that in turn will reduce growth prospects. The Chinese government has developed policies to address the inequality problem, including a new labor law (enacted in June 2007) to strengthen the official trade unions and encourage formal labor contracts, but whether this will suffice to spread the benefits of economic growth more widely and preserve order if the economy suffers a major setback is uncertain.

Inequality, which has been moderately high in India, did not grow during the 1990s and 2000s. Wages appear to have risen overall, also at a rapid pace. One World Bank study estimates that from 1993–1994 to 1999–2000, real wages in India grew by 29 percent—an increase of 4.3 percent a year (Glinskaya and Lokshin 2005)—which is a lower pace than in China but still a sizeable increase. The structure of wages in India has also shifted to favor more skilled and educated labor.

Workers in many of the developing countries in Africa, Asia, and Latin America have not done well in the 1990s and the early 2000s. Employment in Latin America, South Africa, and in parts of Asia has shifted from the formal sectors historically associated with economic advancement to informal sectors, where work is precarious, wages and productivity low, and occupational risks and hazards great. The backlash against the current model of globalization in Latin America reflects this failure. No advanced country has improved its living standards by shifting labor from industry to the informal sector.

Researchers have just begun to explore in depth the causes of the growing informalization of labor in developing countries. I suspect that China and India's entry to the world economy has contributed to the informalization, along with the failure of the Washington Consensus-style policies in many countries. The entry of China and India has transformed many developing countries from low-wage competitors with advanced countries to high-wage competitors with China and India. Wages in Peru or El Salvador are three times those in China or India. Mexico is a more expensive site for manufacturing blue jeans than China. Labor costs in South Africa are also far above those in China and India. Producing generic low-cost goods and services for the global marketplace—activities that if undertaken in the 1980s might have given these developing countries a place in the world economy—is not a recipe for success in the 1990s and the 2000s, given China and India's low-wage competitive advantage.

How workers in the advanced countries will fare in the global economic transition will depend upon how improvements in global productivity and reductions in prices that the new giants will bring to the world economy will interact with the labor market pressure for wage concessions to compete with China and India. Ideally, the increased number of scientists and engineers and the worldwide spread of high-tech sectors will accelerate the rate of technological advance enough to raise living standards in all countries, the United States and other advanced countries will retain comparative advantage in enough leading sectors to remain hubs in the global development of technology, and the world savings rate will rise so that the global capital-labor ratio increases rapidly. In the United States, increased social services and social infrastructure—national health insurance, for instance—may be needed to improve living standards if workers cannot gain real wage increases. As GDP in the United States will continue to grow, a key policy issue should be finding ways to distribute the benefits of this growth beyond the super-wealthy Americans who have benefited the most from the past two decades of economic policy and growth.

## Conclusion

I conclude that in the coming decades, the demographic developments associated with slower population growth will be trumped by the forces of globalization associated with the doubling of the world's workforce. How this "great doubling" plays out will determine the future supply/demand balances in the global labor market. Because the transition to a truly global labor market will be a lengthy, decades-long process, the economic and labor market policies enacted by individual countries, the international community, unions, and firms may help determine whether this process proceeds smoothly, awkwardly, or—invisible hand forbid—aborts.

How long might it take the global economy to absorb the huge workforces present in China, India, and other developing countries? The recoveries of Western Europe and Japan after World War II and South Korea after the Korean War provide some historical guideposts. Under the Marshall Plan, the United States sent capital to Europe that helped those countries reconstruct their economies rapidly. In turn, Europe's recovery created markets for American products, while rapid increases in European wages kept U.S. workers from facing low-wage competition. Similarly, the United States helped Japan develop into a market democracy with the capability of challenging the United States in many technically advanced sectors. South Korea's progress from one of the poorest economies in the world to an advanced economy in about 50 years is even more remarkable, since that country had never before been among the leading global economies. If China maintains its successful development and its wages double every decade, as occurred in the 1990s, in about 30 years Chinese wages would approach levels seen today in the advanced countries. India's wage convergence will take longer. My assessment is that, barring unforeseen difficulties, the successful transition to a truly integrated global labor force will take 40 to 50 years.

Besides the postwar success of Europe, Japan, and South Korea, there are examples of unsuccessful transitions too—the reunification of East Germany with West Germany is the most recent case. The German government acted as if, despite the legacy of nearly half a century of communism, low-income East Germany would meld seamlessly and rapidly with the wealthier capitalist West. Germany offered extensive welfare programs to keep workers in the East, but did not raise taxes to fund a massive Marshall Plan-style program to rebuild the East's economy.

German unions sought wage parity between East and West rather than allowing wage differences to reflect productivity differences. The healthiest economy in Europe was transformed into one of the sickest, with high unemployment and sluggish growth. Reconstruction of the South after the American Civil War was an even greater failure. It took over a century for the South to achieve something akin to economic parity with the rest of the United States. The better part of the history of the American South in the twentieth century was prolonged economic and social oppression of African Americans. By limiting their educational and economic opportunities, rather than joining with African Americans to move their economies forward, the South retarded its economic progress.

If my assessment and predictions are correct, then the overriding goal of global labor market policy during the next decade should be assuring that the absorption of China, India, and the ex-Soviet bloc into world capitalism goes as smoothly as possible. The policy bent in the United States and elsewhere should go in the direction of favoring labor rather than capital, which ought to be able to take care of itself in a global economy with twice as many workers, many available at low wages. There should be sustained international pressure on developing countries to raise their labor standards and to distribute the benefits of economic growth to their workers. And there should be efforts to maintain or improve living standards, if not wages, of all workers in the advanced countries so that even the less-skilled benefit from the movement to a global labor market.

I am not sure what policies would enable the developing countries that cannot compete with China and India in low-wage goods to improve conditions for their workers. Some countries may expand through the sale of natural resources, but mining and other resource industries employ relatively few people. Some emerging nations may be able to expand their domestic markets. I suspect that there is no simple answer about what to do in the face of the doubling of the global workforce, and that each country will have to craft a strategy dependent on its own unique circumstances.

Finally, if I am wrong and there is instead a great labor shortage in the foreseeable future, I believe that it will come not from demography but from catastrophic events that the shortage soothsayers ignore: a global pandemic that kills millions of people; climate change that destroys significant parts of economies; and/or political insanity that produces barriers to trade, migration, and capital flows around the world. With reasonable policies and a bit of luck, however, none of these events should be able suspend the movement toward a single and more egalitarian world economy.

## References

Association of American Universities. 2006. "National Defense Education and Innovation Initiative: Meeting America's Economic and Security Challenges in the 21st Century."Available at http://www.aau.edu/reports/NDEII.pdf.

Aspen Institute, Domestic Strategy Group. 2003."Grow Faster Together or Grow Slowly Apart." Available at http://www.aspeninstitute.org/atf/cf/%7BDEB6F227-659B-4EC8-8F84-8DF23CA704F5%7D/DSGBROCHURE_FINAL.PDF

Atkinson, Richard C. 1990. "Supply and Demand for Scientists and Engineers: A National Crisis in the Making." *Science* 248(4954): 425–432.

Bannister, Judith. 2005. "Manufacturing Earnings and Compensation in China." *Monthly Labor Review* 128(8): 22–40.

Fisher, Anne. 2003. "Believe It or Not, a Labor Shortage Is Coming." *Fortune*, online. October 7. Available at http://www.saveyourfactory.com/articles/FORTU NE%20%20Believe%20it%20or%20not,%20a%20Labor%20Shortage%20is %20Coming.pdf

Freeman, Richard B. 1979. "The Effect of Demographic Factors on Age-Earnings Profiles." *Journal of Human Resources* 14(3): 289–318.

Freeman, Richard B. 2005a. "Does Globalization of the Scientific/Engineering Workforce Threaten U.S. Economic Leadership?" Working Paper No. 11457. Cambridge, MA: National Bureau of Economic Research.

Freeman, Richard B. 2005b. "Can We Improve Worker Well-Being in the Global Economy." W.J. Usery Distinguished Lecture Series, Georgia State University.

Freeman, Richard B. 2006a. "What Does the Growth of Higher Education Overseas Mean for the U.S.?" Presented at the ASGE / ASSA Meetings Session, *U.S. Higher Education in Global Perspective*, Boston, January 7.

Freeman, Richard B. 2006b. "Is A Great Labor Shortage Coming? Replacement Demand in the Global Economy." Working Paper 12541. Cambridge, MA: National Bureau of Economic Research.

Freeman, Richard, Tanwin Chang, and Hanley Chiang. 2005. "Supporting the Best and Brightest in Science and Engineering: NSF Graduate Research Fellowships." Working Paper 11623. Cambridge, MA: National Bureau of Economic Research.

Glinskaya, Elena, and Michael Lokshin. 2005. "Wage Differentials Between the Public and Private Sector in India." Policy Research Paper 3574. Washington, DC: World Bank.

Gomory, Ralph, and William Baumol. 2001. *Global Trade and Conflicting National Interest*. Cambridge, MA: The MIT Press.

Government-University-Industry Research Roundtable of the National Academy of Science (GUIRR). 2003. "Envisioning A 21st Century Science and Engineering Workforce for the United States: Tasks for University, Industry, and Government." Available at http://laborsta.ilo.org/.

National Academy of Sciences, Committee on Science, Engineering, and Public Policy. 2006. "Rising Above The Gathering Storm: Energizing and Employing America for a Brighter Economic Future." Available at http://books.nap.edu/openbook.php?isbn=0309100399.

Organisation for Economic Co-operation and Development. 2007. "Education at a Glance." *OECD Indicators*. Paris: OECD. Available at www.sourceoecd.org/upload/9607051e.pdf

Overholt, Alison. 2004. "The Labor Shortage Myth." *Fast Company* 85: 23. Available at http://www.fastcompany.com/magazine/85/essay.html.

Toossi, Mitra. 2002. "A Century of Change: U.S. Labor Force, 1950-2050." *Monthly Labor Review* 125(5): 15–28. Available at http://www.bls.gov/opub/mlr/2002/05/art2full.pdf

United Nations, DESA (Department of Economic and Social Affairs), Population Division. 2002. *World Population Ageing 1950–2050*. Available at http://www.un.org/esa/population/publications/worldageing19502050/index.htm.

U.S. Chamber of Commerce. 2006. *The State of American Business 2006*. Washington, DC. Available at http://www.uschamber.com/NR/rdonlyres/ezykof6trlip32srd2uynfhuit2vr55zkh3tf2u3u2eepq76smynipiwpy2xhnbvzy6dcwji6uopvxfvcxic2nspoya/06sab.pdf.

Welch, Finis. 1979. "Effects of Cohort Size on Earnings: The Baby Boom Babies' Financial Bust." *Journal of Political Economy* 87(5): S65–S97.

Weinstein, Eric. (undated). "How and Why Government, Universities, and Industry Create Domestic Labor Shortages of Scientists and High-Tech Workers." Available at http://www.nber.org/~peat/PapersFolder/Papers/SG/NSF.html.

# Comments on "Labor Market Imbalances: Shortages, Surpluses, or What?" by Richard B. Freeman

Surjit S. Bhalla

It is a real pleasure to comment on Richard Freeman's paper, especially as I agree with much that he says. Freeman offers a lot of very interesting data to substantiate the view that looming labor shortages are a mythic scenario and not a realistic one. Actually, my one major criticism of the paper is that he gives too much credence to the labor shortage view. I will dismiss it even more quickly than Freeman does. In my remarks, I want to emphasize the *other* side involving labor surplus, and to present some research that I have been working on that supplements Freeman's view. My main conclusion is that far from a labor shortage, the probability of an emerging global labor *surplus* has not been emphasized enough.

Labor surplus—where and how can it arise? Since we are now in a global economy, it will arise from increased global supply of labor. In this regard, two influences are operating. First, fertility rates around the world are dropping. We are witnessing the start of the great fertility decline in the developing world, not unlike that which happened in the developed world a half century earlier. Several developing countries, such as Iran, have fertility levels below 2 or below replacement levels. Other highly populated developing countries, such as Bangladesh and India, have rapidly falling fertility rates. In India the fertility rates are dropping by 0.1 child a year and should be close to 2 children per adult woman by 2010 or so.

The fertility decline should support the labor shortage view; however, the reason it does not is because such declines are strongly accompanied by an increase in the labor force participation rates (LFPR) of women. In India, female LFPR levels in urban areas are very low, registering only 15 percent in 1999–2000. These levels, however, are rising sharply, by about

1 percentage point a year. Parallel developments in other South Asian economies—along with the Middle East, the last remaining center of low female LFPR—means that effective labor supply will be increasing at a sharp rate.

The effects of this supply shock will be like what happened in the United States as women increasingly entered the labor force beginning in the 1960s. For instance, between 1960 and 1990, there is a well-known statistic that the U.S. real median wage rate stayed constant. A popular and convincing explanation for this unchanging real wage was the large increase in the labor supply that came from women's increasing labor force participation rates. In my view, the same pattern is going to take place in the developing world, and because of increasing education levels, it is likely to take place toward the upper end of the distribution. As Freeman has shown, the developing countries will continue to make large investments in education, particularly India and China. Some statistics on the evolution of labor supply at the upper end are revealing. The fastest growing segment is workers with postsecondary degrees. The growth rate of this segment is around 3.3 percent per year, double the rate of growth of the secondary school graduates, which is 1.6 percent per year. This relative pace is expected to continue, even though the overall growth in world labor supply is expected to decline to a 1 percent rate over the next decade, as compared to a 1.4 percent growth rate at present.

Let's examine some statistics on scientists and engineers, fields where the expected labor shortage is supposed to be high. The big numbers are that India produces 400,000 scientists and engineers a year, and China about 50 percent more, or 600,000, every year. That is a million new scientists and engineers from these two countries alone. In contrast, each year the United States produces about 70,000 to 100,000 scientists and engineers, while Europe doubles that amount. On the surface, these headline numbers are scary, but are exaggerated if the concern is, as it should be, with the quality of these highly skilled workers. Two points on quality: first, in the past, the *quality-adjusted ratio* in relative supplies was most likely unity, meaning that an Indian or Chinese worker had only one-tenth the quality of an American-trained engineer. Thus, ten times the supply might mean only one-tenth of effective quality-adjusted supply. Second, this quality is fast increasing because of pressures from globalization. If one adds up the quantity and the quality, one obtains a skilled labor *surplus* scenario as the most likely outcome. This increase in supply will obviously have an effect on the wages of high-skilled workers around the world. When I say "wages," I am specifically thinking of "U.S. wages," but through those implications we can derive what is likely to happen elsewhere. And the effect will be to compress the present advantage of the skilled U.S. worker, a parallel development to the compression obtained at the low-skill end over the last three decades.

This conclusion indicates one of the few points of disagreement that I have with Freeman. He says that, to date, the expected increases in low-skilled wages have not shown up. For 100 years between the mid-nineteenth and the mid-twentieth centuries, world inequality increased steadily, and peaked around 1970. But global inequality declined considerably over the following 35 years, and that decrease is really attributable to the large increase in low-skilled workers, primarily from India and China. These two countries account for 40 percent of the world's population. This is the big supply shock that people have not, in my view, correctly appreciated or understood. The joint per capita income growth of these erstwhile poorest countries has been around 5.5 percent per year for the last 30 years. This movement has been a major cause for the decline in world inequality from its peak Gini of 66 in 1969 to around 62 today.

There have been many shocks to the world economy over the last century, but the China-India shock is likely to be the largest. Starting in the late 1950s, economic growth in Japan began to accelerate; joined with fast reconstruction growth in Europe, the world witnessed the first major postwar shock of fast world growth. (Interestingly, world growth in the last few years has just equaled this mid-1960s fast pace.) The second postwar phase of world growth, but on a lower scale, was provided by the East Asian economies in the 1970s and 1980s. The world's economic system absorbed these shocks very well. Yet these were small shocks—a little rainfall compared to the typhoon from China and India that has been unleashed on the world, starting in 1980 and continuing even now. It is this typhoon, and its consequences, that we are discussing today.

Some idea of the magnitude of this phenomenon can be gleaned from the following fact. Between 1500 and 1980, China and India moved from having a share of world income (in purchasing power parity prices) equal to their own population share (meaning, average income in these two countries was equal to the world average income during the years 1500 to 1700), to a share in income equal to only 8 percent of world income (and 40 percent population share) in 1980. This low share was reflected in low average income, which was reflected in figures of large absolute poverty. Then came the period of fast growth in these two populous giants: by 2020, the joint income share of these two economies is likely to be 40 percent, and equal to their share in the world population. Thus, what China and India lost in 480 years (from 1500 to 1980), they are projected to regain in 48 years. This *is* the shock to the world economic system that promises to be the largest one ever experienced by the world, much bigger in terms of its impact than even the industrial revolution.

This raises the obvious question: how is it that very large countries like India and China have been able to grow so fast, and sustain this pace over such a long period? A major factor, in my view, has been the nature of the exchange rate policies of the developing countries, primarily those of China but also including India. By keeping its exchange rate deeply undervalued, China has been able to grow fast, and faster than expected. Its GDP growth rate over the last 45 years has averaged more than 9 percent per annum, India 5.7 percent. One of the major stylized facts of development is that a country's "real exchange rate" appreciates with economic growth. (The real exchange rate is defined very simply as the ratio of the exchange rate in terms of the purchasing power parity and the exchange rate in terms of the U.S. dollar ). This is the Balassa-Samuelson effect, meaning that as countries grow, the price level in these developing countries gravitates toward the price level in the developed world. This increase in the price level, an appreciation in the real exchange rate, is accompanied by increasing productivity. In the postwar era, every developing country has shown a large increase in the real exchange rate (RER). In China and in India, the ratio of the price level (the RER) was .4 or .5 in 1980, but today it is half that level. In every other country and region, the RER had a tendency to increase. In China, this pattern of development has been reversed with the real exchange rate declining with development. Instead of Chinese goods becoming relatively expensive, these have become relatively cheaper. This has been accomplished by the policy of not allowing the real exchange rate to appreciate; this nonappreciation helps exports to grow faster, imports to grow less. The net result is faster absolute growth, especially with regard to China's competitors and more especially with regard to the Western world.

Just to give you one statistic as to how distorted the situation is: if Chinese growth rates continue at the current levels or even decline somewhat—let's say to 7 percent per year for the next 20 years—the real exchange rate will have to appreciate by more than 300 percent in order for its per capita income level to reflect the RER and income relationship of a "typical" country. China's ultracompetitive exchange rate compounds the competitive situation for developed countries, and even the developing countries. This is the global imbalances problem.

We return to the idea of income inequality. The good news that emanates from this growth rate in developing countries is a decline in world income inequality. This decrease was caused first by *extra* wage growth among low-skilled workers, a major reason why the median real wage in the United States has stagnated. My prediction, consistent with what Freeman has discussed happening from 1960 to 1990 at the low end of the wage scale, is that in the future we will witness a compression of wages at the high end of the wage scale.

I will conclude by briefly touching on policy. What can the United States do to address these effects of globalization? Not much really. Training more people will not change the relative labor supply levels—the magnitudes are very different. The coming increase in global labor supply is a shock for which I do not think there is any policy response for any developed, or developing, economies. Economic theory says that if wages in the developing countries, particularly India and China, rise much faster, then less labor will be exported abroad. If technological and productivity changes occur, then everything changes. Freeman wrote a book titled *The Overeducated American,* which was published in 1976, but I think he was 30 years too early in his predictions. Yet the phenomenon he foresaw will now happen soon—there will be a dampening in the relative wage of highly skilled workers in the United States.

So, to conclude, there is not much the developed economies can do in terms of labor market policy or interest rate policy. I think there is a lot that can be done to reduce the pressures through macroeconomic policies and, in particular, through exchange rate policies. The U.S. dollar needs to depreciate, especially with regard to East Asia, and this prescription is doubled with regard to the Chinese yuan. This depreciation will have the desired double effect—faster export and total growth in the United States, and somewhat less faster growth in China than 10 percent per year. This policy alone will help considerably in redressing the global imbalance problem of 10 percent current account surplus in China and a 6 percent deficit in the United States. This policy can help create more jobs in America and less overheating in China: a win-win situation for the global economy.

# Comments on "Labor Market Imbalances: Shortages, Surpluses, or What?" by Richard B. Freeman

Alan V. Deardorff

I'm a person from the trade theory side of international economics. I suppose my purpose here is to provide the perspective of a standard trade economist on this issue, although at least one of my views is not a standard perspective shared among trade economists.

First of all, on the question of whether there is a looming labor shortage, Freeman's answer is no. Indeed, it is pretty obvious that is the right answer. Based on the addition to the world markets of China, India, and the former Soviet bloc, is there a labor surplus? On that score Freeman says yes. The real question is, what are the implications of this surplus?

Along the way, he mentions that China, by educating its workers so rapidly and through advances in technology, is going to leapfrog comparative advantage. I will come back to this point later, but for now I will remark that for a trade economist, that is an interesting idea. The underlying concern, although it was not mentioned much in what Freeman said today, is that from this process the United States and other developed countries are going to lose comparative advantage.

Freeman also mentioned that other developing countries are going to lose out in competition with China and India. What I want to do is address some of these ideas. On the labor shortage issue, I will say practically nothing because I agree with him. On the surplus issue, I disagree. While it is true that in some sense the world's labor supply has grown, I disagree with Freeman on what the implications of that will be. I have a few small points to say about trade theory and how that fits into all of this. These are quibbles with his argument, as I'm not exactly disagreeing with him, but simply going a little beyond what he said.

I'll begin with my quibbles about trade theory. Freeman cites two standard models of trade theory. The first is the Heckscher-Ohlin model, in which rich countries have a comparative advantage based on skilled labor, what we usually mention today rather than capital. In the context of that model, if a big part of the world with a lot of unskilled labor suddenly appears on the global economic stage, then that's going to benefit the skilled labor in the rich countries. There are also going to be some gains for countries as a whole, but perhaps some losses for unskilled labor. That is very standard stuff in the Heckscher-Ohlin model. Freeman also cites what he calls the North-South model, but I am not exactly sure which model this is—it rather sounds like Vernon's product-cycle model. Regardless of the name, the North-South model is a very sensible model in which the rich countries have a technological advantage. These countries have some technologies that their southern neighbors do not have, so even if the goods that the rich countries produce with these technologies use resources the rich do not have much of, the rich countries may still have a comparative advantage. These high-technology nations export the goods they produce to the rest of the world. Again, if the world economy gets bigger as a result of these less-technologically advanced "southern"countries suddenly joining in, then this addition expands the demand for everything, and the rich countries benefit too. The traditional trade theoretic way of looking at this development would say, hey, no problem. Welcome China and welcome India—they are going to make us better off. Well, Freeman says things are not quite playing out this way. However, we have some variations on traditional trade theory to address this scenario. One is that China is adding an awful lot of skilled workers to the global economy. Freeman gave us some numbers on China's educational investment in science and engineering, so China is getting an awful lot of skilled workers. As a result, it is starting to export some goods that we thought were our prerogative because of our supposed comparative advantage in skilled workers. In terms of comparative advantage, that is one way that leapfrogging can happen.

China is exporting the types of goods that we in the United States used to export, and that is going to hurt us. Similarly, China is engaging in a lot of research and development. Now it makes sense that in order to catch up, they would try to acquire the technologies that we have and they do not. That's a standard part of the traditional trade model: countries that are behind will move ahead in technology by imitating the technologically advanced countries. But Freeman's paper discusses the fact that China is not just imitating, but innovating, and in some areas moving the frontier of technology. He mentions that they are working in nanotechnology; again, presumably, this is going to allow them to acquire advantage in some products and services that we used to think were more exclusively our domain of expertise.

Freeman's paper suggests that at least two of these things are somehow contrary to trade theory, but in terms of the implications, these are exactly what trade theorists have considered. To the extent that the rest of the world acquires the resources or technology to produce the same goods more cheaply that we have been exporting, our terms of trade are going to worsen. In 2004 Samuelson got a lot of press for an article he wrote that described this aspect of globalization, but the fact is that there was nothing new about it when he published the article. For a long, long time, trade economists have been aware that we can lose some of our gains from trade if the rest of the world acquires whatever it was that provided our comparative advantage. That type of loss is quite consistent with traditional trade theory. What trade theorists might find interesting is why these countries are acquiring the technology or the resources to move ahead in the particular way that they are proceeding. Since they have a shortage of education, it seems pretty obvious that they should want to acquire it. As for the technology, I admit to a bit of bemusement as to why China is pursuing nanotechnology when presumably there are plenty of on-the-shelf technologies that they could pick up more cheaply. But since they are not exactly behaving according to the standard market economy model in all aspects of what they are doing, maybe that is why they are pursuing nanotechnology. It is possible that they see the benefits of being a leader in technology to be worth the costs, even though it draws heavily on what is for them a scarce resource. We've done some silly things, too, and some of them have actually worked out.

So, is this a problem for us? Is it really true that we Americans are likely to lose from all of this? In the standard textbook trade model that we teach our lowest-level undergraduates, where there are just two goods and two countries, the answer would be yes, we are going to lose. If your country is only exporting one good, but the other country learns to produce the same good, then you lose. You continue to lose until they surpass you enough so that you can start exporting the other good and restore some gains from trade. But move a little bit beyond that model to a world with lots of countries and lots of goods, and then it's not such a problem. Suppose we manufacture and export a lot of goods for which we have a comparative advantage. Then if other countries do indeed leapfrog and find one, two, or a hundred goods that they can export, that's just fine. We can stop exporting those things, but doing so does not mean we will not continue to gain from trade in many other goods and services.

There is no necessary reason why this leapfrogging is going to be a problem for us. Remember that this whole story of these countries' gains eroding our comparative advantage is a story only of our losses from the traditional gains from trade, meaning that the original terms of trade have simply worsened. But these terms of trade can only really worsen if the point is reached where we do not trade with these countries at all. If they end up actually exporting stuff to us cheaply, we start gaining from getting the cheap stuff. Again, getting beyond those very simple trade models, there are lots of other reasons for gains from trade, which these models do not address. Among these are gains in consumer welfare from having a variety of products from which to choose, technological spillovers that benefit the less-developed countries, increasing returns to scale, and so forth. I am not so worried that we in the advanced nations are going to lose our gains from trade. Or that we, on net, are going to lose at all from these developments, which seem a natural evolution of the world economy. Again, that does not mean that particular groups within our economy won't lose, such as the unskilled labor mentioned earlier, or some more-skilled workers whose counterparts become competitive abroad. But our country as a whole is most likely to benefit, and our attention should focus more on harvesting those benefits so as to compensate those who are hurt.

There is repeated mention of developed countries losing out because they have high wages. Trade economists continually hear this line that "oh dear, trade is going to be harmful for us because our wages are higher than the countries we have to compete with." That sentiment forgets that there is a reason for those higher wages: some sort of productivity advantage to justify those wage differentials. Of course, there is the possibility that the wages could be artificially high because of labor market imperfections, union bargaining agreements, and those sorts of things. But given the normal functioning of markets, high wages reflect some actual productivity differential. Even I have been prone to misdiagnosing the problem. When I first heard the idea of the North American Free Trade Agreement, my initial thought was, how can we compete with the Mexicans? I had forgotten what I'd been teaching my students, and the same analysis applies when talking about South Africa not being able to compete with China. It is true, of course, that these two countries cannot compete across the board in everything. But trade theory tells us that each country will have a comparative advantage in some products, and the market will help them define what these advantages are. The worst that can happen is that they suffer some loss of their terms of trade, if the particular products that they were gaining from exporting get replaced by products from China, India, or whomever.

On the issue of a potential labor shortage, Freeman is right—it is just silly to seriously entertain this possibility. How about the idea of labor surplus? His point is that China's opening and the entry of all these other countries almost doubles the global labor supply. That assessment really seems right. Since there is no corresponding doubling of the capital stock, this does suggest that in an integrated world economy—where factor prices are going to be determined by the relative amounts of these various factors—labor's wages are going to fall worldwide, and capital is going to be better off. This is exactly what happens in the trade model taught to undergraduates. The Heckscher-Ohlin model predicts that global factor prices will equalize. Once an equalized factor price equilibrium is reached, world factor prices not only are the same everywhere but these are based upon world factor endowments. One can legitimately argue that, although the actual world endowment of labor hasn't gone up, the part that is participating in world markets has risen, and that ought to cause a big problem.

As a result, we will get increased competition in all labor categories because each one is expanding, partly due to the educational investment taking place in some developing countries. I don't disagree with the directional effects that Freeman identifies. I think he is absolutely right that worldwide, on this account alone, there is going to be some downward pressure on wages, and some upward pressure in various countries on returns to capital. The downward wage pressures will differ by the different types of labor—we must not forget that technology is marching forward all the time and may well be bidding up the prices of skilled labor worldwide at the same time that other types experience downward pressure. In any case I think Freeman is quite right about the general pressures on wage rates.

My disagreement comes with the size of the effect: I expect these wage changes to be small. My reason for thinking that these are going to be small certainly does not derive from standard trade theory. As I said, the Heckscher-Ohlin model incorporates factor price equalization, but more and more in recent years I have been having some doubts about that prediction of the model, as I think have many other trade economists. We have always known that particular equilibrium of the model to be an extreme case of the more general trade model. It predicts what will happen if you have perfectly frictionless trade and factor endowments across the world that differ by small enough amounts. These conditions are what enable the result of factor price equalization. But more and more the evidence suggests that we are not in a world that conforms to this equilibrium of the Heckscher-Ohlin model. The question then becomes, what is the simplest manageable approximation to reality that we ought to be looking at when trying to model these effects? Is it the Heckscher-Ohlin integrated world economy of factor price equalization, or is it perhaps a situation of autarky in which we do not trade at all? Lately I have been thinking that autarky may provide a better approximation for understanding worldwide factor prices than does the extreme assumption of factor price equalization. Now the truth, of course, lies somewhere between the extremes, but much depends on which end we are closer to. If it is the case that we are closer to autarky than to the factor-price equalization equilibrium, then the globalization of world markets is going to pull the factor prices in the direction Freeman describes. However, these prices are not going to be very far from autarky, in the sense that the United States is going to stay rich. Our aggregate wages are going to stay high, but some wages may go down a little bit. In China and India, aggregate wages are going to come up a little bit. Will developing-country wages stay low forever? Hopefully, no, but most of their increase will result not from trade but from capital accumulation, education, and acquisition of technology.

What evidence supports the idea that the world may be closer to autarky than to the most extreme model of free trade? I will touch briefly on three reasons. In the trade literature, Daniel Trefler has noted the large amount of trade that is "missing." Of course we are all very impressed with how much world trade has grown in the last 50 years, but it is still a negligible fraction of what it ought to be according to the standard model of free trade. The current level of world trade is so small that you cannot see it on a graph compared to what would be needed to achieve factor price equalization according to our theories.

Second, much more obviously, there are international differences in factor prices. These differences are large and seem to be reasonably sustainable, which suggests that we may have a long, long way to go before global factor prices equalize.

Finally, what we have known for a long time but have only recently woken up to for the implications for trade, is that distance and borders are a whole lot more important than allowed for in the Heckscher-Ohlin model of factor price equalization. There is something going on in the contemporary world that is restraining the integration process. Measurable transportation costs are not large enough to explain why factor prices are not converging more rapidly than is currently the case, but we really do not know what it is that is impeding the process of integration. I do not dare call the culprit "dark matter," but there is something at work that is causing countries to behave much more like autarkic economies than like economies where factor prices equalize. I admit that none of these reasons are definitive, but all this evidence suggests to me that we should at least consider the possibility that the economic typhoon predicted from China and India is going to wash over us rather gently.

# 5

## The Essential Complements to Capital

# Capital and Its Complements in Economic Growth

J. Bradford DeLong

We economists are professionally required by our discipline to be of at least two minds on every issue: on the one hand, but on the other hand. This sense of detached objectivity prompted Harry S. Truman's oft-repeated remark that he desperately wished to find a one-handed economist. Usually, however, the "on the one hand, on the other hand" structure of economic argument is more of a pose than a reality. It is pro forma to give the arguments on both sides of an issue, but one of the hands usually is strong and capable, while the other one is palsied. The mind behind one hand is strong, confident, and loud; the other whispers "but what if?" in the deep recesses of our brain.

Yet on today's issue—capital and its complements, the role of saving, investment, and international capital flows in modern economic growth—the "on the one hand, on the other hand" structure of the argument is definitely not a pose. On this topic economists today should be and must be of at least two minds, while vigorously gesturing with two if not three hands, as they try to assess what is going on in the global capital markets and what impact this has had and will have on modern global economic growth. This mode of proceeding has its benefits: we are genuinely uncertain, and we are genuinely confused. It has costs as well: the thread of the argument is hard to follow, if indeed there is a dominant thread, or a coherent, sustained argument to be advanced. After all is said and done, one ends up confused—but at least one's confusion has been raised to a more sophisticated, subtle, and complex level.

This paper will therefore present a wide-ranging and rambling look at the issue of capital and its complements in promoting economic growth. The analysis proceeds in five stages:

- Historical patterns: what has been the relationship between capital and growth in the past, and what economists have thought about that relationship.

- The capital accumulation gradient: the increasing difficulty, as industrialization proceeds, that poor developing countries have in raising their capital intensities to levels that allow use of the most modern productive technologies.

- The neoliberal bet: the hope so confidently and widely shared a couple of decades ago that international capital mobility would greatly aid in helping poor countries climb up the capital accumulation gradient—that heightened capital mobility would be able to produce rapid industrialization and growth throughout the world.

- The unexpected reversal: the fact that international capital mobility over the past two decades has expanded much more rapidly than almost anybody had predicted, but has expanded in the wrong direction. The poor have not been borrowing from the rich to finance their investment and industrialization; instead, the rich have on net been borrowing from the poor to finance their own consumption.

- What is to be done?: the conclusion is the least confident part of the paper, because it is not at all clear what is to be done.

Think of this paper's discussion as a classically structured five-act tragedy. The tragic flaw is the assumption that the relationship between capital flows, investment, and growth today and tomorrow would be the same as it had been in the past—specifically, in the late nineteenth century, when capital flows to capital-scarce but resource-rich regions had powerfully fueled industrialization and development. The critical reversal of fortune comes when the unblocking of the barriers to large net capital flows sees the flows proceed at an unexpectedly large intensity—but in a large and destructive way. The dénouement has yet to be written; in fact, it will be our job over the next decades to write it.

## Act I: Capital, Growth, and History

Let's begin with economic history by reviewing what professional economists have thought about the capital stock and its importance for economic growth over the past two centuries, starting with Adam Smith, the founding father of modern economics, and his magnum opus, *An Inquiry into the Nature and Causes of the Wealth of Nations* (1776). For Smith and his successors up until 1950 or so, capital was absolutely essential for economic growth. At the foundation you needed good institutions: "security of property and tolerable administration of justice," as Smith called it in 1776, little more than which was required, in his view, to raise a country's economy to the maximum feasible heights of prosperity. If these fundamental institutions were right, then landlords, merchants, and manufacturers would invest and improve their assets. In investing and improving, they would add to the nation's capital stock:

In all countries where there is a tolerable security [of property], every man of common understanding will endeavour to employ whatever [capital] stock he can command, in procuring either present enjoyment or future profit.... A man must be perfectly crazy, who, where there is a tolerable security, does not employ all the stock which he commands, whether it be his own, or borrowed of other people. (Book II, Chapter I)

And a larger capital stock would mean thicker markets, a finer division of labor, and a more productive economy. A society that has a sophisticated division of labor would have very high productivity, and that process was how you got to the wealth of nations.

Reverse the process and you had the poverty of nations, a result that Smith believed he saw in the Asia of his time:

In those unfortunate countries, indeed, where men are continually afraid of the violence of their superiors, they frequently bury or conceal a great part of their stock, in order to have it always at hand to carry with them to some place of safety, in case of their being threatened with any of those disasters to which they consider themselves at all times exposed. This is said to be a common practice in Turkey, in Indostan, and, I believe, in most other governments of Asia. (Book II, Chapter I)

Over the first 175 years of the economics profession, Smith and his successors viewed capital as absolutely essential for any episode of sustained economic growth. We economists were by and large capital boosters, and our mantra was that thrift, saving, investment, and wealth accumulation is the magic formula that gets us to where we want to be. The last and fullest expression of this line of thought came in 1960 with W.W. Rostow's *The Stages of Economic Growth: A Non-Communist Manifesto*. In Rostow, a nation's key to joining the industrial economies and triggering self-sustained modern economic growth came when the economy (and the polity) reached the point where it could suddenly—over a decade or a little more—double its private and national savings and investment rate. That, and of course, the sociological, political, and other economic processes that triggered that doubling and sustained it, was what was most needed.

It was in large part because this line of thought elevating the overwhelming importance of capital had been so dominant—essentially unquestioned—that the work of Solow (1956, 1957) and Abramovitz (1956) came as such a shock and had such great influence. They made the assumption that the social marginal product of capital is well captured by the individual returns that corporations and other businesses earn as profits and that savers and investors receive as income. Essentially, they each said: "Wait a minute. Under that assumption, capital is not that important after all." Looking at the sources of productivity growth and increases in living standards in the United States over the twentieth century, both Abramovitz and Solow calculated that something like 75 or 80 percent did not come from increasing the capital-output ratio—at least not if the private marginal product of capital was taken as an indicator of the social marginal product. Instead, the keys to growth and development appeared to be things other than a rise in capital intensity as measured by the capital-output ratios: skills, education, technology broadly understood, and improvements in organizational management.

Then in the 1990s there came a partial reaction against the conclusions of Abramovitz and Solow. Mankiw, Romer, and Weil's very influential 1992 cross-country growth study found, in its final and preferred specification, as capital's half-share $\alpha$ in the Cobb-Douglas production function, signs that capital was more important in growth the further down the income scale you looked. Profit share-based estimates had produced estimates of $\alpha$ in the range of one-third to one-quarter. It makes a significant difference whether output per worker is linear in the savings-investment rate, as Mankiw, Romer, and Weil's coefficients suggested, as opposed to the alternative of growing with the square or cube root of the savings-investment rate.

DeLong and Summers (1991) found that the post-World War II cross-country dataset contained an extraordinarily strong correlation between growth and *private* investment in machinery and equipment. Public investment by state-owned monopolies did not do it. Investment in structures did not do it. The correlation was very strong in OECD-class and middle-income economies. And it appeared to remain even when you looked far down at the very bottom of the cross-country income distribution—high-investment low-growth Tanzania and Zambia being neutralized in the dataset by still higher investment and extraordinarily rapid growth in their neighbor Botswana. The correlation appeared to arise whether the high rate of equipment investment was driven by a high domestic savings rate, large capital inflows, or low relative prices of machinery and equipment that translated a moderate savings effort into a substantial investment outcome.

At the conceptual level, this makes considerable sense. A lot of what we economists think of as total factor productivity is, in one way or another, embodied or has essential requirements in the shape and magnitude of the collective capital stock. It is not unreasonable to think that simply piling up more capital without having better organizations or better technology does not do much good. Yet it is also not unreasonable to think that a high level of capital is an essential complement to accomplishing the things that really do matter—and that the things that do matter the most matter the most only if capital is not a significant constraint. In the framework of Rodrik (2004), a shortage of capital can be but not must be a binding growth constraint: a place where "the biggest bang for the reform buck can be obtained" if it is "the most significant bottleneck in the economy." But if this is not the case, then a lack of capital is not the main problem.

From this perspective, large estimated coefficients in cross-country growth regressions found either for investment in the aggregate capital stock, as shown in Mankiw, Romer, and Weil (1992), or for investment in the machinery capital stock, as in DeLong and Summers (1991), means three things: first, that high investment serves as a marker that other binding constraints to growth are absent. Causation thus runs both ways: a rich country where things are going well, profits are high, and property is secure will be a natural place to invest. High investment is a cause of prosperity and also a signal of prosperity, showing that things are going right. Second, policies aimed at spurring investment may well prove unsuccessful and counterproductive if there are other binding constraints to growth—and if investors are smart enough to recognize that these other binding constraints mean that the rate of private return on investment is not likely to be high. Third, in a significant fraction of times and places a shortage of new capital is the binding constraint on growth, and that relaxation of this constraint does indeed reveal a very high marginal social product of capital.

## Act II: Population, Relative Price Structures, and Growth

There are several steps to argue that a shortage of capital is frequently an important binding constraint on growth in developing countries. The first step is to note that poor countries are still, for the most part, rapid-population-growth countries. China and India either are approaching zero population growth, or would be approaching zero population growth if not for the enormous momentum currently embedded in the age structure. But there are still a huge number of countries—and not just the countries in Africa—where populations are growing rapidly. This is because countries with low levels of prosperity and low levels of literacy are countries where people find it advantageous, for private insurance reasons, to have relatively large numbers of children. High mortality rates mean that only ample reproduction can now ensure that one is outlived by one's descendants. And low education levels mean that children soon turn from mouths into hands, and so add to the household's productive potential in the relatively short run. These facts of life mean that population and labor force growth is relatively fast, which means that unless domestic savings in these countries goes through the roof, domestic capital-output ratios will be relatively low.

When, as in Mexico today, your population is growing at between 2 and 3 percent per year, it requires a huge domestic savings effort to increase your capital-output ratio—unless, that is, you can ship a huge share of that increase of the labor force north over the border and lessen your own domestic problems of growth. Thus rapid population-growth countries will be relatively poor countries, which will be rapid population-growth countries.

The second step is to take a look at relative poverty and real investment, as depicted in two interesting figures from a paper by Chang-Tai Hsieh and Peter Klenow (2003). Figure 5.1 shows investment rates as a share of GDP plotted against GDP per worker, using a purchasing power parity concept and common international prices worldwide. Figure 5.2 shows the same investment rates at domestic prices. While Figure 5.2 is flat, Figure 5.1 shows a sharp rise from 5 percent to 25 percent of GDP as you move from the poorest to the richest countries in the world.

Relative to the price of output, the price of capital broadly understood, according to Hsieh and Klenow, varies by a factor of five and varies systematically with income. If you are Tanzania or Mali or even Bangladesh, it takes 4 percent of GDP devoted to national savings and domestic

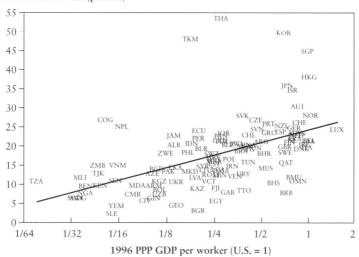

1996 investment rate (percent)

1996 PPP GDP per worker (U.S. = 1)

**Figure 5.1**
Investment Rates at International Prices
*Source:* Hseih and Klenow (2003).

1996 investment rate
at domestic prices (percent)

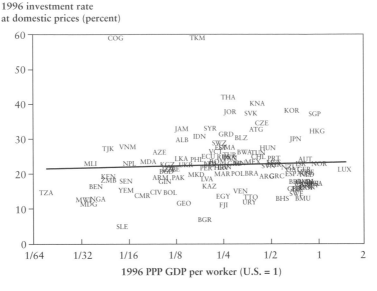

Figure 5.2
Investment Rates at Domestic Prices
*Source:* Hseih and Klenow (2003).

prices to produce a 1 percent real investment share of GDP when real investment is measured at standard international prices. This implies an extraordinary tilting of relative price structures against the poor countries of this world: it requires enormous domestic savings efforts to get even tolerable amounts of real capital to use for development.

If we are right in our guess that capital is close enough to being a composite commodity such that we can talk about capital and labor, and still make coherent sense looking all the way across the world's income distribution, then for this reason alone a relatively poor country is going to find it next to impossible to achieve a reasonable capital-output ratio solely through its domestic savings, because of this tilting effect of relative price structures. This is a much stronger disadvantage of backwardness than the crowding of markets for primary products stressed by the original statements of the price-structure-and-underdevelopment thesis in, for example, Prebisch (1959). It also points out a defect in the thesis that holds that one reason poor countries are poor is that their citizens or their leaders or their governments have by and large chosen to consume rather than to save. That is simply not the case: savings rates on a national level have little or no partial correlation with prosperity. It is relative price structures, and thus real investment shares of GDP as measured in international dollars, that have this high correlation.

The reason for this striking association is clear. Modern transportation via container ships makes the cost of transporting durable commodities across oceans essentially zero. Thus the nominal prices of tradeable manufactured goods will be close to the same all across the globe. What will not be the same are the nominal prices of services provided by unskilled labor: those will be roughly proportional to the product of the real wage—for which read "real labor productivity"—and the equilibrium real exchange rate. Any exchange rate that balances trade will thus produce a very high price of manufactured goods in terms of services and unskilled labor in poor countries. And that is the tilt of the relative price structure against investment, which is heavily weighted toward the price of manufactured tradeable goods.

## Act III: The Neoliberal Bet on International Capital Mobility

Thus for poor countries to bootstrap themselves by their own efforts alone into rapid sustainable growth is very difficult. Hence the neoliberal bet: the hope that international capital mobility would come to the rescue, first by relaxing this binding capital constraint imposed by the tilt of relative price structures, and second, by reducing the scope for corruption and rent seeking via the economic controls imposed to prevent international capital mobility. Courtesy of Christopher Meissner and Alan Taylor at this conference, we have already heard about the historical precedent: Britain before 1914. According to Meissner and Taylor, Britain's net foreign assets in 1913 were equal to 20 months' GDP. Net foreign assets in 1913 equaled 60 percent of Britain's domestic capital stock.

A huge amount of industrialization before 1913 in the resource-rich, temperate periphery was financed by the willingness of British investors to commit their capital overseas—not just to build up Britain's capital stock, but to build up capital stocks abroad as well. (Let's ignore the fact that the British investors in the Erie Railroad found that Jay Gould stole two-thirds of their money, not least by taking a huge leveraged long position in the stock and then announcing his retirement from the company. He retired, the stock price boomed, and he pocketed something like 50 percent of the present discounted value of the fact that he would no longer be around to loot the company.) The point is that this pattern of British foreign investment between 1870 and 1913 worked according to the textbook expectation that capital would flow to regions where it was scarce and boost growth there. Thinking that we would learn from history, and that this history would repeat itself at the end of the twentieth century and the start of the twenty-first, has proven to be the tragic flaw of the contemporary era of globalization that we are now witnessing.

Fifteen years ago I certainly shared this neoliberal belief that international capital mobility was perhaps the best thing that could help the world economy. It held the promise of allowing the relatively rich core to fund the industrialization of the poor periphery. Back in 1993 at then-current exchange rates, China's entire capital stock was $2 trillion, at a time when the capital stock of the United States was $20 trillion. All that you would have had to do to double the capital stock of China through international capital mobility was to gradually, over the course of a decade, move 10 percent of the capital stock of the United States across the Pacific. That would have done truly wonderful things.

Thus the neoliberal hope at the start of the 1990s was essentially to place a large economic policy bet on capital mobility: to trust that very large and very poor labor forces across the world would turn out to be very attractive to global capital free to flow. If relatively small amounts of technology transfer could be used to make such labor even a small fraction as productive as industrial core labor, the incentives for capital to flow toward the periphery like a mighty river would be overwhelming. Before 1914 it was natural resources that had provided the irresistible incentive for international capital mobility toward a periphery composed of economies like Australia, Canada, New Zealand, and the United States, but also Argentina, Chile, Hong Kong, Kenya, Malaysia, Singapore, South Africa, and Uruguay. The hope was that, in some respects, this pre-1914 process could be replicated. That would cut at least a generation off the time needed to make a truly humane and prosperous world economy.

## Act IV: The Unexpected Reversal

But that is not what has happened. We know the unexpected outcome: the current situation of global imbalances. Yes, there have been large flows of capital going both ways around the world. But the huge increase in gross flows is not the big story. The big story is that the expected large net flow of capital from the rich to the poor countries of the world seeking high profits from reducing disequilibria between the wages and the relative productivity of labor has simply not happened. Instead, the principal thing that occurred was an enormous flow of capital from the periphery to the core, a flow perhaps best tracked in real time by Brad Setser of the Council on Foreign Relations, which is available on his weblog, http://blogs.cfr.org/setser/.

Personally, I first saw this reversed trend at work in 1994, when I was sitting at the Treasury, blithely writing memos about the North American Free Trade Agreement (NAFTA). This agreement promised to provide Mexico with guaranteed tariff-free access to the largest consumer market in the world. Thus, we modeled that there would be an extra $20 to $30 billion a year of capital outflow from the United States to Mexico as companies sought to take advantage of Mexico's new long-term comparative advantage as a manufacturing production platform. The expectation was that capital inflow into Mexico would support a relatively high value of the peso for a substantial time—and hence produce immediate benefits from NAFTA to Mexico in terms of an investment boom and a higher level of real consumption because American imports would be available on easier terms. Hence, I argued, the late Rudiger Dornbush was almost surely wrong when he worried in the early 1990s about the state of the Mexican peso and the possibility of yet another Mexican devaluation crisis.

Well, as so often happened, Dornbusch proved smarter than me. It turned out that $20 billion to $30 billion of capital a year did flow from the United States to Mexico as American firms sought production platforms. But it also turned out that what looked to be $30 billion to $40 billion a year of capital flowed from Mexico to the United States. Relatively rich Mexicans took a look at the country's monetary and political instability. They decided that in the event that something went really wrong from their perspective in Mexico and they had to flee across the Rio Grande in a rubber boat, it would be much better to get to Texas and have a large dollar-denominated asset account waiting for them in New York, rather than run the risk of having all of one's money back in Mexico in the wake of whatever political instability led one to flee in the first place.

In addition, there was and is a belief, stronger outside the United States than within it, that the marginal product of capital within the United States is high, that there is a capital-technology complementarity, and that investing in the United States is the way to take advantage of this differential and make a profit from this special relationship. It is indeed the case that U.S. labor productivity is now 35 percent higher than it was back in 2000, with, as best as we can see, real wages remaining exactly the same. That difference represents a huge shift of income in the direction of capital. These ratios represent huge potential profits, which attract foreign investment. It is not just political risks of investing abroad that are driving the long-term inflow of capital to the United States, but attributes in the American economy that make it attractive for foreign capital investment.

Yes, there are benefits to international capital mobility. But for most of the past generation and looking into the future for the next, the market's message is that those benefits do not include a relaxation of the capital constraint and thus an acceleration of growth in the global periphery. The dominant factor is not that the periphery does not offer an attractive labor force from which capital can profit. The compelling attraction is that the core—especially the United States—offers a form of protection for capital against unanticipated political disturbances. Since 1990 global investors have valued the American-provided political risk insurance that they can obtain by placing their money in the United States more than U.S.-based companies have liked the idea of producing abroad in places where the wages of labor are lower.

Dwarfing whatever private insurance against political risk was purchased by the inflow of private capital to the United States was the public purchase of political risk by emerging market governments, especially the government of China. Such large inward capital flows are a very good thing for China's state council: 300 million Chinese people living on the coast, largely in the cities, and 900 million people, most of whom are still desperately poor, residing in the interior. There are enormous pressures to move China's workers into more productive urban and nonagricultural occupations as fast as possible. The only guaranteed way to do this is to put them to work in coastal manufacturing and in supporting occupations.

This development strategy requires that somebody be willing to buy the products of China's manufacturing sector. Who is the world's importer of last resort? The United States. What would the consequences for China be if it could no longer think of increasing its exports by 25 percent or more per year? With its current rates of internal migration, there would be extraordinary economic, extraordinary social, and probably extraordinary political consequences as well if this export growth were curtailed. Inward capital flows are good for the world's rich, who are diversifying their portfolios into the core in a major way. The rich in the periphery can now sleep soundly, knowing that they have assets in a safe place, in case they have to flee the country in a rubber boat. Or, if their great-grandchildren might want to live in the United States, having lots of property in the United States now is a good way to get a senator to write a supporting letter to the Immigration and Naturalization Service. But as the record of the last two decades has shown, contrary to prior expectations, global capital mobility does not appear to be a good way to relax whatever aggregate capital shortages serve as severe growth constraints on emerging markets.

Yet recognition of these facts came relatively slowly.

At first the consensus was that the inflow of capital to the United States was largely due to cyclical factors. The 1990s, now an eternity ago, saw U.S. Treasury Secretary Lawrence Summers attribute the pattern of capital flows to imbalances in the business cycle, and warn that the world economy had to get the business cycle back into balance and could do so either "by balancing up or balancing down." In Summers's view, the U.S. current account deficit could not be long sustained at its then extraordinary level of $200 million a year for very long. 2007 saw an American current account deficit nearly four times as large as the one that Secretary Summers had said was about to become unsustainable nearly a decade before.

Then the consensus shifted to believing that the large net capital inflows to the United States were mostly the result of policy mistakes that had recreated the large U.S. budget deficits of the Reagan era. Somebody had to buy the newly issued debt of the U.S. Treasury, and foreigners were a natural set of people to buy and hold it. Then the consensus shifted to seeing the capital inflow as the result of the U.S. housing bubble—the fact that all of my neighbors in California have been using their houses as gigantic automatic teller machines to pull out huge amounts of equity to then spend on the style to which they would like to become accustomed.

Those who warned—most aggressively, economist Dean Baker of the Center for Economic and Policy Research—that the housing price appreciation of the 2000s was not entirely the result of what Ben Bernanke termed the global savings glut, but was instead a bubble that would prove a dangerous source of financial instability, have been proven correct. In retrospect it is difficult to imagine what those who approved adjustable-rate low downpayment mortgages were thinking. There were always large tail risks involved in such mortgages coming either from employment or interest rate changes, and it would have been proper for these risks to have been much more thoroughly diversified. Doctors living in suburban San Francisco should not be in the business of bearing such risks. Neither should highly leveraged investment banks, which have an originate-and-sell business model.

But does this mean the low interest rate policies of the United States in the early 2000s were a policy mistake? Would we really have a better world if interest rates had not been lowered so much in the early 2000s, and all the labor structurally displaced from the dot-com and telecommunications busts had gone into unemployment? I do not believe so—although one has to grant that financial regulators would have served the public better had their communications strategies placed more emphasis on the inappropriateness of individuals bearing idiosyncratic financial risk, and both low downpayments and adjustable-rate mortgages are large sources of idiosyncratic risk.

The net flow of capital into the United States has been good for American consumers, who have been able to borrow very cheaply and spend $90,000 on a kitchen renovation. But is this easy feeding of America's appetite for consumption truly a good thing? Shouldn't the United States's domestic savings rate be higher? The old Solow model's golden rule of thumb is that national savings rates should be equal to capital shares. Moving to a framework that, appropriately, allows for greater time discounting, either through more steeply declining marginal utility of wealth or pure time preference, reduces that prescription somewhat, but still leaves America more likely than not to be in a situation in which it is short of savings.

This influx of capital to the core has been good to savers and governments abroad seeking insurance and—so far—better investment returns. It may well have been good for the core by offering it capital to fund consumption on favorable terms at low interest rates. But it has not been so good for labor in the periphery. The hopes of seeing capital flowing from the rich core to the poor periphery, producing higher capital-output ratios out on the periphery, and transferring technology and boosting real wages for those who are not at the top of the income distribution, have really not been realized.

And there remain today the risks of sudden stops and reversals in international capital flows that could make the subprime crisis of 2007–2008 look like a Sunday afternoon picnic in Battery Park.

## Act V: Remains to be Written

This brings me to the final act: what is to be done? That is for us to decide. And I have no answers, in part because the causes that have led us to this somewhat unexpected point are complex in origin, and so must be the solutions. I will, however, suggest three things that must be considered as we grapple with the situation we now face. First, we need to recognize that the core is not a net capital provider to the periphery in the current generation, there is no sign that it is going to be, and that is a bad outcome. Second, even though net international capital flows are going the wrong way, there are still substantial gross capital flows outward. We can hope that the gross outward capital flow from the core to the periphery will carry along with it the institutions and managerial expertise that have made people so wealthy in the advanced economies. Third, we need to worry about tail risks, sudden stops, and why financial markets have not been appropriately pricing the risks generated by large-scale persistent inflows of capital to the core of the world economy.

In 2008 the global economy is developing magneto trouble, as John Maynard Keynes put it 75 years ago. What it needs is a push—more aggregate demand. In the United States, the weak dollar will be a powerful boost to net exports, and thus to aggregate demand. But from the perspective of the world as a whole, net exports are a zero-sum game. So we will have to rely on other sources of aggregate demand to fuel the global economy.

## References

Abramovitz, Moses. 1956. "Resource and Output Trends in the United States since 1870." *American Economic Review* 46(2): 5–23.

Delong, J. Bradford, and Lawrence H. Summers. 1991. "Equipment Investment and Economic Growth." *The Quarterly Journal of Economics* 106(2): 445–502.

Hseih, Chang-Tai, and Peter J. Klenow. 2003. "Relative Prices and Relative Prosperity." Working Paper No. W9701. Cambridge, MA: National Bureau of Economic Research.

Mankiw, N. Gregory, David Romer, and David N. Weil. 1992. "A Contribution to the Empirics of Economic Growth." *The Quarterly Journal of Economics* 107(2): 407–437.

Prebisch, Raul. 1959. "Commercial Policy in Underdeveloped Countries." *American Economic Review* 49(2): 251–273.

Rodrik, Dani. 2004. "Rethinking Growth Policies in the Developing World." Available at http://ksghome.harvard.edu/~drodrik/luca_d_agliano_lecture_oct_2004.pdf.

Rostow, W. W. 1960. *The Stages of Economic Growth: A Non-Communist Manifesto*. Cambridge: Cambridge University Press.

Smith, Adam. 1776. *An Inquiry into the Nature and Causes of the Wealth of Nations*. London: Millar.

Solow, Robert M. 1956. "A Contribution to the Theory of Economic Growth." *Quarterly Journal of Economics* 70(1): 65–94.

Solow, Robert M. 1957. "Technical Change and the Aggregate Production Function." *Review of Economics and Statistics* 39(3): 312–320.

# Comments on "Capital and Its Complements in Economic Growth" by J. Bradford DeLong

Abhijit V. Banerjee

I approached this question from almost the opposite end as Brad, but ended more or less in the same place as he does. The equalization of the capital-labor ratio, which is depicted in the first slide of Brad's presentation, is the idea that the capital-labor ratio varies a lot across the world. Wouldn't it be nice if capital moved to those countries that had less capital, and equalized the capital-labor ratio? Well, the fact is that everything we know in development economics says that capital just does not move in this manner. Let's forget about capital flowing from the United States to India, and instead talk about how fast capital moves within a developing country. I'll spend some time making this point.

One way of looking at the cost of capital mobility is to compare lending and deposit rates within the same sub-economic region. This answers the question of what is the cost of moving capital from someone who has money to someone who needs money. The examples I will cite will usually be within the same town or same region, and often even within the same marketplace.

Another way to consider this matter is to compare lending rates for different borrowers by asking, what would be the additional cost of moving capital from borrower A to borrower B? Let me just give you some facts. One of the biggest reports on this topic was financed by the Asian Development Bank. The study was conducted in many countries, and I'll come back to the overall results, but for now I will concentrate on a subreport for India (Dasgupta 1989). For a variety of significantly sized nonbank intermediaries, it examined the difference between deposit rates and lending rates. The differential is on the order of 25 to 30 percent, when the base deposit interest rate is 10 to 12 percent. So the gap between the lending rate and the deposit rate is much bigger than the deposit rate itself. This is a scenario where inflation rates average 5 percent and are pretty stable, not a scenario where there is a huge amount of inflation risk. The figures are very similar for Pakistan—in a very well-known study by Irfan Aleem (1990), the average interest rate charged by lenders was 78.5 percent, while the opportunity cost of capital to these lenders was 32 percent. These lenders were already borrowing money at very high rates. If the average Pakistani put his or her money in the bank, s/he would have earned a 10 percent interest rate. These gaps reflect huge orders of magnitude, and under these conditions capital is not moving to those people who are saving money at a 10 percent interest rate. In principle, household savers could be lending to those guys who are paying 78.5 percent, but that is not what is happening.

Many of these cross-country studies report similar facts about different borrowers. Once again, from the report on India by Dasgupta that I mentioned earlier, you see interest rates on term loans for less than a year vary between 48 percent annually and 5 percent per day. Five percent per day is 16,000 percent per year. For longer loans the variation is less, but still enormous. In the Asian Development Bank study I mentioned, the mean interest rate was 78 percent, while the standard deviation was 38 percent. So, if you do standard division, the mean was between 2 percent and 150 percent. This wide divergence is not just some South Asian perversion of financial markets; it is also true of other countries located elsewhere in the developing world. In Thailand, the interest rate differentials go from 2 percent to 7 percent per month, so that's an enormous difference. I could go on and on. Suffice it to say that this is a very established fact of micro-level development economics: interest rates within very small markets are not equalized.

A common first reaction to this idea often assumes that this inequality of rates is due to huge default risks, but default risk plays a very small role. In the Indian study I cited, while the handloom financiers and the financial companies have big differences in their default risk, this only explains 7 percent of the total interest cost. But since the total interest cost is 70 percent, this default risk only explains about 5 percent of the interest cost. So default risk really does not explain anything. In terms of default rates, the study from Pakistan documents a median default rate of 2 percent.

A second response is to ask if the market is competitive. The study by Aleem was conducted in 1980–1981 in exactly one semiurban marketplace in Pakistan with 14 professional moneylenders, all of whom individually calculated the cost of lending. The study found that the cost of lending essentially explained the interest rate, and there was no obvious evidence of excess profits. So why is moving capital between subregions so costly? There is very little actual default but a very high risk of default. I think that this risk is not emphasized enough. Passive default is very important. Small businesses often have very poor cash management practices and these firms often do not deal very well with risk. Active default can also take place; assets can vanish overnight. People can just walk away. Courts can take forever to rectify such situations, so all of these risks make collecting loans very hard. So, the obvious answer is that lending rates are high because preventing default is costly.

Why is preventing default so costly? One of the things necessary to understand is the economics of preventing default. I think at the core of this concept is one idea, which I will call the monitoring multiplier. It goes the following way: when the cost of monitoring goes up a little bit, the interest rate goes up to cover that cost. When the interest rate goes up, of course default becomes more likely, so then you have to monitor a bit more to deal with this extra increased default risk. In turn, this raises interest rates a little bit more, so eventually that multiplier can become very large. You can sort of compute that multiplier on a specific model and that multiplier can be very large. So, the default multiplier says that small difference in monitoring costs can lead to large difference in interest rate.

Another very key fact is the fixed cost of monitoring. For example, someone has to go and check addresses to make sure you know where the borrower lives—that's a fixed cost. The smaller the loan, the greater is the burden of the fixed cost. So, one might ask, why don't you just make large loans. Well, big loans carry the opposite risk. If you allow someone to borrow a hundred times more than he may need, his incentives to use the money properly go down. In sum, a potential lender is between a rock and a hard place. You don't want to lend a lot to people because of the collective default risk, but if you lend only a little, then the margin costs kill you. Between these two alternatives, it is not hard to understand why interest rates behave this way in developing countries.

Consequently, we observe the behavior that these observations predict. First, lots of funds can't borrow because they are the wrong scale. You've already seen that certain funds are willing to pay interest rates of 50 or 60 or 70 or 80 percent. These are not small funds. These finance companies essentially lend to large traders. We did a study where we use the fact that there was a policy change in directed lending to a particular set of funds in India, and estimated a marginal product of capital from that change. We found that these loans were made to very large firms in the 95th percentile of the fund size distribution. The funds that are affected by this particular manipulation have a 90 percent marginal product of capital. This does not mean that every firm in India is earning 90 percent on their capital investments because if you look at the increment of capital output ratio (ICOR) and invert it, you get an upper bound on the marginal product of capital. If you take that upper bound, you find that it is less than 25 percent, so some funds must have very low returns on capital as well. This is exactly what you would expect to find in a situation where capital is immobile. If you happen to have money, you keep it to yourself. If you happen not to have money, you don't get it. Hence, the marginal product of capital varies enormously. I think the core consequential fact for growth is not that India is incredibly productive economically, but that there are huge gaps in productivity between those who have access to capital and those who do not.

We also looked at the specific fact that in India we get what I call a poor match between talent and money. We looked at family firms connected to cash-rich families. If you happen to be from a family that has lots of cash resources, what does your firm look like in terms of size? Your firm is enormously large. It has a scale that is three times bigger than your competitors, and by every measure your productivity is much lower. If you happen to be cash rich, you go into this business because you want to use the money, and that choice does not generate the right selective use of capital.

So, the first thing I want to say is that this misallocation of capital exacts an enormous productivity cost. Hsieh and Klenow, who Brad mentioned, have another paper where they fit the production function to India and China and conclude that total factor productivity could double if capital and labor were officially allocated within four-digit industries.

So just within the four-digit industries, reallocated capital and labor pro-ductivity would double.

Speaking to global imbalances, the conference topic at hand, every problem that afflicts within-country lending is worse for cross-border lending. Lenders often are unfamiliar with the legal system in another country. They may be unable or unwilling to participate in extralegal systems of enforcements. In India, at some point Citibank took to doing what many Indian lenders do, sending somebody around to check on borrowers and mildly threaten people to deliver. Of course, this prac-tice was immediately reported by the newspapers, and Citibank had to retract that policy. In fact, they stopped lending in that sector very quickly. Internal monitoring is harder given local business practices, so all of this makes lending in developing countries problematic and hard. How can these constraints be overcome? Well, I think that there are three strategies. One is agency. You basically get someone to set up a lending subsidiary there, but this must be a monitoring-intensive business. The agent must be able to provide verifiable support for his lending deci-sions, and only well-organized and formally documented borrowers can get these loans. Another strategy is to trade credit in a specific form, which is a very standard way of lending. Merchandise is often produced, and credit provided to the suppliers, using the carrot of new contracts to get them to repay the loan. This method works well in countries that are part of an established supply chain, but it is much less effective where the buyer is footloose. In China trade credit works well—you can give credit to your suppliers because you are going to be there for a long time. In Ghana you are less likely to do this because you are not sure that your firm is going to be there much longer. Moreover, the suppliers are not sure that you are going to be there, so this mutual commitment does not exist. As another strategy, foreign direct investment is really interesting, and I think it works well if foreigners are willing to spend lots of time in the country. This is less of a problem if the investors are returning émigrés or are living in countries that are attractive to foreigners. What is inter-esting about this strategy is that something noneconomic is at play here, which is potentially a big problem for Africa and for smaller countries.

My concluding message is that it is hard to imagine that the world-wide imbalances in the allocation of capital will be fixed by the world's capital markets. It seems particularly implausible that most small countries in the developing world, and countries in Africa, many of which are politically fragile, will manage to attract much foreign capital, even with substantial institutional improvements.

## References

Aleem, Irfan. 1990. "Imperfect Information, Screening, and the Costs of Informal Lending: A Study of a Rural Credit Market in Pakistan." *World Bank Economic Review* 4(3): 329–349.

Dasgupta, A. 1989. *Reports on Informal Credit Markets in India: Summary*. New Delhi: National Institute of Public Finance and Policy.

# Comments on "Capital and Its Complements in Economic Growth" by J. Bradford DeLong

Lixin Colin Xu

In the standard international trade model between two countries, capital and labor are perfectly mobile within a country or region. Thus, in theory, free trade would lead to the equalization of factor prices, including rental prices of capital. Without distortions (such as tax rate differences), the marginal product of capital (MPK) should be equal in all locations. But we observe widely differing MPK both across countries, and across regions within a country. Based on a recent World Bank investment climate survey in China, we find that the interquartile range of MPK is almost 6. In 2004, the per capita GDP in Shanghai was 42,818 renminbi, but was 4,082 renminbi in the rural province of Guizhou, a ten-fold difference in income. In terms of the inflow of foreign direct investment (FDI), Shanghai attracted 362 U.S. dollars of FDI in 2004, while the province of Gansu attracted only 1 dollar. These observations suggest that capital/labor intensity and capital productivity not only differ greatly between countries, but within countries as well. What explains the huge variations in MPK and capital flow across regions in China? In this short note I will discuss what recent studies, based on the World Bank Investment Climate Surveys (mostly those that I've been conducting with my co-authors), have found to augment Brad DeLong's discussion on capital and its complements.

## Existing Evidence

Substantial regional protectionalism is the first reason for MPK and capital inflow differing within China. There are trade restrictions between regions, and there might be price differences between regions. Various regions may not charge the same prices for the same product. The reasons for such protectionism include the desire to keep large firms within a region in order to collect more taxes to improve local infrastructure and to keep the jobs local.[1] Indeed, there is evidence that local Chinese leaders get rewarded if the local economy performs well (Li and Zhou 2005). Regional protectionalism can manifest itself in many ways. Local governments, for instance, can impose quantity quotas for outside manufacturers, can charge higher taxes or offer local producers tax breaks for selling locally, and can impose different technical standards for outsiders. Regional protectionalism explains why each region has its own car and refrigerator manufacturers instead of the scenario that efficiency could dictate: larger, more nationwide car and refrigerator producers.

The second reason is the well-known one regarding differences in human capital in different localities. Complementarity of physical and human capital in the production function essentially leads to differing technology for different regions, thus violating the standard Heckscher-Ohlin assumptions. There used to be an explicit Hukou (or household responsibility) system that prohibited formal employees from moving to different locations. This restriction was loosened over time, especially for unskilled workers. However, for skilled workers, such restrictions are still in effect. Moreover, given the large wage differences across cities—as one can imagine that would exist with the huge differences in GDP per capita—high-skilled workers tend to stay in more developed regions, such as Shanghai, Beijing, and Shenzhen. The complementarity between human and physical capital suggests that there would be more capital attracted in cities with more skill endowment. Table 5.1 reports the share of employees with college education in 120 Chinese cities in 2004 based on the World Bank Investment Climate Survey. Beijing tops all cities with a share of 42 percent, and Sanming is only about 8 percent.

Do we have evidence that skill-intensive cities have higher MPK or attract more capital inflow in China? In a word, yes (later I shall present evidence that MPK is higher in firms located in cities with more college graduates).

The third reason that MPK and capital inflow differ within China is due to regional differences in infrastructure or geography. An important aspect of infrastructure is transportation, which the investment climate

**Table 5.1**
Cities and the Shares of Employees with University Education

| | | | | | | | |
|---|---|---|---|---|---|---|---|
| Anqing | 0.119 | Guiyang | 0.287 | Liuzhou | 0.191 | Taizhou | 0.140 |
| Anshan | 0.153 | Haerbing | 0.376 | Luoyang | 0.180 | Tangshan | 0.116 |
| Baoding | 0.200 | Haikou | 0.298 | Maoming | 0.142 | Tianjin | 0.273 |
| Baoji | 0.172 | Handan | 0.141 | Mianyang | 0.200 | Tianshui | 0.179 |
| Baotou | 0.180 | Hangzhou | 0.261 | Nanchang | 0.289 | Weifang | 0.130 |
| Beijing | 0.421 | Hefei | 0.285 | Nanjing | 0.222 | Weihai | 0.118 |
| Benxi | 0.126 | Hengyang | 0.164 | Nanning | 0.240 | Wenzhou | 0.129 |
| Cangzhou | 0.120 | Huanggang | 0.113 | Nantong | 0.155 | Wuhan | 0.356 |
| Changchun | 0.290 | Huhehaote | 0.229 | Nanyang | 0.159 | Wuhu | 0.151 |
| Changde | 0.149 | Huizhou | 0.132 | Ningbo | 0.123 | Wulumuqi | 0.268 |
| Changsha | 0.289 | Huzhou | 0.112 | Qingdao | 0.175 | Wuxi | 0.145 |
| Changzhou | 0.131 | Jiangmen | 0.169 | Qinhuangdao | 0.192 | Wuzhong | 0.091 |
| Chengdu | 0.312 | Jiaxing | 0.054 | Qiqihaer | 0.186 | Xiamen | 0.169 |
| Chenzhou | 0.108 | Jilin | 0.179 | Quanzhou | 0.096 | Xian | 0.363 |
| Chongqing | 0.209 | Jinan | 0.231 | Qujing | 0.104 | Xiangfan | 0.180 |
| Chuzhou | 0.108 | Jingmen | 0.139 | Sanming | 0.080 | Xianyang | 0.250 |
| Dalian | 0.255 | Jingzhou | 0.178 | Shanghai | 0.231 | Xiaogan | 0.174 |
| Daqing | 0.193 | Jinhua | 0.124 | Shangqiu | 0.106 | Xining | 0.180 |
| Datong | 0.149 | Jining | 0.154 | Shangrao | 0.107 | Xinxiang | 0.170 |
| Deyang | 0.133 | Jinzhou | 0.220 | Shantou | 0.127 | Xuchang | 0.095 |
| Dongguan | 0.122 | Jiujiang | 0.119 | Shaoxing | 0.130 | Xuzhou | 0.209 |
| Foshan | 0.146 | Kunming | 0.202 | Shenyang | 0.305 | Yancheng | 0.121 |
| Fushun | 0.192 | Langfang | 0.179 | Shenzhen | 0.175 | Yangzhou | 0.108 |
| Fuzhou | 0.155 | Lanzhou | 0.193 | Shijiazhuang | 0.201 | Yantai | 0.190 |
| Ganzhou | 0.125 | Leshan | 0.143 | Suzhou | 0.210 | Yibin | 0.101 |
| Guangzhou | 0.259 | Lianyungang | 0.157 | Taian | 0.239 | Yichang | 0.182 |
| Guilin | 0.236 | Linyi | 0.157 | Taiyuan | 0.243 | Yichun | 0.110 |
| Yinchuan | 0.183 | Yuxi | 0.129 | Zhengzhou | 0.209 | Zhuzhou | 0.248 |
| Yueyang | 0.183 | Zhangjiakou | 0.117 | Zhoukou | 0.179 | Zibo | 0.209 |
| Yuncheng | 0.141 | Zhangzhou | 0.133 | Zhuhai | 0.150 | Zunyi | 0.187 |

Source: World Bank Investment Climate Data.

survey quantifies as the share of sales due to losses, theft, and break-age during transportation. This measure captures partly the efficiency of the transportation sector. This ratio ranges from less than 1 percent in Hangzhou to almost 10 percent in Leshan and Ningbo. In studies of FDI inflow into Chinese cities using the World Bank Investment Climate data, Clarke and Xu find that sales losses due to infrastructure problems do not really lower foreign equity ownership, as shown in Table 5.2. Poor infrastructure in China thus does not hinder capital inflow to some Chinese regions.

**Table 5.2**
Determinants of FDI Inflow across Chinese Cities

Dependent variable = share of foreign ownership in a district

| | (1) | (2) | (3) | (4) | (5) | (6) |
|---|---|---|---|---|---|---|
| ln(L) | 0.014 | 0.018 | 0.027 | 0.014 | 0.014 | 0.014 |
| | (1.31) | (1.65)* | (2.47)** | (1.35) | (1.35) | (1.36) |
| age | −0.079 | −0.075 | −0.077 | −0.076 | −0.076 | −0.076 |
| | (3.76)*** | (3.46)*** | (3.48)*** | (3.68)*** | (3.68)*** | (3.71)*** |
| ln(city pop) | −0.000 | 0.007 | 0.017 | 0.010 | 0.010 | 0.009 |
| | (0.01) | (0.43) | (1.23) | (0.60) | (0.60) | (0.56) |
| Ln(GDP PC) | 0.077 | 0.092 | 0.088 | 0.072 | 0.072 | 0.074 |
| | (3.13)*** | (3.90)*** | (3.79)*** | (3.09)*** | (3.09)*** | (3.21)*** |
| Dist. to port | −0.007 | −0.009 | −0.009 | −0.006 | −0.006 | −0.006 |
| | (2.08)** | (2.76)*** | (3.10)*** | (2.10)** | (2.10)** | (1.92)* |
| Ln(city average wage) | −0.084 | −0.039 | −0.077 | −0.102 | −0.102 | −0.110 |
| | (1.85)* | (0.97) | (1.82)* | (2.49)** | (2.49)** | (2.48)** |
| open city | 0.105 | 0.125 | 0.093 | 0.072 | 0.072 | 0.071 |
| | (1.55) | (2.38)** | (1.80)* | (1.13) | (1.13) | (1.14) |
| Mean share of employees with college edu. | 0.111 | 0.102 | 0.101 | 0.111 | 0.111 | 0.106 |
| | (1.42) | (1.27) | (1.26) | (1.47) | (1.47) | (1.42) |
| Ln(road/pop) | 0.017 | | | 0.021 | 0.021 | 0.021 |
| | (0.93) | | | (1.19) | (1.19) | (1.21) |
| ln(city phone per capita) | 0.014 | | | 0.009 | 0.009 | 0.011 |
| | (0.76) | | | (0.50) | (0.50) | (0.60) |
| Mean ln(days passing customs) | −0.128 | | | −0.102 | −0.102 | −0.104 |
| | (5.18)*** | | | (4.16)*** | (4.16)*** | (4.12)*** |
| Mean index of property rights protection | | 0.064 | | 0.004 | 0.004 | 0.008 |
| | | (1.75)* | | (0.12) | (0.12) | (0.22) |
| Mean share of loans need bribes | | −0.201 | | −0.126 | −0.126 | −0.134 |
| | | (3.26)*** | | (2.06)** | (2.06)** | (2.24)** |
| Mean tax/sales | | −0.992 | | −0.583 | −0.583 | −0.602 |
| | | (3.01)*** | | (1.97)** | (1.97)** | (2.04)** |
| Air quality | | | 0.228 | 0.108 | 0.108 | 0.105 |
| | | | (4.63)*** | (2.15)** | (2.15)** | (2.08)** |
| Restaurant density | | | 0.137 | 0.133 | 0.133 | 0.132 |
| | | | (3.07)*** | (2.94)*** | (2.94)*** | (2.89)*** |
| Mean share of loss of sales due to transportation | | | | | | 1.126 |
| | | | | | | (1.42) |
| Mean share of loss of sales due to electricity | | | | | | −0.034 |
| | | | | | | (0.19) |
| City GDP growth | | | | | | 0.000 |
| | | | | | | (0.69) |
| industry shares for the district | yes | yes | yes | yes | yes | yes |
| Observations | 916 | 916 | 910 | 910 | 910 | 910 |

* significant at 10%; ** significant at 5%; *** significant at 1%. White-corrected error, and clustering at the district-year level.

Source: From Clarke and Xu (Ongoing). Based on investment climate survey in China, World Bank. Unit of observations is by districts within a city.

The fourth reason for MPK variations among different regions is the inefficiency of China's financial system. Ideally, an efficient financial system should carry out the role of channeling capital into locations with higher MPK. If the financial system works well, then there should not be the huge variations in MPK across regions. But the Chinese financial system has many well-known problems, such as favoring the state sector at the expense of the booming private and TVE sectors (Brandt and Li 2003; Cull and Xu 2000, 2003; Allen, Qian, and Qian 2005), and state-owned enterprises (SOEs) not using loans productively (Cull and Xu 2000). Yet there is also evidence that there might be mechanisms at work to compensate for the inadequacies of the formal finance system in China (Allen, Qian, and Qian 2005). Cull, Xu, and Zhu (2007) find, for instance, that SOEs may act as secondary financial intermediaries to channel bank loans into private firms. In particular, SOEs without good growth opportunities are found to be more likely to extend trade credit when these firms have access to bank loans, while the SOEs that grew faster tend to extend less trade credit when they have access to bank loans.

The importance of finance in affecting capital allocation is also demonstrated in international comparison. An ongoing investigation finds that the significantly higher growth of business firms in China (relative to India) is largely due to the significantly higher capital growth in China (see Mengistae, Xu, and Yeung 2006). Although Chinese firms have less access to finance in terms of the share of firms claiming access to bank loans (or line of credit), the same access translates into a much higher total factor productivity (TFP) level in China than in India.

Our recent surveys find that Chinese regions differ greatly in effective tax burdens. Sales taxes range from 0.038 in Jiangmen (a city in Guangdong) to 0.179 in Yuxi (Yunnan), and 0.163 in Jinzhou (Liaoning); see Table 5.3. In general, inland and more backward regions feature higher effective tax burdens, perhaps because these lagging areas have smaller tax bases, yet the demand for public sector jobs there tends to be higher. If we assume constant returns to scale, perfect competition, and profit maximization by firms, local firms then maximize $(1 - t)Lq(k) - wL - rk$, so we would have $q'_k = r/(1 - t)$. Then we should observe a negative correlation between the local tax burden and local FDI inflow. Indeed,

**Table 5.3**
Differences in Effective Tax Rates and Foreign Direct Investment Among Chinese Cities

| City | Foreign | Effective Tax Rate | City | Foreign | Effective Tax Rate | City | Foreign | Effective Tax Rate |
|---|---|---|---|---|---|---|---|---|
| Anqing | 0.078 | 0.098 | Jining | 0.067 | 0.116 | Wulumuqi | 0.036 | 0.146 |
| Anshan | 0.040 | 0.148 | Jinzhou | 0.110 | 0.163 | Wuxi | 0.173 | 0.126 |
| Baoding | 0.061 | 0.114 | Jiujiang | 0.073 | 0.127 | Wuzhong | 0.000 | 0.128 |
| Baoji | 0.015 | 0.120 | Kunming | 0.046 | 0.107 | Xiamen | 0.561 | 0.086 |
| Baotou | 0.056 | 0.126 | Langfang | 0.160 | 0.100 | Xian | 0.076 | 0.128 |
| Beijing | 0.265 | 0.114 | Lanzhou | 0.024 | 0.130 | Xiangfan | 0.058 | 0.138 |
| Benxi | 0.039 | 0.133 | Leshan | 0.034 | 0.118 | Xianyang | 0.050 | 0.114 |
| Cangzhou | 0.043 | 0.123 | Lianyungang | 0.202 | 0.111 | Xiaogan | 0.064 | 0.166 |
| Changchun | 0.141 | 0.125 | Linyi | 0.130 | 0.088 | Xining | 0.035 | 0.121 |
| Changde | 0.060 | 0.135 | Liuzhou | 0.071 | 0.131 | Xinxiang | 0.049 | 0.120 |
| Changsha | 0.080 | 0.151 | Luoyang | 0.010 | 0.144 | Xuchang | 0.041 | 0.139 |
| Changzhou | 0.118 | 0.139 | Maoming | 0.129 | 0.126 | Xuzhou | 0.075 | 0.153 |
| Chengdu | 0.126 | 0.115 | Mianyang | 0.057 | 0.118 | Yancheng | 0.051 | 0.138 |
| Chenzhou | 0.031 | 0.153 | Nanchang | 0.099 | 0.096 | Yangzhou | 0.114 | 0.120 |
| Chongqing | 0.059 | 0.135 | Nanjing | 0.211 | 0.138 | Yantai | 0.192 | 0.097 |
| Chuzhou | 0.067 | 0.115 | Nanning | 0.080 | 0.136 | Yibin | 0.009 | 0.147 |
| Dalian | 0.441 | 0.094 | Nantong | 0.184 | 0.104 | Yichang | 0.106 | 0.109 |
| Daqing | 0.013 | 0.182 | Nanyang | 0.033 | 0.130 | Yichun | 0.041 | 0.182 |
| Datong | 0.056 | 0.140 | Ningbo | 0.209 | 0.140 | Yinchuan | 0.042 | 0.091 |
| Deyang | 0.044 | 0.138 | Qingdao | 0.203 | 0.090 | Yueyang | 0.053 | 0.087 |
| Dongguan | 0.807 | 0.081 | Qinhuangdao | 0.194 | 0.098 | Yuncheng | 0.013 | 0.175 |
| Foshan | 0.348 | 0.125 | Qiqihaer | 0.014 | 0.097 | Yuxi | 0.079 | 0.179 |

| | | | | | | | | |
|---|---|---|---|---|---|---|---|---|
| Fushun | 0.079 | 0.142 | Quanzhou | 0.486 | 0.139 | Zhangjiakou | 0.107 | 0.104 |
| Fuzhou | 0.390 | 0.116 | Qujing | 0.035 | 0.149 | Zhangzhou | 0.395 | 0.100 |
| Ganzhou | 0.299 | 0.128 | Sanming | 0.078 | 0.136 | Zhengzhou | 0.066 | 0.115 |
| Guangzhou | 0.459 | 0.106 | Shanghai | 0.413 | 0.123 | Zhoukou | 0.039 | 0.101 |
| Guilin | 0.082 | 0.150 | Shangqiu | 0.009 | 0.082 | Zhuhai | 0.692 | 0.093 |
| Guiyang | 0.071 | 0.137 | Shangrao | 0.027 | 0.134 | Zhuzhou | 0.051 | 0.173 |
| Haerbing | 0.083 | 0.111 | Shantou | 0.274 | 0.119 | Zibo | 0.073 | 0.110 |
| Haikou | 0.226 | 0.149 | Shaoxing | 0.078 | 0.132 | Zunyi | 0.028 | 0.138 |
| Handan | 0.047 | 0.174 | Shenyang | 0.210 | 0.141 | Jilin | 0.073 | 0.125 |
| Hangzhou | 0.254 | 0.112 | Shenzhen | 0.674 | 0.075 | Jinan | 0.057 | 0.124 |
| Hefei | 0.205 | 0.101 | Shijiazhuang | 0.059 | 0.129 | Jingmen | 0.115 | 0.125 |
| Hengyang | 0.006 | 0.105 | Suzhou | 0.665 | 0.082 | Jingzhou | 0.058 | 0.130 |
| Huanggang | 0.071 | 0.184 | Taian | 0.070 | 0.103 | Jinhua | 0.053 | 0.157 |
| Huhehaote | 0.056 | 0.098 | Taiyuan | 0.019 | 0.156 | Weifang | 0.105 | 0.116 |
| Huizhou | 0.696 | 0.081 | Taizhou | 0.055 | 0.158 | Weihai | 0.167 | 0.079 |
| Huzhou | 0.106 | 0.121 | Tangshan | 0.124 | 0.113 | Wenzhou | 0.051 | 0.176 |
| Jiangmen | 0.586 | 0.038 | Tianjin | 0.294 | 0.134 | Wuhan | 0.108 | 0.118 |
| Jiaxing | 0.190 | 0.119 | Tianshui | 0.027 | 0.151 | Wuhu | 0.101 | 0.143 |

Source: From Clarke and Xu (ongoing). Based on investment climate survey in China, World Bank. Unit of observations is by districts within a city.

this is what we find in China (Clarke and Xu, ongoing): the higher the district-level average tax burden, the lower the foreign direct ownership in the district.

The cross-country literature has emphasized the role of property rights protection in ensuring investors' rights and their willingness to invest. Keefer and Kanck (1997), for example, find that developing countries with better institutions grow and converge faster than similar countries with bad institutions. Fan et al. (2006), using a subsample of low institution countries, find that FDI inflow per capita is positively related to government quality and expected growth. Similarly, research done within China also finds the importance of property rights for firms' decision to reinvest. Cull and Xu (2005) use firm-level evidence, coupled with city-level variations in property rights protection, and find that the reinvestment rate increases with government's contract enforcement mechanisms (as proxied by the percent of disputes resolved via courts), and decreases with government expropriation (as proxied by the lack of government helpfulness in firm-government interactions, and informal payment as a share of sales).

A final factor that I consider for MPK differences and capital inflow is the differences in livability. Some cities simply are more attractive, featuring such amenities as nice beaches, fewer traffic jams, better quality of air and water, and so on. Not surprisingly, many of these cities, such as Dalian, Qingdao, and Shanghai, also attract much more FDI than other cities. This is not surprising since the amount of FDI is often associated with the expatriates working for multinational corporations who live in the investment destinations, as better amenities would be more attractive to them. Indeed, Clarke and Xu (ongoing) find that FDI inflow are larger in districts that feature better air quality and a higher restaurant density, holding constant the usual suspects like the level of development, infrastructure, wage rates, tax burdens, and the protection of property rights.

### New Evidence

To further shed light on why firms differ in their MPK, and what is the role played by the various usual suspects and unusual suspects,

I directly estimate the determinants of MPK in the following equation:

$$MPK_{ijt} = f(K/L, M/L, L; X).$$

Here $K/L$ is the capital-labor ratio, $M/L$ is the material usage per capita, and $L$ is the number of employees. $X$ represents the other determinants of MPK and includes the firm's effective tax rate, the amount of corruption, protection of property rights, managerial time costs in dealing with government regulation and other burdens, access to finance, the corruption of the financial sector, judicial efficiency, customs efficiency, local leaders' age, tenure, and the owners' promotion from within. (This list can be derived from the standard Cobb-Douglas production function in which the technical efficiency part depends on the local business environment, broadly defined to include those market-supporting institutions [finance, court, customs], direct government expropriation [tax, time burden, corruption], managerial ability, and time horizon [age, promotion from within, and average tenure of the past three top local leaders].)

The data we use to calculate MPK is the most recent World Bank Investment Climate Survey, which contains information from 120 cities in almost all the Chinese provinces. These cities jointly account for 70 to 80 percent of China's GDP, and are thus quite representative of China as a whole. The MPK is derived from the estimates of the firm-level Cobb-Douglas output-capital-labor-material production function.[2] In the estimation we allow for firm fixed effects and industry-specific coefficients of factors. As illustrated in Table 5.4, the results suggest that marginal product of local Chinese firms is very sensitive to how the local economy is governed:

1. MPK is not related to the region's tax rate or amount of corruption, contrary to conventional wisdom.

2. The time costs of dealing with regulators and officials also do not affect MPK.

3. Market-supporting institutions matter a great deal:

   a. Banks: Access to finance increases MPK, while corrupt banks reduce MPK. Thus inefficiency in the financial sector may partly account for the large variations in MPK across regions.

## Table 5.4
## Determinants of Marginal Product of Capital in Chinese Firms: Y = log(MPK)

| | | | |
|---|---|---|---|
| log(K/L) | −0.793 | −0.794 | −0.798 |
| | (184.44)*** | (183.72)*** | (184.15)*** |
| ln(M/L), M=material | 0.458 | 0.450 | 0.448 |
| | (85.71)*** | (82.25)*** | (81.75)*** |
| ln(L) | 0.015 | 0.024 | 0.015 |
| | (3.89)*** | (6.13)*** | (3.83)*** |
| mean effective tax burden | 0.042 | 0.093 | 0.121 |
| | (0.22) | (0.47) | (0.62) |
| mean entertainment/travel costs in sales | −0.963 | −0.886 | −0.839 |
| | (1.24) | (1.16) | (1.11) |
| mean share of managerial time in dealing with four specific gov't bureaus | −0.290 | −0.153 | −0.151 |
| | (0.80) | (0.42) | (0.42) |
| mean share of managerial time in dealing with government officials | −0.114 | −0.165 | −0.153 |
| | (0.59) | (0.86) | (0.79) |
| mean share of loans needing bribes | −0.392 | −0.334 | −0.343 |
| | (4.45)*** | (3.82)*** | (3.89)*** |
| log(court time to resolve commercial disputes) | −0.175 | −0.186 | −0.185 |
| | (4.05)*** | (4.27)*** | (4.23)*** |
| mean share of college-educated employees | 1.035 | 1.089 | 0.987 |
| | (13.40)*** | (14.40)*** | (12.85)*** |
| mean access to loans | 0.247 | 0.261 | 0.269 |
| | (7.40)*** | (7.78)*** | (8.02)*** |
| log(mean days passing customs) | −0.161 | −0.127 | −0.127 |
| | (10.70)*** | (8.35)*** | (8.30)*** |
| dummy: city secretary internally promoted | 0.038 | 0.036 | 0.038 |
| | (2.92)*** | (2.79)*** | (2.90)*** |
| ln(city secretary age) | 0.175 | 0.140 | 0.138 |
| | (2.26)** | (1.81)* | (1.79)* |
| avg tenure of city secretary | 0.009 | 0.010 | 0.009 |
| | (1.50) | (1.56) | (1.46) |
| log(firm age) | | −0.031 | −0.038 |
| | | (4.81)*** | (5.77)*** |
| collective ownership | | 0.155 | 0.156 |
| | | (6.23)*** | (6.31)*** |
| legal-person ownership | | 0.198 | 0.194 |
| | | (10.39)*** | (10.20)*** |
| domestic private ownership | | 0.133 | 0.130 |
| | | (7.11)*** | (6.90)*** |
| foreign ownership | | 0.289 | 0.278 |
| | | (12.11)*** | (11.73)*** |
| CEO years of schooing | | | 0.030 |
| | | | (11.96)*** |
| CEO experience in this firm | | | 0.006 |
| | | | (5.87)*** |
| ind, year dummies | yes | yes | yes |
| Observations | 25315 | 25303 | 25276 |
| R-squared | 0.78 | 0.78 | 0.78 |

* significant at 10%; ** significant at 5%; *** significant at 1%. White-corrected error, and clustering at the district-year level.
Source: From Clarke and Xu (ongoing). Based on investment climate survey in China, World Ban.

b. Judicial/Legal System: if courts are not efficient, as measured by long times needed to resolve a commercial dispute, this leads to lower MPK.

c. Customs: a long customs delay is associated with lower MPK.

4. Human capital matters: Cities with a higher share of college graduates have higher MPK. This finding is consistent with a common explanation for cross-country variations in capital intensity.

5. The characteristics of chief executive officers (CEOs) matter: MPK is higher when CEO schooling and CEO experience increases.

6. A city's leadership matters: MPK is higher for firms located in cities whose top leaders are more experienced, are promoted internally within the city, and have long tenure.

7. Ownership matters: In China, MPK is highest in foreign-owned firms, followed by legal-person ownership, private and collective firms, and finally state-owned firms. This difference again indicates that within China there is room for improvement in capital allocation, mainly for state-owned firms.

## Conclusion

The evidence from China suggests that regional variations in inflows of FDI and marginal productivity of capital can readily be explained by some of the usual suspects as well as ones that are surprising. These include a region's tax burden, level of corruption, expected growth rate, infrastructure, access to financial services, the efficiency of customs and the judicial process, and quality of life. Given the vast variations in all these aspects among in various regions in China, due to the country's decentralized nature and geography, the large variations in capital-labor ratio and marginal product of capital are not too difficult to reconcile. The fact that MPK depends on ownership, local leadership, and financial services suggests that allocative inefficiencies may well play a part in these regional variations. The fundamental causes of these differences—their relative importance, and how important is the magnitude of inefficiency—requires further investigation.

## Notes

1. It is assumed that it is easier to collect taxes from larger firms than from small firms (Gordon and Li 2004).

2. In particular, the MPK is derived as follows. Let technology be $y = AL^\alpha k^\beta m^\gamma$, where $y$ is output (as proxied by sales in constant value) per worker, $k$ is capital-labor ratio, $m$ is material expenditure per employee, and $L$ is the number of employees. Then MPK $= \beta AL^\alpha k^{\beta-1} m^\gamma$. Capital is measured as the net value of fixed assets, the only proxy we have for capital. The production function is estimated industry by industry, allowing for firm fixed effects.

## References

Allen, Franklin, Meijun Qian, and Jun Qian. 2005. "Law, Finance, and Economic Growth in China." *Journal of Financial Economics* 77(1): 57–116.

Brandt, Loren, and Hongbin Li. 2003. "Bank Discrimination in Transition Economies: Ideology, Information, or Incentives." *Journal of Comparative Economics* 31(3): 387–413.

Clarke, George, Lixin Colin Xu. Ongoing. "Explaining FDI Inflow into Chinese Cities." World Bank.

Cull, Robert, and Lixin Colin Xu. 2000. "Bureaucrats, State Banks, and the Efficiency of Credit Allocation: The Experience of Chinese State-Owned Enterprises." *Journal of Comparative Economics* 28(1): 1–31.

Cull, Robert, and Lixin Colin Xu. 2003. "Who Gets Credit? The Behavior of Bureaucrats and State Banks in Allocating Credit to Chinese State-Owned Enterprises." *Journal of Development Economics* 71(2): 533–559.

Cull, Robert, and Lixin Colin Xu. 2005. "Institutions, Ownership, and Finance: The Determinants of Profit Reinvestment among Chinese Firms." *Journal of Financial Economics* 77(1): 117–146.

Cull, Robert, Lixin Colin Xu, and Tian Zhu. 2007. "Formal Finance and Trade Credit during China's Transition." Policy Research Working Paper 4204. Washington, D.C.: World Bank.

Fan, Joseph, Randall Morck, Lixin Colin Xu, Bernard Yeung. 2006. "Does 'Good Government' Draw Foreign Capital? Explaining China's Exceptional FDI Inflow." Background paper prepared for the Singapore conference on China-India Comparison, World Bank.

Gordon, Roger, and Wei Li. 2004. "Tax Structures in Developing Countries: Puzzles and Possible Explanations." Working Paper, University of Virginia.

Keefer, Philip, and Stephen Knack. 1997. "Why Don't Poor Countries Catch Up? A Cross-National Test of Institutional Explanation." *Economic Inquiry* 35(3): 590–602.

Li, Hongbin, and Li-An Zhou. 2005. "Political Turnover and Economic Performance: The Incentive Role of Personnel Control in China." *Journal of Public Economics* 89(9-10): 1743–1762.

Mengistae, Taye, Lixin Colin Xu, and Bernard Yeung. 2006. "China vs. India: A Microeconomic Look at Comparative Macroeconomic Performance." Background paper prepared for the Singapore conference on China-India Comparison, World Bank.

# 6

# Imbalances between Savings and Investment

# Understanding Global Imbalances

Richard N. Cooper

Two contemporary issues provide reason to focus on national savings and investment. First, the debate over public pensions, and pensions more generally, taking place in all rich countries. Second, the large global current account imbalances that conceptually represent the difference between national savings and domestic investment. Are all of us living in advanced economies saving enough to provide adequate retirement income for our rapidly aging populations? This question is especially pertinent to Americans, whose household savings rate seems to have disappeared altogether in 2005. And are the countries with large external deficits—notably the United States—inappropriately mortgaging the income of future generations, not to mention courting financial calamity in the meantime?

This paper will not answer either question definitively, but I hope to shed some light both on the issue of saving adequately for retirement, and especially on the second issue of the potential risks posed by large external deficits. The United States will be the focus of attention, but in an increasingly interconnected global economy it is anachronistic to focus on domestic factors alone—and it is simply inappropriate when the issue is the country's external deficit: equal attention must be devoted to the counterpart surpluses elsewhere in the world.

Let's start with some factual background. Table 6.1 shows that the U.S. current account deficit rose steadily from 1995 to 2006, except for a brief pause in the recession year of 2001, both in dollar terms and as a percentage of GDP. This deficit rose from 1.2 percent of GDP in 1995 to 6.0 percent in 2006, the highest annual current account deficit recorded in U.S. history, before receding to 5.3 percent in 2007. In accounting terms, with

**Table 6.1**
U.S. Current Account, Investment, and Saving[a]

| | Current Account Deficit | | | Saving | | Statistical Discrepancy |
|---|---|---|---|---|---|---|
| | ($bn) | (    <= | Investment | Private Percent of GNP | Public | =>    ) |
| 1993 | 72 | 1.1 | 17.5 | 16.2 | −1.8 | −2.1 |
| 1994 | 107 | 1.5 | 18.5 | 15.7 | −0.6 | −2.0 |
| 1995 | 92 | 1.2 | 18.5 | 16.2 | −0.3 | −1.4 |
| 1996 | 101 | 1.3 | 18.9 | 15.8 | 0.7 | −1.2 |
| 1997 | 111 | 1.3 | 19.7 | 15.6 | 1.9 | −0.8 |
| 1998 | 188 | 2.1 | 20.2 | 15.2 | 3.1 | 0.2 |
| 1999 | 279 | 3.0 | 20.6 | 14.3 | 3.7 | 0.4 |
| 2000 | 397 | 4.0 | 20.7 | 13.5 | 4.4 | 1.3 |
| 2001 | 371 | 3.7 | 19.1 | 13.8 | 2.5 | 0.9 |
| 2002 | 460 | 4.4 | 18.3 | 14.9 | −0.7 | 0.2 |
| 2003 | 515 | 4.7 | 18.3 | 14.8 | −1.6 | −0.4 |
| 2004 | 626 | 5.3 | 19.2 | 14.9 | −1.2 | −0.2 |
| 2005 | 739 | 5.9 | 19.8 | 14.3 | −0.4 | 0.0 |
| 2006 | 798 | 6.0 | 19.9 | 13.5 | 0.5 | 0.1 |
| 2007ᴾ | 739 | 5.3 | | | | |

[a]National accounts basis; differs from balance of payments basis in coverage and timing.
Current account deficit in 2006 was $811 billion in the balance of payments.
*Source:* Bureau of Economic Analysis.

small qualifications, the current account deficit represents both net foreign investment in the United States, and the difference between domestic investment and national saving. Thus a 5 percentage point rise over a decade suggests either that U.S. investment must have increased, or that U.S. saving must have declined.

Table 6.1 provides information on gross domestic investment (including government investment) and on gross private and public saving in the United States over the period 1993–2006. If we compare 2004 with 1995, there was a modest increase in investment and a modest decline in private saving, together amounting to 2.0 percent of GDP, or only about half the change in the current account. Investment grew strongly to 2000, and private saving declined sharply (4.9 percentage points together), but investment declined during the subsequent recession and then recovered somewhat, while private savings grew to 2004. Compared with the current account, it is interesting how little variation domestic investment and private saving showed over the decade, with a range of barely more than 2 percentage points each, although in 2000 saving reached its low point when investment was at its highest. There are however two additional columns in Table 6.1: government savings and statistical discrepancy. Both columns show substantial variation. The public sector was in rough balance in 1995, with state and local government saving almost offsetting federal government dissaving. The federal budget then improved significantly, running surpluses for the four fiscal years between 1998 and 2001. On national account definitions, gross government saving was positive from 1996 through 2001, reaching a peak of 4.4 percent of GDP in 2000. With the 2001 recession, the federal tax cuts of 2001 and 2003, and increases in federal spending associated with homeland security, the war in Iraq, and farm support, the federal budget moved into deficit again and in 2004 gross government saving was negative by 1.6 percent of GDP—a swing of 6 percentage points from 2000. Yet state and local governments remained gross savers throughout this period, their capital expenditures exceeding their collective modest budget deficits in 2002 and 2003.

To sum up, over the past decade the movements of U.S. domestic investment and private saving alone should have been associated with a deterioration of the nation's current account deficit of 4.9 percent points of GDP 1995 to 2000, compared with the actual deterioration of 2.8 percentage points, and with an improvement during the 2000–2006 period of 0.8 percentage points, compared with a further deterioration of 2.0 percentage points. The discrepancies are explained partly by movements in public saving, which increased by 4.7 percentage points from 1995–2000, but declined by an astonishing 5.6 percentage points over 2000–2004, and by 3.9 percentage points during 2000–2006. Moreover, all such figures are subject to measurement errors, and the statistical discrepancy swung positively by 2.7 percentage points in the 1995–2000 period, which suggests that the investment boom was stronger than actually measured, or that private U.S. saving declined by more than measured. In the 2000–2006 period, the statistical discrepancy swung by 1.2 percentage points in a negative direction.

As shown in Table 6.1, the modest decline in U.S. private saving over the 1995–2006 period is at odds with frequent media references to a sharp decline in savings rates in the United States. Indeed, household saving as a percent of disposable income declined from around 10 percent in the early 1980s, a period marked both by high inflation and a severe recession, to 4.6 percent in 1995, then 1.8 percent in 2004, and apparently became negative in 2005 and 2006. Private savings, as reported in Table 6.1, cover the entire private sector, including corporate retained earnings, and these figures are gross amounts, meaning these include corporate depreciation allowances. Such an inclusion is entirely appropriate in a world of rapid technological change. We should care less about net additions to the measured capital stock than about improvements in the quality of capital, and improvements are usually possible with replacement investment. Almost all investment is new in this sense, and a well-governed corporation assesses any major investment afresh, whether it is financed out of depreciation allowances, retained earnings, or new capital.

The "saving" reported in Table 6.1 is drawn from the national income and product accounts, which have the advantage of being embedded in a well-considered, internally consistent accounting framework. But there are a number of reasons that the current set of national accounts, which were developed in the 1930s and the 1940s, do not well serve the modern knowledge economy, nor do these accounts adequately capture savings from the perspective of the individual household, whose reported saving rate is now near to zero.

Economists define "saving" as consumption that has been deferred in the current period with the objective of raising future consumption—if not one's own, then perhaps that of one's progeny. By this standard definition, much current U.S. spending on education should be counted as saving (and investment). Most people do not attend school or college for its current consumption value (although there may be some); rather, individuals pursue education, and forego earnings, because they or their parents (or society, through free compulsory education) believe it will improve their life prospects, including their future income. Evidence supports this belief: a summary of empirical work suggests that for individuals in the United States, an additional year of schooling increases annual earnings by roughly 10 percent (Card 1999). The rate of return on a college education for a white male has been reported to be 13 percent (CEA 1996). Americans spend a lot on education—7.2 percent of GDP in 2004 counting public and private spending together—and U.S. expenditures on education are notably higher than in most other countries. Yet educational spending is treated as public or private consumption in the national accounts. A similar claim could be made for certain health-related expenditures, such as immunization programs.

Consumer durables are a large part of household expenditure in the United States, 8.4 percent of GDP in 2004. While the services provided by these durables are, for accounting purposes, consumed in the year of purchase, these durables provide a stream of services for many additional years: over 10 years for the average automobile and over 20 years for some household furniture and appliances. Thus the purchase of consumer durables represents "saving"(and investment) in the strict sense of the term. Yet in the national accounts household purchases of appliances, automobiles, furniture, home computers, pianos, and television and audio equipment are treated as nondurable consumption goods (the purchase of new residential housing, including original appliances, *is* treated as investment). While many such durable goods are discarded every year, the total U.S. stock of household durable goods is rising by about $250– 300 billion a year. In many cases, the replacement equipment is superior to discarded equipment, thanks again to continuing technical improvement, and promises to last even longer; thus, such purchases should more properly be regarded as investment.

Among American households, 70 percent own their residences, and for many years houses and condominiums increased in value, as have equities in the long-term trend. Capital gains do not add to the national stock of productive capital (although these may reflect retained earnings and intangible investments, on which more below), but such gains do add to the accessible wealth of individual households, hence to their ability to consume in the future. Thus from its perspective a household is "saving" by investing in housing or in the stock market. The net worth of American households has continued to rise from year to year (excepting modest setbacks in 2001 and 2002), averaging 6.4 percent a year from 1990–2006, to reach nearly $58 trillion at the end of 2006, which is over five times disposable income. Over 60 percent of gross household assets were held in the form of financial assets, the remainder being in home equity and durable goods. (These figures for household assets include nonprofit organizations, but they account for less than 10 percent of the total.)

This increase in U.S. household net worth has occurred despite substantial mortgage refinancing, and the consequential withdrawal of home equity, making it available for other purposes—to repay other consumer debt, to buy consumer durables (especially automobiles), or to finance vacations. Financial market innovations, such as home-equity loans and reverse mortgages, have increased the liquidity of home equity, making it increasingly available for other purposes. Of course, home equity as a potential liquid asset depends on home prices, which rose significantly over 1995–2005, but dropped from 2006, strongly in some regions, which reduces some of the "saving." Smith and Smith (2006), however, find house prices in many U.S. markets still below values justified by fundamentals such as rents, mortgage interest rates, and tax treatment. In the longer run, one of the fundamental factors is new household formation, which is likely to hold up better in the United States than in most other rich countries where birth rates have fallen more sharply and where immigration is less important.

Extensive net worth, especially among older U.S. households, suggests the likelihood of significant bequests to the next generation. For example, the 2004 Survey of Consumer Finances shows Americans in the 55-64-year-old age group with a mean net worth of $844,000, and those aged 65–74 years with a mean net worth of $691,000. Given high and increasing longevity, these bequests are likely to be received by persons in their late 50s or 60s and nearing traditional retirement age in the United States. Such generational transfers of course do not add to national productive wealth, but they do add to household wealth just as people are entering a period when they might need more financial capital to fund potentially long retirements. To the extent that such transfers are anticipated by the recipients, these expectations might act to reduce household savings out of current income.

Last but not least, there is the consideration of pension entitlements from both public and private sources. Publicly financed Social Security provides virtually all future American retirees, after the age of 66, with an annual income up to a maximum of $23,000, escalated for inflation. Career military and government employees have much more generous government-supported pension rights. Many private corporations have promised defined benefit postretirement pensions to their employees. While these defined benefit programs are in decline, and not all are fully honored due to corporate bankruptcy, they remain an important claim by millions of workers, for which corporations are enjoined to save—one reason for the growth in corporate saving in recent years, to a cumulative total of $1.8 trillion in pension assets (Wilcox 2006). These pensions are publicly guaranteed up to a maximum annual amount of $48,000 (escalated for inflation), and while the Pension Benefit Guaranty Corporation is now technically insolvent, few doubt that it will somehow be preserved by government action. (Defined benefit plans have gradually given way to defined contribution plans, but their value is included in the household net worth discussed above.)

The United States is noted, among rich countries, for having relatively generous terms for personal bankruptcy, and only modest social inhibitions for invoking this status in case of burdensome personal debt. It remains to be seen whether the recent tightening of the conditions for personal bankruptcy will result in a discernable increase in personal savings.

In short, the average U.S. household appears to have many sources of future income. It is not clear that it needs to save more, as such behavior is measured in the current system of national accounts, or that it will do so. Of course, there is a wide dispersion of household net worth; direct equity ownership in particular is highly concentrated. Many households should no doubt save more given their own self-interests. But if concern is really with destitution or even genteel poverty for some people in retirement, that should be the focus of policymakers' attention, rather than lamenting the low total of private household savings in the United States.

Yet an entire society is less than the sum of its parts when it comes to savings behavior. A private perspective differs from an all-encompassing social perspective. Nations need to be concerned with an adequate flow of total income, not counting transfers between buyers and sellers or between benefactors and heirs. Capital gains per se do not add to a country's capital stock, although these may reflect additions to the capital stock, including especially the growth of intangible capital, as we shall see.

But the United States does not do a good job of measuring corporate saving either. This is most obvious in the case of spending on research and development (R&D), which is clearly motivated by the expectation of future payoffs (and is thus, strictly speaking, savings and investment). Except when undertaken directly by government, spending on research and development does not enter into the national accounts at all, but rather is handled as an intermediate business expense, netted out in calculating final demand and output. (Apparently an agreement has been reached within the OECD to change this practice in the coming years.) Yet on such evidence as we have, U.S. spending on research and development produces exceptionally high rates of return, roughly 25 percent in terms of private return and 50 percent in terms of social return (see Fraumeni and Okubo 2005, p. 279), and a mean of 100 percent on agricultural research (see Frederico 2005, p. 112). But the point is not limited to expenditures on research and development. Corrado, Hulten, and Sichel (2006) estimate that there may be $3.6 trillion of intangible capital in the U.S. corporate sector and $1 trillion annual investment, built through systematic expenditure on research and development, personnel training, and branding, that is not recorded either as investment or as part of the capital stock, even though this intangible capital generates future value. It exceeded investment by the business sector in tangible capital (excluding housing) by 120 percent. Counting it would have added nearly $1 trillion annually to GDP during the period 2000–2003.

The basic system of national accounts was developed in the 1930s and 1940s, at the height of the industrial age, and strongly emphasizes physical capital as the major source of future earnings. This legacy does not serve well a knowledge-based economy, where value lies increasingly in teams of highly skilled employees operating in complex interdependent systems. Physical capital of course plays an important role in the contemporary economy, but the key to generating future income streams is building the teams and product innovation.

Expenditures to build intangible capital may be expected to raise equity prices, so some of the "capital gains" that are not recorded as personal income or saving may in fact reflect the accumulation of capital, both tangible and intangible, through retained earnings (including depreciation allowances) by corporate business. In addition to funding defined benefit retirement plans, corporations in this way are saving on behalf of individuals.

Government investment is now included in the national accounts as investment rather than consumption (with allowance made also for depreciation), but with the same emphasis on bricks and mortar (and on durable weapons platforms such as aircraft carriers) as private investment. Expenditures on research and development, education, and public health are counted as consumption, not investment. If American expenditures on durable goods, education, and research and development are reclassified as saving, U.S. private saving, plus public expenditure on education and research and development, is one-third of GDP. Allowing for expenditures on intangible capital beyond R&D would raise the savings ratio even further. This does not sound like shortchanging the future. (This reclassification should also be made for other countries, of course, but the magnitude of the additional contribution would be considerably smaller in all but a few countries.)

The federal budget went from deficit to surplus to deficit again during the past decade, while the U.S. current account deficit grew continuously. Thus there is no easy one-to-one relationship between the government deficit and the external deficit, as the current experiences of Australia, with its budget surplus and large current account deficit, and of Japan, with its large budget deficit and large current account surplus, should remind us. Other things equal, however, a larger budget deficit increases the current account deficit by raising yields on long-term U.S. Treasury securities, regarded around the world as attractive investment instruments, higher than these would otherwise be.

The foreign exchange market for the U.S. dollar is not subject to systematic U.S. intervention; the U.S. dollar floats against other currencies that are allowed to float. The U.S. current account deficit is large because foreign investment in the United States is large. Table 6.2 shows foreign capital inflows, private and public, and U.S. capital outflows for the 2000–2007 period. Over $1 trillion in foreign private funds entered the United States in 2004—much larger than the current account deficit in that year—and again in 2006 and 2007. Indeed, foreign private capital inflows have exceeded the U.S. current account deficits, usually by substantial amounts, in every year since significant deficits began in the early 1980s. In addition, nearly $400 billion of foreign official funds, reflecting a buildup of foreign exchange reserves in central banks, also entered the United States in 2004, dropping to $259 billion in 2005 but exceeding $400 billion in 2006 and 2007. It has been said that foreign central banks are financing the U.S. current account deficit and, incidentally, the U.S. budget deficit. This is an inappropriate attribution of selective inflows against selective outflows in the U.S. balance of payments. It would be as true to say, as France's President de Gaulle did in 1963, that foreign central banks (partially) financed U.S. capital outflows.

Why are so many foreign funds being invested in the United States? The answer lies partly in the attractiveness of U.S. financial assets, which are claims on a robust, innovative economy offering good returns, liquidity, security, and relative stability. But the answer lies also in the high savings relative to investment opportunities present in other economies, particularly but not exclusively in other rich countries. Investment opportunities have been limited in Japan and continental Europe, while savings remain relatively high in these countries. The excess private savings have been partially, but only partially, absorbed by large budget deficits in other major countries, such as Japan and Germany. The difference has been invested abroad. In addition, since the rise in world oil prices started in 2003, oil-exporting countries have seen their export revenues soar, and with that also their current account surpluses. Table 6.3 provides data on the allocation of current account positions in 1997, 2000, 2005, and 2006. An increase in the U.S. current account deficit of about $400 billion over the 2000–2006 period was accompanied by even greater increases in the current account surpluses of Japan, Germany plus its close economic associates the Netherlands and Switzerland, China, Russia, and the nations of the Middle East; the last two listings mainly reflect

**Table 6.2**
Capital Flows in the U.S. Balance of Payments
($ billion)

| | 2000 | 2001 | 2002 | 2003 | 2004 | 2005 | 2006 | 2007ᴾ |
|---|---|---|---|---|---|---|---|---|
| Foreign Capital Inflow | 1047 | 783 | 798 | 864 | 1462 | 1204 | 1860 | 1864 |
| Private | 1004 | 755 | 682 | 586 | 1064 | 945 | 1419 | 1451 |
| Official | 43 | 28 | 116 | 278 | 398 | 259 | 440 | 413 |
| U.S. Capital Outflow | 561 | 383 | 295 | 325 | 905 | 427 | 1055 | 1206 |
| Private | 559 | 377 | 291 | 327 | 910 | 447 | 1063 | 1183 |
| Official | 1 | 5 | 3 | −2 | −4 | −20 | −8 | 23 |
| Stat. Discrepancy | −69 | −10 | −42 | −13 | 86 | −18 | −18 | 84 |

p = preliminary
*Source:* www.bea.gov

**Table 6.3**
Current Account Balances
($ bn)

|                                          | 1997 | 2000 | 2005 | 2006 |
|------------------------------------------|------|------|------|------|
| United States                            | −141 | −417 | −755 | −811 |
| Japan                                    | 97   | 120  | 166  | 170  |
| Germany, Netherlands, Switzerland        | 41   | 5    | 230  | 263  |
| Hong Kong, Korea, Singapore, Taiwan      | 39   | 80   | 88   | 91   |
| Other advanced economies                 | 29   | −58  | −166 | −230 |
| China                                    | 34   | 21   | 161  | 250  |
| Other Developing Asia                    | −27  | 18   | −4   | 28   |
| Central and Eastern Europe               | −21  | −32  | −62  | −88  |
| Commonwealth of Independent States       | −9   | 48   | 88   | 98   |
| Middle East                              | 11   | 72   | 197  | 234  |
| Western Hemisphere                       | −67  | -48  | 35   | 45   |
| Africa                                   | −6   | 8    | 16   | 29   |
| Discrepancy                              | 14   | −179 | 7    | 87   |
| NB: fuel exporters                       | 16   | 151  | 348  | 423  |

*Source:* IMF *World Economic Outlook,* September 2005 and April 2008

the impact of higher oil prices on their current account balances. Central Europe and other rich countries (mainly Spain, Britain, and Australia) experienced negative movements in their current accounts, while Latin America (including oil-exporting Venezuela but also Brazil) experienced a significant positive movement. For most years there is a significant statistical discrepancy, indicating higher recorded deficits than surpluses.

The surpluses of the members of the Organization of Petroleum Exporting Countries (OPEC)—mainly the Middle Eastern countries plus Venezuela and Nigeria—will undoubtedly decline after several years, either as oil prices decline or as the oil-exporting countries learn to spend their higher income, which accrues initially to governments in almost all significant oil-exporting countries. The International Monetary Fund, however, projects these surpluses to rise somewhat in 2008 and to recede but remain high through 2009 (IMF 2008, p. 258). Thus these surpluses can be considered transitory, although enduring for several more years.

Augmented Germany, China, and Japan have the largest surpluses after the oil-exporting countries. Table 6.4 provides data for recent years on national saving and domestic investment in Japan and Germany, along with the newly rich Asian economies of Hong Kong, Singapore, South Korea, and Taiwan, and developing Asia. Saving has declined in Japan, and private saving even more since 2000, as the large public sector deficit declined from 7.7 to 5.8 percent of GDP, 2000–2005. In Germany alone, savings rose slightly, and private savings even more, since the government deficit rose by 4 percentage points between 2000 and 2005. Savings levels remained roughly unchanged in the four Asian Tigers, and rose a remarkable 8 percentage points in developing Asia, which is dominated quantitatively by China but also includes India, Indonesia, and a number of other significant developing countries. All these regions record significantly higher saving rates than the United States, as indeed do other regions of the world, including Latin America and Africa, but for reasons discussed earlier, the real difference is lower than the recorded difference.

What is more noteworthy is the decline in investment in most other rich economies, including Japan, Germany, and newly rich Asia. Recorded

**Table 6.4**
Savings and Investment
(percent of GDP)

|  |  | 1992–1999 | 2000 | 2005 | 2006 |
|---|---|---|---|---|---|
| Japan | S | 30.6 | 27.8 | 27.2 | 27.8 |
|  | I | 28.1 | 25.2 | 23.6 | 24 |
| Germany | S | 21 | 20.1 | 21.7 | 22.8 |
|  | I | 21.9 | 21.8 | 17.1 | 17.8 |
| Newly Rich Asian Economies[a] | S | 33.8 | 31.9 | 31.3 | 31.4 |
|  | I | 31.1 | 28.4 | 25.9 | 26 |
| Developing Asia | S | 31.8 | 30.3 | 41.3 | 43.8 |
|  | I | 32.3 | 28.2 | 37.2 | 37.9 |

[a]Hong Kong, South Korea, Singapore, Taiwan
*Source:* IMF, *World Economic Outlook*, September 2006 and April 2008

physical investment remains higher in most places than in the United States. Germany (along with the United Kingdom) is the major exception; there investment has been in a slump for some years. In developing Asia, by contrast, investment has risen sharply, led by China where investment exceeds 40 percent of GDP, an amount that is considered to be too high both by Chinese authorities and by some foreign analysts. This is the only such case of a developing country with too much investment (as distinguished from investment in the wrong places) that I can recall. But the growth of investment in China has fallen short of its increase in saving. Rapid economic growth permits China's consumption to rise rapidly even when the rate of saving increases.

Recall that, apart from measurement errors, a country's current account position (which equals net foreign investment) is the difference between domestic investment and national savings. Thus saving in excess of domestic investment (or private saving in excess of investment plus government deficits) implies investment abroad, net of inward flows of foreign investment. Why are several of the world's major economies investing so much abroad?

A major part of the answer, I believe, lies in demographic trends. Birth rates have declined in all rich countries, although differentially, and in many developing countries as well, most notably China, which introduced its one-child policy in 1979. The result is the prospect, or the actuality in Japan and Germany, of declining population growth, despite an increase in longevity. More pertinent than total population for saving and investment is the change in the age composition of populations. In most advanced economies, the aging of societies, with its implications for pensions and healthcare, has been widely discussed. Less widely discussed has been the decline in the population of young adults—those individuals who receive contemporary education, enter the labor force, form new households, and require housing and, for their children, schooling. For China, Germany, Japan, and the United States, the world's four largest economies, Table 6.5 shows the population aged 15–29 years in 2005 and this age cohort's projection to 2025. Apart from the United States, where birth rates have declined less than in other rich countries, and where immigration continues to be an important source of new young adults, the projected decline in this age group is remarkable. Yet this is the age

**Table 6.5**
Population Aged 15–29 Years

| | (million) | | (percent) |
|---|---|---|---|
| | 2005 | 2025 | Change |
| China | 321 | 259 | –19 |
| Germany | 14.2 | 11.9 | –16 |
| Japan | 22.6 | 17.8 | –21 |
| United States | 61.9 | 66 | 7 |

*Source:* U.S. Census Bureau

group that provides the most educated, most flexible (occupationally and geographically) new members of the labor force. A decline in this age group not only implies a loss in economic flexibility, but also a decline in the need for investment to equip new members of the labor force, for investment in housing and its accoutrements, and for investment in education. Residential housing investment, in particular, is reduced to less than full replacement plus some allowance for geographic mobility in rich countries. In poor growing countries such as China, demand for housing will remain robust as the population upgrades housing quality, as well as moves from rural to urban areas.

With these demographic trends, the prospects for significant increases in domestic investment in rich countries are limited. Replacement of obsolete equipment, necessary in a world of continuous technical change, will continue to take place. Some capital deepening will continue to occur, although that implies lower returns to capital, making such investment unattractive compared with investment abroad. Investment in Germany and Japan is closely related to export prospects. If these weaken due to appreciating currencies, investment is likely to suffer.

The United States stands out among the world's rich countries as having a prospective continued rise in young population, partly because the fertility rate has declined noticeably less in the United States than in other rich countries (to 2.1 children per woman of childbearing age, compared with 1.4 in Japan and Germany, and 1.0 in Hong Kong and Singapore), partly because of continuing immigration on a significant scale.

The future needs of aging, low-growth societies with limited domestic investment opportunities can be met by profitable external investment. (Excess private savings can be, and in Germany and Japan have been, absorbed in financing budget deficits, but most government expenditures are not oriented toward increasing future income.) This is what is happening now. Most countries with prospective declines in new entrants to the labor force show significant current account surpluses, reflecting their foreign investment. Spain is a notable exception, as are several central European countries. These nations are below the rest of Europe in per capita income and are still in a catch-up phase, requiring additional productive investment; Spain is building vacation and retirement homes for many northern Europeans, as well as upgrading its housing stock.

This adjustment is what financial globalization is all about: a decline in home bias in the disposition of savings and investment, especially when indicated by structural economic changes, such as the demographic developments discussed above. Where should such investment take place? Conventional economic theory suggests it should take place in relatively poor countries, with low ratios of capital to labor, because returns in such environments should be higher there. But conventional theory is a vast oversimplification of the complex conditions that both attract global investment (investors want assurance that their investments are secure, subject only to business risk) and that make investment productive. These conditions require an appropriate social and political infrastructure—social order, physical security, rule of law, secure property rights, impartial dispute settlement, and so on. Many of these institutional conditions are not present in the world's poorest countries, and some of these are not present even in middle-income countries. Argentina, Bolivia, Russia, and Venezuela have reminded investors in recent years how insecure private property can be from political action, particularly foreign private property. So today global investors hardly approach very poor countries, unless these nations have exploitable natural resources, and they approach many emerging markets warily. And after the series of financial crises between 1994 and 2001, many emerging markets also approach international borrowing with a great deal of caution. As the memory of these painful experiences has receded with time, however, private foreign investment in emerging markets has begun to pick up, aided by low interest rates in capital-exporting countries and investors' desire for higher returns. During 2006, for instance, an estimated $650 billion in private funds flowed to developing countries, up from $187 billion in 2000. These went mainly to East Asia (primarily equity) and to central Europe (primarily debt), but a significant amount of foreign direct investment also occurred in Latin America (World Bank 2007, Tables 2.1–2.11).

However, it is not surprising that over the last decade much of the surplus saving in other rich countries went to the United States. The U.S. economy accounts for between 25 and 30 percent of world economic output. The social/political system is stable, private property is respected, and dispute settlement is reasonably quick and fair. Nearly half of the world's marketable securities (stocks and bonds) are issued in the United States. Returns there are better on average than in other rich countries, and more secure and reliable than in emerging markets. The American economy is innovative and relatively flexible. Its long-term future prospects are bright. Given these circumstances, it is not surprising that a growing fraction of world saving should be invested in the United States.

Indeed, in a fully globalized world economy, with no home bias, one would expect roughly 25–30 percent of world saving outside the United States to be invested in the United States—and 70-75 percent of U.S. saving to be invested abroad. Saving outside the United States in 2006 was $9.3 trillion, 27.5 percent of which is $2.5 trillion. U.S. private saving was about $1.8 trillion, 72.5 percent of which is $1.3 trillion. The difference is $1.2 trillion, which is larger than the U.S. current account deficit of $0.8 trillion in that year. Of course, home bias continues to be important, so investment abroad has not yet reached these large two-way amounts. But 15 percent of world saving, which will rise in value from year to year, does not seem to be an unsustainably large number; if anything it is on the low side. Yet that was enough to cover American investment abroad (less loans by U.S. banks, which are directly financed abroad) plus its current account deficit.

Some people are troubled that a significant amount of foreign investment in the United States, but still a minority of total foreign investment, is made by foreign monetary authorities, in the form of additions to their foreign exchange reserves that are held in U.S. Treasury or other securities. Japan added $480 billion to its reserves during the 2000–2005 period, and together the newly rich Asian economies added over $300 billion. Emerging markets and developing countries taken together (including OPEC members) added an astounding $1.5 trillion to their reserves, exceeding the net private capital inflow into these countries, and a further $1.9 trillion in 2006 and 2007. Why?

The reasons are varied. Oil exporters have experienced an unexpected increase in export receipts because of strong world demand and rising oil prices over the past five to seven years. Their imports have not grown correspondingly, but this is likely to be largely a question of timing. Oil prices may be expected to decline in the future, and oil-exporting countries will gradually move the higher earnings, initially accruing to their governments, into the income stream, which will ultimately lead to a higher demand for imports.

It should be noted that total foreign exchange reserves have grown enormously since the introduction of floating exchange rates in the mid–1970s, contrary to expectations of the advocates of floating exchange rates. Clearly countries are not comfortable with freely floating rates, desire at least to have the possibility of managing these rates, and therefore feel they need higher reserves as economies and foreign trade grow in value. This sentiment was strongly reinforced by the financial crises that took place between 1994 and 1999, in which reserves in several important countries proved to be totally inadequate to deal with the financial pressures on their currencies, initially more from residents than from nonresidents. Since 1999 the major exceptions to this trend of building up dollar reserves are the United States, Canada, and the European Central Bank.

In some cases the growth in reserves is the incidental by-product of an active exchange rate policy, designed to slow appreciation of the domestic currency or even to prevent appreciation altogether. The growth in reserves is not necessarily unwelcome in these circumstances, but it does create problems of monetary management since this buildup is the equivalent of open-market purchases in foreign rather than domestic securities. But the currency policy may itself be motivated by fundamental factors. As noted above, it makes sense for an aging Japan to invest heavily in foreign assets with positive yields rather than investing at home for lower yields or, worse yet, investing in government securities that finance construction projects with negligible social return. Yet private Japanese savers have been extraordinarily conservative; households keep much of their saving in the postal system, which is backed by the government but offers very low returns to the savers and perhaps, given the use of these funds, none to the nation as a whole. Through buying foreign exchange reserves, Japan's Ministry of Finance is assuring future real returns—command over real resources in the international market—to the entire nation, which through their conservative behavior would not be obtained by relying on private savers alone. In short, the Japanese monetary authorities are acting as financial intermediaries, converting what private savers want now into what they will need in future years. Foreign exchange risk is real to the individual investor, but it is not to the nation: by investing abroad, even in U.S. bonds, it secures a future claim on goods and services in the international market. (Given the magnitude of their reserves, Japanese authorities might be well advised to diversify them into some higher-yield foreign investments, as a number of other countries have done, and as China and South Korea decided to do in 2007.)

The most dramatic growth in U.S. dollar reserves, besides the OPEC member nations, has been taking place in China: an increase of $1.5 trillion from the end of 2000 to the end of 2007, outstripping even its very rapid growth in imports. This growth in reserves has been made possible by China's current account surplus, modest and without trend until 2005, when it shot upward to $159 billion, 19 percent of exports, and further to $250 billion in 2006; and by continued net private capital inflow, particularly of foreign direct investment.

But China still maintains severe restrictions on resident capital outflow. Given the rapid income growth in China in recent years, the high savings rate, and the limited domestic menu of financial investments that Chinese households can hold, mainly in bank savings accounts, the latent private Chinese demand for investment abroad is probably very high. Partly on residual communist doctrinal grounds, partly for the pragmatic reason of not wanting to undermine their fragile banking system, Chinese authorities are hesitant to move soon to full currency convertibility and free movement of capital. Nonetheless, the Peoples Bank of China, its central bank, can be thought of as investing abroad on behalf of the public, and against the day in which the Chinese currency will be fully convertible (a stated Chinese objective) and capital outflow may be large. It is undoubtedly true that China, unlike Japan, has many potentially profitable investments at home. But it is also true that the banking system as it is currently constituted does a poor job of allocating capital, and that, as noted earlier, in recent years Chinese authorities have considered aggregate domestic investment to be excessive. A similar argument may be made with respect to the more modest, but still significant, buildup of reserves by India and a number of other developing countries that continue to maintain controls on resident capital outflow.

Presumably savings will decline in other rich countries as their populations age; this is implied by the life-cycle hypothesis. But the decline may be a very gradual one. Simple versions of the life-cycle hypothesis assume individuals know when they will die, or purchase annuities to minimize this uncertainty. But longevity is increasing, remarkably but unpredictably, so people do not know when to expect to die. Relatively few people in the rich countries currently purchase annuities on top of their defined benefit pensions (whether state-sponsored or private). Nonfinancial assets such as houses or family businesses are not easily liquefied in most countries. So saving continues into postretirement ages. This behavior is especially noteworthy in Germany and Italy (McKinsey 2004), but it is true even in the United States. Table 6.6 shows the median net worth, in constant dollars, in the United States by age bracket for 1995 and 2004. Looking at either column alone suggests a decline in net worth, or dissaving, as people age past 65 years. But different groups are being compared. People aged 55–64 years in 1995 were nearly a decade older in 2004, and their net worth increased despite passing age 65. Those aged 65–74 years in 1995 also increased their net worth further by 2004 through increased savings. This behavior can also be observed by comparing 2001 with 1992. Thus it cannot be taken for granted that in the future aging societies will dissave, at least quickly and reliably, as predicted by standard life-cycle theory; increased but uncertain longevity complicates this assumption.

**Table 6.6**
Median Family Net Worth
(Thousands of 2004 dollars)

| Age Bracket | 1995 | 2004 |
| --- | --- | --- |
| <35 years | 14.8 | 14.2 |
| 35–44 years | 64.2 | 69.4 |
| 45–54 years | 116.8 | 144.7 |
| 55–64 years | 141.9 | 248.7 |
| 65–74 years | 136.6 | 190.1 |
| >75 years | 114.5 | 163.1 |

*Source:* U.S. Statistical Yearbook, 2007, Table 702

While the rest of the world may continue to produce savings that are available for investment in the United States, can the United States accommodate an ever-increasing amount of such investment? Table 6.7 shows total financial assets in the United States for the 1980–2007 period, financial assets owned by households (the figures include nonprofit institutions), and gross foreign claims on the United States. Several points stand out. First, both total financial assets and household ownership of financial assets have grown faster than GDP over this period, 9.0 percent a year for total financial assets compared with 6.2 percent growth for nominal GDP. This growth in assets reflects increasing financial innovation and layering of financial assets over the physical capital stock, but it also reflects the growth in intangible capital discussed earlier.

Foreign claims on the United States have grown even faster, by 13.7 percent a year over this same period. The foreign share of total financial assets has risen from under 4 percent in 1980 to nearly 11 percent in 2007. Obviously a rise in the share of U.S assets held by foreigners cannot continue indefinitely, although 11 percent remains far below the foreign share expected in a fully globalized economy. But a rise in value can continue indefinitely, so long as the U.S. economy and its financial asset superstructure continue to grow. And growing foreign investment in the United States can be serviced indefinitely so long as directly or indirectly

Table 6.7
U.S. Financial Assets

|      | ($trillion) | | | (percent) |
|------|-------|------------------|---------------|---------------|
|      | Total | U.S. Households[a] | Foreign-owned[b] | Foreign Share |
| 1980 | 13.9  | 6.6  | 0.48  | 3.4  |
| 1985 | 23.5  | 9.9  | 0.96  | 4.1  |
| 1990 | 35.9  | 14.6 | 1.99  | 5.5  |
| 1995 | 53.5  | 21.6 | 3.4   | 6.4  |
| 2000 | 89.5  | 33.3 | 6.42  | 7.2  |
| 2005 | 119.7 | 39.5 | 11.63 | 9.7  |
| 2006 | 132   | 43.2 | 13.85 | 10.5 |
| 2007 | 141.9 | 45.3 | 15.42 | 10.9 |

[a]Includes nonprofit organizations
[b]Includes net interbank claims; includes foreign direct investment at current cost.
*Source:* Federal Reserve, Flow of Funds

this investment adds to the nation's productive assets at yields as least as high as those that must be paid to foreigners.

The risk profile of foreign private claims on the United States is very different from the risk profile of U.S. private claims on the rest of the world; the foreign risk profile is tilted much more toward debt instruments, both short-term and long-term. In contrast, 61 percent of private U.S. claims on foreigners are equity investment (foreign direct investment plus corporate shares), while only 35 percent of foreign private claims on the United States are equity instruments. In this respect foreign claims on the United States mirror their investment behavior at home, at least for the largest rich countries for which data are readily available: Japan, Germany, Britain, France, Italy, and Canada, in order of economic size. At end of 2004, equities constituted only 21 percent of German household financial assets (62 percent of disposable income), 16 percent in Britain (64 percent of disposable income), and 8 percent in Japan (39 percent of disposable income), compared with 28 percent (116 percent of disposable income) in the United States (OECD 2005, annex Table 58). Foreign official investment in the United States includes virtually no equity, so the bias is even greater with respect to total foreign claims on the United States.

The difference in risk profile goes part way toward explaining the fact that although the United States is a substantial net debtor to the rest of the world, U.S. earnings on its overseas investments continue to exceed its payments to foreigners on investments in the United States.

There is another significant asymmetry, seen from the U.S. perspective: foreign claims on the United States are denominated overwhelmingly in U.S. dollars, while U.S. claims on the rest of the world reflect a mixture of U.S. dollar-denominated assets and foreign currency denominated assets. Thus the net international investment position (NIIP) of the United States is sensitive to movements in exchange rates between the U.S. dollar and other currencies. Concretely, depreciation of the dollar, ceteris paribus, reduces the net debtor position of the United States, measured in dollars. Valuation changes other than those arising from currency movements also affect the NIIP, in particular movements in share prices and in the valuation of foreign direct investment. Thus while the cumulative U.S. current account deficit in the 1990–2006 period was $5.2 trillion, the increase in the net debtor position of the United States was "only" $2.0 trillion, well under half. Largely because of the dollar's depreciation, the NIIP of the United States actually increased by $114 billion in 2003, despite that year's current account deficit of $539 billion, and on preliminary figures did not change in 2006 despite a deficit of $811 billion.

Many observers have argued that the large U.S. current account deficit is unsustainable. If they mean recent trends in the deficit cannot continue, that is surely correct; the deficit cannot continue to rise indefinitely as a share of U.S. GDP, as it did (with a brief pause in 2001) 1996–2006. However, if they mean that a large U.S. deficit cannot continue indefinitely, that argument is not correct. Demographic trends in Japan, Europe, and East Asia are likely to call forth current account surpluses for a number of years, so as to build up external assets that can be drawn upon in later decades as populations continue to age. Central banks are sometimes endogenous in this process, intermediating between domestic savers whose behavior (such as in the case of Japan) is too conservative to serve well the national needs or who (as in the case of China) are not permitted to invest freely abroad.

The United States has a vibrant, innovative economy. Its demographics are markedly different from those of other rich countries, in that birth rates have not fallen nearly so much and immigration, heavily concentrated in young adults, can be expected to continue on a significant scale. In these respects the United States, although rich and politically mature, can be said to be a young and even a developing country. It has an especially innovative financial sector, which continually produces new products to cater to diverse portfolio tastes. The United States has a comparative advantage, in a globalized market, in producing marketable securities and in exchanging low-risk claims for higher risk assets. It is not surprising that savers around the world will want to put a small but growing part of their savings in the United States. The U.S. current account deficit as a consequence is likely to remain large for some years to come.

## References

Card, David. 1999. "The Causal Effect of Education on Earnings." In *Handbook on Labor Economics*, Vol. 3A, ed. O. Aschenfelter and D. Card, 1801–1863, Tables 4-6. Amsterdam: Elsevier.

Corrado, Carol, Charles R. Hulten, and Daniel E. Sichel. 2006. "Intangible Capital and Economic Growth." Working Paper No. 11948. Cambridge, MA: National Bureau of Economic Research.

Council of Economic Advisers (CEA). 1996. *Economic Report of the President.* Washington, DC: Government Printing Office.

Fraumeni, Barbara M., and Sumiye Okubo. 2005. "R&D in the National Income and Product Accounts: A First Look at Its Effect on GDP." In *Measuring Capital in the New Economy*, ed. Carol Corrado, John Haltiwanger, and Daniel Sichel, 275–316. Chicago: University of Chicago Press, 2005.

Frederico, Giovanni. 2005. *Feeding the World: An Economic History of World Agriculture, 1800–2000.* Princeton, NJ: Princeton University Press.

International Monetary Fund (IMF). 2005. *World Economic Outlook* (September). Washington, DC: International Monetary Fund.

International Monetary Fund (IMF). 2006. *World Economic Outlook* (September). Washington, DC: International Monetary Fund.

International Monetary Fund (IMF). 2008. *World Economic Outlook* (April). Washington, DC: International Monetary Fund.

McKinsey Global Institute. 2004. *The Coming Demographic Deficit: How Aging Populations Will Reduce Global Savings.* San Francisco: McKinsey Global Institute.

Organisation for Economic Co-operation and Development. 2005. *Economic Outlook*. Paris: OECD.

Smith, Margaret Huang, and Gary Smith. 2006. "Bubble, Bubble, Where's the Housing Bubble?" *Brookings Papers on Economic Activity* 1: 1–50.

Wilcox, David W. 2006. "Reforming the Defined-Benefit Pension System in the United States." *Brookings Papers on Economic Activity* 1: 235–285.

World Bank. 2007. *Global Development Finance*. Washington, DC: World Bank.

# Comments on "Understanding Global Imbalances" by Richard N. Cooper

Guy Debelle

Australia has had a long history of current account deficits, or capital account surpluses if I were to use the terminology of the 2006 Economic Report of the President. The current account deficit in Australia is currently around 6 percent of GDP and has averaged 4.5 percent over the past 20 years, as shown in Figure 6.1. Net foreign liabilities are around 60 percent of GDP, with much of that being in the form of debt.

In Australia, we had an extensive debate about the sustainability of current account deficits during the 1980s. A lot of the arguments that are being aired at the moment regarding the current situation in the United States bear a striking similarity to the debate that occurred in Australia two decades ago. Now, over 20 years later, by and large, the majority of economists in Australia hold views that are very similar to those put forward in this excellent paper by Richard Cooper. Although it must be said that while most Australian economists are relaxed about the country's current account deficit, it still can engender a significant amount of fear among politicians and the public, almost the reverse of the situation in the United States. The view reached by economists in Australia is akin to the "consenting adults" view of the Lawson doctrine, although it should be noted that this argument was originally made by Australians John Pitchford and Max Corden some time before Lawson.[1]

While it is true that compared to the United States, Australia is a much smaller player in the global capital markets, I don't think that for this analysis, absolute size matters as much as the two countries' respective proportional shares in global investment portfolios. Taking this perspective, the lessons from the Australian experience in the 1980s broadly scale up to compare with United States's current account deficit today.

Percent

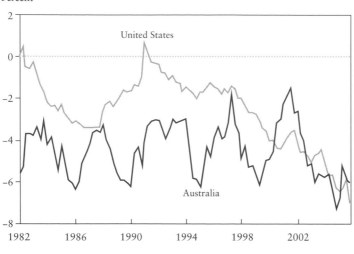

**Figure 6.1**
Current Account as a Percent of GDP
*Source:* Australian Bureau of Statistics, U.S. Bureau of Economic Analysis.

Given that I broadly share Cooper's views, whereas a sizeable share of the economics profession, including a number of the economists attending this conference, do not, in my comments I will generally try to amplify a number of the arguments Professor Cooper makes, rather than dwell on the few small issues where he and I may disagree.

Cooper's analysis of the U.S. current account deficit, made from a savings-investment and a capital account perspective, provides some useful insights which are ignored if one only focuses on the current account itself. It offers quite a different perspective on the issue of sustainability, and calls into question whether what we are observing are indeed imbalances. To his analysis, I would like to add a balance-sheet perspective. In the end, global imbalances are an issue of stocks as much as flows, but the current debate about these imbalances only focuses on the flows. Stocks can change not only because of flows but also from price changes, which are valuation effects. A balance sheet analysis that focuses on the stocks leads one to examine issues such as the treatment of capital gains and valuation effects more generally than in the traditional measures.

Valuation effects are not in included in the balance of payments equation, nor in the national income accounts.

## How Are People Saving?

Cooper provides interesting details on the movements in saving and investment in the United States, which have been the counterpart of the nation's widening current account deficit. He makes a number of arguments as to why the traditional measure of saving may give an inaccurate picture of the true financial position of U.S. households. In terms of the imbalances argument, however, one has to argue that these issues of mismeasurement are more relevant for U.S. households than these are for households in other countries, and I think it would be interesting for the paper to spend more time examining this point. U.S. households may spend more on education than do households in other countries, but to have an impact on current account positions, it would have to be the case that the share of education spending is rising faster in the United States than in other countries, or that the rate of return on education is rising faster in the United States than elsewhere. I don't think this is likely to be the case.

The stronger argument that Cooper makes, which I would like to develop further in these remarks, is that the nature by which U.S. households are saving differs substantially from that in other countries, although it is similar to the United Kingdom and Australia. U.S. households have a greater share of their savings in the form of equity investments than do households in other countries. This has important implications about how one thinks about imbalances. The capital gains on these equity holdings are not recorded in the national accounts. These gains are, however, recorded when one looks at national balance sheets (more on this detail later). One can debate the issue as to whether the capital gains that U.S. households have experienced from the rise in house prices also constitutes a source of saving. To my mind, these do not, so in what follows my arguments will focus only on saving in the form of equity holdings. If one treated capital gains from housing in the same way, the argument is even stronger.

Take the case where households in country A save only in the form of bank deposits or the purchase of government securities, but households in country B invest all their savings in equity. Assume that total returns are equalized across these two investments. The national accounts record the interest income earned by the households in country A on their savings as household income, but these accounts only record the dividend payments on the equity holdings in country B as income. The capital gains on the equity investments are not recorded in either the national accounts or balance of payments. Yet the capital gain is a significant part of the return on the equity investment for the households in country B. From the national accounts perspective, the households in country B will be doing less saving than those in country A.

Now take the case where the households in country A lend their savings to the households in country B, who in turn invest the borrowed funds by purchasing equity in country A. Again assume the interest on the loan is equal to the return on the equity investment, which comprises dividend payments and a capital gain. The national accounts will again show less saving in country B than in country A. And country A will be recording a current account surplus while country B will be recording a current account deficit. This is because the net income flows, as recorded in the balance of payment statistics, will be from country B to country A, as the interest payments will exceed the dividend payments (assuming a positive capital gain). Wealth holdings will be the same in both countries, and households' expected permanent income will also be the same. Country B's current account deficit will be persistent, yet I would not say that there is an imbalance here. The argument is even stronger if one allows for an equity risk premium on these investments.

Obviously, the rest of the world, and particularly East Asia, are broadly akin to country A, and the United States, the United Kingdom, and Australia are broadly akin to country B.

So the bottom line is that these measurement issues need to be taken into account when examining the current global imbalances. The problem doesn't necessarily go away but it does result in a different perspective on the scale of the problem. Valuation changes do not make it into the current account, but these shifts do affect the measurement of the stock of liabilities.[2]

## A Balance Sheet Approach to Global Imbalances

Extending Cooper's argument that the national accounting system may not be providing the most appropriate metric for assessing global imbalances, I would like to argue that the standard analysis of the current capital account flows should be combined with a balance sheet or stock analysis.

Most analyses of global imbalances start from either the size of a nation's current account or the size of its foreign liabilities relative to GDP. However, measuring foreign liabilities relative to GDP is not necessarily the most appropriate benchmark to use, as it is deflating a stock (foreign liabilities) by a flow (GDP). When assessing a corporation's borrowing, a balance sheet perspective is generally used in the form of gearing ratios, which measure debt against assets or equity. Measures of debt service are used to assess the ability to service that borrowing.[3]

Using a balance sheet approach to assess the external position of the United States suggests that the stock of foreign liabilities should be deflated by the assets held by U.S. residents, which, in other words, is a measure of wealth. One can regard these assets as representing wealth held as collateral against the stock of liabilities. Again, one can debate whether housing wealth should be included in this calculation, so for the purpose at hand, I have performed the analysis with and without incorporating housing.[4]

As one can see from Figure 6.2, this balance sheet analysis presents quite a different picture of U.S. assets and liabilities. Foreign liabilities have risen at a much smaller pace relative to wealth than these have relative to nominal GDP. Obviously this reflects the fact that the value of U.S. households' equity holdings, and financial wealth more generally, have been rising faster than GDP. This situation illustrates valuation effects are at work. Hence, expressing U.S. foreign liabilities as a share of the nation's wealth gives quite a different picture of sustainability or vulnerability. The same analysis holds true for Australia.

As U.S. households are doing more of their saving through equity than other households, then this sort of analysis presents a much more benign picture. In net terms, foreign liabilities have been stable as a share of household wealth over the past few years. In Australia, this share has actually declined, as shown in Figure 6.3.

Percent

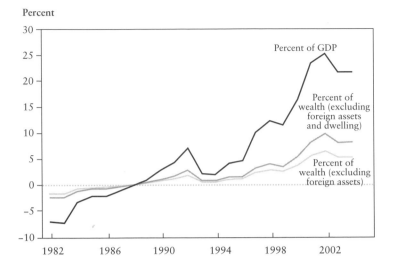

**Figure 6.2**
A Balance Sheet Analysis of U.S. Net Foreign Liabilities
*Source:* Australian Bureau of Statistics, Federal Reserve Board, Reserve
Bank of Australia, U.S. Bureau of Labor Statistics.

Percent

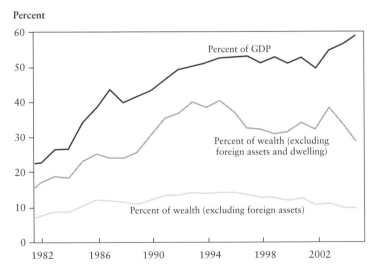

**Figure 6.3**
Australia's Net Foreign Liabilities
*Source:* Australian Bureau of Statistics, Federal Reserve Board, Reserve
Bank of Australia, U.S. Bureau of Labor Statistics.

In addition, in the event of any depreciation of the U.S. dollar, net foreign liabilities will decrease significantly because of valuation effects, further bolstering the balance sheet of U.S. households.

**Why Are the Flows Going to the United States?**

Cooper asks an important question: why is it that the bulk of global capital flows are all going to the United States? I think the answer he gives is the correct one, namely that the United States possesses a developed secure financial system that offers a respectable and reliable rate of return. I place particular emphasis on the words "secure" and "reliable." A recent paper by Ricardo Caballero, Emmanuel Farhi, and Pierre-Olivier Gourinchas (2006) formalizes this argument, and concludes that the current alignment of capital flows is stable and liable to persist for quite some time to come.

A conclusion that one can draw from this "secure and reliable" analysis is that in terms of global imbalances, one of the greatest benefits from economic reform in Japan and Europe is to make them more attractive destinations for the world's savers. Similarly, developing secure financial systems in Asia would yield a similar outcome. But this type of institutional change is a slow process that does not take place overnight. Hence as these reforms take root, one would expect investors' perceptions and the ensuing international portfolio adjustment to be quite gradual too.

Is the share of U.S. assets in global portfolios likely to reach saturation soon? Cooper notes that perhaps the United States is slightly underweight in the global portfolio. There has been a notable decline in home bias over the past decade or so, as the process of financial globalization has proceeded, but primarily the destination of these funds has been to the United States. So ignoring home bias, the U.S. portfolio allocation is about right, whereas most other countries are underweight.

A crude characterization of the present situation might be as follows: there has been a general decline in home bias over the past two decades, but there has not been a general portfolio diversification. Instead investors have tended to put their funds in markets which are seen as secure and dynamic. Thus far, private investors in East Asia, and more recently, the oil-producing countries, have judged that the United States provides them with the investment characteristics they are seeking.

Given that their strategy has been to invest predominantly in U.S. assets, and importantly, U.S. dollar-denominated assets, an interesting question arises. If I have a large portfolio in the United States, measured in U.S. dollars, and the U.S. dollar depreciates, do I increase my investment in the United States to bring my U.S. allocation back up to my benchmark, or do I rush for the exits and thereby generate further capital losses on my U.S. investments, which is a large share of my overall wealth portfolio? With their large U.S. dollar portfolios, this is clearly an issue for the world's central banks. Again, valuation effects matter here, which an analysis solely based on flows will overlook.

A final variant on this question is: do we expect to see a rapid portfolio readjustment, or in other words, is there likely to be a sudden stop in the United States? Gabriele Galati and I have looked at the issue of current account reversals from the capital account perspective.[5] We find that there is almost no evidence of a sudden stop taking place in developed countries. By and large, capital flows adjust quite seamlessly, particularly in a floating exchange rate regime.

## If the U.S. Current Account Deficit is a Problem, What Might be Done About It?

If, after one has examined the issue from a balance sheet perspective, one still concludes that the U.S. current account per se is a problem, or is symptomatic of some other problem, what should be done about it?

If household saving is too low in the United States, what are the distortions that are causing this inadequate saving? What policies can be put in place to encourage higher saving? I don't think we have good answers to those questions.

One can argue that the U.S. administration needs to address the fiscal situation, but that is an issue of sustainability of the public debt, regardless of whether it is held by foreigners or domestic residents. Moreover, the twin deficits are probably distant cousins rather than identical twins.[6] The Australian experience certainly highlights this point: our budget position has swung from deficit to surplus a number of times with little obvious effect on the current account.[7] Even if one allows for a near twin-like relationship, then the U.S. current account would only decline to a level that many considered excessive only a few years ago.

If one is concerned about the capital flowing into the United States, then would the policy recommendation be that United Stated reimpose capital controls? The capital that is flowing in is coming in willingly: the United States is not forcing the rest of the world to lend to it. This is evident in the fact that U.S. interest rates have been generally low. The rest of the world is providing the funding to the United States (and Australia) at low cost, whose residents can then turn around and invest profitably. Why would you say no to such funding?

Should policymakers in the United States engineer a recession to make U.S. assets less attractive? Or should they adopt policies that make the United States a less attractive place to invest? Clearly that is nonsensical, although it appears that some lawmakers in the United States are considering this solution. Self-imposed restrictions such as the Dubai Ports decision are perhaps the greatest threat here. Financial protectionism may be more of a threat to global stability than trade protectionism in goods and services.

## Conclusion

In the very long run, I expect that the configuration of capital flows would not look like these currently do. Eventually, I expect capital to be flowing from the developed world to the less-developed world. I do not expect to see such an extreme allocation of net capital flows where the flows of capital are disproportionately going to a small number of countries. So in that sense the current configuration of capital flows is probably unsustainable, but that does not mean we are on the verge of catastrophe.

Changes such as developing sound and trusted financial institutions that will enhance the attractiveness of Europe and Japan as destinations for international investment flows are very slow moving, and are not likely to result in a rapid reallocation of portfolio flows. Moreover, the large long positions that many global investors hold in U.S. dollars means that there is probably a built-in stabilizer. I do not expect to see a sudden stop in the United States or Australia.

The experience of Australia, as depicted in Figure 6.4, shows that current account deficits or capital account surpluses can persist for quite some time. Cooper's paper provides a number of sound reasons why this might be also the case for the United States; see Figure 6.5. The issues he

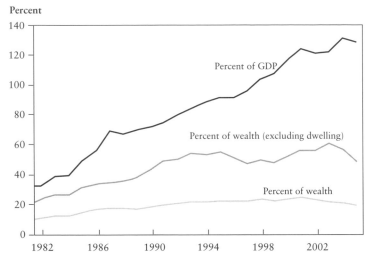

**Figure 6.4**
Australia's Gross Foreign Liabilities
*Source:* Australian Bureau of Statistics, Federal Reserve Board, Reserve
Bank of Australia, U.S. Bureau of Labor Statistics.

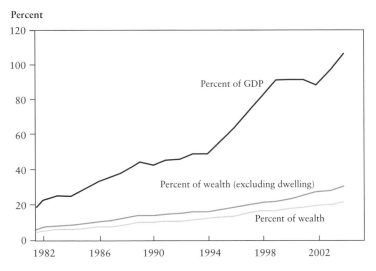

**Figure 6.5**
U.S. Gross Foreign Liabilities
*Source:* Australian Bureau of Statistics, Federal Reserve Board, Reserve
Bank of Australia, U.S. Bureau of Labor Statistics.

raises about the means by which U.S. households save and the treatment of capital gains on those investments are important and often neglected in the analysis of the current global imbalances. In general, a more considered analysis of the balance sheet of the United States would lead to a more balanced assessment of the global "imbalances," and the sustainability of the current configuration of global capital flows.

■ *The views expressed are those of the author and not necessarily those of the Reserve Bank of Australia.*

## Notes

1. Pitchford (1989); Corden (1991).

2. Gournichas and Rey (2005) and Lane and Milessi-Feretti (2004) have written extensively on this, as has Tille (2006).

3. A similar argument applies to the measurement of household borrowing, where household debt should be scaled by the value of household assets, rather than household income, which is generally used.

4. The wealth numbers for the United States are from the Flow of Funds statistics.

5. See Debelle and Galati (2007).

6. See Enders and Lee (1990).

7. See Gruen and Sayegh (2005).

## References

Caballero, Ricardo, Emmanuel Farhi, and Pierre-Olivier Gourinchas. 2006. "An Equilibrium Model of 'Global Imbalances' and Low Interest Rates." Working Paper No. 11996. Cambridge, MA: National Bureau of Economic Research.

Corden, Max. 1991. "Does the Current Account Matter? The Old View and the New." *Economic Papers* 10: 1–19.

Debelle, Guy, and Gabriele Galati. 2007. "Current Account Adjustment and Capital Flows." *Review of International Economics* 15(5): 989–1013.

Enders, Walter, and Bong-Soo Lee. 1990. "Current Account and Budget Deficits: Twins or Distant Cousins?" *The Review of Economics and Statistics* 72(3): 373–381.

Gourinchas, Pierre-Olivier, and Helene Rey. 2005. "International Financial Adjustment." Working Paper No. 11155. Cambridge, MA: National Bureau of Economic Research.

Gruen, David, and Amanda Sayegh. 2005. "The Evolution of Fiscal Policy in Australia." *Oxford Review of Economic Policy* 21(4): 618–635.

Lane, Philip, and Gian Maria Milesi-Feretti. 2004. "International Investment Patterns." Working Paper No. 2004/134. Washington, DC: International Monetary Fund.

Pitchford, John. 1989. "A Sceptical View of Australia's Current Account and Debt Problem." *Australian Economic Review* 86(2): 5–14.

Tille, Cédric. 2006. "On the Distributional Effects of Exchange Rate Fluctuations." *Journal of International Money and Finance* 25(8): 1207–1225.

# Comments on "Understanding Global Imbalances" by Richard N. Cooper

Laurence J. Kotlikoff

Richard Cooper's paper provides a highly sanguine view of the U.S. current account deficit, notwithstanding its historically high current value. He marshalls ten points to make this case.

First, the federal government's borrowing and spending, rather than low private saving rates, explain the recent increase in the current account deficit. Second, the rate of private saving has been relatively constant, with increases in corporate saving offsetting the dramatic decline in personal saving that has received so much attention from the press. Third, the concept of private saving is not well measured in the national income accounts because it excludes the acquisition of durable goods, capital gains, and increases in intangible capital. Fourth, older Americas have a lot of wealth and a lot of it will be left to the baby boomers, keeping them afloat during potentially long retirement periods. Fifth, our country spends a lot on research, development, and education, and this type of investment is a form of unmeasured saving. Sixth, the U.S. economy is vibrant, growing, and safe, so it makes a lot of sense for foreigners to invest here. Seventh, the United States is a big economy, so it should attract a large share of international investment. Indeed, according to Cooper this share is lower than one might expect. Eighth, current and projected future demographic changes should lead to more investment in the United States and less in Japan and Europe. Ninth, given the nature of their investments, Americans earn, on average, a higher return on foreign asset holdings than foreigners earn on U.S. asset holding. And since our national income accounts record book, not market, positions, these accounts omit the capital gains Americans earn abroad and, thereby, overstate our current account deficit. And tenth, we can expect to see ongoing large current account deficits as foreign nationals use the United States to seek a safe haven for their money, and as foreign governments seek large U.S. dollar reserves to protect the values of their currencies.

In short, Cooper tells us not to worry about our current account deficit or its underlying causes.

I have a much darker and, I believe, a more accurate view of our current account deficit.

Let me begin by pointing out that current account deficits per se are not, in my mind, a matter of concern. If foreigners want to invest in the United States, God bless them—that's a major plus for U.S. workers and taxpayers. Were the term "current account deficit" banned and were we always forced to use the term "foreign additions to the U.S. capital stock" instead, we economists would stop looking at the difference between domestic investment and national saving and start looking at the levels of each on a one-off basis. This is what Cooper is doing, and properly so.

I'm going to do the same, but I'm going to focus on net domestic investment and net national saving. As you can see from Figure 6.6, both have declined as a share of national income since 1960, with the gap between these measures increasing over time.

The main culprit for the recent rise in the U.S. current account deficit is our country's low rate of national saving. Today foreigners are investing four dollars in the United States for every dollar Americans are investing here. Cooper suggests that the government's dissaving is primarily to blame for the current account deficit. I think this view is off base. Like almost all economists, Cooper treats measures of the federal deficit, taxes, transfer payments, personal disposable income, private saving, and government saving as well-defined economic concepts, when these are content-free accounting measures that reflect an economically arbitrary labeling of government receipts and payments. If, for example, we label our Social Security and Medicare contributions to the government as "loans," rather than as "taxes," our measures of the federal deficit, private saving, and government dissaving will radically change. Using this alternative language or a zillion other relabeling schemes would wreak havoc on Cooper's analysis of the sources of the rise in our current account deficit.

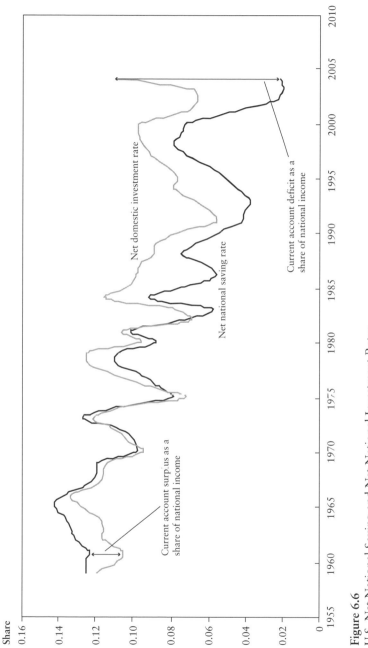

**Figure 6.6**
U.S. Net National Saving and Net National Investment Rates
*Source:* U.S. Bureau of Economic Analysis.

I've been belaboring this point for years now, but to little effect on current government accounting practices. My most recent admonition to the profession, entitled "On the General Relativity of Fiscal Language" is co-authored with Jerry Green and is posted on my web site. This paper provides a general proof that neoclassical economic theory does not define any of the conventional fiscal and saving measures included in Cooper's study.

This argument is not meant to be nihilistic. We can study well-defined economic variables, like the current account, but we need to do so using well-defined economic variables, not purely linguistic constructs. In the case of the U.S. current account, the decline in the net national saving rate is not, in fact, due to increased government spending. Government consumption as a share of national income has declined since the early 1960s. The government's share of spending has risen since 2000, but it's still a much smaller share of national income than it was in 1960.

The reason our rate of national saving has declined is because household consumption has risen dramatically as a share of national income. And the group within the household sector that has enjoyed the sharpest rise in consumption is the elderly. This is no surprise. What we've been doing for the past 50 years is transferring ever larger resources from young savers to old spenders and, as the life-cycle consumption model clearly predicts, this practice has led to a decline in national saving. Much of these transfers to the elderly, of course, come in-kind, in the form of medical goods and services, which cannot be saved and consumed later.

Today, we're handing each and every elderly American, on average, more than $30,000 per year in Social Security, Medicare, and Medicaid benefits—roughly 80 percent of per capita U.S. GDP. The real level of the Medicare and Medicaid benefits has been rising at over 4.5 percent per year for the last 30 years. This is pure consumption and this, in part, is why our national saving rate is so low. The rest of the explanation for why the household sector is spending at such a high rate is that we are telling today's baby boomers and even today's younger workers that they too will be able to rip off their progeny through an ongoing policy of pass-the-generational buck.

In short, I view our large current account deficit as symptomatic of an ongoing fiscal policy of intergenerational expropriation. This fiscal child abuse has effectively delivered the United States to the point of national

Percent

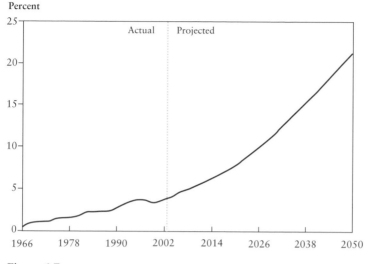

**Figure 6.7**
Total Federal Spending for Medicare and Medicaid as a Percent of GDP
*Source:* U.S. Congressional Budget Office. See *The Long-Term Budget Outlook*
(December 2003).

bankruptcy. Careful calculations by economists Jagadeesh Gokhale and
Kent Smetters indicate that a $63 trillion present-value gap separates our
government's projected future expenditures and receipts. As shown in
Figure 6.7, the projected costs for Medicare and Medicaid alone will
amount to 20 percent of GDP by 2050, and these combined liabilities
account for the bulk of the $63 trillion gap. Once U.S. government bond
holders, both domestic and foreign ones, start to understand that the
United States is, indeed, insolvent, and will be forced to pay its bills by
printing money, we will see a financial meltdown of unprecedented proportion.

So, while I agree with much of what Cooper says, I disagree most
strongly with his central thesis that the U.S. current account deficit
portends no major problems in the future. To the contrary, the current
account deficit is symptomatic of a long-term generational policy that has
been slowly, but surely, driving our nation broke. When the last straw
hits the camel's back, which could happen any day now, we're going to
see the bond and stock markets crash, interest rates soar, the value of the

dollar plunge, and inflation take off, notwithstanding the Fed's supposed independence in not reacting to such adverse financial market events.

## Reference

Gokhale, Jagadeesh and Kent Smetters. 2006. "Fiscal and Generational Imbalances: An Update." In *Tax Policy and the Economy,* Volume 20, ed. James M. Poterba, 193–223. Cambridge, MA: The MIT Press.

# 7
## Adjustment Mechanisms

# Interest Rates, Exchange Rates, and International Adjustment

Michael P. Dooley, David Folkerts-Landau, and Peter M. Garber

## Introduction

In June 2003, we published the first of a series of notes that developed our views of the key features of the global monetary system and its future direction. Taken together, this series has come to be known as the "Bretton Woods II" view, a reference to analytical parallels made with the postwar fixed rate system.[1]

When we first wrote on the nature of the global financial system, the general view was that the global current account imbalances were generated by U.S. savings and fiscal behavior, and that the problem would have to be solved by sharp dollar depreciation. Interest rates would have to rise, both to implement a secular shrinkage of U.S. demand and to control the rapid growth phase of the business cycle, then just taking off following the 2001 recession. Asian countries were thought to be tangential to this central problem: their growing surpluses and reserves were believed to be excessively cautious hangovers from an effort to build precautionary reserves after the 1997–1998 Asian financial crisis. To the extent that China's currency policy was discussed, it was raised in order to warn China that its economy might overheat rather than to warn about the global macroeconomic effects of Asian development strategies. Analysis was carried out on a country-by-country basis, either of the U.S.-centric or small open economy sort, without much attention paid to why the global macroeconomic system had assembled itself together, and how it was operating as a whole.

We argued in 2003 and early 2004 that due to the nature of the de facto global system, nominal and especially real interest rates would remain unusually low at any given phase of the business cycle. Our view was that the huge underemployment and tremendous savings in China and the rest of Asia were the driving forces of the global system, and that the United States was essentially a passive center country, but willing to absorb these low cost savings. As its development strategy, China/Asia would continue to pump out savings and therefore cheap goods to the rest of the world. This state of affairs would keep real interest rates and inflation low in the long term, while at the same time financing the U.S. current account deficit. Other currencies would appreciate against the dollar, but only the floating currencies would jump immediately. The currencies of the countries actually driving the system would appreciate only gradually. This delayed appreciation would cause regions with problematic economies, particularly Euroland, to stagnate even more, putting intense political pressure on their monetary authorities.

We also argued that the prevailing effect of the system was to neutralize somewhat the forces of protectionism that always arise in industrial countries when a poorer country tries to develop via industrial exports. This decrease in protectionist sentiment would occur through allowing rich countries industrial capital access to the cheap labor in the developing country's export sector, thereby splitting and co-opting the usual protectionist political coalitions.

At the time these were published, these notes provided a strong explanation and fit for the then-current state of the global economy, and for many of the anomalies that existed. More than that easy fit, these notes provided a strong contrarian forecast on global and regional interest rates, exchange rates, inflation rates, economic growth, and global imbalances. Also at the time of publication, these forecasts on asset prices and the duration of the system were many sigmas away from the conventional analysis and forecasts, so these attracted more than their share of attention and criticism.

That the forecasts have been on target for the last three years may be a matter of good analysis or good fortune. But this analysis has, in the nature of things, led to a more general acceptance of the view in the financial markets, to the extent that clients, accepting of these forecasts, now just want to hear the risk scenarios revolving around this central view. This is much less true of the academic and official sector discourse, where even after several years we are still often on the defensive against strongly held views that the global financial system will collapse very soon, all the more likely for not having collapsed already.[2]

Whatever the judgment that hindsight will deliver on these academic disputes, it is clear that the global monetary system that we have described has some legs to it. So rather than fight old battles over the probability of imminent collapse, we think it is time to analyze the dynamics and evolution of the system *given that its basic parameters will last for some time.*

## A Differing Base of Premises

In this paper, we set out in greater detail how we think about the dynamic forces emanating from the emergence of China and Asia as major players in world capital and foreign exchange markets. Conventional analyses have been based for several years on the assertion that the Bretton Woods II system cannot hold together for much longer. This judgment may or may not turn out to be correct, but this contention does not offer any guidance if the system does survive for an extended time period, as we believe it will. The framework developed below also provides a guide to the dynamics of the system following a variety of changes in the economic environment.

For the sake of simplicity, our framework has divided the world into three regions, emerging Asia, the United States, and Euroland.[3] Euroland includes all countries outside the United States with open capital markets and market-determined exchange rates. We will use the euro to stand for the currencies of these countries, since it is the dominant currency among them. Asia includes all countries with relatively closed capital markets and managed exchange rates, and we use the renminbi to stand in for their collective currencies.

Some observers have questioned the usefulness of aggregating the managed rate countries into a single zone because of the differing incentives and constraints facing these countries. We agree, for example, that current account surpluses and reserve growth for China, oil-exporting countries, and Japan are products of quite different developments and incentives, and are likely to have different degrees of persistence over time.[4] Our forecast is that individual countries will join and exit the bloc of countries that manage their dollar exchange rates, and their various management regimes will find different degrees of success, but the bloc will nevertheless remain a lasting and economically important feature of the international monetary system.[5]

The analysis will lean on four assumptions, which we believe are realistic. These four tenets dramatically simplify the dynamics of a three-region analysis:

1. *Asian financial markets are poorly integrated with the other two regions because of capital controls and the threat of sovereign interference with capital flows.* This situation allows Asia to manage the dollar-renminbi exchange rate so that the renminbi appreciates in real terms slowly over an adjustment period of many years.

2. *The U.S. and Euroland financial markets, in contrast, are very well integrated and their respective assets are very close substitutes.* This assumption is consistent with a great deal of empirical work, especially on the inefficacy of sterilized intervention. The United States and Euroland do not manage the euro-dollar exchange rate.

3. *The dominant change in the economic environment that is driving the main features of the world economy is the rapid growth of savings rates and the level of savings in Asia, and their exportation of this surplus to the rest of the world.*

4. *The United States and Euroland differ in their capacities to utilize Asian savings, with the United States having a much greater absorptive capacity.*

Some of the significant departures of our analysis from the conventional approach include the following points:

1a. Conventional analysis considers Asian financial markets sufficiently integrated with international markets so that Asian governments will not be able to manage real exchange rates at reasonable costs. In particular, this view holds that they will be unable to fend off hot money inflows. Moreover, they will not want to distort real exchange rates for much longer in order to encourage export-led growth.

2a. Conventional analysis assumes that the United States and Euroland financial markets are not well integrated. Diversification of Asian reserves is thought to have an important effect on the dollar-euro exchange rate.

Yet this assumption seems to us inconsistent with substantial evidence that intervention and reserve management by U.S. and Euroland authorities have not had a large or lasting effect on industrial country exchange rates.

3a. The conventional analysis usually identifies a fall in the U.S. household savings rate or a rise in the government fiscal deficit rate as the driving force behind the U.S. current account deficit.

4a. Yet U.S. interest rate movements have not been consistent with this assumption—these rates have been falling instead of rising. To circumvent this contradiction, it is conventionally asserted that interest rates and asset prices are being driven by incorrect expectations, a misunderstanding of the dangerous nature of the system, or bubbles.

## Analysis

In our framework, the fundamental shock to the system is a change in the supply of savings from Asia and a suspension of the usual home bias in allocating these savings across world markets. It may not seem all that important to decide whether it will be because U.S. savings fell or Asian savings increased to drive the pattern of current accounts we now see. But determining this is, in fact, crucial for understanding the current system and the direction it will take.

Asian real exchange rates are not market-determined prices, but instead are heavily and successfully managed by Asian governments. As noted above, the conventional analysis assumes this troublesome fact will soon go away. We argue that this policy behavior will *eventually* go away, but that right now it is a central feature of Asian development policies and will not dissipate for a long time. It follows that if the rest of the world now is to adjust to a savings shock emanating from Asia, the primary adjustment mechanism will not be changes in Asian real exchange rates.

To manage real exchange rates in today's environment, Asian governments must intervene in foreign exchange markets. The part of the intervention that is sterilized is, in fact, intervention in credit markets. Asian finance ministries or central banks sell domestic securities, thus reducing the supply of loanable funds to domestic borrowers, and buy foreign securities, thereby increasing the supply of loanable funds in the United States and Euroland. The resulting shift in interest rate differential is possible because of effective capital controls. In other words, Asian governments can manage exchange rates and interest rates because, as a matter of official policy, if not private preference, their domestic assets are made imperfect substitutes for foreign assets in private portfolios.

Figures 7.1 and 7.2 summarize the current state of the global financial system. Long-term U.S. real rates fell to half their previous cyclical peak for two years during the rapid growth phase of this business cycle. These rates have recently begun to rise, but are still substantially below their cyclical peak. This situation is reflective of low real interest rates throughout the industrial world. Simultaneously, the U.S. current account deficit has grown steadily as a ratio to U.S. GDP. Whatever one might think about low saving rates in the United States, this is clear evidence that the supply of savings pushing into the United States, regardless of price, has dominated a demand-pull effect of foreign savings coming into the United States for half a decade.

Because Asian exchange rates are actively managed, the eventual adjustment must proceed through current account balances, other cross

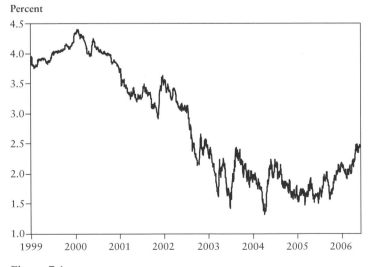

**Figure 7.1**
10-Year Treasury Inflation-Protected Security Yield
*Source:* Federal Reserve Board.

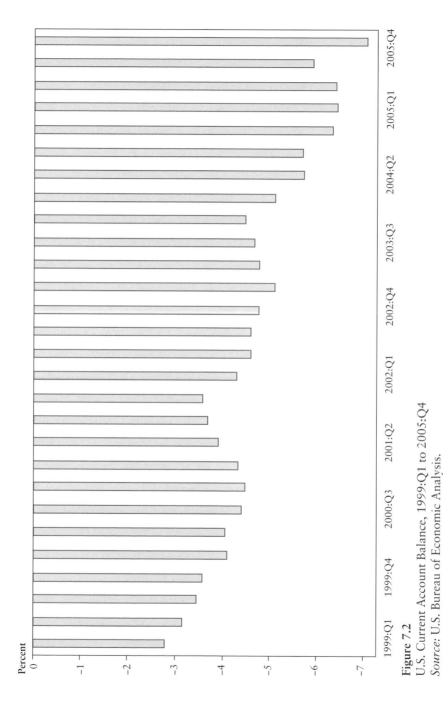

**Figure 7.2**
U.S. Current Account Balance, 1999:Q1 to 2005:Q4
*Source:* U.S. Bureau of Economic Analysis.

rates, and real interest rates. To understand current accounts we have to understand savings and investment behavior. The question is, how are savings and investment changed in the United States, Euroland, and elsewhere as Asian savings are offered to the rest of the world? In particular, can we understand why real interest rates might fall in both the United States and Euroland, while current account balances adjust by very different amounts? In our view, this is a very easy case to understand.

We can illustrate our approach first with a set of figures focusing on interest rates and current accounts for Asia, the United States, and Euroland, and then with another set focusing on net foreign debt positions and exchange rates.

Figure 7.3 shows real interest rates for the United States, Euroland, and Asia on the vertical axes. The horizontal axes represent the domestic savings, investment, and current accounts for these three regions. The upward sloping curves labeled S are national savings. The curves labeled S' are national savings augmented by imports or exports of savings through horizontal shifts. The downward sloping curves labeled I are investment. For convenience, we start with balanced current accounts at a common interest rate, but any starting point for the separate economies will do as long as real rates are the same in the United States and Euroland.

A policy to divert Asian savings to the United States and Euroland reduces the supply of savings available in Asia, and shifts the Asian supply curve to the left. In Asia, a current account surplus is generated and Asian interest rates rise. In this exercise, we assume that savers in Asia are paid the initial interest rate $r_0$, investors are charged $r_1$, and the resulting excess of savings is dumped on the global financial market for whatever rate of return it may bring. The financial markets allocate these new savings to the United States and Euroland to re-equate the real rates of interest in the two zones.

In the United States and Euroland, as Asian savings push in, the augmented savings supply curves shift to the right. The real interest rate in the United States and Euroland falls as we move down the investment demand curves, and the financial markets distribute the added savings across the two zones. The demand curves are downward sloping because investment increases relative to domestic savings as interest rates fall.

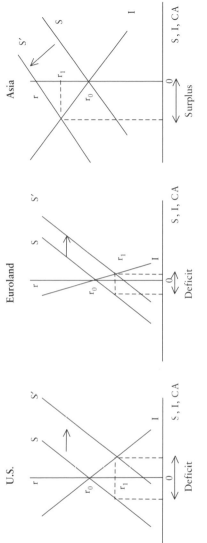

**Figure 7.3**
Current Account and Interest Rates in the U.S., Euroland, and Asia
*Note:* S stands for savings, I for investments, CA for the current account, and r for the interest rate.
*Source:* Authors' calculations

Moreover, consumption rises with a fall in interest rates, so domestic savings fall as well. The rise in consumption and investment is matched by an inflow of foreign savings and, by definition, the current account deficit, initially marked at zero, increases. The increase in Asia's current account surplus is matched by the sum of the increases in the current account deficits of the United States and Euroland.

In the United States, the increase in savings demanded is large because investment and savings are quite sensitive to the rate of interest.[6] Euroland sees the same qualitative changes. But its investment and the current account deficit increase only slightly because there are few profitable investment opportunities, and personal consumption is not very responsive. The fundamental factor driving the different responses of the United States and Euroland current account deficits is the different amount of opportunities to efficiently use foreign savings as the interest rate falls in both regions.

An important aspect of the adjustment process is how private arbitrage fosters the equalization of real rates of return on capital invested in the United States and Euroland. Later, when we turn to exchange rate determination, we will use the result that real interest rates are equalized by flows of savings. It is clear, however, that expected rates of return on capital in the United States and Euroland could be equalized by expected real exchange rate changes, in addition to real interest rates.

During the adjustment period, this apparent indeterminacy between real interest rates and expected changes in real exchange rates is resolved at the end of the period. When the new equilibrium is established, there is no reason to predict that the real exchange rate between the euro and the dollar will continue to change over time. Since looking forward at the end of the adjustment period, the capital stocks must have the same expected rate of return, it follows that real interest rates must be the same at that time. Across time, arbitrage will ensure that during the adjustment period any capital put in place in the United States and Euroland that will remain in place in a new steady state must have the same rate of return.

For Asian governments, the preferred policy over time is to allow gradual real exchange rate appreciation. This adjustment over time reduces their intervention in credit markets and their exports of savings. By the end of the adjustment period, real interest rates will have equalized across the three regions.

Turning now to the foreign exchange markets, there are three keys to understanding the behavior of the three cross exchange rates.

First, looking ahead for some years, Asian governments can and will manage the real dollar value of their currencies. They can do so because capital controls make Asian domestic assets imperfect substitutes for U.S. and Euroland assets in private portfolios. Yet over time, as capital controls become less effective and their domestic asset markets are integrated with international capital markets, their ability to manage their real exchange rate will erode. The Asians' desire to maintain the system will also erode as their surplus labor is absorbed. But they will manage rates as long as they can because undervaluation is an important part of their development strategy.

Second, in the long run, say ten years more or less, the real value of the three currencies will have to adjust to changes in the three region's international investment positions generated during the adjustment period. Asia's net asset position will improve while the U.S. and Euroland positions will deteriorate by relatively large and small amounts, respectively.

The relationship between the long-run exchange rate and the net foreign debt position of each region is not controversial, and is the centerpiece of most analyses about the ultimate depreciation of the U.S. dollar. As a country's net foreign debt increases, larger trade balance surpluses are needed to service its net debt. So a fall in net foreign assets is associated with a depreciation of the real exchange rate. The implication of these increasing current account deficits is that the dollar and the euro must depreciate against the renminbi, but the dollar must depreciate by more. Therefore, the dollar must depreciate against the euro.[7]

Third, normally today's exchange rates would reflect these long-run expectations to some degree. But intervention by Asian governments is sufficient to manage the strict dollar-renminbi exchange rate. Intervention will not keep the renminbi undervalued forever, but it can extend the adjustment period. As we have argued elsewhere, from China's perspective, the preferred path for Asian real exchange rates is a gradual appreciation toward their new long-run values.

In contrast, the euro cross rates both today and along the adjustment path are determined by private investors. The relevant context for these portfolio choices is that dollar and euro assets are close substitutes.[8] The key implication is that once the system is fully understood, the euro and the dollar must depreciate at the same rate over time relative to the renminbi. Recall that real interest rates on capital invested in the United States and Euroland are equalized by net savings flows. It follows that investors must expect the euro-dollar exchange rate to remain unchanged. Put another way, both currencies must depreciate, and be expected to depreciate, at the same rate against the renminbi.

The result of a leftward shift in Asian savings exports is then an immediate euro appreciation against the dollar and the renminbi, followed by a constant dollar/euro exchange rate. This means that there will be immediate, maximal political pressure for relief in a Euroland unable to absorb the shock easily and continuous, though declining, pressure thereafter.

These results are illustrated in Figure 7.4. Starting from an initial value of the renminbi-dollar rate in the top panel and a renminbi-euro rate in the bottom panel, we can follow the effects of an increase in Asian savings exports and intervention. These increases raise interest rates faced by domestic investors in Asia and lower interest rates in the United States and Euroland. Asia generates a current account surplus matched by deficits in the United States and Euroland. This situation continues until Asian savings exports and intervention return to normal levels. In the top panel of Figure 7.2, this interval is from 0 to T. The eventual fall in the dollar against the renminbi from A to B is required to close the trade deficit, and even to generate the trade surplus needed to service the higher level of U.S. debt at time T and after.

Absent intervention, we would expect an immediate depreciation of the dollar; but this can and will be delayed by intervention.[9] Along the adjustment path AB, the dollar is supported by a flow of outside intervention. Private investors know the dollar will depreciate but nevertheless are willing to hold the stock of dollars, reduced by Asian purchases of U.S. assets.[10] U.S. debt to foreigners is growing more rapidly than it would have if the fall in interest rates had been partially offset by a market-determined depreciation of the dollar.

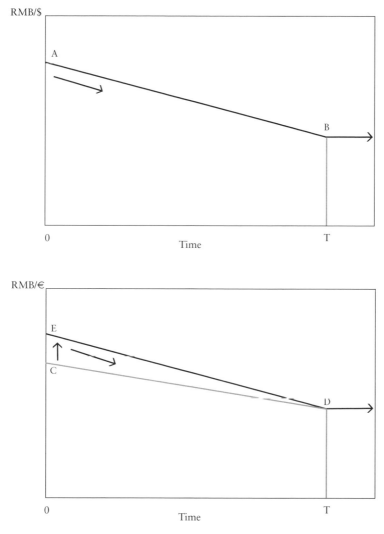

**Figure 7.4**
Exchange Rates
*Source:* Authors' calculations

In the bottom panel of Figure 7.4, the renminbi-euro rate starts at C and must eventually move to D, a much smaller depreciation. Like the United States, Euroland will accumulate debt (or reduce net assets below their previous path) during the eventual adjustment period. But in this case Asian governments are not intervening to manage the exchange rate either at point C or along the adjustment path. The question is then, where will the market set euro exchange rates?

We can make our analysis more realistic and much more transparent by assuming that U.S. and Euroland assets are close substitutes in private portfolios. This is an important departure from the usual portfolio balance model because it implies that the currency composition of Asian intervention is of secondary importance. If euro and dollar assets are close substitutes in private portfolios, Asian governments could intervene in either dollars or euros to stabilize the dollar value of their currencies. Moreover, diversification of Asian reserves would have little or no lasting effect on the dollar-euro exchange rates, contrary to a key conclusion of the conventional view.[11] This is because the irrelevance of Asian reserve diversification is consistent with a very large body of empirical evidence that sterilized intervention has had no lasting effect on exchange rates among industrialized countries.[12]

The practical importance of this assumption is that the two adjustment paths in Figure 7.4 must have the same slope. If these did not, more rapid dollar depreciation against the renminbi, relative to euro depreciation against the renminbi, implies an expected depreciation of the dollar against the euro. Since interest rates in the United States and Euroland are the same, arbitrage would be profitable. Private investors would immediately bid for euros against dollars and would do so until the euro jumps to E. From this initial appreciation, the euro now depreciates against the renminbi at the same rate as the dollar. Note that along this adjustment path the euro, as the key and only freely priced currency in the global financial system, overshoots and remains "overvalued" relative to the dollar and the renminbi throughout the adjustment interval, although the degree of overvaluation shrinks over time.

Therefore, for senior European financial officials to claim that a small Euroland current account position means that the European Union is neither part of the problem nor of the solution is a position divorced from reality. In particular, successfully arguing that *China should not speed up the appreciation of the renminbi, for this would place maximal pressure on the euro to appreciate against the dollar* is exactly opposite of the intent.

We can now review our current account analysis. The euro has appreciated against the renminbi and the dollar, so Euroland's current account deficit, already increased by the fall in interest rates, tends to widen. The dollar is unchanged against the renminbi and has depreciated against the euro, so the already increased U.S. current account deficit is reduced. These second-round effects on the current account positions of the three regions do not alter our basic story, assuming that the reactions to absorbing interest rates changes will be very different in the United States and in Euroland.

## Interest and Exchange Rates with Disturbances Along the Adjustment Path

Of course, changes in many domestic and international economic conditions will shift the dollar-euro exchange rates along the adjustment path set out in the previous section. The framework we have developed is useful to evaluate changes in the economic environment during the adjustment process, and the peculiar nature of the global system produces some remarkable and unanticipated results.

### 1. *A Stronger Euroland Outlook*

Suppose, for example, that at time $t_1$ an improved outlook for profits in Euroland generates a positive shift in the demand for investment in Euroland. Figure 7.3 suggests that Asian savings will shift from the United States to Euroland for the balance of the adjustment period and that interest rates in both regions will rise.

The effects on exchange rates are illustrated in Figure 7.5. With more Asian savings going to Euroland and less to the United States, at the end of the adjustment period, at T, the euro will be weaker and the dollar stronger than would have been the case. If Asian intervention at $t_1$ keeps the dollar from jumping from its initial value at F in Figure 7.5, the euro

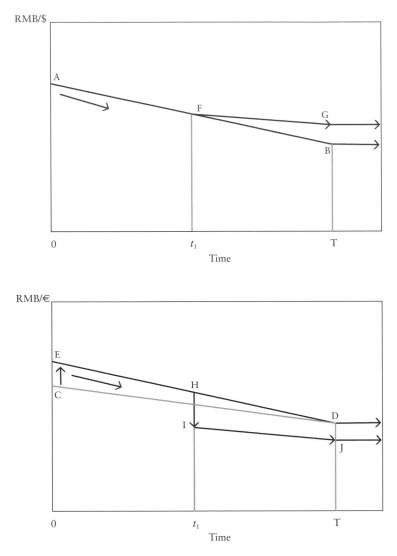

**Figure 7.5**
Exchange Rates
*Source:* Authors' calculations

depreciates sharply at $t_1$ for two reasons. First, it must now reach level J at T, and it must now depreciate more slowly to match the dollar's reduced rate of depreciation.

## 2. *A Weaker Euroland Outlook*

A weaker outlook for Euroland investment would have symmetric effects. In this case there would be deterioration in the final expected debt position of the United States and an improvement in the final debt position of Euroland. This scenario would require a more rapid rate of dollar depreciation against the renminbi and another move up for the euro. Interest rates in both regions would fall.

## 3. *A Stronger Outlook for the United States*

Changes in U.S. growth and investment would have similar effects. As U.S. growth increases, so does the expected stock of U.S. debt. The greater long-run depreciation would not affect the current level of the renminbi-dollar exchange rate, but would require a more rapid appreciation of the renminbi against the dollar for the balance of the adjustment period.

The euro would appreciate against the renminbi and the dollar for two reasons. First, its long-run level would jump, as Euroland would have a higher net asset position than before, and second, the euro would have to appreciate immediately in order to match the dollar's higher expected depreciation rate against the renminbi.

This situation is illustrated in Figure 7.6. The expected renminbi-dollar exchange rate at T shifts down from B to G, and the expected renminbi-euro rate moves up from D to K. The euro immediately jumps from H to I as again the change in the euro is amplified by arbitrage between dollar and euro assets. Interest rates in both regions would rise.

## 4. *More War or Katrina*

The United States might not experience the strong growth discussed earlier. For instance, expanded expenditures for war or a larger fiscal deficit and demand for capital following destruction of U.S. capital would increase U.S. demand for foreign savings and lead to increased U.S. indebtedness at T. Therefore, the analysis in scenario 3 still applies. The euro appreciates against the dollar. Global interest rates rise.

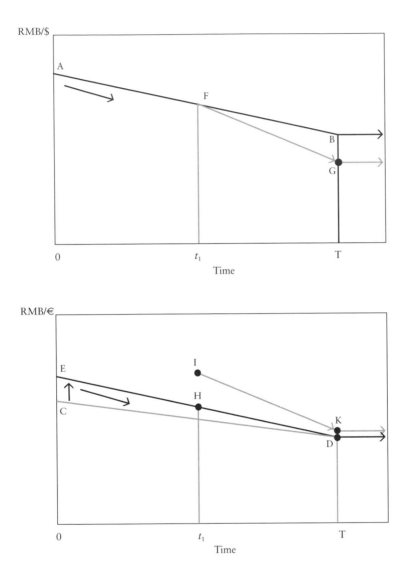

**Figure 7.6**
Exchange Rates
*Source:* Authors' calculations

### 5. Protectionism Surges; Oil Exporters Start Consuming Asia's Surplus Savings

It turns out that all of these potential events have the same impact on interest and exchange rates.

*5a.* For example, effective protectionist measures against Asian exports in both the United States and Euroland would forcibly reduce net savings transfers to the United States and Euroland from Asia by forcing a reduction in Asia's net trade surplus.

*5b.* Similarly, a decline in net Asian savings exported to the United States and Euroland would occur if a larger share of U.S., European, and Asian income is transferred to oil exporters via terms of trade shifts. As the oil exporters start to consume a high fraction of this transfer, fewer excess savings are available to accumulate U.S. and Euroland debt.

Each of these developments can be analyzed as illustrated in Figure 7.7.

In all these events, expected U.S. net debt at T is reduced, which raises the terminal exchange rate from B to G. Euroland net debt also falls, which raises the renminbi-euro rate from D to K. We assume that on its new path, the renminbi-dollar rate does not jump up at $t_1$, but the rate of dollar depreciation is reduced, so that the new path for the renminbi-dollar rate is FG. The renminbi-euro rate must reach K at T, and the path from $t_1$ must have the same slope as FG; that is, the renminbi-euro rate must have the same expected rate of depreciation as the renminbi-dollar rate. The conclusion is that the euro can either depreciate or appreciate immediately against the dollar, depending on the relative change in debt stocks in response to the new environment. There is no necessary direction of effect for this key exchange rate. Interest rates will rise both in the United States and Euroland because of the reduction in available savings.

A useful rule of thumb is that events that change expected U.S. and Euroland debt stocks and real exchange rates in opposite directions generate large and immediate changes in the dollar-euro rate when these expectations change. The market rate changes in the same direction as the change in the expected future rates. Events that move both expected debt stocks in the same direction have ambiguous effects on the exchange rate at the point where expectations change.

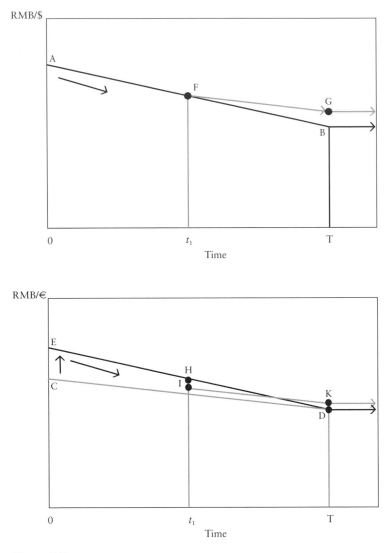

**Figure 7.7**
Exchange Rates
*Source:* Authors' calculations

## Further Thoughts on Asset Markets

The apparent failure of dollar exchange rates to respond to unprecedented recent and projected U.S. current account deficits is an important challenge for economic analysis. It is generally agreed that a substantial increase in projected debt levels should be associated with expectations that the real exchange rate will eventually depreciate. If private investors regard financial assets denominated in different currencies and issued by residents of different countries as perfect or very close substitutes, then the current exchange rate should be tied to the expected future exchange rate through the interest parity condition. Taken together, these ideas suggest that the dollar should have declined several years ago against the floating currencies when expectations about future U.S. debt levels were revised.

Suppose, for example, that some event generates a forecast that U.S. debt will increase from 0 to 60 percent of U.S. GDP, and then stabilize at that level at some arbitrary future date, T. Most analysts would agree that a real depreciation of the dollar by time T will be a part of the adjustment process required to service this higher level of debt.[13] If the dollar is expected to be lower at T, if interest parity holds, and if real interest rate differentials are not affected by the shock that generated the increase in expected debt, then the real exchange rate must depreciate immediately, and by the same amount as the long-run expected value when expectations change.

Research on exchange rates since the early 1970s has been dominated by attempts to reconcile the data to this elementary notion that increases in projected debt levels should be accompanied by expectations in real exchange rate depreciation. In the early years of floating rates, the question was why exchange rates were much more variable than reasonable estimates of long-run expected values. The current debate asks why market rates now are so stable in the face of strong presumption that the long-run expectation for the U.S. net foreign indebtedness has changed by a large amount.

To be sure, the market could have gotten it wrong then and could be getting it wrong now. If so, a crisis with sharply rising interest rates and sharply falling dollar exchange rates could be imminent, as conventional analysts predict. But it seems prudent to carefully consider alternative possibilities that are *currently* consistent with the salient evidence.

### An Attempt to Reconcile Current Exchange Rates and Expectations

Market exchange rates need not move in lockstep with expected exchange rates if interest rates change or if interest rate parity does not hold. An approach that was popular in the early 1980s to explain "excess volatility" of market exchange rates explored the assumption that interest rate parity may not hold if assets denominated in different currencies or issued in different countries are not close substitutes.[14] That is, if residents of a country for some reason prefer domestic assets, they would have to be compensated with higher expected yields to move away from their preferred portfolio. If rates of change toward a stable long-run equilibrium varied, it follows that current exchange rates could be much more variable than long-run expected exchange rates. Moreover, sterilized intervention alters relative supplies of securities, and could have some influence on expected rates of change and the levels of exchange rates.

In the current context, the implications of this portfolio balance approach are straightforward. If foreign residents prefer home securities and those preferences are unchanged, U.S. residents must pay a premium to finance a current account deficit. If we assume domestic interest rates are not affected by the shock that increases U.S. foreign debt, foreign investors must be induced to hold the growing stock of dollar-denominated claims on the United States by an extra expected return in the form of expected appreciation of the dollar. Since at T the dollar has to be below its current level because of increased U.S. indebtedness to foreigners, and since it must be expected to appreciate from now to T, the dollar must depreciate by even more now.

At first glance, this does not seem to help much in understanding the current situation where, it is argued, the dollar has not depreciated enough. But this can be rationalized by assuming the initial shock was a spontaneous increase in preferences for dollar assets (Blanchard, Giavazzi, and Sa 2005). If foreigners want dollar assets, they can obtain them through current account surpluses and in the interim will accept a lower expected yield on the dollar assets they do hold. It follows that even though the dollar is expected to be lower at T, it may not fall much initially because an expected depreciation is consistent with an otherwise unsatisfied demand for dollars during the adjustment period.

## Is Exchange Rate Intervention a Plausible Driver of the System?

Identifying plausible reasons for a shift in preferences toward dollars remains a serious problem.[15] One explanation holds that if changes in governments' balance sheets are not systematically offset by private investors, the shift in currency preferences could be associated with government policies. In particular, sterilized intervention could account for expected increases in U.S. net international debt, but only gradual adjustment in dollar exchange rates.

But there are a number of reasons that the portfolio balance approach was placed on a back burner of the profession's research agenda. First, a very large empirical literature was unable to find any lasting effect of intervention on interest rates or exchange rates. Second, imperfect substitution is usually modeled as aversion to exchange rate volatility. But sensible estimates of the degree of risk aversion needed to match exchange rate data seemed implausible. Third, imperfect substitution could be related to default risk or capital controls, but this has generally been assumed to be irrelevant for industrial countries.

Finally, Dornbusch (1976) showed that monetary policy and associated changes in real interest rate differentials could account for exchange rate volatility with perfect substitution and stable long-run expected values for real exchange rates. In an era where monetary policies were quite variable, this solved the theoretical puzzle of the day and moved portfolio balance models to the history of thought reading list.

Nevertheless, it is clear that home bias in goods, equities, and other financial assets remains a central fact and puzzle for international economics.[16] Obstfeld (2004) presents a thoughtful review of these issues; he suggests that a new theoretical basis for the portfolio balance approach will emerge from his work with Ken Rogoff on the implications of imperfect goods market integration. Such an explanation would be welcome, but in the interim we remain largely in the dark about the source of home bias for assets and its implications for models of portfolio behavior.

Our own home bias in these matters is that capital controls and the threat of sovereign interference with foreign investment is the most compelling argument behind a portfolio balance framework.[17] It follows that the portfolio balance approach is more likely to be useful in understanding the behavior of countries or groups of countries whose governments dominate private portfolio decisions through controls and intervention and manage their exchange rates.

In our framework, the shift in preferences toward dollars is not just *qualitative* but is *measured* by increases in international reserves of governments managing their exchange rates. Moreover, sterilized intervention is effective in altering interest differentials and exchange rates *between* managed economies and an integrated international capital market. But shifts in the composition of reserves do not change exchange rates *within* the larger integrated market.

While we use China/Asia and the renminbi as shorthand for the managed fixed-rate region and its currency, we do not argue that China alone is large enough to dominate international interest and exchange rates. However, we estimate that countries that actively manage their exchange rates comprise about one-third of world GDP and savings. The shock to the global system that we model is a substantial increase in savings rates and levels among this group. These effects are coupled with a decision of governments in the managed-rate region to put a large share of the increase, about half, into foreign assets.

We could extend the portfolio balance model as well to economic relationships within the international capital market, meaning to the relations between the United States and Euroland, but we do not do so for two reasons. First, the reasons for rejecting this model in the past are still very powerful. Second, a three-zone portfolio balance model is very difficult to work with, particularly when we are interested in studying the endogenous responses of exchange rates and real interest rates to various shocks. Since such models have a low insight to equation ratio, we stick with the perfect substitutes model for the United States and Euroland. Our guess is that introducing a little bit of home bias in these portfolios will do little violence to our results.

## Conclusion

To summarize the results presented in this paper, given the shift to a global financial system with a long-term rise in exports of Asian savings, and an understanding that this system will persist, includes recognizing that:

• A substantial immediate appreciation of the euro against the dollar will take place. As one of the only key prices allowed to move freely, this will entail a painful overshooting.

• Real interest rates in the United States and Euroland will remain low relative to historical cyclical experience, but will converge slowly toward normal rates as Asian financial markets become integrated with international markets.

• The dollar and the euro will gradually depreciate relative to the renminbi but, after the initial euro appreciation against the dollar, these currencies will *remain constant relative to each other in the absence of further disturbances.*

• A shift to a more rapid expected growth in Europe would *depreciate* the euro relative to the dollar and renminbi and raise interest rates in the United States and Europe.

• More rapid expected growth in the United States would tend to *depreciate* the dollar relative to the euro and renminbi. Because the dollar–renminbi exchange rate is managed, the dollar would not fall immediately but would begin to depreciate more rapidly. The euro would appreciate immediately and then match the dollar's more rapid rate of depreciation against the renminbi.

• Shifts in the currency composition of Asian reserves from dollars to euros would have little or *no lasting effect* on dollar-euro exchange rates.

• Effective protection in the United States and Euroland or a fall in the savings rate in Asia would generate a stronger dollar in the long run. The immediate effect would be less rapid dollar depreciation against the renminbi. The euro could go either way against the dollar.

• In real terms, the dollar will eventually have to depreciate relative to the renminbi. But most of the adjustment in the U.S. trade account will come as U.S. absorption responds to increases in real interest rates. Slow adjustment in the composition of U.S. output toward traded goods over an extended time period will not require unprecedented dollar depreciation.

• High oil prices and high consumption by oil exporters would generate a slower rate of dollar depreciation against the renminbi and higher interest rates in the United States and Euroland. The dollar-euro rate could go either way.

## Notes

1. See Dooley, Folkerts-Landau, and Garber 2003a, 2003b, 2004a, 2004b, 2004c, 2004d, 2005a, 2005b, and Dooley and Garber 2005. Many of these can be found at http://www.frbsf.org/economics/conferences/0502/index.html.

2. See Eichengreen 2004, Obstfeld and Rogoff 2004, Obstfeld 2005, and Roubini and Setser 2005.

3. Because there is no necessity of geographic contiguity, we have referred to these regions in other essays from the functional viewpoint as the trade account region, the center country, and the capital account region.

4. See Dooley and Garber 2005, p. 158–160.

5. We have consistently argued that the system, *not its current manifestation in the orientation of particular countries to these three blocs*, would last for the foreseeable future: "Fixed exchange rates and controlled financial markets work for twenty years and countries that follow this development strategy become an important periphery. These development policies are then overtaken by open financial markets and this, in turn, requires floating exchange rates. The Bretton Woods system does not evolve, it just occasionally reloads a periphery." See Dooley, Folkerts-Landau, and Garber 2003b, p. 3.

6. This means that there are many viable projects or confident consumers ready to go with a small improvement in financing costs relative to Euroland.

7. In our view, the amount of the eventual dollar depreciation is often overestimated. Recall that the primary factor driving the increase in the U.S. trade and current account deficit is the relatively strong response of U.S. investment and consumption to a decline in interest rates. Over the adjustment period interest rates will rise, thereby causing an equally strong reverse effect; this will help reduce the U.S. deficit. The exchange rate adjustment therefore must be consistent with a slow shift in U.S. output toward traded goods.

8. See Henderson and Leahy (2005) for a three-country analysis of intervention where imperfect asset substitution is assumed for all three regions.

9. We could replace time with net debt on the horizontal axis and have a diagram similar to that presented in Blanchard, Giavazzi, and Sa (2005). The case we present here is similar to their discussion of intervention following a shift in preferences away from U.S. goods. The interested reader is encouraged to work

through their analysis of an imperfect substitutes model. Their analysis assumes that interest rates are unchanged and changes in absorption are assumed to be related to fiscal policies.

10. The portfolio balance equilibrium is based on the idea that residents of all countries prefer home assets but can be moved away from their preferred portfolio by differences in expected yields; that is, by interest differentials adjusted for expected changes in exchange rates.

11. See Eichengreen 2005.

12. We have also explored the effects of diversification under the assumption of imperfect substitution between dollar and euro assets. Our conclusion was that it is not in the interests of Asian governments to diversify, and recent data from the International Monetary Fund shows that they have not done so through the end of last year. See Dooley, Folkerts-Landau, and Garber (2004a). The argument presented here suggests that Asian governments can diversify if they choose to do so, but that this would have no lasting effect on dollar exchange rates.

13. See Lane and Milesi-Ferretti 2004 and 2005 for discussion and evidence.

14. See Branson and Henderson 1985 for a survey.

15. Cooper (2001, 2004) offers a compelling argument for a change in private preferences for U.S. assets. We agree that this is part of the story but focus here on governments' portfolio choices.

16. See Obstfeld and Rogoff 2000.

17. See Dooley and Isard 1980.

# References

Blanchard, Olivier, Francesco Giavazzi, and Filipa Sa. 2005. "The U.S. Current Account Deficit and the Dollar." Working Paper No. 11137. Cambridge, MA: National Bureau of Economic Research.

Branson, William, and Dale Henderson. 1985."The Specification and Influence of Asset Markets." In *Handbook of International Economics*, Vol. 2, ed. Ronald W. Jones and Peter B. Kenen, 749–806. Amsterdam: Elsevier Science/ North-Holland.

Cooper, Richard N. 2001. "Is the U.S. Current Account Sustainable? Will It Be Sustained?" *Brookings Papers on Economic Activity* (1): 217–226.

Cooper, Richard N. 2004. "U.S. Deficit: It Is Not Only Sustainable, It Is Logical." *Financial Times*, October 31.

Dooley, Michael, David Folkerts-Landau, and Peter Garber. 2003a. "Dollars and Deficits: Where Do We Go From Here?" Paper written for Deutsche Bank Global Markets Research. Available at http://www.frbsf.org/economics/ conferences/0502/DollarsandDeficits.pdf.

Dooley, Michael, David Folkerts-Landau, and Peter Garber. 2003b. "An Essay on the Revived Bretton Woods System." Working Paper No. 9971. Cambridge, MA: National Bureau of Economic Research.

Dooley, Michael, David Folkerts-Landau, and Peter Garber. 2004a. "The Revived Bretton Woods System: The Effects of Periphery Intervention and Reserve Management on Interest Rates and Exchange Rates in Center Countries." Working Paper No. 10332. Cambridge, MA: National Bureau of Economic Research.

Dooley, Michael, David Folkerts-Landau, and Peter Garber. 2004b. "Direct Investment, Rising Real Wages, and the Absorption of Excess Labor in the Periphery." Working Paper No. 10626. Cambridge, MA: National Bureau of Economic Research.

Dooley, Michael, David Folkerts-Landau, and Peter Garber. 2004c. "The U.S. Current Account Deficit and Economic Development: Collateral for a Total Return Swap." Working Paper No. 10727. Cambridge, MA: National Bureau of Economic Research.

Dooley, Michael, David Folkerts-Landau, and Peter Garber. 2004d. "The Revived Bretton Woods: Alive and Well." Paper written for Deutsche Bank Global Markets Research. Available at http://www.frbsf.org/economics/conferences/0502/BrettonWoods.pdf.

Dooley, Michael, David Folkerts-Landau, and Peter Garber. 2005a. "Savings Gluts and Interest Rates: The Missing Link to Europe." Working Paper No. 11520. Cambridge, MA: National Bureau of Economic Research.

Dooley, Michael, David Folkerts-Landau, and Peter Garber. 2005b. "Interest Rates, Exchange Rates, and International Adjustment." Working Paper No. 11771. Cambridge, MA: National Bureau of Economic Research.

Dooley, Michael, and Peter Garber. 2005. "Is it 1958 or 1968? Three Notes on the Longevity of the Revived Bretton Woods System." *Brookings Papers on Economic Activity* (1): 147–187.

Dooley, Michael, and Peter Isard. 1980. "Capital Controls, Political Risk, and Deviations from Interest Parity." *Journal of Political Economy* 88(2): 370–384.

Dornbusch, Rudiger. 1976. "Expectations and Exchange Rate Dynamics." *Journal of Political Economy* 84(6): 1161–1176.

Eichengreen, Barry. 2004. "Global Imbalances and the Lessons of Bretton Woods." Working Paper No. 10497. Cambridge, MA: National Bureau of Economic Research.

Eichengreen, Barry. 2005. "Sterling's Past, Dollar's Future: Historical Perspectives on Reserve Currency Competition." Working Paper No. 11336. Cambridge, MA: National Bureau of Economic Research.

Henderson Dale, and Michael Leahy. 2005. "A Note on Alternative Exchange Rate Policies with Three Currencies." Available at http://mysite.verizon.net/resr6xul/.

Lane, Philip R., and Gian Maria Milesi-Ferretti. 2004. "The Transfer Problem Revisited: Net Foreign Assets and Real Exchange Rates." *Review of Economics and Statistics* 86(4): 841–857.

Lane, Philip R. and Gian Maria Milesi-Feretti. 2005. "Financial Globalization and Exchange Rates." Working Paper 05/03. Washington, DC: International Monetary Fund.

Obstfeld, Maurice. 2004."External Adjustment." *Review of World Economics* 140(4): 541–568.

Obstfeld, Maurice. 2005 "Sustainability and the U.S. Account: Dark Musings." Available at http://www.frbsf.org/economics/conferences/0502/Obstfeld.ppt.

Obstfeld, Maurice, and Kenneth Rogoff. 2000. "The Six Major Puzzles in International Macroeconomics: Is there a Common Cause?" In *NBER Macroeconomics Annual 2000*, ed. Ben S. Bernanke and Kenneth Rogoff, 339–390. Cambridge, MA: MIT Press.

Obstfeld, Maurice, and Kenneth Rogoff. 2004. "The Unsustainable U.S. Current Account Position Revisited." Available at http://www.frbsf.org/economics/conferences/0502/Obstfeld.pdf.

Roubini, Nouriel, and Brad Setser. 2005. "Will the Bretton Woods 2 Regime Unravel Soon? The Risk of a Hard Landing in 2005–2006." Presented at Federal Reserve Bank of San Francisco symposium, Revived Bretton Woods System: A New Paradigm for Asian Development?, February 4. Available at http://www.frbsf.org/economics/conferences/0502/index.html.

# Comments on "Interest Rates, Exchange Rates, and International Adjustment" by Michael P. Dooley, David Folkerts-Landau, and Peter M. Garber

Catherine L. Mann

Are global imbalances here to stay for a long while or are the adjustment mechanisms of our economic theory classes soon to come into play? When this comment was originally written in June 2006 for delivery at the conference, the dollar had been depreciating against the major freely traded currencies for about four years, but had moved much less against the managed currencies of the other important trading partners, including, in particular, the Chinese renminbi. The Dooley, Folkerts-Landau, and Garber (DFG) collection of papers have been described as "Bretton Woods II" for the central role the near-peg of the renminbi to the dollar plays in the world's current account imbalances.

Then and now, my framework for assessing global imbalances takes the form of the four Cs. The first C is consumption. In mid-June 2006, U.S. consumption had been driving both GDP growth and import growth, contributing to the U.S. side of the global imbalance. The second C is codependency, which describes the nature of the relationship between the U.S. current account deficit and the capital inflows from other countries. The U.S. imbalance occurs in a global context of policy choices and habits. Complacency is the third C—the apparent stability of the global macroeconomic situation contributed to complacency on the part of both policymakers and the private financial community that this situation of "balanced imbalance" could continue indefinitely. The fourth C is crisis. At the Boston Fed conference held in mid-2006, I noted that while we surely had the first three Cs in place, the important question was whether the fourth C is on the horizon, and if not, why not?

In the end, DFG predicted that forces of constancy (a fifth C!) would prevail, meaing that a crisis would not ensue. At the time, I tended to agree with them, although our analyses took somewhat different paths. The different paths yielded different implications for how long the stability of global imbalances could last, and, in the end, I was less sanguine than DFG about the path of stability they foresaw continuing indefinitely.

Indeed, in the intervening two years, U.S. consumption has slowed, and the current account has narrowed. Codependency, and its associated buildup of financial assets, has become more noticed by the countries lending to the United States, with the rise of sovereign wealth funds a consequence. Complacency reigned until it did not—with the subprime crisis delivering the "proper jolt" that I noted in my closing remarks would change the dynamics of the system.

## Overview of DFG and Where I Differ

First, DFG see the main factor driving the global imbalance as Asian savings. While I agree that Asian saving is important, it takes two domestic imbalances to create a global imbalance. The U.S. household consumption story is our domestic part of the global imbalance. A second part of DFG's analysis is the relationship between the dollar exchange rate and the U.S. current account deficit. They argue that the dollar exchange rate, as of June 2006, had not responded to the large U.S. current account deficit. In contrast to this view, in an essay written in 2002 and published in 2003, titled "How Long the Strong Dollar?," I argued that the dollar exchange rate did respond at that time to the projected high share of U.S. assets in private portfolios of global investors. What has happened subsequently to the exchange rate, particularly evinced in the different movement of the Federal Reserve Board's "major trading partners" currency index versus that of the other important trading partner (OITP) index, is that Asian official purchases have taken up the slack in private investors' purchases of U.S. assets. Subsequent to 2006, although Asian official purchases remain large, there has been an accelerated appreciation against the dollar by those managed currencies.

The third key part of the DGF analysis is that, in their view, future adjustment will take place in two steps. As the first step, U.S. domestic demand would slow in response to rising real interest rates, which would be a consequence of the second step—a gradual integration of Asian private finance into global capital markets and the associated equalization of higher real interest rates around the world. In contrast, I argued then and maintain now that, while there was (and in fact did occur, over the last year) certainly the potential for the first step of their analysis, this was not on account of integrating Asia into global capital markets, which is too gradual a transition to explain near-term changes in interest rates. Rather, any rise in interest rates would more likely be due to a Federal Reserve policy shift that was accompanied by other central banks around the world. Removing the accommodative monetary stance would represent the recognition by U.S. policymakers of their possible awakening from complacency regarding the role of U.S. consumption in maintaining these global imbalances. On the other hand, the continued (as of 2006 anyway) low-risk, low-inflation, and low-term premia on longer-term U.S. assets suggested a continued complacency on the part of the private financial markets. At the June 2006 conference I asked, "Does this complacency raise the prospect for crisis, or is this complacency well founded in the constancy of exchange rates underpinning Bretton Woods II?"

## The Cs Framework and Data

Codependency of habits and policies here and abroad has yielded global imbalances both on the real side and on the financial side. What habits are these? The habit on the part of the United States to consume more than it produces and the habit on the part of some of other countries abroad to consume less than they produce. Policies here and abroad have tended in the past to exacerbate those habits. For example, the personal income tax cuts in the United States have tended to promote personal consumption as well as reduce national savings. The extended period of low interest rates tended to support equity and housing prices, both of which tended to promote U.S. consumption through increased wealth. With the change in monetary stance (up until the 2007 subprime crisis), at least one U.S. policy had moved toward neutral. By contrast, abroad, the policy to maintain relatively depreciated exchange rates (although less so starting in mid-2006) had tended to buttress the habit of production in excess of consumption, which was most evident in parts of Asia.

Codependency, even now as of mid-2008, is stable and this apparent stability can produce policy and private complacency about assessing risks. In addition, this apparently stable situation does not necessarily yield a desirable trajectory. Why is this stable codependency undesirable? The stable production-consumption imbalances are mutually reinforcing, so they are stable. On the other hand, these production-consumption imbalances yield undesirable domestic trajectories because these are associated with resource misallocations that damage potential growth. The capital, sectoral, and geographical misallocations in China, and to some degree in India, were noted in other papers and comments during the conference. A persistently undervalued exchange rate undermines the development of a nation's banking system, directs credit away from services toward tradeable goods, and focuses investment to port areas.

Resource misallocations also can be measured from the standpoint of potentially vulnerable financial asset positions. One is the growing U.S. net international investment obligation that is increasingly exposed to changes in interest rates and the increasing concentration of foreign official holders of U.S. official assets. The financial vulnerabilities probably matter more in the short run given the liquidity of the markets. Overall, policymakers, who can change course, should not exacerbate the habits and behaviors that are much more difficult to alter.

What is the evidence for the four Cs framework? The adjustment challenges facing the United States, and in the context of global exchange rates the rest of the world too, is daunting, as shown in Figure 7.8. The present imbalances observed in the U.S. current account and trade deficit are unprecedented over the floating rate period. Some observers of these data look to exchange rate adjustment as a way of achieving U.S. external balance—a twenty-first century redux of the late 1980s and early 1990s. But those observers must be careful what they wish for. Although the current account deficit was relatively narrow during these years, and the dollar very competitively priced, the overall macroeconomic situation in the United States and some other parts of the world was not so salubrious. A decomposition of the U.S. trade deficit reveals that it is not just Asian savings that drives global imbalances, as shown in Figure 7.9. Nearly the entire U.S. trade deficit in most recent years, and in fact for virtually all of the last 25 years, comes from large and widening deficits on consumer

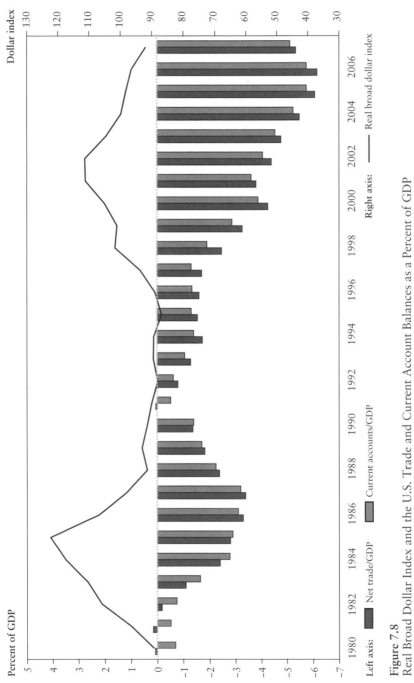

**Figure 7.8**
Real Broad Dollar Index and the U.S. Trade and Current Account Balances as a Percent of GDP
*Source:* U.S. Bureau of Economic Analysis.

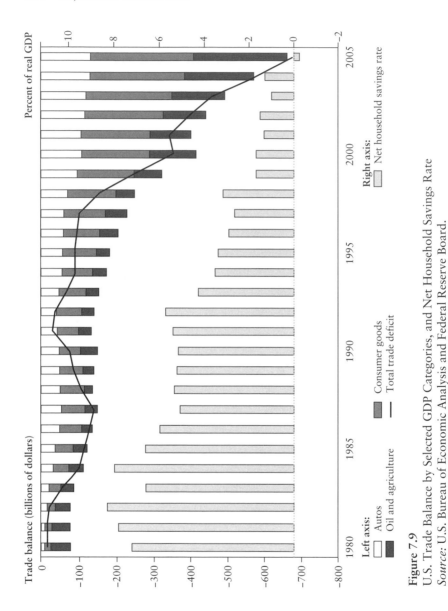

**Figure 7.9**
U.S. Trade Balance by Selected GDP Categories, and Net Household Savings Rate
*Source:* U.S. Bureau of Economic Analysis and Federal Reserve Board.

goods, autos, and energy. Placed against the trade deficit is the household saving rate, which has trended downward, significantly so since the early 1990s. The "ocular regression" of the correlation between consumer-type imports, overall net imports, and the household saving rate is supported by more sophisticated econometric techniques (Mann and Plück 2007). Some researchers have questioned the calculation of household saving (for instance, see Cooper 2005). Making adjustments to wealth, education, and so on may adjust the level, but does not change the downward trend, and it is the trend that drives the important relationship. Finally, note that the overall U.S. trade deficit is in categories of trade that are not investment-related: capital goods and industrial supplies and materials account for about 30 percent of imports and 44 percent of exports, but are not shown because this category is about in-trade balance.

Examining the current accounts and trends for a range of countries further indicates that the Asian savings phenomenon is not the whole story behind these global imbalances, as illustrated in Table 7.1. The trend toward net external saving is most pronounced for Asia, but it is not exclusively an Asian story.

The second part of the DFG argument, at least through mid-2006, was that the dollar was not responding to the U.S. imbalance. Well, then and

Table 7.1
Increases in Savings: Current Accounts as a Percent of GDP

|  | 1998 | 2004 | 2005 | 2006 | 2007 |
|---|---|---|---|---|---|
|  | | | (percent) | | |
| European Union | 2.6 | 0.5 | −0.2 | −0.7 | −1.0 |
| Japan | 3.0 | 3.7 | 3.0 | 3.9 | 4.5 |
| China | 3.3 | 3.6 | 7.2 | 9.4 | 11.7 |
| Developing Asia | 2.6 | 2.6 | 4.1 | 5.9 | 6.9 |
| Western Hemisphere | −4.5 | 1.0 | 1.4 | 1.5 | 0.6 |

Source: International Monetary Fund, World Economic Outloook Database, 2007.
Note: Data for 2007 are projections.

now, I'd argue both yes and no. The behavior of the exchange value of the dollar in recent years is similar to that observed during the 1990s—the major currency index has adjusted relatively more whereas the OITP index has adjusted a lot less. The differential adjustment may matter more today than in the early 1990s because of the changing shares of the United States's trading partners, particularly for imports; see Figure 7.10. Clearly, against some currencies, the dollar has adjusted. But why more against some compared to others? In 2002, I calculated that the widening trajectory for the U.S. current account deficit implied that a growing share of the increase in global financial wealth would have to be invested in U.S. securities, so as to not exert downward pressure on the dollar and upward pressure on interest rates (Mann 2003). Those calculations showed that more than 100 percent of the increase in global non-U.S. financial wealth would have had to be invested in U.S. securities in order to support the dollar at that time. Well, that shift in investment did not happen, and so a general downward move in the dollar started in 2002.

However, the dollar has not completely adjusted, and the relatively less adjustment in Asia and the region's financial means used to avoid adjustment is partly contributing to the financial vulnerability of the global economic system. This situation is shown in Figure 7.11. As the depreciation of the dollar started against the major currencies, the United States' share in global capital imports started to contract, consistent with the pullback by foreign investors from maintaining a too-high share of U.S. assets in their portfolios. However, official investors came in to augment demand for U.S. securities so as to maintain the U.S. share in global capital imports. The preponderance of official investors from the OITP countries explains the differential behavior of the two exchange rate indexes. This official behavior is not new and it continues even in 2008. It has frequently been the case that the official share in U.S. capital imports has been high in periods when the dollar has been under downward pressure.

### Scenarios of Adjustment

So, how might adjustment take place? One partial-equilibrium approach is to consider only adjustment via changes in growth—a slowdown in U.S. economic activity and a boom abroad. At the other partial-equi-

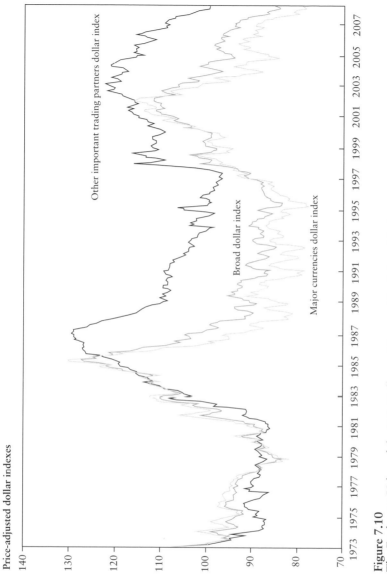

Price-adjusted dollar indexes

**Figure 7.10**
The Exchange Value of the U.S. Dollar as Measured by Selected Indexes
*Source:* Federal Reserve Board.

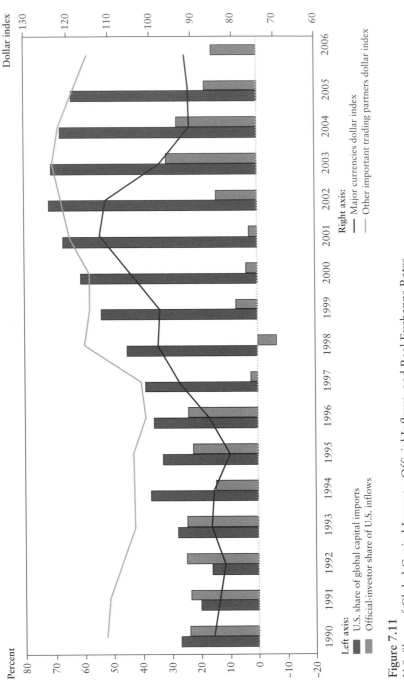

**Figure 7.11**
U.S. Share of Global Capital Imports, Official Inflows, and Real Exchange Rates
*Source:* IMF *World Economic Outlook Database,* U.S. Bureau of Economic Analysis, and Federal Reserve Board.

librium extreme, all adjustment could take place via movements in the exchange value of the dollar.

Based on parameters estimated in Mann and Plück, an "average" non-U.S. domestic demand boom improves, albeit slightly, the U.S. trade deficit. On the other hand, a modest U.S. slowdown dramatically reduces the U.S. side of the global imbalance. With regard to exchange rate changes, estimates using the exchange rate scenario in Truman (2005) show that a big exchange rate change vis-à-vis Asian currencies shifts U.S. consumer spending dramatically away from those imports and raises and shifts U.S. exports away from Europe toward Asian markets. The magnitude of the shifts in net exports to Asia could sum to about 7 percent of the region's GDP.

Therefore, both growth and relative price adjustments are needed. Ending global codependency requires big adjustments to U.S. domestic demand and to currencies in Asia. Part of this adjustment must be led by changes in policy. But that requires a change in policymakers' complacency regarding the current situation. This is exactly why it is not likely to happen any time soon. (And indeed, the response to sluggish consumption growth in the United States is to lower interest rates and issue tax rebate checks, policies which are opposite to the adjustment in consumption necessary to narrow the U.S. side of the external imbalance.) As with DFG's Bretton Woods II, codependency and complacency suggest that the current situation will persist, but for somewhat different reasons than these authors propose.

In 2006, I was less sanguine than DFG. On the real side, the misallocations of resources were already noted, and were leading to political pressures, at least in the United States, to remedy the situation. On the financial side, the U.S. share of global capital imports remains high, private inflows are a smaller share of those capital imports, and the official purchases of U.S. assets are increasingly concentrated nationally. I suggested in 2006 that the private financial markets may be waking from their complacency, or could do so quickly given a proper jolt. I argued then that, from the standpoint of politics and private finance, the situation may be more vulnerable than DFG suspect. Only future research will show the extent to which the magnitude of the subprime meltdown was related to global external imbalances.

## References

Cooper, Richard. 2005. "Living with Global Imbalances: A Contrarian View." Policy Brief 05-03. Washington, DC: Institute for International Economics.

Mann, Catherine L. 2003. "How Long the Strong Dollar?" In *Dollar Overvaluation and the World Economy*, ed. C. Fred Bergsten and John Williamson, 57–76. Washington, DC: Institute for International Economics.

Mann, Catherine L., and Katharina Plück. 2007. "Understanding the U.S. Trade Deficit: A Disaggregated Perspective?" In *G7 Current Account Imbalances: Sustainability and Adjustment*, ed. Richard Clarida, 247–277. Chicago: University of Chicago Press.

Truman, Edwin M. 2005. "Postponing Global Adjustment: An Analysis of the Pending Adjustment of Global Imbalances." Working Paper 05-6. Washington, DC: Institute for International Economics.

# Comments on "Interest Rates, Exchange Rates, and International Adjustment" by Michael P. Dooley, David Folkerts-Landau, and Peter M. Garber

Eswar S. Prasad

This is a paper by Dooley, Folkerts-Landau, and Garber, so almost by construction it is an interesting paper and when all is said and done you know exactly where they stand on the issue of global imbalances. Given that this is an issue that a lot of us worry about, after a first reading of the paper you get the sense that it is time to go home and catch up on your sleep because all is well in the world, things are going to adjust smoothly, and life is going to be all right.

Beginning in 2003, these three authors went out on a limb in a very constructive way. Not only did they come up with an internally consistent approach that rationalizes global imbalances, but they also made a prediction that, as they note in this conference paper, was "many sigmas away" from the conventional wisdom. So, in this new paper they take a brief moment to gloat, and while conceding that some of what has happened since may be chalked up to fortune, overall they contend that their analysis got it all right.

The basic thesis of the paper is that global imbalances are an equilibrium outcome, that they are sustainable over the medium-term horizon, and that they will eventually fade away without any major disruptions in the countries involved. I would like to focus on whether this sort of laissez-faire approach to the adjustment process is ideal. In my view, sustainability is not really the issue. The issue is whether the current state of policies is optimal, and one can think about this question in two ways. First, we should consider whether the risks of a bad outcome have increased very significantly. Second, even if the potential risks do not pan out in a disruptive manner, is this approach the right way that policy-makers should be thinking about these global imbalances?

The first question is about whether there are really significant risks, or whether the whole notion of global imbalance is just an organizing principle that perhaps gives my former employer, the International Monetary Fund, a new mandate to go around banging heads by saying, "Look, global imbalances are a problem. Let's all sit down at the table and figure out what you need to do for yourself and for the greater good of the world economy." I think there is some truth to that point of view, because ultimately what might be a way of trying to resolve the global imbalances will, in a sense, resolve imbalances in the individual countries. This will entail attempting to get China and much of emerging Asia to increase domestic consumption, trying to get more flexible exchange rates, reducing government consumption in the United States, and perhaps starting Europe on the process to real growth. These are all goals that are intrinsically valuable and perhaps will reduce the risks associated with global imbalances, so it may be a very useful organizing principle to get reforms started that are really essential to the long-term health of the international financial system and global economy. Such reforms would address the distortionary consequences that should be part of the welfare calculations resulting from the current state of global imbalances. See Figure 7.12, which shows how total capital flows (private plus official) have been going from relatively poor nonindustrial economies to advanced industrial economies, a direction exactly opposite the one predicted by theory; Figure 7.13 shows a similar calculation but excludes the United States.

There is still the question of whether the current situation is really one of reserve imbalances, where the huge and growing hoards of reserves by some emerging market countries portend dysfunctionality somewhere else. But remember that no one is forcing the Chinese to accumulate more reserves and to use their foreign exchange to buy more U.S. government bonds and finance U.S. consumption. Is it simply just puritanical tendencies on our part that are causing us to think about the behavior of certain consenting adults as abnormal?

Some argue that maybe we just have to get ourselves in tune with the new reality. I think, however, that view ignores a number of potential problems because at present we are at an equilibrium that is sustained at some level by official flows. Peter Garber and his co-authors have nicely

Ratio

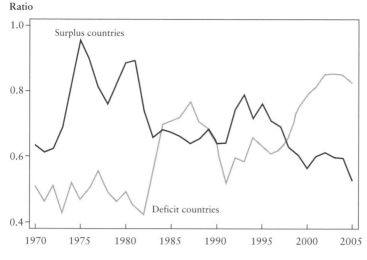

**Figure 7.12**
Relative Incomes of Capital-Exporting and Capital-Importing Countries
(Relative Per Capita GDP, Weighted by Current Accounts)
*Source:* Prasad, Rajan, and Subramanian (2006).
*Note:* For each year, we separate our sample of countries into two groups—
those with current account surpluses and those with deficits in that year.
For the first group, we then take each country's share of the total current
account surplus accounted for by all countries in that group. We then
multiply that share by the relative PPP-adjusted per capita income of that
country (measured relative to the per capita income of the richest country
in the sample in that year). This gives us a current account-weighted measure
of the relative incomes of surplus countries. We do the same for current
account deficit countries. This enables us to compare the relative incomes
of surplus versus deficit countries in each year.

pointed out how this current situation, which has been sustained for a
number of years, makes a great deal of sense. For instance, by putting
its reserve accumulation in U.S. dollars, China could in fact be locking
itself into its current exchange rate regime and creating a sustainable
equilibrium. But again, I think the importance of official flows tends to
be overstated in some cases because at the margin—and the margin is
typically where the action takes place—there are some trigger events,
although Peter was quick to dismiss some of them, which can tip the balance rather quickly. Some of these events could generate enough shifts in
private capital flows that you would have broader effects.

Ratio

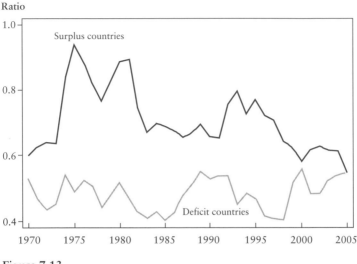

**Figure 7.13**
Relative Incomes of Capital-Exporting and Capital-Importing Countries, Excluding the United States (Relative per Capita GDP, Weighted by Current Accounts)
*Source:* Prasad, Rajan, and Subramanian (2006).

In sum, I believe that it is important for us to be thinking about the underlying issues that need to be resolved in order to deal responsibly with these global imbalances. Yet I should add that the connection between the current state of doing nothing and doing the right thing is not immediately obvious. If you did in fact have China doing the right things, it is not entirely obvious that these actions would have the desired effect of reducing current account imbalances. For instance, if China undertook serious financial sector reforms, it is not immediately obvious that this would help redress the global current account imbalances. This reform would of course help China make its long-term growth more stable and sustainable.

Perhaps the excessive focus on global imbalances as *the* problem to be contained may not be the right angle to approach what are in many respects larger structural issues that need to be addressed. Having framed the issue this way, one can then ask whether the scenario that Peter and his co-authors have laid out is the right one. What they posit is a gradual adjustment scenario where, for instance, there is a gradual appreciation of China's currency and other things adjust slowly. Here is where I take issue with their framework because, although this paper does not explicitly state it, the underlying assumption is that benign neglect is the right approach. Their argument hangs on the notion that so long as there are no huge shocks to the international financial system, there is going to be a very sensible and smooth adjustment process. I take issue with this stance because it essentially takes as its foundation maintaining the exchange rate regime as a crucial part of the adjustment strategy. This requires certain policy distortions—in my view major policy distortions—like financial repression and capital controls.

I will use China as a specific example partly because I know China a little better than other economies, and also because I think it highlights some of the key issues. Ultimately, my contention is that the right way for China to be generating growth is not through repressing its domestic financial and capital markets. Now, in this conference paper and in earlier work, Peter has argued that foreign direct investment is going to be the way around financial sector problems within China, which he views as essentially unsolvable in the near future. As Larry Lau pointed out in an earlier session, however, foreign direct investment really comprises a very small portion of the financing that is available for China's domestic investment. So a robust domestic financial system is really crucial for the intermediation of capital that drives investment. As do many of the East Asian countries, the Chinese save a lot, but much of this savings is intermediated through a very weak financial system.[1] So unless you get that adverse situation sorted out, things are not going to get much better in terms of China's balance of growth, something that I believe is really important to emphasize rather than just focusing on GDP.

This example illustrates why some policies that remain on the periphery of the current consideration of global imbalances start to play an important role in the inevitable adjustment. This is why I think it is crucial to consider the interacting relationships between different policies. Ultimately it is difficult to foster financial sector reform; in the case of China this mostly involves banking sectors. It is difficult to have banking sector reform unless you have market signals acting through interest rates from which the banks can take cues. Moreover, it is really difficult to have an autonomous monetary policy, notwithstanding moderately effective capital controls, unless you have exchange rate flexibility. Having exchange rate flexibility is hardly an end in itself, but it does deliver some very important benefits by providing a way in which the central bank can generate market signals to manage investment and credit growth. Flexible exchange rates enable financial sector reforms and, in a sense, enable a more efficient allocation of credit, which I think is really important for the economy (Prasad 2008).

Ultimately, the approach I think that will work in redressing these imbalances will look at the overall policy landscape on the underlying distortions and institutional weaknesses that represent departures from a first-best situation. I have emphasized the investment side but I think the consumption side is important as well. It is only if and when you have financial market development that some of the liquidity constraints in China's economy are going to start loosening up and perhaps increase consumption. Again, the effect on the current account in the short term is far from obvious. You could have the net effect on saving and investment going the other way such that current account surplus even rises. But in terms of the longer-term objectives, I think the focus should be on strengthening internal financial markets in these developing countries. This is why I'm concerned that maintaining the current stance of policies that make the current equilibrium hang together might lead to a much more adverse outcome in the longer run. For instance, Figure 7.14 shows how the faster-growing developing countries have been exporting capital during this decade, some of this in the form of official accumulation of international reserves. The net effect, however, is reducing the amount of capital available for investment in developing nations, and this is not conducive to long-run growth.

Ultimately, even though we live in a second-best world, I think there is some truth that underlies Peter's notion that trying to undertake a big bang sort of financial sector reform in China or trying to solve the Europe's structural problems in a very rapid way may not quite work. But I think that the Dooley, Folkerts-Landau, and Garber papers may be shifting the balance toward complacency, as Cathy Mann pointed out. This is not really the ideal way to approach the problem of global imbalances. Even if these imbalances do not require a crisis to get resolved, they do really serve as an opportunity to focus on some of the underlying

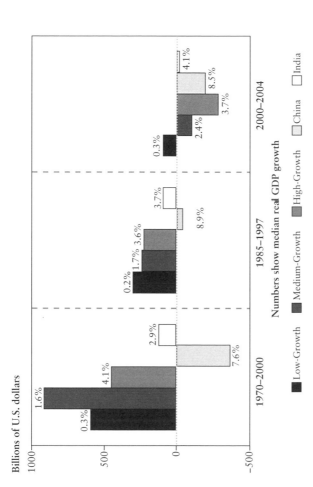

**Figure 7.14**
Allocation of Capital Flows to Nonindustrial Countries (Cumulative Real Current Account Deficits)
*Source:* Prasad, Rajan, and Subramanian (2006).
*Note:* The nonindustrial countries in our sample are split into three groups with roughly equal total populations in each group. China and India are treated separately. Each panel shows the cumulative current account deficits (in billions of U.S. dollars, deflated by the U.S. CPI indexed to 1 in 2004) summed up within each group over the relevant period. A negative number indicates a surplus. Median real GDP growth rates for the countries in each group (after averaging over the relevant period for each country) are also shown.

problems enabling their continuation. I would prefer policymakers to focus on these long-term issues.

In an ideal world, relatively capital-poor economies would have better financial systems that would effectively intermediate both domestic savings and foreign capital, and thereby achieve higher growth rates through both direct and indirect benefits accruing from financial integration.[2] Advanced economies would generate surpluses to finance investments in developing countries, rather than running deficits to finance consumption. The emphasis on the current state of global imbalances might be refocused to examine what these patterns of international financial flows are signaling about more basic problems in different parts of the world economy. Whether or not these global imbalances are destined to end in a bad manner, they are a sign of things gone awry.

## Notes

1. See Chamon and Prasad (2008) for an analysis of the determinants of China's household saving rate.
2. See Prasad, Rajan, and Subramanian (2006) for an analysis of "uphill" flows of capital, including the possible reasons and consequences.

## References

Chamon, Marcos, and Eswar Prasad. 2008. "Why are Savings Rates of Urban Households in China Rising?" Manuscript, Cornell University and the International Monetary Fund.

Prasad, Eswar. 2008. "Is China's Growth Miracle Built to Last?" *China Economic Review*, forthcoming.

Prasad, Eswar, Raghuram Rajan, and Arvind Subramanian. 2006. "Patterns of International Capital Flows and Their Implications for Economic Development." Jackson Hole Symposium 2006, The Federal Reserve Bank of Kansas City, August 24–26. Available at http://www.kansascityfed.org/publicat/sympos/2006/pdf/11Rajan.pdf.

# 8

## Appropriate Adjustment Considerations and Policies

# An Indian Perspective on Global Imbalances and Potential Policy Responses

Shankar Acharya

I will confine my remarks to two areas. First, I will try to give you an Indian perspective on this issue of global imbalances. (I want to emphasize the article *an*, since we have lots of perspectives on this matter). Second, I will emphasize three or four of the key ideas and assessments that I am taking with me following these two days of stimulating sessions, which, using Brad DeLong's phrase, may have led at times to "higher levels of confusion."

## An Indian Perspective

It is flattering to find India clubbed with China under the rubric of "Emerging Giants." However, honesty compels me to admit that I have to agree with Richard Cooper's point from yesterday that lumping India and China together may not be quite appropriate, at least at the present time, and certainly not as far as the scale of engagement with the global economy is concerned.

Let me give you a few rather obvious indicators and dimensions by way of comparison. If you take merchandise trade (or even if you include services), India's share in global trade is about 1 percent. China's share is, I believe, around 7 percent. If you take inward foreign direct investment, China has received more than U.S. $60 billion annually in recent years. India, on the other hand, gets about U.S. $5–6 billion a year. Even if one adds about U.S. $8–10 billion of portfolio investment, annual inflows of foreign investment into India are running at only about a fifth of the flows into China. A third dimension or indicator, which (surprisingly) we haven't talked much about during this conference, is energy. This surely is a subject with close linkages to the topic of global imbalances. Now, I just happened to look at some numbers recently in *The Wall Street Journal*. The paper was quoting the International Energy Agency (IEA), according to which the incremental increase in oil demand between 2000 and 2005 was as follows: for India it was 300,000 barrels per day, while for China it was 2.1 million barrels a day. So China's demand is about seven times higher than India's. By way of benchmarking, for the United States the incremental increase in oil demand during this same period was 1.1 million barrels per day.

Turning to issues of labor supply and demand, which we discussed yesterday, let me recall the point made by Abhijit Banerjee about weaknesses in the supply chain of India's higher education system. He mentioned that some 15 to 17 professorships were vacant at the elite Delhi School of Economics—this example may be a special case. But there is plenty of other evidence showing major weaknesses at all levels of India's education system, from primary schools upward. Demand for education is not an issue in India. Supply is the problem. We have not got our act together on this. Unfortunately, this problem is likely to have serious long-term effects on skill development in India and the future supply of skilled labor coming into both Indian and global labor markets. In contrast, my impression is that China has had much greater success in getting its higher education system really to forge ahead, providing the kind of numbers that we saw yesterday in Richard Freeman's presentation.

Let me point to one last indicator of differences in achievement between India and China; namely, employment in the organized (as distinct from informal or small-scale) manufacturing sector. That number (if the official data is correct) for a recent year in India was only about 6 million out of a total labor force of over 400 million. This low figure reflects a long history of all sorts of dysfunctional labor laws, among many other factors, but it certainly is an indication of significant labor market problems. Of course this is very different from the numbers that I have seen on China's factory employment in manufacturing, which, depending on the source, varies from somewhere between 50 or 60 to 150 million. If you take all this together and refer back to some of the very interesting discussions we had yesterday during Richard Freeman's session, it's probably not two "typhoons" (to use Surjit Bhalla's colorful phrase) that are on their way to disrupt global labor markets. It is probably one typhoon from China, and perhaps only a gale force 2 storm from India, which may not gather much strength in the foreseeable future.

The second dimension of difference that I want to emphasize between India and China relates to some of the policy issues that typically come up in international forums like the International Monetary Fund (IMF) and G7 when one is discussing the issue of global imbalances. Let me touch on a few aspects. First, if imbalance is a problem (and one of the things I have learned at this conference is that there is a very weighty and respectable intellectual view that suggests it may not be such a big problem), India doesn't seem to be contributing to this problem through a structural current account surplus. In the last 17 years there are only three—2001, 2002, and 2003—in which India had a very modest current account surplus. In every other year it has run a deficit. And in the last couple of years the deficit has been mounting. In 2006–2007 it is probably going to be about 2 percent of GDP. In billions of dollars that's only a modest $15 billion or so. The point is India is not part of the "structural surplus" depicted in one of those diagrams of surpluses and deficits that one commonly sees in papers on global imbalances.

Second, another distinguishing feature between India and China is that the main drivers of aggregate demand in the Indian economy remain domestic consumption plus domestic investment. Exports certainly play a very important supplementary role, especially from an efficiency point of view. But in terms of the macro aggregate demand, India is really a home market-driven economy, which is not what is usually said about recent Chinese experience. Third, with gross domestic savings rate around 29–30 percent of GDP, and gross domestic investment just a shade higher, India is clearly not contributing to any global "savings glut." And finally, I would contend that India's exchange rate policy has been more flexible and variable (in both nominal and real terms) than China's. The variability may not be huge and I'm certainly not arguing that the Reserve Bank does not intervene. Nevertheless, both India's exchange rate policy and outcomes indicate greater flexibility than in China. These are significant differences from a policy perspective, which I hope you find interesting.

## Some Take-Away Themes for Policymakers

To begin with, I found the Meissner and Taylor paper and discussion very illuminating for tracing how imbalances had emerged historically in the 1870 to 1913 period, and how these had been resolved apparently with relatively little distress. Unless, of course, you count the First World War as a consequence of the prior history of global imbalances! Second, I also found very interesting the emphasis placed on balance sheet analysis by Guy Debelle in looking at issues of valuation, dark matter, and so forth. Such valuation issues get bypassed in the standard analyses of balance of payments flows. When one does this kind of balance sheet analysis, it suggests a much more sanguine view of the time profile of U.S. net external liabilities. Third, and perhaps most importantly, I was quite struck by Richard Cooper's analysis of global imbalances in which he appears to view the present pattern of imbalances as pretty much a desirable, perhaps even optimal, outcome. In his view, a number of key countries and regions of the world are presently structural "excess savers" like Japan, "augmented Germany" (to use his term), China, and the oil exporters, which are quite happy (not just now, but perhaps for the foreseeable few years) to put their excess funds into the U.S. financial system, essentially because the U.S. financial system provides far superior financial engineering and intermediation capacities and entrepreneurship than is available at home in the excess saver countries and regions. Hence, a persistent and large current account deficit in the United States is perhaps not a surprising outcome. Indeed, this situation could continue for quite a while.

All three of these take-aways, as well as some of the views expressed this morning by Peter Garber and others, seem to favor the following policy message: don't worry too much about the present pattern of global imbalances. These may well reflect a desirable outcome from the viewpoint of global welfare. And even if these are not an optimal long-term outcome, the imbalances will go away painlessly in due course through the operation of market forces.

However, I am still left with some nagging doubts, which I want to share with you. My first set of nagging doubts relates to the sheer scale of the imbalances, and how quickly these have ballooned in the last or six or seven years. The second set of nagging doubts relates to Laurence Kotlikoff's very worrying assessment of the U.S. government's financial position and his fearsome reference to the $63 trillion "hole" (in present value terms) in U.S. government finances, which he fears could one day be noticed by financial markets with perhaps very unpleasant consequences. Why the markets haven't noticed it up to now, I have no idea. But it certainly leaves a nagging doubt.

Third, with Larry Summers on this panel, I am reminded of a speech he gave eight or nine years ago in Hong Kong, then in his capacity as Deputy Treasury Secretary of the United States, where I happened to be present. If I recall correctly, he was extolling the virtues of U.S. economic performance, describing it as the "1-2-3-4 economy," referring (I think) to a 1 percent current account deficit, a 2 percent fiscal surplus, 3 percent productivity growth, and 4 percent GDP growth. Now, if I just look at those numbers for 2005, these somehow come out a little bit different. It's now a 7 percent current account deficit, a 2 percent fiscal *deficit*, and the other two good numbers are, somewhat surprisingly, still holding up. I do wonder if the 1-2-3-4 economy was a good state for the United States and the world economy back in 1997, and whether the current situation is quite so hunky-dory given today's very different numbers.

If these nagging concerns have some merit, let me close by commending to you the recommendations outlined by the Massachusetts Institute of Technology's Olivier Blanchard at an IMF conference on global imbalances a couple of months ago. He basically advocated a set of policies that would gradually reduce global imbalances, but were also quite worthwhile in themselves for the key country groupings. What are these policies? First, a reduction in the U.S. budget deficit would improve U.S. macroeconomic balances and help reduce the U.S. current account deficit. Second, a shift in favor of domestic demand in China brought about by some combination of appreciation of the renminbi and higher domestic consumption. Third is the good old IMF recommendation of structural reforms in Europe, which can stimulate higher investment and growth and thereby move the Eurozone into taking some of the responsibility for shouldering the deficits to match Asian and oil exporter surpluses. And, finally, there was a call for policies to improve financial intermediation in all economic systems outside the United States, particularly in the structural surplus countries. It seems to me that some sort of coordinated move along these policy lines would not be a bad thing, simply as insurance against the future, whether it is filled with dark matter or not.

# The Effects of Globalization on Inflation and the Implications for Monetary Policy

Donald L. Kohn

Although my discussion will touch on the important topic of global imbalances, I would like to focus on globalization's potential influence on inflation and the associated implications this may pose for monetary policy. This seems a natural emphasis for a policymaker at a central bank; indeed, several of my colleagues on the Federal Open Market Committee (FOMC) have also addressed this issue in the months leading up to this conference.[1] You would see from reading their various remarks that no consensus has yet emerged about how globalization has been influencing recent inflation developments. Part of my intention today is to illustrate some of the considerable challenges that are involved in attempting to identify the extent to which the recent pickup in the pace of global economic integration has influenced inflation dynamics in the United States.[2]

Of course, the trend toward greater international integration of product and financial markets has been established for quite a while; the share of U.S. economic activity involved in international trade (measured by nominal exports plus imports as a share of nominal gross domestic product) has been rising since the early 1970s. However, this trend has accelerated markedly since the early 1990s. Over this period the economies of eastern Europe have become more integrated into the global economy, while China, India, and some other East Asian market economies have emerged as important players in the global trading system.

Although inflation is ultimately a monetary phenomenon, it seems natural to expect, as others have argued, that these developments would have exerted some downward pressure on inflation in the United States. In particular, the economic opening of China and India represents a potentially huge increase in the global supply of mainly lower-skilled workers. It is clear that the low cost of production in these and other emerging economies has led to a geographic shift in production toward these countries—not just from the United States but also from other formerly low-cost producers such as Mexico, Singapore, South Korea, and Taiwan.[3] Trade surpluses in China and in other East Asian countries have increased sharply over the past decade, and from a U.S. perspective, the ratio of imported goods to domestically produced goods has accelerated noticeably in recent years.

However, the extent of the disinflationary effect of this shift in the pace of globalization is less obvious. In the United States, many goods and most services are still produced domestically with little foreign competition. In addition, the significant expansion of production and consumption in China and elsewhere has put substantial upward pressure on the prices of oil and other commodities, many of which are imported for use as inputs to production in the United States. Indeed, the effects of globalization on domestic inflation need not even be negative, especially in today's environment of strong global growth.

In assessing the potential effect of increased globalization on inflation, one challenge is the lack of theoretical and empirical work on this issue. At a research conference on modeling inflation held at the Federal Reserve Board in fall 2005, none of the papers even touched on issues related to globalization. Although some new and interesting research on this topic is emerging from places like the International Monetary Fund and the Bank for International Settlements (BIS), much of this work is still quite preliminary.[4] Nevertheless, the existing research does highlight several channels through which globalization might have helped to hold down domestic inflation in recent years. These channels include the direct and indirect effects on domestic inflation of lower import prices, a heightened sensitivity of domestic inflation to foreign demand conditions (and perhaps less sensitivity to domestic demand conditions), downward pressure on domestic wage growth, and upward pressure on domestic productivity growth.[5]

In trying to clarify my own thinking about the likely magnitude of these effects, I find it useful to start with a simple reduced-form equation that attempts to explain movements in inflation, and then to ask whether and how the statistical relationships embedded in this equation have been affected by globalization. The equation, a standard one used at the Board and elsewhere, relates core consumer price inflation—using, say, the index for core personal consumption expenditures (PCE) or the core consumer price index (CPI)—resource utilization, lagged inflation, changes in relative prices of food and energy, and changes in relative import prices. Using this framework, we can look for globalization's effect in several ways. First, we can look for influences that the model directly controls for—notably, how changes in import prices affect domestic inflation. Second, we can look for evidence of globalization-related structural change in the model by examining the stability of the parameter estimates. Third, we can see whether our standard model has omitted any variables that might be interpreted as representing changes in globalization. Finally, we can look for evidence of model errors that would be consistent with the hypothesis that globalization has been restraining inflation. I will focus in particular on the years since 2001, which, judging from the data on U.S. trade shares, is when the pace of globalization appears to have picked up; the end point for the data is early 2006.

I will start with the import price channel—the hypothesis that increased globalization has depressed import prices and thus dampened domestic inflation. Importantly, the estimated strength of this channel should capture not only the direct effects of import prices on the cost of living in the United States but also at least a portion of the indirect effects of actual and potential import competition on the prices of goods produced domestically. In the reduced-form model that I have just described, the effects of import prices on inflation show up quite clearly. Furthermore, the estimated effects appear to have increased over time, with the increase apparently stemming primarily from the upward trend in the share of imported consumer goods in household spending.[6]

We can use the model to get a rough idea of how relative changes in import prices have influenced domestic inflation by simulating how core consumer prices would have behaved if relative import prices had instead remained constant. In particular, the increase in core import prices since the mid-1990s has averaged about 1.5 percentage points less per year than the increase in core consumer prices. According to the model simulation, which also builds in the associated reduction in inflation expectations, the direct and indirect effects of this decline in the relative price of imports held down core inflation by between 0.5 and 1 percentage point per year over this period, an estimated effect that is substantially larger than it would have been in earlier decades. However, much of the decline in import prices during this period was probably driven by movements in exchange rates and the effects of technological change on goods prices, rather than by the growing integration of world markets.[7]

In addition, since 2004, import prices have risen at about the same average pace as core consumer prices, and thus no longer appear to be acting as a significant restraint on inflation in the United States. This step-up in the rate of change of import prices obviously reflects, to some extent, recent movements in the dollar, especially its depreciation in 2004. However, it also reflects large increases in the prices of a number of imported commodities, which have been attributed in part to the rapid expansion of economic activity in China and other Asian countries.

A second hypothesis is that increases in global manufacturing capacity have held down U.S. inflation in recent years—by limiting the ability of U.S. producers to raise prices in response to increases in the domestic costs of production. At a basic level, the elevated profit margins of U.S. producers over the past few years seem inconsistent with this hypothesis. But it does raise a broader issue about the determinants of inflation, meaning whether U.S. inflation is now less sensitive to domestic demand pressures and more sensitive to foreign demand conditions than it was during earlier periods. In the context of the inflation model, we can examine this issue in two ways. First, we can look for evidence that the coefficients on the domestic output or unemployment gaps have fallen over time. Second, we can add a measure of foreign excess demand to the model to see whether it helps to explain domestic inflation in recent years.

With regard to the first test, we do find evidence that the coefficient on the unemployment gap has fallen in the United States. In particular, the coefficient from a model estimated over the past 20 years appears to be about one-third lower than when the model is run over a 40-year period. Of course, globalization is not the only potential explanation for this result. Numerous other researchers have cited persistently low inflation and the improved credibility of monetary policy as having played a more important role. In fact, in rolling regressions, the timing of the decline in the sensitivity of inflation to the unemployment gap appears to be too early for it to be associated with the more recent acceleration in the pace of globalization.

This aspect of the globalization hypothesis would be bolstered if the decline in the sensitivity of inflation to domestic demand was accompanied by an increased sensitivity to foreign demand. Efforts to find such a link have met with mixed results, with some researchers having found large effects and others having found no effect.[8] Our own analysis of this issue indicates that these results are sensitive to how the foreign output gap is defined and to how the inflation model is specified, suggesting that any effect may not be especially strong.

Similarly, the evidence that globalization has helped to restrain unit labor costs in recent years is mixed. One hypothesis is that the increase in the supply of low-skilled workers associated with the emergence of China and other East Asian countries as low-cost centers of production has put downward pressure on the growth of nominal wages in the United States. However, a model of changes in aggregate labor compensation that is similar in structure to the price-inflation model that I described earlier does not detect a stable relationship between measures of globalization (for example, import price changes or the BIS estimates of the foreign output gap) and aggregate wage dynamics in the United States. That said, the recent changes in some, though not all, measures of aggregate compensation seem to have been somewhat lower than such models would have predicted. Of course, several purely domestic factors could help to account for any shortfall, such as the aftereffects of the unusually sluggish recovery in job growth early in this expansion, or a possible downward drift in the nonaccelerating inflation rate of unemployment. But it also is a pattern that would be consistent with downward pressures from an expansion in global labor supply. In support of this link, some cross-section studies have found a relationship between industry wage growth and import penetration, while the research on wage inequality tends to relate some of the relative decline in wages of low-skilled workers to trade, although in both types of studies the effects are generally relatively small.[9] Similarly, research from the Federal Reserve Bank of New York shows a modest relationship between exchange rate fluctuations and wage growth, with larger effects evident for the wages of lower-skilled workers.[10]

A second possibility is that globalization has restrained unit labor costs by raising productivity. Increasing volumes of trade should bolster productivity as economies concentrate their resources in those sectors in which they are relatively more efficient. But I have seen little direct evidence on the extent to which in recent years globalization may have boosted aggregate productivity growth in the United States. Nevertheless, research at the Board finds that multinational corporations, which may have greater opportunities to realize efficiencies by shifting production locations, accounted for a disproportionate share of aggregate productivity growth in the late 1990s.[11] And some microeconomic studies have found a relationship between global engagement and productivity at the firm level.[12] Thus, it seems possible that the persistently high growth rates of multifactor productivity in recent years may partly be due to the productivity-enhancing effects of globalization.

In this regard, I would note that a potential shortcoming of my approach to assessing the effects of globalization on inflation is that these effects may be too recent to be captured adequately by the data. That is, it may be too soon for globalization to have generated statistically observable changes in the parameter estimates or structure of the standard inflation model. Nonetheless, if the influence of globalization on inflation is as substantial as many claim, we might have expected the standard model to have had difficulty in predicting recent inflation trends. For example, if recent increases in world labor supply are restraining domestic unit labor costs to a significant degree, or if there are other important influences on inflation that are related to globalization but difficult to quantify in the context of the standard model, we would expect to have seen sizable model errors over the past several years.

Again, the evidence indicates that globalization has some limited influence on U.S. inflation. If we use out-of-sample dynamic simulations of a model for core PCE price inflation estimated from 1985 through the end of 2001, we find that, although the model overpredicts inflation over the past several years, the errors average only 0.1 to 0.2 of a percentage point per year, considerably less than one might have expected given the anecdotes in the popular press. In contrast, the forecast errors from a model of core CPI inflation are larger (averaging roughly .5 to 1 percentage point per year since mid-2001), and perhaps suggestive of some influence from globalization.

What do I conclude from all of this evidence? My own assessment is that, quite naturally, the greater integration of the U.S. economy into a rapidly evolving world economy has affected the dynamics of inflation determination. Unfortunately, huge gaps and puzzles remain in our analysis and empirical testing of various hypotheses related to these effects. But for the most part the evidence seems to suggest that, to date, the effects have been gradual and limited. There is a greater role for the direct and indirect effects of import prices; possibly some damping of unit labor costs, though judging from high profit margins, less so for prices from this channel; and potentially a smaller effect of the domestic output gap and a greater effect of foreign output gaps—but here too, the evidence is far from conclusive. In particular, the entry of China, India, and other countries into the global trading system has in recent years probably exerted a modest disinflationary effect on prices in the United States.

Moreover, we should recognize that these disinflationary forces could dissipate or even be reversed in coming years. These reflect, at least in part, the global imbalances that are the subject of this conference, rather than just the integration of emerging-market economies into the global trading system. For example, the fact that China and some other emerging-market economies have resisted upward pressure on their exchange rates and are running trade surpluses has undoubtedly contributed to their disinflationary effects on the rest of the world. The prices of their exports are lower than these would be if market forces were given greater scope in foreign exchange markets, and they are supplying more goods and services to the rest of the world than they themselves are demanding. These imbalances are not likely to be sustained indefinitely. The elevated rates of national saving in these economies—and, in some, relatively restrained rates of investment—are not likely to persist in the face of ongoing improvements in the functioning of their financial markets, increases in the depth of their product markets, and fuller developments of economic safety nets. As individuals in these countries are increasingly drawn to investing at home and consuming more of their wealth, and as their real wages catch up to past productivity gains, the upward pressures on their currencies will intensify, their domestic demand will come into better alignment with their capacity to produce, cost advantages will decline, and these economies will exert less, if any, downward pressure on U.S. inflation.

This observation brings me to my final point, which is about monetary policy. Clearly, the greater integration of the world's economies does leave the United States more open to influences from abroad. In one sense, a more open economy may be more forgiving as shortfalls or excesses in demand are partly absorbed by other countries through adjustments of our imports and exports. And, to the extent that the United States can draw upon world capacity, the inflationary effect of an increase in aggregate demand might be damped for a time. But we are also subject to inflationary forces from abroad, including those that might accompany a shift to a more sustainable pattern of global spending and production, or those that might emanate from rising cost and price pressures. Moreover, a smaller response of inflation to domestic demand also implies that reducing inflation once it rose could be difficult and costly. And, from another perspective, integrated financial markets can exert powerful feedback, which may be less forgiving of any perceived policy error. For example, if financial market participants thought that the FOMC was not dedicated to maintaining long-run price stability—a notion that I can assure you is not correct—they would be less willing to hold dollar-denominated assets, and the resulting decline in the dollar would tend to add to inflationary pressures. Clearly, policymakers need to factor into their decisions the implications of globalization for the dynamics of the determination of inflation and output.

In the end, however, policymakers here and abroad cannot lose sight of a fundamental truth: in a world of separate currencies that can fluctuate against each other over time, each country's central bank determines its inflation rate. If the FOMC were to allow the U.S. economy to run beyond its sustainable potential for some time, inflation would eventually rise. And this pickup would become self-perpetuating if it became embedded in inflation expectations. Thus, while a better understanding of the implications of globalization will aid in our understanding of inflation dynamics, it is also clear that such developments do not relieve central banks of their responsibility for maintaining price and economic stability.

## Notes

1. For example, Richard W. Fisher, "Globalization and Monetary Policy" (Warren and Anita Marshall Lecture in American Foreign Policy, Harvard University, Cambridge, MA, November 3, 2005); and Janet L. Yellen, "Monetary Policy in a Global Environment" (speech at The Euro and the Dollar in a Globalized Economy Conference, University of California at Santa Cruz, May 27, 2006).

2. See, for example, International Monetary Fund (2005), "Mexico: Staff Report for the 2005 Article IV Consultation," October; and Alan G. Ahearne, John G. Fernald, Prakash Loungani, and John W. Schindler (2003), "China and Emerging Asia: Comrades or Competitors?" (International Finance Discussion Paper 2003-789, Board of Governors of the Federal Reserve System, Washington, DC, December).

3. See, for example, International Monetary Fund (2005), "Mexico: Staff Report for the 2005 Article IV Consultation," October; and Alan G. Ahearne, John G. Fernald, Prakash Loungani, and John W. Schindler (2003), "China and Emerging Asia: Comrades or Competitors?" (International Finance Discussion Paper 2003-789, Board of Governors of the Federal Reserve System, Washington, DC, December).

4. Thomas Helbling, Florence Jaumotte, and Martin Sommer, "How Has Globalization Affected Inflation?," in *IMF World Economic Outlook* (Washington, DC: IMF, 2006), 97–134; and Claudio Borio and Andrew Filardo, "Globalization and Global Disinflation: New Cross-Country Evidence on the Global Determinants of a Domestic Inflation" (unpublished paper, Bank for International Settlements, March 2006).

5. Ken Rogoff also argues that globalization has increased the incentives for central banks to keep inflation low. Kenneth S. Rogoff, "Globalization and Global Disinflation," in *Monetary Policy and Uncertainty: Adapting to a Changing Economy* (symposium sponsored by the Federal Reserve Bank of Kansas City, August 28–30, 2003), 77–112.

6. As is standard in such models, we use a price measure for "core" imports, defined as imports of goods excluding energy, computers, and semiconductors. When the change in relative import prices is weighted by the import share, the coefficient in the model is fairly stable.

7. Research at the Board examined the direct effects of Chinese exports on global import prices from the mid-1990s to 2002 and found only a modest effect on U.S. import prices. Of course, it is possible that China's influence on import prices has grown in recent years as its trade share has expanded. Refer to Steven B. Kamin, Mario Marazzi, and John W. Schindler (2004), "Is China 'Exporting Deflation'?" (International Finance Discussion Paper 2004/791, Board of Governors of the Federal Reserve System, Washington, DC, January).

8. Borio and Filardo (see note 4) and Gamber and Hung 2001 found that foreign resource utilization had sizable effects on U.S. inflation, while Tootell 1998 found little to no effect. See Edward N. Gamber and Juann H. Hung, "Has the Rise in

Globalization Reduced U.S. Inflation in the 1990s?," *Economic Inquiry* 39 (2001): 58–73; and Geoffrey M. B. Tootell, "Globalization and U.S. Inflation," *New England Economic Review* July/August (1998): 21–33.

9. For example, Helbling, Jaumotte, and Sommer (see note 4) and William R. Cline, *Trade and Income Distribution* (Washington, D.C.: Institute for International Economics, 1997).

10. Linda Goldberg and Joseph Tracy, "Exchange Rates and Wages" (unpublished paper, Federal Reserve Bank of New York, 2003).

11. Carol Corrado, Paul Lengermann, and Larry Slifman, "The Contribution of MNCs to U.S. Productivity Growth, 1977–2000" (unpublished paper, Board of Governors of the Federal Reserve System, 2005).

12. For example, Mark E. Doms and J. Bradford Jensen, "Productivity, Skill, and Wage Effects of Multinational Corporations in the United States," in *Foreign Ownership and the Consequences of Direct Investment in the United States: Beyond Us and Them*, eds. Douglas Woodward and Douglas Nigh (Westport, CT: Quorum Books, 1998): 49–68.

# Five Policy-Relevant Observations and an Epilogue for 2008

Lawrence H. Summers

My broad views on the U.S. current account imbalances—what the United States should do and what other countries should do—have been documented in other speeches and are available on my web site. As I have explained my reasoning elsewhere, what I would like to do here is to make five policy-relevant observations bearing on various aspects of the situation. These observations responded to the situation in late June 2006, when these remarks were first delivered. At the end of this essay, revised for the conference volume, I will offer some further observations in light of the changed economic circumstances that have occurred since then.

First, Alan Greenspan was right some years ago when he urged that monetary policymakers must take a risk management approach to their task, meaning that they need to think about risks, even if it is not certain that these risks will materialize. The general costs to economic policy of thinking these real imbalances are not a real problem are, I would suggest, much smaller than the risks of remaining complacent if that complacency proves unwarranted. Therefore, making a case that this problem of current account imbalances should be taken seriously by policymakers does not require establishing that a hard landing will happen or is highly likely—only that there is a risk that something could happen, and that it would be good to be prepared to deal with such an event.

One lesson that I draw from economic history is that every bubble has its wise guys. On its face, it is not entirely unreasonable to suggest that U.S. stocks were properly valued in the summer of 1929, as Brad DeLong has quite aptly argued. In late 1988, Jeff Sachs published a paper using various urban economic theories to explain why land was properly valued in Tokyo at that time. In late 1999, when it was clear that the Internet was a fantastic innovation, I asked a group of high-tech executives whether they could determine what fraction of this wave of transformation we had already ridden. They clearly regarded the question as a slightly odd one, and then one of them told me, "You don't understand, Larry. It's a river, not a wave, and it's going to go on forever." Likewise, as of mid-2006, the dollar has not plummeted, and there are a reasonable set of arguments that can be constructed as to why its value could go either way. One should assume that at any given moment in any financial market, people will always develop arguments for why the situation could go either way. Yet this recognition does not mean that those who advocate for policy complacency are wrong; it just means that one should not take too much comfort from the fact that these arguments are out there.

Looking back to the 1985 situation, which I think is instructive, it seems to me that there are two ways of reading that experience. One reading is that it was a huge crisis. The other interpretation is that the United States had a high dollar and a big current account deficit, and so if you look at the GDP statistics, in hindsight you would not think that something very dramatic had happened.

I lean toward the more negative reading of the 1985 situation. It seems to me that with 20 years of historical perspective, if you had to pinpoint something that triggered the global stock market crash on October 19, 1987, probably the best thing to examine was a certain amount of skirmishing between Jim Baker and the Germans over what was going to happen to the dollar, who should cut interest rates, and who should not. It seems to me that the Japanese monetary policy response of loosening to avoid excessive dollar depreciation had a great deal to do with the bubble that set the stage for 15 years of deflation in that country. But using this 1985 experience as the basis for predictions about the contemporary situation might not lead to particularly sanguine assessments of what lies ahead. You could say, for example, that given the current situation, the United States is going to have an experience like 1985, but it is probably going to be bigger because now the U.S. current account deficit is twice as big. If this is the likely effect, I doubt we would feel any better if someone tried to point out that the late 1980s correction wasn't so bad in the larger scheme of things.

So the first thought I want to leave you with is that in the face of this potentially severe unwinding, prudent monetary policy and prudent planning should err on the side of paying attention to the alarmists. You will go very wrong if they are right, but you will not go so wrong if they are wrong.

My second observation is simply that on the question of resolving these global imbalances, I think everyone must be very careful about what they wish for. I believe Peter Garber and his colleagues are completely right to draw attention to at least one of the anomalies with respect to the traditional alarmist view: the observation that around the world, real interest rates are low, not high. If the U.S. failure to save was the dominant feature of the global system in creating these new imbalances, as Larry Kotlikoff has suggested, then you would expect new interest rates to be abnormally high, not abnormally low. Garber's observation, taken from the level of real interest rates, is quite probative in its suggestion that understanding much about the imbalance has to come from understanding not what is happening in the United States, but what is happening in the rest of the world. Contra Ben Bernanke, I think the term "investment drought" is probably more correct as a description of what has been going on than his term "savings glut."

Now I would like to comment on one persistent fallacy and make one prescriptive observation. The greatest, most enduring fallacy in official economic circles—a fallacy sometimes perpetuated in the financial community—is what I shall call the "Immaculate Conception" theory of current account improvement. This theory posits that if a country has a current account deficit and then decides to save more, its current account deficit will improve. The value of its currency will remain constant or appreciate because a higher savings rate will engender more confidence, while its economy will get stronger and grow faster. No European central banker in the last decade, with the exception of Mervyn King, has addressed the question of current account deficits without committing this fallacy.

Constant repetition does not make the Immaculate Conception theory any less fallacious. For a nation's current account deficit to improve when it increases its savings, something must happen that changes the level of imports or exports. This adjustment can either be a change in the relative price—in other words, a fall in the exchange rate—or it can be an economic slowdown that reduces the demand for imports. There is no other way that a current account deficit can improve.

Current G7 communiqués elide these tradeoffs by suggesting that if only the United States increased its savings, then there would be a stronger global economy, a stronger dollar, and all will be right with the world. These theoretical assertions are simply not supported by practical experience, and are similar to suggesting that if only people could fly, transportation would be easier. These comments were successfully excised from the communiqués during the time when I had some influence over their content, but they have since found their way back in.

Economic reality implies that if we wish to find a policy that will correct these global imbalances, we need to be very careful what we wish for. If the United States successfully increases its savings rate, and nothing else happens, the result will be a decline in global aggregate demand to the extent that the reduced pressure on U.S. interest rates reduces capital inflows into the United States and causes the dollar to fall. If this adjustment happens without a recession, then expenditures will switch from the rest of the world to the United States. After all, that is the idea, and the global result will be deflationary and contractionary.

It is far from clear that this would be a good thing. Remember that while the United States is a leading nation—and therefore U.S. political support is crucial to any effective global solution—the fact that the real interest rates have fallen, not risen, suggests that the dominant impulse observed here reflects in important ways the policies that are being enacted in the rest of the world.

Thus, those who wish to see this situation addressed need to focus on the question of what is happening with monetary and fiscal policy in the international macroeconomy. I have already discussed what European central bankers say about these issues. In the developing world, central bankers often resort to a common refrain: "Isn't it terrible that the United States is running this huge current account deficit because of its huge budget deficit, and therefore is sucking capital out of the developing world where it could do so much good?" This sentiment rings hollow, to put it mildly, when the central banker in question has accumulated $50 billion in U.S. Treasury bills on behalf of his country's citizens that in the preceding year paid a real interest rate of about 1 percent. The finance minister in India is not innocent of this particular sin, and I choose to believe that it is being committed in order to bolster domestic consumption, rather than being reflective of a conviction that this is the best policy course for the global economy.

The moral of the second observation is that while the United States should not be complacent about its role in creating global imbalances, what takes place in the rest of the world is probably even more important to a resolution of these imbalances than what happens in the United States.

The third observation pushes a hobbyhorse of mine, which I touched on earlier. One thing that is most remarkable about the global economy is the rate at which reserves are being accumulated in developing countries. If we use what seems to me to be an extremely cautious standard proposed some years ago, the so-called Guidotti-Greenspan rule, this maintains that a country is well reserved against financial crisis if it holds reserves equal to all of its short-term debt coming due in one year. But even if we are hyperconservative and assume that the necessary reserves are twice that amount, then today in the developing world there is approximately $2 trillion of excess reserves beyond what is necessary for insurance against financial crisis. That $2 trillion figure is rising at about $500 billion a year.

It is a mystery to me why these funds are being invested at rates that in dollar terms probably average a 2 percent yield. In local currency terms, given that appreciations will happen at some point, these funds are earning close to zero. It seems to me that while we essentially have an international financial architecture that is designed entirely with a view to promoting the flow of capital from industrial countries to poor countries, we have a global financial system in which the dominant flows are going in the opposite direction. Thinking through how that reversal is going to take place is, in my opinion, a question of profound importance.

My own view is that the developing world could receive the "least expensive lunch" if it more prudently invested its reserves in risk-bearing assets that earn a comparably high return. It seems to me the question of how these resources are invested is a matter of great importance.

All three of these observations lead to my fourth observation: what does this current situation of global imbalances say about U.S. monetary policy in particular, and what does it say monetary policy more generally? In a world that is changing very rapidly—a world that is financially integrated and very different than any we have seen before—this is no time for slavish adherence to mechanistic rules of any kind, even if adherence to such rules might create the possibility of greater predictability. The most important rule for stability is to remain responsive to what is happening in the world, rather than to behave predictably at the cost of being unresponsive to the things that are most important in this brave new world. In a world where asset prices and currency fluctuations are ever more important, it would be quite unwise to straightjacket monetary policy. My hope is that in the future the Federal Open Market Committee would, as it has in the past, take a catholic view of the variables that need to be considered in the context of monetary policy. If past monetary policy deserves any criticism—and I am not sure any criticism is merited—it is due to an excessive focus on Taylor Rule variables, like output gaps relative to asset prices. I would be sorry to see any set of changes in monetary policymaking directed at pushing further in those predetermined directions.

I would like to make one comment on the general monetary policy framework as it currently stands. It seems to me that a very crude history of business would suggest that individual business cycles end. Eventually, expansions end for one of two reasons. The canonical pre-World War II reason held that business cycles ended because of the kinds of things that Henry Kaufman and Al Wojnilower understand much better than I do: excessive credit cycles, excessive risk-taking, inflated asset prices, overbuilding, overinvestment, nonsustainability, nervousness, collapse, withdrawal, falling asset prices, and reduced demand. That's the story, I would argue, of most business cycles before World War II.

Before 1999, the tale of postwar business cycles was very different. It was a story of expansion, rising inflation, and a nervous Federal Reserve that, in trying to hit the brakes without causing a skid, braked a bit too hard, skidded, and caused a recession. This is the story of the recessions or slowdowns in 1958, 1967, 1971, 1974, and 1989, as well as what happened after 1979 with the oil supply shift. In contrast, the story of the 2000 business cycle reflects the fact that we actually had achieved credibility by reestablishing a low-inflation environment, so it was not surprising that when the business cycle ended, it ended for the same reasons that cycles ended in the pre-World War II era.

As of June 2006, we are in a situation where we do not know what the expansion will die of, but there are two risks in the environment. One risk is a contraction prompted by falling house prices, falling demand, and a falling dollar. A second risk is rising inflation, an increase in the Federal Funds rate, and an ensuing economic slide. Precisely because of the presence of both of these risks, this seems to be a more difficult and fragile moment for monetary policy then we have seen in a long time. In a way, the dilemma that monetary policy faces now is a mild version of the classic postcrisis dilemma of Mexico in 1994 or Asia in 1998, which I hope the United States will not experience in the next five years. This is the dilemma in which is the economy is slowing, the financial system is failing, and people are taking money out of their banks and selling their currency. In such a situation, there are two plausible money policy responses. Because people are selling the currency, one option is to print less currency so that it will hold its value. The second option is to print more currency because the banks have no liquidity. Unfortunately, it is not possible to print less currency and more currency at the same time.

It is important to avoid a crisis precisely because it is not possible to solve the tension between the liquidity provision objective of U.S. monetary policy and the basic stabilization objective of monetary policy once a crisis has occurred. Today we are seeing a situation that has a little bit of both elements of this tension, as we have signs of bubbles bursting at the same time as there are signs of rising inflation.

My fifth and final observation is of a different kind. I am struck not only by how much of the conversation here is about China, an emerging Asia, or the oil-exporting countries, but also by how ill-equipped Americans are to participate in this conversation. Our average citizen has a very limited understanding of other countries, the opportunities they present, the challenges they face, and how these nations interact with the United States. Shankar Acharya's remarks provide a good example of this problem. On a trip to India in March 2006, I learned that Shankar is right: the gap between India and China is much greater than we realize. In other words, the set of impressions I had formed before my trip by reading the American media reasonably assiduously were wrong. The gulf between the economies of China and India now is vastly greater than what I imagined prior to my trip to India. I am sure that this misapprehension reflects sloppiness and lack of careful thought on my part, but perhaps it was fueled by all the U.S. media accounts I read, which had a certain tendency to generalize.

It seems to me if the United States is going to be successful in the twenty-first century, we are going to need a large cadre of people in the private sector, in the public sector, and in the academic sector who are much more knowledgeable about the countries with which we will have to cooperate than has been the case traditionally. On my trip to India I learned that while its population is about one-sixth of the world's entire population, while it is a country of immense strategic importance to the United States, and while a large percentage of its population speaks English, only 1,100 American students studied in India last year. That is about one-seventh of the combined number of Americans who studied in Australia and New Zealand. Without in any way denigrating the pedagogical and intellectual benefits of study in Australia and New Zealand, it seems to me that in terms of broadening the U.S. perspective with respect to the rest of the world, we have a very long way to go.

It is hard to believe that we Americans will realize our potential without making a much greater effort to understand the world outside our borders. It is a combination of what does and does not happen in our universities, what prestige does and does not attach to joining our foreign service, and what attitudes our national leaders project. I am continually stunned by the contrast between the detailed knowledge of political, social, and economic developments in the United States that exists on the part of elites in other countries that I visit, and the shallow knowledge of other major countries that is pervasive among American elites. Redressing this imbalance is also an important challenge if we are to find our way forward.

## An Epilogue: 2008

The late Rudi Dornbusch was fond of remarking that in economics, "things take longer to happen than you think they will, and then they happen faster than you thought they could." Almost two years have passed between when these original remarks were delivered in late June 2006 and their revision in May 2008. In mid-2006, we were in a situation that many thought could continue for a long time—in a show of hands, the overwhelming majority of conference attendees indicated that they expected a smooth correction. Yet a similarly large majority responded affirmatively when Jeff Fuhrer, the Boston Fed's research director, asked if there was at least a 10–20 percent chance that a financial crisis would force such an adjustment to occur.

While it is too soon to tell if current events will prove decisive in permanently reversing the long-standing global imbalances, we have had a financial crisis, a crisis precipitated by problems in the U.S. subprime mortgage market. This tipping point was predicated on related but distinctive patterns of excessive valuations in housing markets, and excessive complacency in credit markets—issues experienced observers have drawn attention to for many years. The cracks took longer to appear than many expected, and these fissures have subsequently proven to be far more structurally damaging than almost anyone predicted.

While we are still debating whether this episode will be counted as a "true" recession according to the textbook definition, this business cycle has clearly slowed down, and it has closed down according to the pre-World War II script outlined above: excessive credit cycles, excessive risk-taking, inflated asset prices, overinvestment, nervousness, and withdrawal. We are now confronting a combination of the risks envisioned in June 2006, including falling house prices, a falling dollar, and rising inflation that has been stoked by rising commodity prices. The increasing demand for oil and food, particularly from China and other emerging economies, does seem to augur a permanent shift in the global demand for scarce resources that will only become more pronounced in the coming years. The falling value of the U.S. dollar may help our trade deficit to some degree, but given our oil-dependent economy, in the near-term this gain may be offset by higher energy prices that feed through to other cost increases.

In terms of globalization, there is a very real danger that the mood among Americans will shift toward protectionist tendencies—we are already seeing evidence of such tendencies in the 2008 presidential campaign. Yet there is a very real reason for this sentiment. Americans are feeling much less certain about their economic security and future, and this is not just a sudden shift given the current problems with energy prices and the housing market. U.S. factory workers have seen their jobs outsourced to other countries, medical costs have been skyrocketing for years, income disparities have grown, and real incomes have stagnated for the vast majority of Americans. Promoting internationalism in an open global economy must work on successfully aligning the interests of working people and the middle class in rich countries with the success of the global economy.

One of my observations from 2006 remains particularly relevant today: what takes place in the rest of the world is critically important to how both the global economy and the U.S. economy weather the current storms. Will the tipping point in the U.S. economy, and its spillover effects in the rest of the world, call forth policies elsewhere that may help mitigate a global downturn? Will the policies have the capacity to manage some of the long-term structural adjustments that have been prescribed for years, even as the day of reckoning had been continually postponed?

It has always seemed to me that those of us involved with financial and monetary policy have a great responsibility. To have well-functioning capital markets and a credible currency are immensely important. But much more important is the reality that when the economy is successfully managed, people's fortunes are largely determined by their own choices and efforts. When the wrong economic policies are pursued, people's lives can be wrenched apart as they lose their jobs, their homes, and their ability to provide for their families because of complex forces entirely beyond their control. The U.S. economy and the world economy stand at a critical juncture, and as economic policymakers search for sensible solutions, they bear a tremendous responsibility.

# Contributors

**Shankar Acharya** is honorary professor and member of the Board of Governors at the Indian Council for Research on International Economic Relations (ICRIER) and chairman, Kotak Mahindra Bank. Previously, he was a member of the Prime Minister's Economic Advisory Council, chief economic adviser to India's Ministry of Finance, and a member of the Securities and Exchange Board of India. Acharya has played a key role in formulating India's budget and tax policies, monetary policy, and foreign trade and payments policies, as well as helping steer the development of the country's capital markets. While serving at the World Bank, he was the principal author of the World Development Report (1979). Acharya's two most recent books are *Essays on Macroeconomic Policy and Growth in India* (2006) and *Can India Grow without Bharat?* (2007). Acharya earned his B.A. at Oxford University and his Ph.D. in economics from Harvard University.

**Abhijit V. Banerjee** is the Ford Foundation Professor of Economics at the Massachusetts Institute of Technology (MIT), the director of the Poverty Action Lab, and a past president of the Bureau for Research in Economic Analysis and Development (BREAD). His areas of research are development economics, the economics of financial markets, and the macroeconomics of developing countries. Before joining the MIT faculty in 1996, Banerjee taught at Princeton University and at Harvard University. He is a fellow of the Econometric Society and the American Academy of Arts and Sciences, and has been a Guggenheim Fellow and Alfred P. Sloan Research Fellow. Banerjee was awarded the Mahalanobis Memorial Medal in 2000 and received the Malcolm Adishesiah Award in 2001.

He received a B.Sc. from the University of Calcutta, an M.A. from Jawaharlal University (New Delhi), and a Ph.D. in economics from Harvard University.

**Selva Bahar Baziki** is a graduate student in economics at the Johns Hopkins University, where in August 2008 she began her Ph.D. studies in economics. From 2005–2006 she was a research assistant, and from 2006–2008 a senior research assistant at the Federal Reserve Bank of Boston, where she worked under the direction of Jane Sneddon Little. A native of Turkey, Baziki has a B.A. in economics from Bryn Mawr College, and spent her junior year abroad studying at the London School of Economics.

**Suzanne Berger** is the Raphael Dorman and Helen Starbuck Professor of Political Science at the Massachusetts Institute of Technology (MIT), where she serves as director of the MIT International Science and Technology Initiative and as director of the MIT-France Program. Berger's research focuses on comparative politics and the political economy of advanced industrial countries. Her current research program is investigating the impact of globalization on domestic economies and politics. Berger has published extensively on issues of international economic competitiveness. As a member of the MIT Commission on Industrial Productivity, she co-authored the Commission's report, "Made in America: Regaining the Competitive Edge." Berger is a fellow of the American Academy of Arts and Sciences. She holds a B.A. from the University of Chicago, and an M.A. and a Ph.D. from Harvard University.

**Surjit S. Bhalla** is the principal of Oxus Research and Investments, a New Delhi-based economic research, asset management, and emerging-markets advisory group. Prior to joining Oxus in 1996, he worked at the Rand Corporation, the Brookings Institution, the World Bank, Goldman Sachs, and Deutsche Bank. Bhalla has served as executive director of the Policy Group in New Delhi, the first non-government-funded think tank in India, and he currently serves on the board of India's National Council of Applied Research. A frequent advisor to the Indian government on financial and securities markets, Bhalla has written books and articles on poverty and inequality in India for both academic and general publications. Among his works are articles on economics, politics, and cricket published in Indian newspapers and magazines. Bhalla holds a B.S. in electrical engineering from Purdue University, an M.P.A. from the Woodrow Wilson School of Public and International Affairs at Princeton University, and a Ph.D. in economics from Princeton University.

**Stephen W. Bosworth** is dean of the Fletcher School of Law and Diplomacy at Tufts University, a position he assumed in February 2001. Prior to being appointed at the Fletcher School, he served as the U.S. Ambassador to the Republic of Korea from 1997–2001, to the Philippines from 1984–1987, and to Tunisia from 1979–1981. From 1995–1997 Bosworth was the executive director of the Korean Peninsula Energy Development Organization, and from 1987–1995 he was president of the United States-Japan Foundation. He has served in a number of senior positions in the U.S. Department of State, and has been an adjunct professor at Columbia University's School of International and Public Affairs. In 1987 he received the American Academy of Diplomacy's Diplomat of the Year Award and twice received the Department of State's Distinguished Service Award, first in 1976 and then in 1986. Bosworth currently serves as a director of the Council on Foreign Relations and the Japan Society of Boston, is a member of the Trilateral Commission, and is on the International Board of Advisers for the President of the Republic of the Philippines. He is a graduate of Dartmouth College.

**Richard N. Cooper** is the Maurits C. Boas Professor of International Economics at Harvard University and vice-chair of the Global Development Network. His recent research, some conducted jointly with others, has focused on country-level fiscal booms and crises, international macroeconomic management, and global environmental policy. He served in the U.S. government as chair of the National Intelligence Council from 1995–1997, Under-Secretary of State for Economic Affairs from 1977–1981, Deputy Assistant Secretary of State for International Monetary Affairs from 1965–1966, and as senior staff economist for the Council of Economic Advisers from 1961–1963. From 1990–1992 Cooper chaired the Federal Reserve Bank of Boston's Board of Directors. Currently he is a member of the Brookings Panel on Economic Activity, the Council on Foreign Relations, and the Trilateral Commission. Cooper holds an A.B from Oberlin College, an M.Sc. in economics from the London School of Economics, and a Ph.D. in economics from Harvard University.

**Alan V. Deardorff** is the John W. Sweetland Professor of International Economics at the University of Michigan, where he holds dual appointments in the economics department and the Gerald R. Ford School of Public Policy. He has written extensively on issues of international trade theory and policy. Deardorff, with his co-author Robert M. Stern, has developed a computable general equilibrium (CGE) model of production, trade, and employment in 34 major countries. They have used this model for a variety of purposes, including analysis of the Tokyo and Uruguay Rounds of multilateral trade negotiations and possible outcomes of the ongoing Doha Round. Along with Drusilla K. Brown, they have also developed a series of four- and eight-country CGE models to evaluate the sectoral employment implications of various regional trading arrangements in North America, the Western Hemisphere, Asia, and Europe. Deardorff has been a consultant to numerous government and non-government agencies, including the Asian Development Bank, the Organisation for Economic Development and Cooperation, the U.S. Agency for International Development, the U.S. Senate, the U.S. Treasury Department, and the World Bank. He earned a B.S. from Stanford University, and a Ph.D. in economics from Cornell University.

**Guy Debelle** is the assistant governor in charge of the Financial Markets Group at the Reserve Bank of Australia, a position he assumed in March 2007. Prior to this, he headed the Reserve Bank's International Department from 2004–2007 and its Economic Analysis Department from 2001–2003. Debelle has researched and published in the areas of financial markets, inflation, inflation targeting, and monetary policy. He first joined the Reserve Bank in 1994 as an economist in its research department, but Debelle has also worked at the International Monetary Fund from 1995–1997, as a visiting professor of economics at the Massachusetts Institute of Technology in 2003, and at the Bank for International Settlements in 2004. He has an undergraduate degree from the University of Adelaide, and a Ph.D. in economics from the Massachusetts Institute of Technology.

**J. Bradford DeLong** is a professor in the department of economics at the University of California at Berkeley, and chairs the interdisciplinary program major in political economy for the Berkeley International and Area Studies Teaching Program. His research interests range broadly in the fields of macroeconomics and economic history, including work on business cycle dynamics, economic growth, inflation, international finance, political economy, the history of economic thought, and behavioral finance. DeLong is a research associate at the National Bureau of Economic Research, a visiting scholar at the Federal Reserve Bank of San Francisco, and served as the U.S. Treasury Department's deputy assistant secretary for economic policy from April 1993 through May 1995. He has an A.B. in social studies and a Ph.D. in economics from Harvard University.

**Michael P. Dooley** is a professor of economics at the University of California at Santa Cruz, which he joined in 1992. His research interests cover a range of issues in open economy macroeconomics, crises in emerging markets, debt management, capital controls, capital flight, and liberalization in financial markets. Dooley is a research associate at the National Bureau of Economic Research, a research fellow at the Kiel Institute of World Economics, and is one of the three main editors of the *International Journal of Finance and Economics*. His prior positions have included working as an economist in the division of international finance at the Board of Governors of the Federal Reserve System from 1971–1983, including as assistant director of this division from 1982–1983; serving as the assistant director for the research department at the International Monetary Fund from 1983–1991; and being chief economist for Latin America at Deutsche Bank from 2002–2003. Dooley has a B.S. in economics from Duquesne University, an M.A. in economics from the University of Delaware, and a Ph.D. in economics from Pennsylvania State University.

**David Folkerts-Landau** is a managing director and head of Global Markets Research (Equities and Fixed Income) at Deutsche Bank AG in London. He is also a member of the Bank's Global Markets Executive Committee. Prior to joining Deutsche Bank in 1997, Folkerts-Landau was the division head of international capital markets and surveillance and financial markets research at the International Monetary Fund, a position he held since 1992. Before beginning at the International Monetary Fund in 1985, Folkerts-Landau was an assistant professor of economics and finance at the University of Chicago's Graduate School of Business. He has a Ph.D. in economics from Princeton University.

**Richard B. Freeman**, a labor economist, is the Herbert Ascherman Professor of Economics at Harvard University, and co-directs the Labor and Worklife Program at the Harvard Law School. He directs the Labor Studies Program at the National Bureau of Economic Research (NBER). Freeman is a senior research fellow at the London School of Economics' Centre for Economic Performance and visiting professor at the London School of Economics. Freeman has published over 300 articles and 35 books on a wide range of research interests, including the effects of immigration and trade on inequality; the job market for scientists and engineers; the growth and decline of unions; Chinese labor markets; self-organizing non-unions in the labor market; employee involvement programs; and income distribution and equity in the marketplace. Currently he is co-directing the NBER/Sloan Science Engineering Workforce Project. Freeman is a fellow of the American Academy of Arts and Sciences. He has served on five panels of the National Academy of Sciences, including the Committee on National Needs for Biomedical and Behavioral Scientists. He earned his B.A. at Dartmouth College and his Ph.D. at Harvard University.

**Peter M. Garber** is a global risk strategist at Deutsche Bank and a research associate at the National Bureau of Economic Research. Previously, he was an economics professor at the University of Virginia, the University of Rochester, and Brown University. Garber has written extensively on international financial markets, trade regimes, and speculative investment bubbles, both for academic audiences and general readers. His most recent book is *Famous First Bubbles: The Fundamentals of Early Manias* (The MIT Press). Garber has been a consultant to and a visiting scholar at the Inter-American Development Bank, the International Monetary Fund, and the World Bank. He has an A.B. from Princeton University and a Ph.D. in economics from the University of Chicago.

**John. F. Helliwell** is the Arthur J.E. Child Research Fellow of the Canadian Institute for Advanced Research, where along with George Akerlof he co-directs its program on "Social Interactions, Identity, and Well-Being." Helliwell's wide-ranging research interests include applied macroeconomics, comparative economic growth, international economics, natural resource economics, social capital, and well-being. He is a member of the National Statistics Council, a research associate at the National Bureau of Economic Research, and an emeritus professor of economics at the University of British Columbia. From 2003–2004 Helliwell was a visiting special advisor at the Bank of Canada, in 2003 was a visiting research fellow at Merton College, Oxford University, and in 2001 was a visiting fellow at St. Catherine's College, Oxford University. He was the Mackenzie King Visiting Professor of Canadian Studies at Harvard University from 1991–1994, and during 1995–1996 he was a Fulbright Fellow and co-chair of Harvard University's Canada Program. Helliwell has an undergraduate degree from the University of British Columbia, and spent a year as a Rhodes Scholar at Oxford University, where he earned an M.A. and a D.Phil. in economics.

**Donald L. Kohn** took office in August 2002 as a member of the Board of Governors of the Federal Reserve System for a full term ending January 31, 2016. On June 23, 2006, Kohn was sworn in as vice chairman of the Board of Governors of the Federal Reserve System for a four-year term. Kohn has written extensively on issues related to monetary policy and its implementation by the Federal Reserve. Prior to becoming a member of the Board, Kohn served on its staff as adviser to the Board for Monetary Policy from 2001–2002, secretary of the Federal Open Market Committee from 1987–2002, director of the Division of Monetary Affairs from 1987–2001, and deputy staff director for Monetary and Financial Policy from 1983–1987. He also held several positions in the Board's Division of Research and Statistics: associate director from 1981–1983, chief of Capital Markets from 1978–1981, and economist from 1975–1978. He is chairman of the Committee on the Global Financial System, a central bank panel that monitors and examines broad issues related to financial markets and systems. Before joining the Board of Governors, Kohn began his career as an economist at the Federal Reserve Bank of Kansas City, where he worked from 1970 to 1975. Kohn received a B.A. in economics from the College of Wooster and a Ph.D. in economics from the University of Michigan.

**Laurence J. Kotlikoff** is a professor of economics at Boston University, where he has taught since 1984 and twice served as chair of the department. From 1977–1984 Kotlikoff was a postdoctoral fellow in the economics department of the University of California at Los Angeles, and from 1980–1984 he taught in the economics department at Yale University. In 1981–1982 Kotlikoff served as a senior economist with the President's Council of Economic Advisers. He specializes in macroeconomics and public finance, and has published extensively, both in academic journals and in popular media, on issues of fiscal deficits, the tax structure, Social Security, Medicare, healthcare reform, generational accounting, pensions, saving, insurance, and personal finance. Kotlikoff is a research associate of the National Bureau of Economic Research, a fellow of the Econometric Society, a fellow of the American Academy of Arts and Sciences, and president of Economic Security Planning, Inc., a company that specializes in financial planning software. He earned his B.A. in economics from the University of Pennsylvania and his Ph.D. in economics from Harvard University.

**Jane Sneddon Little** is a vice president and economist in the research department of the Federal Reserve Bank of Boston, where she leads the macroeconomic applications and policy studies section. Little's research focuses on international macroeconomic issues. In the past few years she has written or co-authored papers on asset prices and economic stabilization, the evolution of the international monetary system, the offshoring of jobs, and the practice of inflation targeting overseas. Recent contributions include editing this volume and the volume entitled *Wanting It All:*

*The Challenge of Reforming the U.S. Health Care System.* In addition to her duties at the Boston Fed, where she has spent her entire career, starting as a research assistant, Little has worked on the Massachusetts Governor's Council on Economic Growth and Technology and on the Task Force on the Health Care Industry. She has also been a lecturer for Simmons College. Little holds a B.A. from Wellesley College and M.A.L.D. and M.A. degrees from the Fletcher School of Law and Diplomacy at Tufts University.

**Catherine L. Mann** is a professor of economics at Brandeis University's International Business School, which she joined in fall 2006 after more than 20 years working in think tanks and policy institutions in Washington, DC. These positions include being a senior fellow at the Institute for International Economics (1997–2006), assistant director of the international finance division at the Federal Reserve Board of Governors (1994–1997), a senior staff economist for the President's Council of Economic Advisers (1991–1992), and a research economist and special assistant at the World Bank (1988–1989). Mann's current research focuses on two related topics: information technology and services trade in global markets, and the U.S. trade deficit and the dollar. She has written many articles and books, including *Accelerating the Globalization of America: The Role for Information Technology* (2006). She received an A.B. from Harvard University and a Ph.D. in economics from the Massachusetts Institute of Technology.

**Christopher M. Meissner** is an associate professor of economics at the University of California at Davis and a research fellow at the National Bureau of Economic Research. He specializes in the economic history of the international economy, particularly the period between 1870 and 1913, and focuses on the history of international financial flows, exchange rate regimes, and the evolution of the gold standard. Before coming to the University of California, Davis, Meissner was at the University of Cambridge, where he was a tenured lecturer, a fellow, and director of studies in economics for King's College. In 2006 he visited at the Bank of England as the Houblon-Norman/George Fellow, in 2005 he was a visiting scholar in the department of economics at Harvard University, and he spent summer 2003 as a visiting researcher at the International Monetary Fund. He has an A.B. in economics from Washington University, and a Ph.D. in economics from the University of California, Berkeley.

**Eswar S. Prasad** has been the Tolani Senior Professor of Trade Policy at Cornell University since 2007. He was previously at the International Monetary Fund (IMF), where he was chief of the financial studies division in the research department and, before that, was the head of the IMF's China division. Prasad's research has spanned a number of areas including business cycles, labor economics, and open economy macroeconomics. His current research interests include the macroeconomics of globalization, the relationship between growth and volatility, and the Chinese and Indian economies. Prasad has co-authored or edited several books and monographs on financial globalization, China, and India. He has contributed op-ed articles to the *Financial Times*, the *International Herald Tribune*, the *Wall Street Journal Asia*, and various other newspapers. Prasad has testified before the Senate Finance Committee and the House of Representatives Committee on Financial Services in China, and his research has been cited in the U.S. Congressional Record. Prasad received his B.A. in economics, mathematics, and statistics from the University of Madras, his M.A. in economics from Brown University, and his Ph.D. in economics from the University of Chicago.

**Lawrence H. Summers** is the Charles W. Eliot University Professor at Harvard University. He served as the 27th president of Harvard University from July 2001 until June 2006. As a research economist, he has also taught on the faculty at the Massachusetts Institute of Technology. Summers has made seminal contributions in labor economics, macroeconomics, monetary economics, and public finance. In 1987, Summers was the first social scientist to receive the annual Alan T. Waterman Award of the National Science Foundation, established by Congress to honor an exceptional young American scientist or engineer whose work demonstrates originality, innovation, and has a significant impact within his or her field. In 1993, Summers received the John Bates Clark Medal, given every two years to the outstanding American economist under the age of 40. Summers has served in a series of senior public policy positions, beginning in 1991, when he left Harvard to serve as the chief economist of the World Bank, and then in various posts in the Clinton administration. Summers was the U.S. Secretary of the Treasury from 1999–2001, following earlier positions as Deputy Secretary of the Treasury and Undersecretary of the Treasury for International Affairs. He currently writes a widely followed column for the *Financial Times*. Summers received his S.B. in economics from the Massachusetts Institute of Technology and his Ph.D. in economics from Harvard University.

**Alan M. Taylor** is professor of economics and director of the Center for the Evolution of the Global Economy at the University of California at Davis. A specialist in international economics and economic history, Taylor has written scores of articles and contributed to books on global market integration, the development of financial markets, and capital and labor flows. He is a research associate at the National Bureau of Economic Research and at the Centre for Economic and Policy Research in London, and a visiting scholar at the Federal Reserve Bank of San Francisco. Before joining the University of California, Davis in 1999 as an associate professor, he was an assistant professor of economics at Northwestern University from 1993–1999. Taylor earned a B.A. and M.A. at the University of Cambridge, and an A.M. and a Ph.D. in economics at Harvard University.

**Lixin Colin Xu** is a senior economist in the development research group at the World Bank. He specializes in the political economy and industrial organization of Chinese firms, and he has published widely on Chinese market efficiency and investment at the national-, industry-, and firm-levels, including his co-authorship of "Improving City Competitiveness through the Investment Climate," the World Bank's most requested Chinese-language study. Xu also serves on the editorial board of the *China Journal of Economics* and is a past vice president and director of the Chinese Economist Society. He holds a B.A. and an M.A. in economics from Peking University and a Ph.D. in economics from the University of Chicago.

# Author Index

# Subject Index